Jaguar Books on Latin America

Series Editors

WILLIAM H. BEEZLEY, Professor of History, University of Arizona
COLIN M. MACLACHLAN, John Christy Barr Distinguished Professor of
History, Tulane University

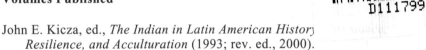

Volumes Published

John E. Kicza, ed., *The Indian in Latin American History*
Resilience, and Acculturation (1993; rev. ed., 2000).
Cloth ISBN 0-8420-2822-6   Paper ISBN 0-8420-2823-4

Susan E. Place, ed., *Tropical Rainforests: Latin American Nature and*
Society in Transition (1993; rev. and updated ed., 2001).
Cloth ISBN 0-8420-2907-9   Paper ISBN 0-8420-2908-7

Paul W. Drake, ed., *Money Doctors, Foreign Debts, and Economic*
Reforms in Latin America from the 1890s to the Present (1994).
Cloth ISBN 0-8420-2434-4   Paper ISBN 0-8420-2435-2

John A. Britton, ed., *Molding the Hearts and Minds: Education,*
Communications, and Social Change in Latin America (1994).
Cloth ISBN 0-8420-2489-1   Paper ISBN 0-8420-2490-5

David J. Weber and Jane M. Rausch, eds., *Where Cultures Meet: Frontiers*
in Latin American History (1994). Cloth ISBN 0-8420-2477-8
Paper ISBN 0-8420-2478-6

Gertrude M. Yeager, ed., *Confronting Change, Challenging Tradition:*
Women in Latin American History (1994). Cloth ISBN 0-8420-2479-4
Paper ISBN 0-8420-2480-8

Linda Alexander Rodríguez, ed., *Rank and Privilege: The Military and*
Society in Latin America (1994). Cloth ISBN 0-8420-2432-8
Paper ISBN 0-8420-2433-6

Darién J. Davis, ed., *Slavery and Beyond: The African Impact on Latin*
America and the Caribbean (1995). Cloth ISBN 0-8420-2484-0
Paper ISBN 0-8420-2485-9

Gilbert M. Joseph and Mark D. Szuchman, eds., *I Saw a City Invincible:*
Urban Portraits of Latin America (1996). Cloth ISBN 0-8420-2495-6
Paper ISBN 0-8420-2496-4

Roderic Ai Camp, ed., *Democracy in Latin America: Patterns and Cycles*
(1996). Cloth ISBN 0-8420-2512-X   Paper ISBN 0-8420-2513-8

Oscar J. Martínez, ed., *U.S.-Mexico Borderlands: Historical and Contemporary Perspectives* (1996). Cloth ISBN 0-8420-2446-8 Paper ISBN 0-8420-2447-6

William O. Walker III, ed., *Drugs in the Western Hemisphere: An Odyssey of Cultures in Conflict* (1996). Cloth ISBN 0-8420-2422-0 Paper ISBN 0-8420-2426-3

Richard R. Cole, ed., *Communication in Latin America: Journalism, Mass Media, and Society* (1996). Cloth ISBN 0-8420-2558-8 Paper ISBN 0-8420-2559-6

David G. Gutiérrez, ed., *Between Two Worlds: Mexican Immigrants in the United States* (1996). Cloth ISBN 0-8420-2473-5 Paper ISBN 0-8420-2474-3

Lynne Phillips, ed., *The Third Wave of Modernization in Latin America: Cultural Perspectives on Neoliberalism* (1998). Cloth ISBN 0-8420-2606-1   Paper ISBN 0-8420-2608-8

Daniel Castro, ed., *Revolution and Revolutionaries: Guerrilla Movements in Latin America* (1999). Cloth ISBN 0-8420-2625-8 Paper ISBN 0-8420-2626-6

Virginia Garrard-Burnett, ed., *On Earth as It Is in Heaven: Religion in Modern Latin America* (2000). Cloth ISBN 0-8420-2584-7 Paper ISBN 0-8420-2585-5

Carlos A. Aguirre and Robert Buffington, eds., *Reconstructing Criminality in Latin America* (2000). Cloth ISBN 0-8420-2620-7 Paper ISBN 0-8420-2621-5

Christon I. Archer, ed., *The Wars of Independence in Spanish America* (2000). Cloth ISBN 0-8420-2468-9   Paper ISBN 0-8420-2469-7

John F. Schwaller, ed., *The Church in Colonial Latin America* (2000). Cloth ISBN 0-8420-2703-3   Paper ISBN 0-8420-2704-1

Ingrid E. Fey and Karen Racine, eds., *Strange Pilgrimages: Exile, Travel, and National Identity in Latin America, 1800–1990s* (2000). Cloth ISBN 0-8420-2693-2   Paper ISBN 0-8420-2694-0

Joseph L. Arbena and David G. LaFrance, eds., *Sport in Latin America and the Caribbean* (2002). Cloth ISBN 0-8420-2820-X Paper ISBN 0-8420-2821-8

Samuel L. Baily and Eduardo José Míguez, eds., *Mass Migration to Modern Latin America* (2003). Cloth ISBN 0-8420-2830-7 Paper ISBN 0-8420-2831-5

Erick D. Langer with Elena Muñoz, eds., *Contemporary Indigenous Movements in Latin America* (2003). Cloth ISBN 0-8420-2679-7 Paper ISBN 0-8420-2680-0

Mass Migration
to Modern
Latin America

Mass Migration to Modern Latin America

Samuel L. Baily and Eduardo José Míguez
Editors

Jaguar Books on Latin America
Number 24

A Scholarly Resources Inc. Imprint
Wilmington, Delaware

Scholarly Resources Inc.
104 Greenhill Avenue
Wilmington, DE 19805-1897
www.scholarly.com

Library of Congress Cataloging-in-Publication Data

Mass migration to modern Latin America / Samuel L. Baily and
Eduardo José Míguez, editors.
       p. cm. — (Jaguar books on Latin America ; no. 24)
    ISBN 0-8420-2830-7 (alk. paper) — ISBN 0-8420-2831-5 (pbk. :
alk. paper)
       1. Latin America—Emigration and immigration—History—19th
century. 2. Latin America—Emigration and immigration—History—
20th century. 3. Immigrants—Latin America—History—19th century.
4. Immigrants—Latin America—History—20th century. I. Baily,
Samuel L. II. Míguez, Eduardo José. III. Series.

JV7398 .M335 2003
304.8'8—dc21   2002036578

∞ The paper used in this publication meets the minimum requirements of
the American National Standard for permanence of paper for printed library materials, Z39.48, 1984.

About the Editors

Samuel L. Baily is a professor of history at Rutgers University, where he has taught Latin American and migration history for thirty-seven years. He is the author of numerous articles and books, including *Immigrants in the Lands of Promise: Italians in Buenos Aires and New York City, 1870 to 1914* (1999) and, with Franco Ramella, *One Family, Two Worlds: An Italian Family's Correspondence across the Atlantic, 1901–1922* (1988). He is currently working on an extensive article on world migration in the twentieth century.

Eduardo José Míguez is a professor of history at the Universidad Nacional del Centro, Tandil, Argentina. He also has been a visiting professor at several other universities in Argentina as well as in Spain and the United States. His published works include *Las tierras de los ingleses en Argentina, 1870–1914* (1985) and, with Fernando Devoto, *Asociacionismo, trabajo e identidad étnica: Los italianos en América Latina en una perspectiva comparada* (1992). He is currently studying the formation of the Argentine middle classes and the history of the Argentine frontier before the so-called Conquest of the Desert.

Contents

Preface

Migration is a worldwide phenomenon that has involved the movement of millions of people across six continents since the beginning of time. The impact of this vast movement of people has been felt in the economies, the politics, the social structures, and the cultures of both the sending and the receiving societies. We have learned much about migration, but our knowledge is nevertheless uneven. We know much more about migration in the United States and Europe, for example, than we do in most other parts of the world—in some cases because there is little written on the subject, and in others because North Americans are unaware of or unable to read what has been written.

Latin America is one of those regions where migration has been important to its history and where there is a great deal written on the subject, but it is not well known in the United States and Europe. Thus, we have solicited and translated the following original articles to make this rich literature available to the North American audience. Eight of the fourteen authors involved are from Latin America—five from Argentina, two from Brazil, and one from Uruguay. In addition, one contributor is from Portugal, one from Japan, and four from the United States. The focus is on Argentina, Brazil, and Uruguay because they are the countries of greatest immigration, but the authors' underlying approach is comparative and thus brings in many other countries as well.

The project has been a joint effort among a number of migration scholars both in Latin America and in the United States. Originally the idea developed in discussions between the two editors, Eduardo José Míguez and Samuel L. Baily, and the distinguished Argentine migration scholar, Fernando Devoto. Due to other commitments, Devoto was forced to withdraw from the editorial process, but we wish to express our deep appreciation for his insightful contributions to the development of the book. There are others whom we wish to thank. Benjamin Alberti, Gustavo Carrera, and Frank Dauster helped with some of the translations. Eduardo would like to acknowledge a grant from the Agencia Nacional de Promoción de la Ciencia y la Tecnología that contributed to this work.

Good editors significantly improve the quality of the text in any book. In a work such as ours, which includes essays translated from a number of different languages, this is even more the case. Yet editors rarely receive the credit they deserve. We therefore wish to acknowledge the splendid work of the three people who were involved in the editing of this book. We are especially indebted to Joan Gaskill Baily who devoted many extra hours skillfully clarifying, refining, and polishing the original translations. Anyone who has done this kind of work understands how difficult and challenging it is. Because of her commitment and dedicated service, *Mass Migration to Modern Latin America* is a much better book. We also wish to thank Linda Pote Musumeci and Ann M. Aydelotte, both editors at Scholarly Resources, for the fine efforts they made to simplify and clarify the text. And, finally, we wish to thank Michael Siegel at the Cartography Lab of Rutgers University for his skill in drawing the maps and graphs and for his patience in dealing with the varied requests we made of him.

Samuel L. Baily
Eduardo José Míguez

Introduction: Foreign Mass Migration to Latin America in the Nineteenth and Twentieth Centuries—An Overview

Eduardo José Míguez

It is common knowledge that the United States is a nation of immigrants. For North Americans, however, the impact of foreign immigration in the formation of Latin American societies is less obvious. The present Latin American population is seen as the descendants of the Spanish conquistadors and the Native Americans, in addition to descendants of the forced "immigration" of African slaves. But, as José Moya shows (Chapter 1), even if we consider only Spanish immigration, the total number of arrivals from the motherland during the colonial period represents merely a fraction of those reaching the new republics and Cuba during the age of mass migration in the second half of the nineteenth and the early twentieth centuries. And Spain was only one of the nations that provided large numbers of immigrants to the new Latin American republics.

The fact is that mass migration during this period had an enormous impact on many Latin American societies. In some cases, such as those of Argentina, Uruguay, and southern Brazil, the number of new arrivals was so large in relation to a relatively small population base that the percentage of foreigners over the total population was even higher than in the United States. For example, in Argentina—the extreme case—in the peak year of 1914, over 30 percent of the nation had been born elsewhere, mostly in Europe. The percentages were much greater if we consider the areas of high foreign concentration such as Buenos Aires and other large cities and the agricultural areas of the Pampas. Between the 1880s and World War I, for example, in the Argentine capital, Europeans constituted one-half of the total population and nearly three-quarters of the adults. Though not quite as high, there were similar percentages for São Paulo, Brazil, and Montevideo, Uruguay.

In other countries, while the number of arrivals was not so significant and the local population was larger, foreign immigrants still played an important role in the formation of the local societies. The following table shows the gross number of arrivals to selected Latin American nations. The United States, Canada, Australia, New Zealand, and South Africa are included for comparative purposes.

Immigrant Arrivals in the Nineteenth and Twentieth Centuries (Selected Destinations)

Destination	Years	Arrivals
United States	1821–1932	32,244,000
Argentina	1856–1932	6,405,000
Canada	1821–1932	5,206,000
Brazil	1821–1932	4,431,000
Australia	1821–1932	2,913,000
Cuba	1901–1931	857,000
South Africa	1881–1932	852,000
Chile	1882–1932	726,000*
Uruguay	1836–1932	713,000
New Zealand	1821–1932	594,000
Mexico	1911–1931	226,000

Source: A. E. Lattes, "Migraciones hacia América Latina y el Caribe desde principios del siglo XIX" (Buenos Aires: CENEP, 1985), 5.
*Incomplete series

Not all of those who arrived stayed in Latin America. As in other countries of mass immigration, return migration was an important phenomenon, but return rates and re-migration were not higher in Latin America than in other recipient nations. Actually, those of Argentina were somewhat lower than in the United States, while in Brazil they were slightly higher.

The timing of migration to Latin America was slightly different than migration to North America. Northern European immigrants—mainly Britons, Germans, and, a little later, the Irish—had begun to arrive in significant numbers in the United States during the first half of the nineteenth century.[1] At that time, there was some migration to certain Latin American destinations from the same areas as well as from France, Spain, and Italy, but the numbers were very small. In Montevideo, for example, 32,000 European immigrants arrived between 1835 and 1842, and an estimated 50,000 were living in the province of Buenos Aires by the latter date. Colonization by Swiss and Germans began in Brazil, as Giralda Seyferth reminds us in Chapter 10, in the late 1810s and early 1820s. On the whole, the total number of European arrivals to the new republics was not important before 1850.

In the third quarter of the nineteenth century the number of immigrants began to increase. Annual arrivals in Brazil for that period were nearly 13,000, consisting mostly of Portuguese and Germans, with smaller influxes of Italians and Spaniards. Argentina received a somewhat smaller number of immigrants at that time, a flow that was already dominated by Italians, Spaniards, and French. In Uruguay over 150,000 immigrants arrived in the few years between 1866 and 1875. The census in Chile for the latter date shows 17,594 foreigners from outside the region, with the British, Germans, and French as the main contributors.

Migration became really massive only after 1880. Argentina and Uruguay received large numbers in the 1880s, with averages of over 100,000 per year for the largest of the River Plate republics. The numbers decreased because of a local economic crisis in the 1890s, but migration recovered by the turn of the century, reaching its peak before World War I. The flow of immigration was not strong during the war, but it recovered somewhat afterward. In Brazil, the expansion of coffee production in São Paulo, the availability of subsidized fares, and the crisis in the River Plate stimulated a great increase in immigration in the 1890s, especially from northern Italy and also from Portugal and Spain. The numbers diminished when in 1902 the Italian government placed restrictions on migration to Brazil and when coffee prices fell due to overproduction in the early years of the past century. After that, the migration cycle to Brazil was not unlike that of the River Plate.

Wars and the situation in Europe had a great impact on the determination of this cycle. However, as in the case of the United States, the evolution of the economy in the recipient society has been the single most significant factor in determining the strength of the migratory flow. A study of Argentina has shown a surprising correlation between the growth of the gross national product—as an indicator of the business cycle—and the inflow of migrants. The results are quite remarkable; Pearson's correlation index for the period from 1875 to 1913 is 0.91, and R square = 0.83.[2] Similar detailed studies have not been done for other nations that received large numbers of immigrants, such as Brazil or Uruguay, but in general there is a close alignment between the economic situation in the recipient society and the number of arrivals. Moreover, periods of economic crisis also witness a sharp growth in the numbers of return migration.

An almost universal characteristic of massive migrations is that the flow was mostly made up of single young men. Latin America was no exception to this rule. As usually happens, the first to immigrate were young men in search of better employment opportunities. In the early stages of the flow between specific European regions and Latin American countries, there was a clear prevalence of this type of migrant. At later stages, brides, sweethearts, sisters, or other members of the family joined the first migrants, and the masculinity rates, which could be as high as three males for every female at the beginning of the flow, became much lower and reached a far more balanced figure. Examples of this process may be seen in such distinct cases as the Japanese in Brazil and Peru (see Chapter 6) or the Spaniards and Italians in Argentina (see Chapter 4). Nevertheless, there are many exceptions to this model, and every local current shows its own pattern of behavior, as Fernando Devoto argues in Chapter 2, which compares the Italian and Spanish migrations to South America.

Perhaps the most notable exception is the migration of entire families to São Paulo, as shown in Chapter 12. Given the characteristics of work on the coffee plantations, the owners needed to hire the whole family for the *fazenda*.[3] The government of the state of São Paulo assumed the task of stimulating this type of immigration with considerable success. Thus, the number of women and children that arrived at the port of Santos was considerably higher than that in most other immigration flows to Latin America. Another atypical current was that of Jewish immigrants, fleeing from the persecutions and lack of liberties in Europe, who went to Buenos Aires and later on to Brazil (see Chapter 11).

If the majority of early migrants were young men in search of opportunities for improving their material well-being, the formation of the migrant currents was in no way the result of an anonymous search for employment by an uprooted population. Several decades of research on migrations to Latin America (following in the wake of other research on the North American case) have shown that rather than considering the migration flow between a country of origin and a country of destination, one should consider a tangle of small local flows between certain European areas and Latin American regions of arrival, an argument developed by Devoto. These local flows were based on kinship relations or other close personal links. The first migrants transmitted vital information to those who followed, and on occasion they would pay new migrants' fares or offer them other types of financial assistance on arrival.

This type of migration mechanism, which is generically called "chain migration," has been distinguished from other forms, particularly those migrations sponsored by governments, usually of the recipient country. In contrast to migration to the United States, which was mostly spontaneous, in several Latin American nations the state played an active role in its promotion. We have already mentioned the case of the state of São Paulo in Brazil, but there are also examples in Argentina, in Peru (see Chapter 6), in Uruguay, and in other Latin American nations. This active participation by the state served to stimulate some specific migratory currents as well as to create some unusual immigrant groups, as was the case with the small contingent of Dutch who arrived in 1889 in Buenos Aires because of subsidized tickets.

In many cases, government promotion policies were complemented by networks of personal relationships, as shall be seen in the cases of the Japanese in Peru and the Italians in Brazil. In comparison, what is known as the *padroni* system does not seem to have been frequent in migrations to Latin America. In the United States and Canada, particularly at later periods, contractors working for businesses that needed large numbers of unskilled workers—to lay track for the railways, for example—tried to hire workers directly in Europe. This independent activity of businesses has not been observed for the Latin American case. The offices in Europe that sought immigrants for Latin American nations generally belonged to the governments of these countries, to land colonization companies—which in turn were usually sponsored by the governments of the receiving societies—or to steamship lines looking for customers. Government policies could not be successful, however, unless there were favorable conditions for the spontaneous increase of migrations. For example, in the case of Peru, a strong immigration policy had little success; at the other end of the spectrum, in Argentina during the period of high immigration after 1900, government participation was minimal.

Another distinctive feature of migrations to Latin America in relation to those to the north was that immigrants arrived in far less-developed capitalist societies, a situation that offered very different opportunities from those in the United States. In North America the local population had developed experience in work, in technology, and in the ways of a market economy that gave them comparative advantages in the labor market. The opposite seems to have occurred in Latin America, as Samuel Baily suggests in his comparative study of Italian immigrants in Buenos Aires and New York (see Chapter 4). There, the immigrants, rather than the residents, frequently seemed better equipped. Thus, even if salaries were higher in the United States, the social position of recent immigrants—particularly those from southern Europe—in relation to the local population was better in Argentina and Uruguay, or in cities such as São Paulo, Rio de Janeiro, or Rio Claro than in New York, Boston, or Newburyport in Massachusetts.[4]

In contrast, on the large estates and plantations in Brazil, immigrant labor replaced slaves—first after the abolition of the trade, and then a few decades later with the abolition of slavery itself. There, working and living conditions for immigrants were usually very harsh and resulted in frequent conflicts. In certain places, such as São Paulo and Cuba (see Chapter 1), European immigrants preferred to settle in the cities because of the difficulties in rural areas, and thus they specialized in urban activities such as commerce and handicrafts. On the other hand, on the Brazilian *fazendas*, working conditions improved with time, and eventually some immigrants managed to acquire their own coffee farms. In other cases, such as the sugarcane and cotton plantations of the Peruvian coast, free migration never became a significant alternative in the local labor market. Both there and in Cuba, semi-servile workers brought from China, known as coolies, were eventually employed for some time.

Meanwhile, in urban centers—Buenos Aires, Rosario, and Córdoba in Argentina, São Paulo, Rio, and Campinhas in Brazil, and Havana in Cuba—immigrants formed important sectors of commerce, handicrafts, or industry and thus became the embryo of the middle classes of the young republics. Thus, it seems accurate to equate the role that the Italians, Spaniards, and Portuguese played in the construction of Latin American capitalism in the half-century after 1875 with the role of the British and Germans in the United States in the half-century before. If in the long run the strength of North American capitalism and the possibilities offered by a stable democracy would finally offer good opportunities to the descendants of the later immigrants who chose to stay in North America, this consequence could not initially have been obvious to the immigrants themselves. How, then, could the migrant choose between the various possible destinations once the decision to migrate had been taken?

There are some objective differences that many prospective migrants must have acknowleged. The distance in miles between Europe and the United States was shorter than it was to most possible South American destinations, and thus the cost and the duration of the journey were also less. Moreover, real wages for equivalent tasks were usually higher in North America. On the other hand, for southern Europeans, the distance in cultures, including the language and religion, was much smaller in destinations such as São Paulo, Montevideo, or Buenos Aires than in New York, Boston, or Toronto. Surely, as suggested by the case of the Italians in Buenos Aires and New York studied by Baily, the possibilities for relative social mobility were also greater in the south. In most cases, however, the choice of a destination was not the result of a strict cost-benefit analysis.

The decision to migrate was usually made within the context of family and social relations. Most of the information on which the decision was made came from the network of family and others who might have already migrated. A few specific currents had a more "objective" economic base. For example, the families from the Veneto in northeastern Italy who escaped from the agrarian crisis in that region took advantage of the demand for family labor and the offer of free tickets to go to São Paulo. The silk artisans of Biella in northwestern Italy found in Paterson, New Jersey, the possibility of plying their trade with better wages. The sailors and fishermen of the Azores found opportunity in the New England fishing ports. Many southern Italians who were working abroad to save money and later return to their homeland preferred the higher wages of the United States. In contrast, northern Italians in the 1870s and 1880s—and much later some Danes, as described by María Bjerg (see Chapter 7)—discovered that the Argentine Pampas offered them a better opportunity than other destinations to become independent farmers with their own land.

Even if these currents had an economic basis, many potential migrants went where their relatives and friends had gone. Frequently, almost all the emigrants from a particular village would migrate to the same destination. This made the process much easier because the migrant knew where he was going and whom he would meet on his arrival. Often, he even knew people who had gone before or had returned from abroad, who could add their personal testimonies to those that had arrived by mail.

Thus, on top of the "objective" reasons related to the labor market, there were "subjective" reasons that influenced the prospective migrants' decision—reasons that in turn may have become "objective," as they also resulted in economic savings. If government policies and the conditions of the labor market were important elements in determining the flow of migrations, probably the most important single factor was the network of personal and community relations through which assistance and information circulated. At the same time, this network diminished the sense of helplessness that could come from abandoning kinfolk and the well-known places of the native village.

There is no doubt that the most effective way to reduce these personal sentimental costs of migrating was the reconstruction of a surrogate community of origin in the new society. As in the United Sates and in the other countries of massive immigration of the nineteenth and twentieth centuries, formal and informal institutions emerged that grouped immigrants together according to their nationality, region or town of birth, or religion, as in the case of the Jews or even of Protestants. In Chapters 6, 7, and 10 the authors tackle the important question of the formation and organization of ethnic communities in Latin America.

From a formal point of view, mutual aid societies and the ethnic press constituted the backbone of these new communities. The informal dynamic that gathered together immigrants of the same town or the same language—and it must be remembered that the profound dialectal differences in Italy and Spain made languages regional rather than national—created an everyday sociability that helped to solve many of their concrete problems, such as landing a job or finding a spouse. The short stories of the lives of the Sola family, Manuel Suárez Martínez, and Santo Codo, or the study of marriage patterns in Argentina (Chapter 8), or the work on Italian families in Brazil (Chapter 12) all illustrate this point.

Possibly, however, the construction of an ethnic leadership was the most important factor in the formation of the community. Naturally, all human groups confer power on some of their members—that is, the capacity to influence or mediate in collective matters and even to exert ascendancy over its individuals. In formal organizations, some aspects of this power are incorporated into their structure: the owner and the editor of a newspaper, the president and the board of directors of a mutual aid society, or the principal of an ethnic school. In informal organizations, the social standing and individual charisma of the actors allow them to take power. Of course, the two spheres coincide. The positions directing formal institutions are generally occupied by the most prominent members of the associations or those who are the most capable and charismatic.

And power is exerted both in formal and informal associations, as illustrated by the cases of Hans Fugl among the Danes in Tandil (in Chapter 7) and Nikumatsu Okada among the Japanese of the Chancay Valley (see Chapter 6). Here, the community leaders were successful immigrants who had achieved some fortune and social standing that were recognized beyond the ethnic enclave. In this respect, many community leaders in late nineteenth-century Latin America were more successful than their North American counterparts (see Chapter 4). Thus, prominent Italians in Buenos Aires or São Paulo, Spaniards in Havana or Buenos Aires, or Portuguese in Rio or Bahia found it easier to transfer their leadership to the recipient society as a whole than did the Italians in New York or Chicago, the Portuguese in Boston or Jacksonville, Illinois,[5] or the Jews in New York. It took several generations for the latter to achieve positions of prestige and power that went beyond the limits of their own communities.

The role and the way in which these communities operated seem to have varied widely according to the characteristics of the different immigrant groups. Within the main communities, as the Gallegos (from northwestern Spain) in Buenos Aires and Havana, or the Portuguese in Rio, the large ethnic societies offered assistance and also a reference of identity, but they did not secure a protective network of social relations or a well-defined space of sociability. These were to be found in a closer circle. The relationship between the president of a society that had thousands of members, such as the Centro Gallego of Buenos Aires, and an ordinary member was surely distant. The social circuit of friendship had to be found in other associations, formal or informal, that grouped together smaller numbers of immigrants on the basis of their village of origin or interests in common.

Smaller ethnic societies could play a more active role in the daily life of their members. Beyond the prestige achieved by leaders such as Fugl for the Danes of Tandil or Okada for the Japanese of Chancay, or the Jews of São Paulo, for small immigrant groups living in a society that, if not hostile, was at least very distant from their own background, community life was an essential part of their existence. It had a crucial role in the preservation of their language, their religion, their culture—in short, who they were.

Another alternative, especially manifested in larger communities, was that immigrants grouped together to create a more or less homogeneous social milieu in which to live. Thus, an ethnic neighborhood such as a Chinatown or a Little Italy secured an ethnic presence in daily life. However, the degree of ethnic concentration in the large Latin American cities—at least in Buenos Aires and Montevideo (see Chapter 5)—does not seem to have been as important as in the large cities of the United States, such as Boston, Chicago, and San Francisco. For smaller immigrant communities, however, spatial segregation did not guarantee ethnic sociability. Not always did the local butcher, baker, or dentist belong to the same ethnic group.

It is no surprise that the family played a crucial role in determining either the continuity of ethnic identities or the process of integration into the host society. Thus, for the case of Argentina, much research has been carried out that has tried to measure the process of integration of immigrants into the local society through marriage patterns (see Chapter 4). Some research along the same lines also has been carried out for Uruguay and Brazil. Though conclusions are far from unanimous, in general they show that in the first generation—the immigrants themselves—there was a strong tendency to form families within tight ethnic boundaries. However, the imbalance between the numbers of male and female immigrants resulted in what Robert MacCaa has called the "marriage squeeze."[6]

If endogamy (marriage within one's own group) was a common feature of immigration both in the United States and Latin America, the higher social prestige of immigrants in São Paulo, Havana, Buenos Aires, or Tandil may have contributed to their easier assimilation into the host society. This integration was much less the case with communities that had profound differences with the host society, such as the Danes of Tandil and the Jews and Japanese of São Paulo. This separation was even wider when the group members tended to establish themselves in isolated ethnic colonies, as did the Germans in southern Brazil (see Chapter 10).

It may be argued that because women had a predominant role in domestic life, they would assume an important role in the preservation of traditions in family life. Therefore, ethnic families might maintain their original identity for one or two generations, while marriages outside the group (between immigrants and host society partners) were the path to bringing up the younger generations as ordinary members of the host society. The role of women, however, was not limited to the preservation of ethnic identity through marriage. Immigrant women played an important economic role. For example, family labor was crucial in the exploitation of the small units of production—in ownership, lease, or sharecropping—

in the Argentine agrarian colonies, the Peruvian haciendas, or the Brazilian coffee *colonato*.[7] Women also were vital participants in the migration process, but this fact has been neglected by traditional historiography. Furthermore, the stereotypical definitions of women's work at the time obscured the active role they played (see Chapter 9).

The dynamics of preservation/integration were not just evident in the formation of families. The residential patterns that showed a lower concentration of immigrants in South American cities relative to those in North America were not only the result of a different process of urbanization but also the consequence of a smaller social distance between the host society and the immigrants (see Chapters 4 and 5). Clearly, this difference is related to the varying degree of capitalist development in both societies. The comparisons in Chapters 3 and 4 show the differences between these processes of integration. It is likely that the integration of immigrants into the local society was faster and more successful in many of the migrant flows that arrived in Spanish and Portuguese America than in their North American counterparts.

There is a well-known saying in Argentina that Mexicans descend from the Aztecs, Peruvians from the Incas, and Argentines from the ships. However exaggerated, it reflects the crucial role of immigration in the formation of some Latin American societies. Of course, the formation of modern Argentina was influenced by the Native Americans and Afro-Americans, a dense crossbreeding among these ethnic groups, and centuries of Spanish colonial rule. In both Peru and Mexico, immigration also contributed to molding their present societies.

To understand some of the most significant features of Latin America, one must consider the impact of migrants. The study of immigration to this region shows the similarities and differences in the process of formation of other American societies. More than any other, the American continent was molded by its contact with Europe after 1492[8] and by the establishment of colonial dependence with different European nations— Spain, Brazil, England, and France. There was also influence by the different pre-existing Native American cultures. However, a common feature of all America was the constant arrival of people of diverse origins— Europeans, enslaved Africans, and, in smaller numbers, Asians and Middle Easterners. For example, Syrian and Lebanese migrants went in significant numbers to several American nations before 1930, particularly to Argentina and Brazil.

Thus, if the diverse social backgrounds of American nations originated in the years of colonial domination, the waves of immigrants in the nineteenth and twentieth centuries also played an important role in the formation of these nations. The migratory currents were different, as was the integration of the new arrivals into the host societies. Understanding how and why these different streams of immigrants were established is a way of approaching the common features and the specific characteristics of the American nations and regions. In turn, grasping these similarities and differences is useful for having a better understanding of each of the American societies, including the United States.

This understanding is made clearer through a comparative perspective—thus the focus on comparison in the various texts in this book. Some chapters are specifically comparative, and others deal with only one case, but they were all written in a comparative frame of mind. In recent years, there has been a significant expansion of research on the history of migrations to Latin America. Moreover, the evolution of the study of immigration in the United States has been one of the most influential factors in this research. European historiography has also made a substantial contribution to the approaches with which the study of migrations to Latin America has been undertaken.

An important debate among scholars of migration for many years has been around the issue of the integration of the immigrants into the recipient societies. In other words, on one hand, how does the new society transform the immigrants and their descendants? And how, on the other hand, do the immigrants transform the host society? The debate focuses on two concepts—the Melting Pot and Cultural Pluralism. The American version of the Melting Pot theory viewed the immigrant as an essentially passive individual, uprooted from his or her culture of origin and absorbed into the dominant culture of the host society. In Latin America, particularly in Argentina, scholars such as Italian sociologist Gino Germani argued that a process of fusion had taken place, thereby creating a new society that incorporated both the old Argentine and new immigrant traditions into a single new culture.[9] Cultural Pluralism, by contrast, which was a response of scholars in the 1960s and 1970s who rejected the view of the Melting Pot theory, argued that instead of disappearing, much of the immigrants' culture of origin persisted in the new host societies and created a new society of cultural pluralism. Many of the essays in this book move the debate into a more nuanced understanding of these interpretations.

The contributors have brought together a sample of the diverse lines of research adopted by scholars from Latin America, the United States, and Europe who have tackled this subject. The variety of historic problems as well as research paths and approaches is so wide that it would not be possible to assemble in one book a complete discussion of the themes and problems of the field. Neither has it been our purpose to present a general synthesis of the subject. What we have tried to do is to bring together a group of research results that allow us to visualize the research lines in progress and that present some of the specific problems of migrations to Latin America. We hope that our selections will open new areas of thought on the impact of migrations on the formation of the American societies and thereby contribute the Latin American experience to the rich study of the global process of migrations.

The following chapters are grouped in three parts. The first presents works that are multicountry comparative studies: in two chapters, primarily between Argentina and Uruguay; in two others, between a specific ethnic group in Argentina, on the one hand, and Brazil, on the other, with the respective groups in the United States; and in two more, a specific ethnic group in Brazil and Peru and another in Argentina and Cuba. The second and third parts extend some of the issues raised in the multicountry comparative studies with single-country case studies: in Part II, three on Argentina, and in Part III, three on Brazil.

Each of the sections begins with a brief story about real people who participated in this migration process—Oreste and Ida Sola, two cousins from a small village in northern Italy who went respectively to Buenos Aires and New York City; Manuel Suárez Martínez, a Gallego who migrated to Argentina; and Santo Codo, an Italian immigrant from northern Italy who went to the coffee plantations of São Paulo, Brazil. They are an important reminder that this book is about real human beings. Although constrained by larger structural forces such as labor markets, they nevertheless made important decisions about their own fates.

Notes

1. For example, an average of over 70,000 immigrants per year arrived in the United States in the decade following 1835.

2. Pearson's index is a standard statistic for the correlation of two variables over time. Zero indicates that there is no relation between them, and 1 that there is a perfect positive relationship. Any figure above 0.50 indicates that there is a significant relation between the variables. R2 is a measure of the degree to which one variable is a determining factor over the other. The GNP tends to present a cumulative growth pattern, and immigrant arrivals also tend to increase over time. Thus, a significant part of this correlation could be attributed to the coincidence of both trends. To avoid this, in order to see if the relation of the variables stood beyond their general growing trend, the relationship between the deviations from the trend values was considered. The calculation of Pearson's index for these deviations still remains considerably high (R = 0.758; R square = 0.575). Eduardo J. Míguez, "Labor Market and Migrant Strategies in the Transatlantic Labor Flow to Argentina—An Overview," paper presented at the Eleventh International Economic History Congress, Session C 38: The Emergence of a Transatlantic Labor Market in the Nineteenth Century, Milan, September 1994.

3. A *fazenda* is a large estate in Brazil, in this case a coffee plantation.

4. The classic books on Rio Claro and Newburyport are Warren Dean, *Rio Claro, a Brazilian Plantation System, 1820–1920* (Stanford: Stanford University Press, 1976); and Stephen Thernstrom, *Poverty and Progress* (Cambridge, MA: Harvard University Press, 1964). For the major cities, there is a bibliography too vast to be quoted here.

5. On the Portuguese immigration to Jacksonville see Don Harrison Doyle, *The Social Order of a Frontier Community, Jacksonville, Illinois, 1825–1870* (Urbana: University of Illinois Press, 1983), 125–31.

6. Robert MacCaa, "Gender in the Melting Pot: Ethnic Marriage Squeeze and Intermarriage in New York City, 1900–1980." Paper presented at the conference "El Poblamiento de las Américas," Veracruz, México, 1992.

7. A form of sharecropping on the Brazilian coffee plantations.

8. The situation was similar in Australia and New Zealand over two centuries later.

9. Gino Germani, *Política y sociedad en una época de transición* (Buenos Aires: Paidós, 1960).

I

Transnational Migration

STORY ONE

An Italian Family in Buenos Aires and New York City

Samuel L. Baily

This account is about two cousins who emigrated from the same town in northern Italy at the beginning of the nineteenth century: one to Buenos Aires, and the other to New York City. Their lives in these different destinations provide insight into the migration process, especially into the way village of origin-based social networks could influence the participants. Their story introduces us to the multinational comparative approach that is adopted by the authors of the six essays in Part I.

Valdengo was a typical northern Italian hill town at the turn of the nineteenth century—one of some eighty small towns in the district of Biella, nestled in the foothills of the Alps. Life was difficult for the people of Valdengo. Most of them were farmers who cultivated grain and raised grapes, but a few were also artisans (shoemakers, blacksmiths) in their struggle to make ends meet. In nearly half of the 230 families in the town, one or more of its members had to find employment elsewhere. This outside income was crucial to a family's survival.

According to the manuscript census schedules, Valdengo in 1904 had a population of 1,128 people, of whom 110, or 10 percent of the total, did not live in the town at the time.[1] Of the 110 who had left, thirty-three were in nearby Biella presumably working in the textile factories there, seventeen were in Rome, Turin, and other parts of Italy, and the remaining sixty were abroad. Of this latter number, nineteen were in the United States, fourteen in Switzerland, thirteen in France, eleven in Argentina, and three in other European countries.

Two of these sixty individuals who were living abroad in 1904 were 20-year-old Oreste Sola, in Buenos Aires, and his 21-year-old second cousin Ida, in New York City. This is the story of how these two cousins who grew up in the same small town in northern Italy migrated to destinations many thousands of miles from each other and from their home. Why did they decide to emigrate? How did they choose these two destinations? With whom did they travel? How did they find a place to live and a job? What was their life like abroad? How did they recreate a social life? Fortunately we can answer these questions because the various members of their respective families wrote many letters that have been preserved.[2]

Although Oreste's father, Luigi, owned a small piece of land in Valdengo, it was not productive enough to support his family. He thus moved to nearby Biella to work in the textile mills, but he kept his small property in Valdengo and later retired there. Oreste's mother, Margherita, also worked in the textile factory, and it was there that she met her husband. They had three children—Oreste, his younger sister Narcisa, and his younger brother Abele. The parents wanted to give their two sons every opportunity, which meant that they worked overtime so that the boys could pursue their education beyond grammar school.

When Oreste graduated from the Biella technical/professional school in 1901, he had several career choices. With his degree he could become an engineer or a technician in one of the local textile mills and do well. Yet he wanted more, and, motivated by a sense of adventure and a desire for economic and social betterment, he chose to emigrate. Here, too, he had several options. As the census shows, there were a number of people from the Biella area who lived in France, Switzerland, the United States, and Argentina. In fact, Oreste had cousins living in France and Cuba. Nevertheless, he chose Buenos Aires, probably because his godfather Zocco was in the construction business there. He sailed to Buenos Aires with several friends (Biellesi) from the Biella area. As he explained in his first letter home, "As soon as we got here, we went to the address of Godfather Zocco, who then introduced us to several people from Valdengo."[3]

Ida's family also had a small plot of land in Valdengo, but her father, Giacomo, was a part-time shoemaker as well as a farmer. He had traveled abroad extensively to various countries in Europe, the United States, and North Africa. Giacomo and his first wife had three children—Ida and her two younger brothers, Abele and Andrea. Ida's mother had died shortly after Ida's youngest brother was born, and her father remarried. Ida did not care for her stepmother and sought ways to get out of the house. She worked as a servant and saved enough money to buy a ticket to New York. It is not clear why she chose New York rather than some other destination, but she sailed to New York with two cousins and went to stay with an uncle who lived there.

In Buenos Aires, Oreste lived with his godfather for six years. After a year of exploration, he found a job as a draftsman with the construction firm that was building the new Argentine Congress. A few years later he took on a second job overseeing the heating and ventilation of these buildings. In 1910 he became an independent contractor whose first job was to lay a short stretch of railroad in the Argentine interior.

Oreste's success enabled him to send money home to his parents, who had by this time retired from the factory in Biella and returned to the family farm in Valdengo. They had supported him so that he could get a good education and become established; now they expected him to support them in return. Although Oreste understood this reciprocal relationship, there was some tension within the family regarding money. His father wrote in one letter: "We keep repeating our plea to remember us, that in the conditions that we are in we cannot do without your continued help." Oreste in reply apologized for his behavior: "Please excuse me then if so much time has gone by since I have carried out my promises . . . and don't think badly of me in your hearts. It is not because of stinginess or carelessness; its just that I can't come up with anything more."[4]

In 1907, Oreste married Corinna Chiocchetti, a young Italian from a village near Valdengo whom he had met in Buenos Aires. Whether through fear of parental interference or insensitivity, the way he announced this fact caused some additional tension within the family. In one letter he told his parents that he was getting married, but he did not mention the name of his future wife. They were distraught because word had gotten back to neighbors in Valdengo from Buenos Aires, and those neighbors knew the name of Oreste's fiancée. As Luigi wrote his son, "One thing that I must tell you and that has not made us too happy. We knew in Biella a good part of your affairs, what you earn . . . and who your wife is. Nothing wrong with that if you had also told us the name of your wife; then we could affirm that which others are saying; instead we must, with displeasure, remain ignorant about that which less concerned people know about your business."[5]

In many ways, living in Buenos Aires at the time was almost like living at home. Most of Oreste's friends and associates were from Valdengo or the Biella area; moreover, many of these people traveled back and forth to Italy and brought with them the latest news from home. Oreste lived with his godfather until he married in 1907. He had met Corinna within this community. Cousin Abele, Ida's brother, arrived in Buenos Aires in 1909 where he and his family remained for the next twelve years. When Oreste became an independent contractor in 1910, he hired his friends and fellow Biellesi to work for him. And in 1912, Oreste's younger brother, also named Abele, migrated to Buenos Aires and lived with him and Corinna for more than a half-dozen years. Oreste not only took in his brother but also helped him to find a job as an engineer and introduced him to his friends in the Biella community.

Ida's story indicates the importance of the Biellese network in her life just as it had been in Oreste's life in Buenos Aires. When Ida arrived in New York, she went to stay with her uncle, who lived in Manhattan. To support herself, she began working at a nearby restaurant owned by a woman from Biella. She met Eugenio Cerruti, a textile worker from a town near Valdengo, at the house of a friend from the Biella area. They were married on April 22, 1905, and over the years raised five children. Eugenio worked in the Paterson, New Jersey, textile mills off and on and also took on a number of other jobs (field hand, manager of a small hotel) in between. He was able to buy a small house in Paterson in 1912. In 1928 he bought a house in nearby Haledon, a town where many Biellesi lived.

Both Oreste and Ida remained close to their families in Valdengo over the years, even though they were separated by thousands of miles and never saw their parents again. Oreste and his father exchanged letters on a fairly regular basis. The family also sent Oreste food, clothes, and books while he and his brother eventually sent money home to support their parents in retirement. They were especially involved during times of crisis. When Narcisa, Oreste's younger sister, died of cancer in 1904, Oreste wrote long letters expressing his grief and sorrow. Later, Oreste and Abele did everything they could to help when their mother, Margherita, suffered from bone cancer. Ida was always close to all the members of her family and served as the principal contact between them. Her two brothers and her father wrote to her even when they refused to communicate with each other.

As close as Oreste and Ida were to their respective families, they never returned to Valdengo except for brief visits many years after they had originally emigrated. Nevertheless, they clearly were ambivalent about the issue of returning. Oreste wrote his parents many times that he soon would be coming home, at least for a visit, and they assumed all along that he would do so. After he married in 1907, Margherita expressed her deep desire to meet her new daughter-in-law and to have a grandchild. The letters, cards, and photographs "sent to us by you and our dear Corinna," wrote Luigi and Margherita, "have convinced us all the more of the love you two have for us, so we anxiously wait for the day when we can embrace and kiss you both with joy."[6] Similarly, a decade later, when Margherita became ill, Luigi pleaded with his sons to return. As he wrote to Oreste in November 1918, "Since the war has finished in Italy's favor, we hope for an honorable peace for everyone that will last and that you will make up your minds to come see us. Oreste, after eighteen years, please don't deprive us of this joy."[7]

Why Oreste never returned home to see his parents before they died is not clear. There was always a reason why he had to postpone the trip: the demands of his business, the war's interruption of transatlantic travel, the cost. After his parents died, Oreste visted Valdengo several times for short periods and kept the family farm. He always maintained his Italian citizenship and never became an Argentine citizen. Oreste died in Buenos Aires in 1949. He was cremated and his ashes were returned to Valdengo, where they were buried beside his father, his mother, and his younger sister.

If, as it seems, Oreste left Valdengo with the idea of going home again, it is not at all certain that this was the case for Ida. She had left Valdengo to escape a difficult stepmother. Ida's husband had no desire ever to return to Italy and did not write to his relatives there. Ida, on the other hand, had maintained contact with her brothers. After her husband died in 1948, she gave some thought to returning to Valdengo. She did visit Valdengo in the summer of 1954 for a reunion with her two brothers, but then went back to Haledon. As she later wrote from Haledon, "If I had been free, I would not have come back here. I was going to settle there for the rest of my life. Now, however, I can't make that change. I'm tied down here. I must stay here."[8] Ida obviously thought that her place was in Haledon with her children and grandchildren. When she died in 1975, she was buried next to her husband in the Paterson cemetery.

Many of the particulars of the experiences of these two cousins differed: they emigrated for different reasons, they chose different destinations, and they had different relationships with their families. Nevertheless, we also see some important similarities in the lives of these two emigrants from Valdengo who went to America at the beginning of the last century: both migrated, settled, and prospered in their new communities. In the end, their stories show the power of the village-of-origin-based networks to shape the immigrants' lives. These networks largely determined how they traveled, where they lived, with whom they worked and socialized, and whom they married.

Notes

1. Comune di Valdengo, Censo di 1901, manuscript schedules. Although the official census was taken in 1901, local officials updated it each year.

2. This story is based on the following sources: the extensive correspondence between Oreste Sola in Buenos Aires and his father Luigi in Italy published by Samuel L. Baily and Franco Ramella, eds., *One Family, Two Worlds: An Italian Family's Correspondence across the Atlantic, 1901–1922* (New Brunswick, NJ: Rutgers University Press, 1988); thirty unpublished letters written between 1916 and 1973 by Ida Sola and various members of her family in Buenos Aires, New York, and Haledon, New Jersey, and Valdengo; a number of interviews between the author and the children and grandchildren of Ida Sola; and Samuel L. Baily, *Immigrants in the Lands of Promise: Italians in Buenos Aires and New York City, 1870 to 1914* (Ithaca, NY: Cornell University Press, 1999), 1–8.

3. Baily and Ramella, *One Family*, 34.

4. Ibid., 76.

5. Ibid., 74.

6. Ibid., 81.

7. Ibid., 204.

8. Letter from Ida to her brother Abele, January 6, 1966.

1

Spanish Emigration to Cuba and Argentina

José C. Moya

In this selection the author examines the enormous impact of the massive Spanish migration after 1870 on the historical development of its two most important destinations in the New World and skillfully places this story in the broader context of European migration. José Moya explores the ways that economic growth in Argentina and Cuba created a demand for labor that was filled in part by Spanish peasants. In both countries, however, most Spaniards settled in urban areas and many were involved in commerce and artisanal activities. Moya reinforces the notion, discussed later in the book, that emigration was essentially a region-based undertaking as he follows emigrants from various areas of Spain to their New World destinations. He notes that Galicians and Catalans migrated to both countries, but the Basques in Argentina and the Canary Islanders in Cuba were considered superior to those from other regions of Spain. In Argentina, with its large Italian population, the Spanish migrants were important in preserving the Hispanic heritage of that country. In Cuba, with its large number of descendants of African slaves, they played a similar role.

The Spanish presence in the New World is often associated with images of sixteenth-century explorers and adventurers. The stories about Cortés, Pizarro, and Ponce de León are part of the curriculum in primary schools of the Western Hemisphere. Yet, most Spaniards reached the Americas as common immigrants rather than as conquistadors, with the vast majority arriving after the colonies had declared their independence from the Iberian Crown. At the most, 1 million Spaniards came to the Indies (as their American possessions were then called) during the more than 300 years of colonial rule from the end of the fifteenth to the beginning of the nineteenth century. More than four times that number came during the half-century after 1880.[1]

These more recent transatlantic migrants not only arrived in greater numbers but they also shifted destinations. During the colonial period, the two jewels of the Spanish overseas empire, silver-rich Mexico and Peru, had attracted the bulk of the *peninsulares* (people from the Iberian peninsula, the common colonial term for Spaniards). During the late nineteenth and early twentieth centuries, Argentina and Cuba drew over three-quarters of the emigrants from Spain: 2 and 1 million, respectively.

In this chapter, I first examine the global context of these population movements. The main question in this section is simple and evidently crucial: What broad social forces could explain the largest transcontinental migration of people in human history? The second section explains why Argentina and Cuba emerged as major magnets for European immigration, becoming, respectively, the second and sixth most important receiving countries in the world. The third and last section examines how Spanish immigrants adapted to their new lands, their image among their hosts, and their contribution to the historical formation of both countries.

The Global Context

Spanish transatlantic migration formed part of a much bigger process that took 56 million Europeans out of their native continent between the end of the Napoleonic Wars in 1815 and the world depression of 1930. No population movement of this magnitude had taken place in human history before. None has surpassed it.[2] These massive transcontinental migrations were caused, and formed part of, a process of modernization that began in Britain and spread from there to the rest of Northern Europe and, later, to the southern and eastern regions of the continent.

The most elemental part of this process was demographic modernization. Before the eighteenth century, high death rates tended to wipe out any gains made by high birth rates, so population growth in Europe, and the rest of the world, was slow and intermittent (periods of high growth rarely lasted more than two decades). In the late twentieth century, low death rates are counterbalanced by low birth rates so that the European population is again static or declining.

In the long transition from the traditional system to the modern one, however, a population explosion took place in Europe for the first time in human history as death rates fell earlier and faster (thanks to improvements in hygiene and the end of plagues) than birth rates. From 1800 to 1900, Europe's population grew from 188 to 420 million (even though 35 million emigrated overseas), and the continent's share of the world's population increased from 19 percent to 26 percent. In Spain this demographic growth affected mostly the northern coastal zones (Galicia, Asturias, Santander, the Basque country, and Catalonia) and the Canary Islands. Not coincidentally, these regions provided the bulk of the exodus to the Americas during the nineteenth and twentieth centuries—in sharp contrast to the colonial period, when most settlers had come from southern Spain (western Andalusia and Estremadura).

The transition from subsistence to commercial agriculture during the nineteenth century fostered emigration in several ways. The countryside's growing ties to the expanding cities—in the form of trade, public administration, and migration—diminished the isolation of the peasantry and promoted the flow of information and mobility, necessary preconditions for the massive transatlantic crossings. Technological innovations and increased productivity fueled further population growth and unemployment, thereby increasing the potential pool of migrants and emigrants. The transformation of communal lands into private plots expelled many small farmers from the land while creating opportunities for others. Reliance on markets, particularly international ones, increased the chances for profits but also made rural economies more vulnerable. In the Canary Islands, for example, a wine-export boom collapsed around the middle of the nineteenth century and was replaced by a boom in cochineal (a natural dye) exports, which in turn fell victim to technological innovation a few decades later as the appearance of synthetic dyes made cochineal obsolete. Capitalist agriculture also awakened a desire for land and profits that often could only be fulfilled through emigration. Saving money to purchase land back home or to expand the family plot became an impetus for rural emigration in Spain as it did in the rest of Europe. Peasants impoverished by the pressures and competition of commercial agriculture did not have the resources to finance a transatlantic trip and tended to migrate internally. Those who traveled overseas were usually better off economically than their neighbors. With some exceptions, ambition and a desire to improve their condition, more than necessity, provided the psychological force behind the overseas exodus from rural areas.

The Industrial Revolution had a similar impact. It encouraged mobility by displacing rural artisans who could not compete with factories and by attracting to urban centers these artisans and the surplus rural labor released by demographic swelling and commercial agriculture. In the manner of stepping stones, many of these migrants or their children would later move on to the Americas. Eventually, industrialization would function as a check on emigration by offering alternative employment, but for a long period it displaced many more workers than it could absorb. As with capitalist agriculture, industrialization also spurred emigration by creating new demands and desires, particularly among the young. In 1912, for example, a Spanish priest blamed the transatlantic exodus on the covetousness of youngsters for patent-leather boots, fancy clothes, guns, phonographs, and other factory-made consumer articles.[3] The easiest way to acquire these desirable goods, it seemed to young people, was to make money in the Americas, where, according to folk humor, "they leash dogs

with sausages." Another product of the Industrial Revolution, the photo-
graph, carried those illusions and yearnings across the ocean, as a Spanish immigrant observed:

> Every time one of these aristocrats of the duster and the broom [Span-
> ish servants in Argentina] takes a picture in her Sunday best ('tailleur'
> [tailor-made] dress, stockings, patent-leather shoes), she immediately
> sends a copy home. The photograph passes from house to house through-
> out the village, and in every one enthusiastic comments are made, see-
> ing in this seignorial attire an enviable well-being. If there is a young
> maid in the house, a desire awakens in her to leave for Argentina, and
> that night the meek bumpkin dreams of faraway lands, of palaces and
> gold, of fortune and happiness. The most determined decide to take the
> trip.[4]

The technological and innovative capacity unleashed by the Industrial Revolution also enabled the transoceanic transportation of not only
dreams and photographs but also of masses of people. From the
midnineteenth century onward, steamships increasingly replaced sailing
vessels, the screw propeller supplanted the cumbersome paddlewheel, and
iron (and later steel) hulls superseded wooden ones. Meanwhile, the sequential introduction of double-expansion, triple-expansion, steam tur-
bine, and diesel marine engines kept cutting down fuel consumption and
pushing up speed on the oceans. On land, new railroad construction increased the pool of potential emigrants beyond port and coastal regions
and into the hinterland.

Another critical element that made mass emigration possible was the
spread of liberalism as a hegemonic ideology. Up to the eighteenth century, the dominant mercantilist tenets held that a kingdom's wealth and
power depended on the number of its subjects and that the State had the
right to prohibit their departure (or the entry of foreigners into colonies).
The demographic revolution or, as it was often called then, the "Malthusian devil," changed many government officials' minds about the benefit
of an ever-expanding population. The liberal emphasis on individual autonomy and personal liberty made it increasingly difficult to defend government restrictions on population movement. During the nineteenth
century European countries—beginning in the north of the continent and
spreading south and east—eliminated most laws banning or restricting
departures. On the other side of the Atlantic, American countries not only
kept the gates open but also encouraged immigration, at times with offers
of free passage and land.

Emigration was not then, and is not now, the result of backwardness
and poverty but of change and modernization (or of a specific early phase
of this process). The most developed countries and richer regions first
joined the flow. Movement and flux—of capital, goods, services, technologies, ideas, and people—became the mark of modernization; as it

spread from England to Germany, to Scandinavia, to southern and eastern Europe, and to Japan, so did overseas emigration. Spain, as a country of relatively late modernization, was among the last European countries to join the nineteenth-century exodus en masse, even though Spaniards had been the first Europeans to cross the Atlantic.

The Receiving Societies—Background

Some of the same forces that caused emigration in Spain and the rest of Europe also helped turn Argentina, Cuba, and a few other countries into recipients of immigrants. Demographic growth in the Old World, particularly in the expanding urban centers where people did not grow their own food, generated the demand for grains and sugar that connected Argentina and Cuba to Europe through trade and transportation networks. This expanding market for food on one side of the Atlantic synchronically created a market for labor on the other, specifically in countries with fertile lands and low population density. Argentina had the pampas, one of the three finest farm belts on the planet,[5] but few farmers. At the time of its independence in 1810, the new country of 1 million square miles—the size of continental Europe—held fewer than 0.5 million inhabitants, about half the population of Barcelona Province, or one-fifth of that of the city of London.

Argentina, in this sense, is a classic country of European settlement. The surplus population created by Europe's demographic expansion and economic modernization did not simply head for countries with flourishing economies. It moved toward specific environments. As Table 1 shows, 96 percent of the 56 million Europeans who left their continent in the century or so after the Napoleonic Wars settled in four regions: North America (in particular the area north of the Mason-Dixon Line and east of the Rocky Mountains), where 67 percent of the total settled; the River Plate (formed by eastern Argentina, Uruguay, and southern Brazil), which attracted more than 20 percent of the total; Australasia, with 7 percent; and in smaller numbers, South Africa. These regions comprise the bulk of the non-European Temperate Zone and have warm-to-cool climates with an annual precipitation of 50 to 150 centimeters, thinly spread aboriginal populations, some of the world's best pasture and wheat-producing lands, immense herds of cattle and flocks of sheep, consistent surplus production of grains, and, with the exception of South Africa, largely Caucasian populations.[6]

Nineteen out of every twenty European emigrants thus settled in what historian Alfred Crosby has aptly called Neo-Europes, and their movement formed part of what the same author termed ecological imperialism, a migration-invasion of Old World animals (humans included) and plants that changed the fauna and flora of these countries. At this level, immigration to Argentina formed part of a much larger demographic-ecological phenomenon.

Table 1. Destination of European Overseas Emigrants, ca. 1820–1932

Country	Number	Percent of Total	Cumulative Percentage
United States	32,564,000	57.9	57.9
Canada	5,073,000	9.0	67.0
Argentina	6,501,000	11.6	78.5
Brazil	4,361,000	7.8	86.3
Uruguay	713,000	1.3	87.6
Australia	3,443,000	6.1	93.7
New Zealand	588,000	1.0	94.7
South Africa	731,000	1.3	96.0
Cuba	1,394,000	2.5	98.5
Mexico	270,000	0.5	99.0
Algeria	150,000	0.3	99.3
Chile	90,000	0.2	99.4
Venezuela	70,000	0.1	99.5
Puerto Rico	62,000	0.1	99.7
British West Indies	60,000	0.1	99.8
Hawaii	40,000	0.1	99.8
Zimbabwe	30,000	0.1	99.9
Peru	30,000	0.1	99.9
Paraguay	21,000	0.0	100.0
New Caledonia	12,000	0.0	100.0
Total	**56,183,000**		

Source: José C. Moya, *Cousins and Strangers: Spanish Immigrants in Buenos Aires, 1850–1930* (Berkeley, 1998), 46.

Cuba, on the other hand, is a peculiar country of immigration and an exception to the rule. An island a bit smaller than Pennsylvania and one-tenth the size of Argentina, it is the only Latin American country outside of the River Plate region, and the only tropical environment in the world, to have received massive numbers of European immigrants (see Table 1). What it had in common with other lands of European settlement was a small aboriginal population. Indeed, the indigenous inhabitants, estimated at 50,000 to 110,000 before Columbus landed on the island in 1492, were virtually exterminated by the violence of the Conquest and by Old World diseases for which they had no immunity. During the next three centuries, Cuba developed as a colony of European settlement with a rudimentary ranching and farming economy. While its strategic position allowed the Caribbean island to become a commercial entrepôt between the American mainland and Spain, it never reached the wealth and importance of the viceroyalties of New Spain and Peru.

The colonial development of Cuba and Argentina resembled each other until the middle of the eighteenth century. They lacked the combination that had made the highlands of Mesoamerica and the Andean region the rich centers of the Spanish empire: precious minerals and a large, sedentary Indian labor force. They also lacked the other combination for a successful exploitation colony: a cash crop and an imported African slave force, as was the case in northeast Brazil or Saint-Domingue (which by the eighteenth century had become the richest colony in the world). By default, they became colonies of European settlement but proved much less able to attract white settlers than, for example, New England or Pennsylvania. Unlike England, Spain did not allow other Europeans to settle in its possessions and did not have the demographic density to provide many colonizers itself before the nineteenth century; indeed, most of those who left preferred to go to the wealthier regions of the empire. But if Argentina and Cuba lacked the wealth of Peru or Pernambuco, they were also spared the extremely unequal social structures of exploitation colonies. Together with a few other regions in the Iberian empires—such as Costa Rica, southern Brazil, and Antioquia (Colombia)—they developed a less affluent but more egalitarian class system that provided a relatively solid foundation on which to build an independent republic.

Cuba: Sugar and Slavery

In the latter half of the eighteenth century, Cuba's historical development took a sharp turn with the growth of the sugar economy and slavery. Although the Spanish Crown had chartered the Havana Company in 1740 to stimulate commercial agriculture and the importation of slaves, it was not until the British ten-month occupation of Havana in 1762 that both goals began to be accomplished. The reforms of the Bourbon monarchs, particularly Charles III, and the collapse of the sugar economy in Haiti after the revolution of 1791–1803 further stimulated the expansion of the plantation system. Between 1763 and 1860, Cuba's population increased from less than 150,000 to more than 1.3 million. Slaves accounted for much of this expansion. During the first half of the nineteenth century, Cuba imported more than 600,000 Africans, and its slave population increased from 4,000 in 1760 to some 400,000 in the 1840s. During the same period sugar exports increased 5,000 times from .02 to 93.45 million arrobas. By then, Cuba had the most advanced and mechanized sugar industry in the world and produced one-third of the global supply. Coffee, introduced by French planters who had fled Haiti during the revolution, and tobacco, grown in large part by immigrant farmers from the Canary Islands, became the two other major export crops.

The end of the slave trade after the middle of the nineteenth century increased the demand for labor. In the late 1840s, Cuban planters brought in hundreds of enslaved rebel Maya Indians from Yucatán and the first of the 150,000 Chinese coolies who arrived from Shanghai and Canton during the next three decades.[7] Ever since the Haitian slave revolt of 1791 the colonial government had also tried to attract white newcomers as a demographic counterbalance to prevent a similar uprising, allowing non-Spanish European Catholics to settle in Cuba. A few thousand came. But a tropical island with a plantation economy based mostly on slave and semi-bondage labor was not exactly the place to attract European immigrants away from the United States, where most of them were then heading.

Cuba, however, offered many attractions to Spaniards. One was its continuing colonial status. Indeed, the independence wars of 1810–1824 on the mainland served to intensify Spain's political and economic connections with the most important of its remaining colonies, which came to contribute almost one-fourth of the Spanish treasury's total revenues. Many loyalists, particularly from Mexico and Venezuela where the emancipation struggle and resentment against Spaniards had been especially virulent, fled to Cuba rather than back to Spain. The continuity and strengthening of formal ties protected and increased informal connections between family, friends, and business partners on both sides of the Atlantic, which in turn spurred immigration. The island's economy was one of the most advanced and dynamic in the Western Hemisphere. At the start of the nineteenth century Havana was larger than New York City. The most important technological innovation of the century, the railroad, appeared in Cuba in 1836, not only before any other Latin American country but also a dozen years before Spain itself and only eleven years after its English birth. The island was also a pioneer in the use of steam engines, the telegraph, and various other technologies. During the first half of the nineteenth century, therefore, some 60,000 Spaniards headed for Cuba—not a large number compared to the peak period in the early twentieth century but more than went to all the other American republics combined.[8]

The inflow of Spaniards into "the ever faithful island of Cuba" acquired greater force in the decades following the middle of the nineteenth century. The failed attempt against colonial rule by the "not-so-faithful" Cubans during the Ten Years' War (1868–1878) brought in 209,000 Spanish soldiers, many of whom stayed after the war was over. The decline of slavery and its final abolition in 1886 intensified the efforts of planters to bring in white laborers and made the Cuban labor market more attractive to free immigrants. Meanwhile, in Spain the emigration-causing forces discussed in the first part of this chapter were gathering strength. And the Spanish-American War brought in an even greater number of *peninsular* conscripts than the Ten Years' War, many of whom stayed after independence.

Unlike the case of the mainland colonies in the early nineteenth century, where emancipation shattered ties with the former metropolis (or state of origin) for decades, Spanish immigration to Cuba actually increased after the island broke away from Spain in 1898. In part because of the U.S. occupation, Cuba avoided the violent aftermath to independence that had afflicted other Latin American republics a century before. The economy, already one of the richest in the Western Hemisphere during the colonial period, continued to grow as sugar production increased tenfold during the first two decades of the twentieth century. The collapse of the beet sugar industry in Europe during World War I raised the international price from 2 to 12 cents per pound leading to a boom, known in Cuban history as "the dance of the millions," that attracted hundreds of thousands of newcomers. Sugar exports also promoted the growth of the secondary and tertiary sectors of the economy, something of particular importance in attracting Spanish immigrants who preferred to settle in cities and work in commercial activities. Already by 1900, Cuba had become the most urbanized country in Latin America after Uruguay and a bit ahead of Argentina. In the following three decades about 800,000 Spaniards entered the island.

Argentina: An Agro-Pastoral Economy

Unlike Cuba, Argentina not only broke away from the Spanish metropolis in the early nineteenth century, but that emancipation also was followed by decades of civil wars and economic disarray. The new republic's first civilian president, Bernardino Rivadavia, tried to encourage agriculture and immigration with a plan to grant public lands to European settlers in emphyteusis, but conditions in the aftermath of emancipation proved propitious for neither. Recurrent civil strife in the countryside prevented planting and repelled settlers. Under the circumstances, only rudimentary ranching, which required little capital or labor input and exploited the natural resource of the pampas, thrived. Relatively few seminomadic gauchos herded and hunted wild or partly tamed cattle and horses in huge unfenced *estancias* (rural estates) for their hide and tallow. In this primitive pastoralism, roaming cattle impeded crop farming and ambitious cattlemen obstructed agricultural colonization projects, viewing them as antithetical to their interests or, at best, costly pipe dreams of liberal ideologues. Yet, indirectly and in the long run, rudimentary ranching facilitated immigration by allowing national capital accumulation at a time when other activities were not viable, by providing government revenues and thus aiding political stability, and by creating the first sustained links with the international economy.

Argentina's pastoral economy also became more complex and labor intensive as the nineteenth century progressed. In the decades after independence, meat-salting plants (*saladeros*) introduced factory methods such as wage levels, a division of labor, and large-scale production on one site. These *saladeros* grew in number and size for much of the century as they supplied the Western Hemisphere's slave markets with jerked beef; they declined only after the abolition of slavery in Cuba and Brazil during the late 1880s. From the 1840s sheep raising grew so fast that by the end of the century sheep outnumbered humans eighteen-to-one and, at 75 million strong, formed the largest flock in the world outside of Australia. Demand from European factories for wool and from European urban dwellers for mutton fueled this expansion; in turn, the expansion of this economy encouraged immigration. Sheep farming was three times as labor intensive as cattle grazing, and the pampas' native plainsmen had neither the cultural inclination nor, given the abundance of wild cattle free for the taking, the material necessity to shepherd. Not surprisingly, sheep tending became so much an immigrant's occupation (mainly Basques and Irish) that an Irish minstrel in the pampas had to set the record straight with the following song:

Usted pensar que los gringos	You thinking [*sic*] that immigrants
no saber nada mas que	don't knowing [*sic*] anything but
cuidar ovejas en campaña.	tend sheep in countryside.
Pero usted se equivoca,	But you are wrong
porque ellos saben también	because they also know how to
tomar mate y chupar caña.[9]	drink *maté* and guzzle booze.

The final phase in the evolution of Argentina's pastoral economy, cattle breeding and beef export, had been delayed for three reasons: by the abundance of the creole livestock whose stringy flesh appealed little to the European palate; by the expansion of sheep raising on the pampas that absorbed grazing lands used by the cattle; and by the difficulty of shipping beef across the Atlantic. After the 1880s these obstacles were overcome by the Argentine *estancieros*, the national army, and new marine technology. Ranchers embraced the practice of importing and breeding pedigreed animals with such enthusiasm that by 1900 the high-grade-beef Shorthorns and Herefords outnumbered all other strains in the national stock. The military conquest of Patagonia from the Araucanian Indians in 1879–80 allowed sheep raising to move south to cheaper and more arid lands whose weeds tasted good enough to the notoriously undiscriminating herbivores, freeing up much of the pampas for cattle grazing. Steamers allowed the transportation of cattle on the hoof, and after the turn of the century refrigerated ships permitted the massive export of frozen and later chilled beef.

By the early twentieth century the 25 million head of cattle outnumbered humans five to one and Argentina had replaced the United States as the major supplier to the British market. The additional element that made this possible was a steady influx of immigrants. Unlike the cattle herding of the decades following independence, where one gaucho could care for 2,000 head, the new cattle-beef economy required armies of laborers to erect the barbed-wire fences that prevented unwanted mixing of thoroughbred animals, to plant the alfalfa that fattened the livestock in a way that the pampas' wild grasses could never do, to milk cows in the mushrooming *tambos* (dairy farms, usually Basque-owned), and to build the wells, windmills, water pumps, and other devices of the modern *estancia*. Cattle barons, who a generation earlier had opposed immigration, now welcomed it with as much enthusiasm as the arrival of Brahma bulls.

The fences that checked the promiscuity of prize bulls also made possible the last stage in Argentina's agricultural revolution—agricultural now in the strict sense of the word and revolutionary in any sense. Cultivated land increased about fiftyfold from 0.5 million hectares in 1870 to 24.5 million in 1914. As late as the first date, the country imported most of its grains; by the second, it had turned into a veritable breadbasket, the world's largest producer of corn and linseed and the second largest exporter of wheat. If the pampas provided the rich and deep topsoil for this boom, Europe provided the *brazos* (literally "arms," and a pseudonym for immigrants often found in the writings and speeches of the country's rural oligarchy). Indeed, Argentina's agro-pastoral economy had steadily evolved toward more labor-intensive forms: from hunting feral cattle and horses for their hides (pre-1810) to herding and slaughtering semitamed animals for the meat-salting plants (ca. 1810–1890), to sheep raising (post-1840), and finally to cattle breeding and crop farming (post-1880). This tendency both fed upon and induced immigration, which increased with each stage. Moreover, the agricultural revolution on the pampas made possible the even more labor-intensive commercial and industrial economy of the urban centers, where 57 percent of the Argentine population resided by 1914.

During the nineteenth century, most Latin American governments had tried to entice European immigrants to "whiten" and "civilize" their countries. These racist agendas, however, were rarely fulfilled. Peru, for example, created dozens of immigration commissions, published and distributed "immigrants' guides," contracted propaganda agents in Europe, and offered would-be immigrants free ship passage, free lodging in Lima, free train transportation to the interior, and free land (fenced, with tools, seeds, oxen, and access to water). And yet for all the racist attitudes and official efforts of its ruling class, Peru attracted in 100 years fewer European immigrants than Argentina in one month and less than the United States in one week at the height of the mass migration period. Only regions with temperate climates and/or with a dynamic export agriculture able to modernize other sectors and create a high-wage economy proved able to attract European newcomers in massive numbers. Argentina clearly fitted both requirements. Cuba fitted only the last, and that is one of the reasons why it was able to attract mostly immigrants from its own colonial metropolis.

Because Argentina broke its colonial ties to Spain in 1810 while Cuba's continued until 1898, Spanish emigration to the Caribbean island was higher than to the River Plate for much of the nineteenth century. Although family connections were never severed completely, the emancipation war and its bitter aftermath reduced the number of Spanish arrivals in Argentina to a trickle until the middle of the 1800s. In 1855, Italians and French already outnumbered Spaniards in the country's capital. However, as the hatreds of the war of independence softened and as Argentina entered into one of the world's most spectacular economic expansions after the 1880s, this country surpassed Cuba as the main destination of Spanish emigrants. By the World War I period, Argentina had by far the largest number of Spanish-born inhabitants in the Western Hemisphere: 830,000, or one-tenth of the country's total population and one-third of its foreign-born population. Cuba followed with 246,000, also about one-tenth of the total inhabitants of the island but almost three-fourths of its foreign-born population. Brazil ranked just below Cuba, and Uruguay, the United States, Mexico, and Chile followed way behind (see Table 2).

Who Came and What Happened

In terms of the regional origin of Iberian immigrants in both countries, there were strong similarities and some differences. Galicians, a people from northwestern Spain whose native language is closer to Portuguese than to Castilian, were the most numerous group in both New World lands. Indeed, they were so predominant that in both Argentina and Cuba, *gallego* became a generic term for all Spaniards. The practice was not completely innocent. Argentines and Cubans knew that other Spaniards resented being called so. Ethnic stereotypes in the Iberian peninsula often depicted Galicians as socially backward and dull-witted. And these stereotypes entered the host societies where "Galician jokes" became a staple of popular ethnic humor (something akin to "Polish jokes" in the United States).

Other groups from the northern seaboard of the peninsula were also overrepresented. Catalans represented about one-tenth of all Spaniards in both countries and were often portrayed as entrepreneurial but stingy—a stereotype that came from the Old World, where they were referred to at times as "the Jews of Spain." The other ethnic cliché about them was that of the "Catalan anarchist," which was not exactly an arbitrary invention. Around the turn of the century, Barcelona had become the most active center of anarchist militancy in the world. Asturians were more numerous in Cuba and Basques in Argentina. Although emigration from the Basque country, one of the most prosperous regions in Spain, declined in the twentieth century, it had accounted for about one-third of the *peninsular* flow

Table 2. Countries with the Largest Number of Spaniards in the Western Hemisphere, ca. 1914–1920

Country	Year	Total Population	Number of Foreigners	(%)ᵃ	Number of Spaniards	(%)ᵇ	(%)ᶜ
Argentina	1914	7,885,980	2,357,952	29.9	829,701	10.5	35.2
Cuba	1919	2,889,004	339,082	11.7	245,644	8.5	72.4
Brazil	1920	30,635,605	1,565,961	5.1	219,142	0.7	14.0
Uruguay	1911	50,000					
United States	1920	105,710,620	13,920,692	13.2	49,535	0.05	0.4
Mexico	1910	30,000					
Chile	1920	3,753,799	120,436	3.2	25,962	0.7	21.6

Sources: Argentina, Comisión Nacional del Censo, *Tercer censo nacional, levantado el 1 de junio de 1914* (Buenos Aires: Talleres Gráficos de L. J. Rosso, 1916–1919), 2:109, 396; Chile, Dirección General de Estadística, *Censo de población de la República de Chile levantado el 15 de diciembre de 1920* (Santiago: Soc. Imp. y Litografía Universo, 1925), 276, 289; Cuba, Dirección General del Censo, *Census of the Republic of Cuba, 1919* (Havana: Maza, Arroyo y Caso, [1920?]), 310; United States, Bureau of the Census, *Fourteenth Census of the United States Taken in the Year 1920* (Washington, DC: Government Printing Office, 1921–1923), 2:693; Brazil, Directoria Geral de Estatística, *Recenseamento do Brasil realizado em 1 de setembro de 1920* (Rio de Janeiro: Typ. da Estatística, 1922–1930), 1:iv, 302–3, 316–17; Mexico, figure for 1910: Mariano González-Rothvos y Gil, *La emigración española a Iberoamérica* (Madrid: Instituto Balmes de Sociología, 1949), 111; Uruguay, figure for circa 1911; Spain, Consejo Superior de Emigración, *La emigración española transoceánica, 1911–1915* (Madrid: Hijos de t. Minuesa, 1916), 219.

ᵃForeigners as a percentage of total population.
ᵇSpaniards as a percentage of total population.
ᶜSpaniards as a percentage of foreign-born population.

to Argentina before the 1880s. Their earlier arrival, and the fact that they were the only Iberian group to settle in the pampas in large numbers and to engage in cattle raising (a prestigious occupation in Argentina with strong links to national identity), made Basques arguably the most admired ethnic group among Argentines, particularly among the elite. Some went as far as to portray Basques as racially superior to other Iberian groups and, consequentially, as less prone to mix with "inferior races" (Africans and Indians) in the New World.

Canary Islanders, on the other hand, hardly went to Argentina but formed the second most important group in Cuba. They never wore the halo of racial superiority that Basques did in Argentina, but they did enjoy a warmer welcome than their other compatriots. Cubans tended to view these fellow islanders as closer to themselves linguistically, culturally, and temperamentally. Tellingly, they, like the Basques in Argentina, were the only Iberian group to settle in the countryside in large numbers. Moreover, they tended to engage in tobacco farming, which, unlike sugarcane growing, was associated with family farming rather than with slavery. Like the pampas and the gauchos in Argentina, the *campiña* (countryside) and the *guajiro* (independent farmer) came to embody the essence of nationality in Cuba. The fact that Basques and Canary Islanders were somehow associated with these icons of national identity helps to explain their respective reputations in both countries.

With the exception of the Basques in Argentina and the Canary Islanders in Cuba, Spaniards tended to settle not in the countryside but in the expanding cities that the wealth from export agriculture made possible. In Argentina, 74 percent of all Spaniards resided in urban centers in 1914, a proportion higher than any other national group in the country (see Table 3). That same year, 18 percent of all non-Spaniards in that country resided in its capital, Buenos Aires; the proportion for Spaniards was twice as high: 37 percent. Similarly, 11 percent of all non-Spaniards in Cuba, but 31 percent of all Spaniards, resided in the city of Havana in 1919.

This preference for urban centers is not easily explained. The majority of immigrants did not come from cities. The proportion represented by those who did was not likely higher than among all the other immigrant groups listed in Table 3, which includes people from much more urbanized countries, such as England, Germany, and France, and particularly urbanized groups in the diaspora, such as Middle Easterners and Russian Jews. Some observers have blamed *latifundia*, the concentration of landed property into a few hands, for impeding the newcomers from accessing farms and forcing them into cities. But why would Spaniards have been more negatively affected by this than all other immigrants? In Cuba they were less than half as likely as blacks to live in rural areas and work in agriculture, and it is impossible to argue that free Spanish immigrants had greater difficulty in accessing landed property than recent former slaves and their descendants. What seems clear, then, is that this concentration in urban centers in both countries was not imposed by structural restraints but represented a culturally informed choice. Perhaps, as Mark Szuchman has put it, "of all the peoples that Rome had brought within its domain, the Iberians most closely imitated their conquerors in the significance they assigned to the city."[10] Unlike in Anglo-American lore, where the city often represents danger and perdition, in Iberian tradition it embodies civilization, a term that tellingly derives from the Latin word for "city."

Table 3. Principal National Groups in Argentina in 1914 and Percentage Living in Urban Centers (Places with More Than 2,000 Inhabitants)

Nationality	Total Number	Percent Urban
Spaniards	829,701	74
Middle Easterners	64,369	73
French	79,491	69
Italians	929,863	69
Germans	26,995	66
English	27,692	62
Russians	93,634	57
Argentines	5,527,285	53
Austro-Hungarians	38,123	49

Source: Argentina, Comisión Nacional del Censo, *Tercer censo nacional, 1914* (Buenos Aires, 1916–1919), 2:395–96.

The urban concentration of Spanish immigrants had its occupational counterpart in their overrepresentation in commerce, as both owners and employees. The "*gallego* grocer" (*bodeguero* in Cuba, *almacenero* in Argentina) became a familiar figure in the towns and cities of both countries. In 1909, Spaniards owned 22 percent of all commercial establishments in Buenos Aires. This proportion was twice as high in some specific ones such as groceries, clothing and notions stores, dairies, bars and cafés, hotels, and bookstores. Their commercial presence in Cuba was even more pronounced. Spaniards accounted for 64 percent of all merchants and 78 percent of all salesmen in Havana at the end of the colonial period (1899). On the entire island, 53 percent of all merchants were foreign-born whites (91 percent of whom were Spaniards). Twenty years later, Spaniards still made up 43 percent of all merchants and 50 percent of all sales personnel in Cuba.

Spanish immigrants also actively engaged in crafts. A large number of the bakers and tailors in Argentina and Cuba were Spaniards. In Argentina, however, Italian immigrants proportionately outnumbered Spanish ones in skilled manual jobs, and the same was true in Cuba with the African-

Cuban population. This in part was the result of Spaniards' concentration in the commercial sector, which, in turn, was facilitated by their higher literacy. Seventy percent of Spaniards in Argentina in 1914 knew how to read and write, as compared to 62 percent of Italians. The literacy gap between Spaniards and Afro-Cubans was even wider: 69 percent versus 25 percent in 1899, and 72 percent versus 53 percent in 1919.

One of the principal differences in the insertion of Spanish immigrants into the labor forces of Argentina and Cuba was their participation in domestic service. In Argentina, Spaniards of both sexes were more likely to work as servants than any other national group. Indeed, the Spanish presence in the domestic service was so predominant that the "*gallega* maid" became a cultural stereotype in Argentine theater, movies, and popular humor. Lino Palacios, the creator of "Ramona," a well-known comic strip about a Spanish maid, remembered in an interview: "In the beginning [circa 1860s] most servants were native girls from the provinces. The *estancieros* brought these *chinitas*, as they used to call them, from the countryside. Then came the flood of Spanish immigrants, and all maids were Spanish, *gallegas*. Italians rarely worked in the house, only outside, as washerwomen and things like that."[11]

In Cuba the domestic service also employed many of the immigrants: about two-thirds of all Spanish women and one-fifth of all Spanish men in the workforce at the end of the colonial period. These proportions surpassed those of native whites (one-half and one-sixth, respectively). But, unlike in Argentina, Spaniards did not become associated with the domestic service in popular culture. One of the reasons is the large black and mulatto population in Cuba, which accounted for 33 percent of the total population in 1899 but for 70 percent of all servants. The other reason was the greater proportion of women among the Spanish residents in Argentina (38 percent of the total in 1914) compared to Cuba (24 percent of the total in 1919). With the feminization of the domestic service in the twentieth century, the relative shortage of Spanish women in Cuba made their presence in that sector of the economy less significant.

Overall, one of the principal characteristics of Spanish immigrants in both Argentina and Cuba was that, unlike many immigrant groups in the United States that concentrated at the bottom of the occupational ladder, Spaniards appeared on all the rungs. In comparison with native whites, Spanish immigrants were underrepresented in the higher professions and (less so in Cuba than in Argentina) in the rural oligarchy. But they were not by any means excluded, and many of the richest landowners, industrialists, bankers, and merchants in both countries had been born in Spain. In the nineteenth century, Spaniards were overrepresented in the middle sectors of the economy, although the degree of overrepresentation may have declined with the growth of a native middle class of European background in the twentieth century. And, of course, Spaniards, particularly the recently arrived and the poorly educated, engaged in all sorts of menial and low-skilled jobs.

The host societies' attitude toward these poor arrivals from Spain could be harsh. In 1859 a North American resident in Cuba wrote the following entry in his diary:

> Even the negroes here seem to look down upon them. The inferiority of the lower classes of Spain, compared with those of Cuba, is even acknowledged by the Spaniards themselves. They may be seen by the cartload, the same as we see the very poorest class of emigrants coming up from Castle Garden in New York, and their appearance is very similar. They stare about, wondering at everything they see, and are pictures of filth, hunger and nakedness. They are called "*sucios blancos*" (dirty whites) by the negroes.[12]

Similar attitudes toward poor Spanish immigrants (or toward poor immigrants from rural backgrounds in general) existed in Argentina, where they were usually described as hardworking but slow-witted and dirty. Contrary to the implications of the quotation above, being white in racist societies had conferred certain advantages for Spaniards in the nineteenth century. But as European immigration increased, particularly in ·Argentina, a light skin became a more common, and thus less valuable, commodity.

Iberian imperialism represented a more serious source of conflict between Creoles and *peninsulares*. The war of independence in Argentina may not have been as bloody as those in Mexico or Venezuela, but it obviously fomented hatreds between natives and Spaniards that lingered past the middle of the nineteenth century. The revival of Spain's imperialist adventurism in Latin America during the 1860s (in Mexico, the Dominican Republic, Peru, and Chile) and its continuing domination of Cuba and Puerto Rico did much to keep resentment against the old colonial power alive. And so did the official history propagated by public education that celebrated the heroic deeds of Argentine patriots against the Spanish oppressors. Despite the continuing colonial status of the island, or perhaps because of it, Cubans developed one of the earliest and strongest national identities in Latin America. Necessarily, this nationalism had a strong anti-Spanish component. The Ten Years' War and the final War of Independence of 1895–1898 were brutal affairs. One-tenth of the population was killed or exiled. And yet, surprisingly, Hispanophobia after emancipation was relatively short-lived and milder than it had been in the mainland colonies under similar circumstances a century before.

Given the linguistic and cultural proximity, one could assume that Spanish immigrants speedily assimilated to their host societies. But this was not the case. In both Argentina and Cuba they created a separate institutional structure that included anything from social clubs and mutual-aid associations to choral societies, hospitals, banks, and newspapers. In

Cuba there is little evidence that creolization advanced faster among Spaniards than among the other immigrants to the island (Chinese, Haitians, Jamaicans, North Americans, and Lebanese). In Argentina, Spaniards consistently exhibited higher rates of residential segregation than Italians, and often higher than the French, British, and Germans. And these rates were particularly high vis-à-vis the native population. The endogamy rates of Spanish males and females consistently surpassed those of their Italian counterparts, who proved more willing to marry out of their own group. Popular stereotypes point in the same direction. Argentine plays and comedies of the earlier part of the twentieth century steadily depicted Italian immigrants as more likely than Spaniards to imitate and adopt local speech, habits, and mannerisms. Indeed, the figure of the *italiano acriollado* (Argentinized Italian) permeated the Porteño thespian scene.

The explanation for this apparent anomaly may lie in the Spaniards' colonial relation to both countries. As citizens of the mother country they thought that their ancestors had discovered and settled Argentina and Cuba; thus, they had special prerogatives not shared by other immigrants. Unlike other groups, many Spaniards believed that they did not have to assimilate to local customs to belong. Indeed, they belonged simply because they were the charter group, the progenitors, the givers of the original culture and language of the American nations. Of course, by the early twentieth century, Argentines and Cubans had long ceased to be transplanted Spaniards, just as North Americans had long ceased to be transplanted Englishmen. Other elements—indigenous, African, Italian—had contributed to the formation of these nations' cultures. But Spanish immigrants tended to downplay these influences or to see them as threats to the Hispanic legacy and predominance.

Conclusion

The influence of Spaniards in the historical development of Argentina and Cuba thus did not end with the Conquest and colonization. Their arrival in massive numbers during the nineteenth and early twentieth centuries significantly contributed to the growth of the population and of the economy in both countries. In Argentina, given the huge immigration of non-Iberians (French, Germans, Russian Jews, Middle Easterners, and particularly Italians, who were more numerous than the Spaniards), they played a pivotal role in preserving the Hispanic heritage of the country. By doing so, they helped to assuage the fears of cultural loss among Argentina's creole elite, giving this ruling group enough confidence in the survival of Argentina's Hispanic legacy to permit immigration and the resulting transformation of the country to continue. In Cuba, with the arrival of large numbers of African slaves during the first half of the nineteenth century, Spanish immigrants played a key role in preserving the island's previous history as a settler society and preventing it from becoming a plantation economy like many of its neighbors in the Caribbean. Cuba, like Brazil and the United States but at a different spatial dimension, ended up as a mixture of a society of free settlement and a society of former slaves. The first component fostered the formation of a well-organized working class and large middle class; the second explains in large part the persistence of racially based socioeconomic inequalities despite decades of socialist redistribution. The presence of Spanish immigrants also explains why throughout the twentieth century Spain has had closer relations with Argentina and Cuba than with any other Latin American country irrespective of political systems.

Notes

1. For a more detailed analysis of Spanish immigration to Argentina see José C. Moya, *Cousins and Strangers: Spanish Immigrants in Buenos Aires, 1850–1930* (Berkeley: University of California Press, 1998).

2. Although intercontinental migration has been increasing since the end of World War II, and particularly since 1980, it has not reached the levels of the earlier part of the twentieth century, in either absolute or relative terms. In 1900 the world had 1.55 billion inhabitants and in the next decade 14.8 million people emigrated from their native continents. By 1980 the world population had tripled, to 4.48 billion, but the number of people leaving their native continents in the next decade had fallen by more than half, to 7.1 million. In absolute numbers the early twentieth-century movement was thus two times larger than that of the 1980s; in relative terms (that is, in proportion to the world population) it was six times larger.

3. Ramón Castro López, *La emigración en Galicia* (La Coruña, 1923), 66–68 [orginally written in 1912].

4. Manuel Gil de Oto, *La Argentina que yo he visto* (Barcelona: B. Bauzá, 1914), 66.

5. The other two are the North American Great Plains (including the Canadian prairies) and the Ukrainian *chernozem*, or black earth of the steppes.

6. The *World Almanac and Book of Facts, 1996*, lists the white population of these countries as follows: United States, 83 percent of the total; Canada, 97 percent; Argentina, 85 percent (in the eastern part of the country the proportion is closer to 95 percent); Uruguay, 88 percent; Brazil, 55 percent (south of São Paulo the proportion has been estimated as between 85 and 95 percent); Australia, 95 percent; New Zealand, 88 percent; and South Africa, 18 percent.

7. The other Latin American country that received a significant number of Chinese coolies during the period was Peru, where 75,000 arrived between 1847 and 1874.

8. Immigration statistics before 1882 are sketchy, but censuses list 39,000 Spaniards living in Cuba in 1846 and 90,000 in 1862.

9. Recorded in David J. R. Watson, *Los criollos y los gringos: Escombros acumulados al levantar la estructura ganadera-frigorífica, 1882–1940* (Buenos Aires, 1941), 16.

10. Gilbert M. Joseph and Mark D. Szuchman, eds., *I Saw a City Invincible: Urban Portraits of Latin America* (Wilmington, DE: Scholarly Resources, 1996), 1.

11. Transcribed in Isabel Laura Cárdenas, *Ramona y el robot: El servicio doméstico en barrios prestigiosos de Buenos Aires, 1895–1985* (Buenos Aires, 1986), 82–84.

12. Louis A. Pérez, ed., *Impressions of Cuba in the Nineteenth Century: The Travel Diary of Joseph J. Dimock* (Wilmington, DE: Scholarly Resources, 1998), 51.

2

A History of Spanish and Italian Migration to the South Atlantic Regions of the Americas

Fernando J. Devoto

Contemporaries and then scholars interpreted the causes of migration of Spaniards and Italians to the countries of the Rio de la Plata at the turn of the past century in two basic ways. Statesmen, Marxists, Malthusians, neoclassicists and others, according to Fernando Devoto, believed that migration was caused either by misery (the pessimists) or by the opportunity to have a better life (the optimists). In addition, he argues, information-diffusion theory is important because it explains why immigrants did not always go where the salary differential between their old and new environments was the best. Finally, the author questions a number of common assumptions that immigrant theorists have made regarding the homogeneity of the migrants, the time frame in which they have been studied, the linear or circular nature of the migration process, and the most appropriate level of analysis (the nation-state, the region, or the village).

The search for the causes of the migration that drove millions of Spaniards and Italians to cross the Atlantic has given birth to a persistent controversy. This controversy was first posed by contemporary observers of the mass migration at the turn of the nineteenth century; these observers were polarized between those who thought that the cause of the exodus was "misery" (pessimists), and those who thought that the motive was a search for a "better life" (optimists). The controversy between the people who judged social development optimistically (that is to say, capitalism) and the pessimists who contested it (or at least contested its nondesirable effects) was certainly ideological. Among those in the first group were liberal economists, who thought that emigration was an advantage for national trade and for the balance of trade, and the politicians in the countries of origin, who believed that free "colonies" were a useful instrument for cultural penetration and, eventually, for other, more aggressive, expansionist activities. Among the pessimists were the European politicians who worried about the social question and who thought that emigration was a necessary evil, a "safety valve" that would prevent worse catastrophes; the nationalists (and demographers) who thought that emigration was draining energy from the body politic; and the Catholic conservatives who imagined that emigration carried with it a loss of faith and a weakening of traditional customs and social mores.

The polemic of these contemporaries continued among historians who, although making different points, were divided into two similar groups: those who viewed the social process with optimism and those who viewed it with pessimism. These historians, while using a more sophisticated language of "pull and push" or "attraction and expulsion," did not differ substantially from the old dichotomy that contrasted the idea of seeking a "better life" with that of escaping "misery."[1]

The pessimist social scientists, who emphasized the existing situation in the migrants' country of origin as the defining cause of emigration, referred to diverse conceptual matrixes that could be schematically grouped into those with an economic orientation (predominantly Marxist) and those with a demographic mindset (in many cases very close to Malthusian stereotypes). The economists' view could be summarized as follows: the development of capitalist economic relationships in Europe carried with it the proletarianization of rural labor, which in turn provided the potential labor pool of the new urban industrial economies whose members were ready to emigrate. This was especially so in underdeveloped economies, that is, for example, in the late-developing economies of the European periphery.[2]

The demographic model has emphasized, instead, the problem of the pressure of population increase associated with the demographic transition that affected the European countries in the nineteenth century. The passage from a system based on high mortality and low birth rates to one of low birth and low mortality rates created a surplus of population that was not able to find enough resources to subsist in its own territory, and therefore had to seek relief in overseas destinations.[3]

The optimists have found support in neoclassic economic theory. Simplified, it could be defined like this: emigration is the result of the construction of a free transatlantic labor market in the nineteenth century, which is the place where surplus supply of labor and labor demand of different national markets converge. Each of these markets is first assumed to be homogeneous and then transparent in that rational individuals aspiring to maximizing their profits operate in them, with uniform access to information and perfect mobility. In that context, the key variable is salary differentials, which leads individuals to maximize their labor opportunities by emigrating. According to this theory, migrants contributed to a relocation of the factors of production and finally to the equilibrium and the general progress of an Atlantic economic system.[4]

Given that one of the most critical topics in the neoclassic model concerns the access to information, other versions of the optimists' perspective focus not on the salary range or on the expectations of profit but on the diffusion of information. This analysis is dominated by an extensive and "epidemiological" idea of the expansion of information. Because of the fact that the principal agent of diffusion of information is the already migrated person, the conclusion is that a critical variable in explaining the rhythm of expansion of a migratory flow is the stock of those who have already migrated.[5] The bigger the flow, the more information about the situation in the country of reception will reach the country of origin. This new information will encourage more people, stimulated by new expectations, to go to the new country.

All of these different perspectives have a solid theoretical base and can be supported with some empirical evidence. The Italian case provided optimists and pessimists alike with much evidence. The pessimists were able to point to the great expansion of emigration in the 1880s that coincided with a difficult situation in the Italian countryside, especially in the Po Valley. This situation developed as a consequence of the fall in agricultural prices that was the result of the influx of Russian, American, and Ottoman grains into Europe. Certainly, this correlation would have been less clear if the researchers had been able to place the expansion in a longer-term context, but national statistics of Italian emigration only began in 1876. Anyway, abundant qualitative literature provided examples about the deleterious effects of capitalist expansion on supplementary sources of income of peasant families, or the influence of rural pauperism that resulted from other processes such as the fragmentation of property or the elimination of communal properties. This same capitalist process once unleashed expanded insufficiently, in a territorially fragmented way, and at times temporarily stopped.

Studied at a macro-aggregated level and in the long term, however, the Italian example also provided solid evidence for the optimists: the immigration flow tended to grow notably over the levels of the 1880s during the first decade of the twentieth century and seemed to respond fairly rapidly to the relative changes in the economic conditions of the American receiving societies. As Graph 1 shows, an interrelationship existed between the oscillations of the Italian flow to Argentina and to Brazil through the 1880s. An especially visible moment was the Argentine economic and political crisis of 1890 during which migratory politics in Brazil "artificially" fed the influx to that country with social groups that would not have been able to migrate to other nations without the advance payment of the cost of passage. There also existed a clear interrelationship between the flow to Argentina and the United States and the economic cycles in both countries from the end of the century up to the American Quota Law in 1921. During the second phase of this period, the flow reoriented itself decidedly to North America, which became the primary destination. Since in the beginning of the twentieth century the Italian economy was also in a strong expansionist phase, the explanation of emigration must be related to the pull factors more than to the push. The diffusion of information and the relative differences between salaries in Argentina and the United States could explain the increased emigration and the change in the primary destination.

Graph 1. Italian Migrations to Argentina, Brazil, and the United States

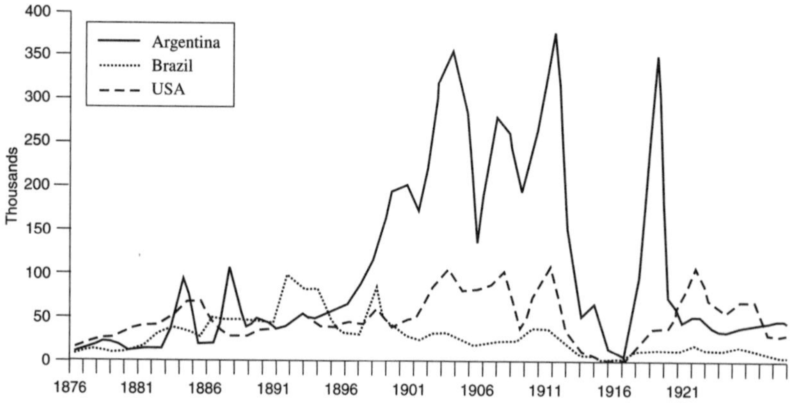

Source: Ministero Agricoltura, Industria e Commercio, Direziones della Statistica.

If the Italian example was able to provide optimists and pessimists alike with supporting evidence, the Spanish example also raises several interesting considerations. In the first place, arguing on the pessimists' side, Spain was not following the rest of the European periphery; its migratory movement began later than the rest of the European movements and not at the time of the great depression of prices. Some authors have suggested that the Spanish delay could be explained by protective state policies (through its monetary policies) that impeded the impact of non-European agriculture on the peninsula.[6] Other authors have said that the Spanish problem was not grains but other agricultural products such as wine, oil, or citrus fruit that were subject to different problems—epidemics such as phylloxera, or foreign markets such as those provoked by the commercial rupture with France. In reality a good argument to explain the cause of the Spanish delay might be the demographic one: Spain had

had a slower population growth during the nineteenth century than a good part of the rest of Europe.

However, the Spanish migratory movement provides us with the best argument against the optimists. Spain is the only country in Europe—together with continental Portugal, and not including the Azores[7]—whose emigrants were not attracted by the opportunities provided by the North American economy. Moreover, Spanish migrations were not only non-elastic in relation to the expansive cycle of the North American urban economy from the beginning of the century, but also were nonelastic in relation to the great agrarian expansion of Argentina in the 1880s. The only exception in the Argentine case was between 1887 and 1889, when the Argentine government offered subsidized fares in its effort to compete for immigrants with the subsidized fares offered by the state of São Paulo. These fares were an especially important enticement for Spanish immigrants to Argentina.[8] The reason why some Spaniards, as opposed to Italians, did not head to those destinations where the salary differential was the greatest can be explained by referring to the model of information diffusion. They had considerably greater opportunities in the old Spanish-American colonies, with which they had a long-standing migratory tradition, than with the opportunities and conditions offered by the North American economy. The Spanish example therefore suggests, with relation to the North American destination, that migrants may be inclined to privilege other nonmaterialistic factors at the moment of making up their minds about where to emigrate.

On the other hand, from the South American point of view, the comparison between the Argentine and Uruguayan cases presents strong evidence against the defenders of the information-diffusion theory. Uruguay provides the clearest example. During the 1860s, Argentina had two to three times as many Italian immigrants as were in Uruguay.[9] However, with the consolidation of the cattle-raising ranches in Uruguay from the mid-1870s, and the expansion of the agriculture and cattle-raising frontier in Argentina from the 1880s, Italian immigration increased most rapidly in Argentina. During the 1880s, the ratio between Italian migrants living in Argentina and Uruguay grew from seven to nine times as many to about thirteen times as many some twenty years later during the first decade before World War I. We can see that, even though there was a significant initial stock in Uruguay and even though the urban adjustment of the Spaniards and Italians was fairly satisfactory, this situation did not sustain a significant flow to Uruguay as compared to its great neighbor.

The Brazilian case provides an almost opposite result. The settlement of steady emigrant flows from Spain and Italy happened later than in the area of the Rio de la Plata, and at its beginning the policies of the state of

São Paulo of publicity and subsidized fares played a fundamental role. This effort coincided with a hostile campaign in Italy and Spain to discourage emigration to Brazil. Often this campaign was orchestrated by economic interests that supported alternative immigration flows like the one to Argentina, or by those who found the conditions in the São Paulo *fazendas* to be the worst possible. Yet in spite of this bad publicity and the fact that the general conditions in Paulista Brazil were probably worse than those in the Rio de la Plata, the flow continued to grow. Certainly, there were three frontiers that permitted social mobility for the peasant families who had emigrated: one concerned the coffee frontier and the potential access of immigrants to the ownership of land in the new areas of cultivation; the second was the urban frontier that would constitute the city of São Paulo with its commercial and industrial development. A third frontier was the strong movement of re-emigration from Brazil to Argentina. Finally, the Uruguayan and Brazilian cases show us how the problem of information is much more complex than neoclassical economists have considered it to be, because it implies a very opaque circuit of messages. At the same time, this circuit is multiple in its channels of transmission but also fragmented (not everyone gets all the possible information at every moment) and, as shown below, costly to its users.

Although the great interpretative lines we have discussed are diverse, they also have some characteristics in common. The first is that they view the immigrant as a homogeneous object on which a stable group of factors acts uniformly. The object is made uniform, and it is thought that it always responds the same way to these factors. The second assumption of these lines of interpretation is that these phenomena can and should be studied at the national level: because theorists see the nation-state as an area of homogenizing experiences (national market construction), because professional historians have used the nation-state as the primary unit in the last century, and because the public and statistical sources in this kind of analysis have been constructed on the basis of the nation-state. Thus, the core argument is built around emigration from Spain to Argentina or from Italy to Brazil. Regional deviations within the places of origin and destination are barely shown as variables of national cases.

The third shared assumption is the limited temporal framework of inquiry. The focus is on the long period of capitalist expansion when there was a greater flow of people and goods that triggered the Industrial Revolution in the economic field, and the extended century between the end of Napoleon's rule in 1815 and the world crisis of 1930 in the political field. The implicit assumption in this time period is that there was a close relationship between capitalist expansion, liberal public policies, and migratory flow. This relationship was perceived as necessary to avoid or minimize the possible impact of other noneconomic or demographic factors on the explanation of migratory movement. Given that most researchers have mainly studied the case of migration to the United States, the periodization reflects the impact of the established migration for that case. The periodization also implies an end point in the U.S. government's Quota Acts of 1921 and 1924 and a sequence of "old emigration," coming from northern and western Europe, and "new emigration," coming from eastern and southern Europe, whose members were less skilled and literate and were predominantly of rural origin.

In regard to migrations to Spanish America, the periodization is certainly different but supported by the same presumptions that underlie the case of the United States and in some regards by the historiography produced in the countries of origin. These theories regarding these migrations are also permeated by the value-loaded stereotypes of the "old" and "new" emigration sequence developed in studies of migrations to the United States. Generally, the shorter periodization proposed relates the delay in the growth of the labor force that would provoke the later capitalist expansion in Spain and Italy, with the later demand of the Spanish-American nations. This later period was dominated by the expansion of the primary exporting economy in the South American continent and by the idea of progress and the Europeanizing utopias associated with the "civilizing" role attributed to European immigration.

Finally, the fourth common assumption concerns the linear progression of the migratory process from origin to destination. This linear direction suggests a sequence of distinct and irreversible stages: expulsion-adjustment-assimilation.

The intent in the rest of this essay is to discuss these four assumptions for the purpose of re-evaluating the schematically presented argumentative lines set forth. The analysis presented is based on the idea that all of these assumptions, irrespective of the polemics and discrepancies, partially share the same conceptual scaffolding. The order of observations will be the inverse of that in which the assumptions were presented above.

Beginning with the last assumption, it seems evident that just by taking a look at the statistics, European emigration to the Americas is a circular rather than a linear process; that is to say, this migration often involved a number of trips back and forth by the same individuals rather than just one trip. Let us pay attention to the Argentine case. Taking a substantial period of time (1861–1920) into account, less than one-half of Italian immigrants returned to Italy, and 35 percent of the Spaniards did the same. In the Brazilian case, the available facts are similar. According to Spanish statistics, around 44 percent of Spaniards who had immigrated to Brazil between 1882 and 1925 returned to Spain.[10] This movement not only included one-time migrants but also those who went back and forth many times during their lives. This circular movement was not confined exclusively to the well-known *golondrinas*, the agricultural

day laborers who harvested crops alternatively on one or the other continent in the same year. For many, these movements included a variable
period around three years between migration and return of people who
engaged in nonagricultural activities.

In reality, the idea of "birds of passage" has been pointed out as a
characteristic of the "new emigration" to the United States; and in more
formalized analytical models, it is indispensable to explain the function-
ing of a secondary labor market for emigrants, characterized by those
labor-intensive activities that provide workers with unstable and low-status
employment.[11] In this sector were immigrant workers who aspired to maximize their incomes in short periods of time and for whom the perfor-
mance of certain less desirable tasks or precarious living conditions were
justified by their perception of the transitory nature of the situation. In
reality all of the classic linear conceptualization rested on an image of
return that poses many problems for the researcher. For many years, the
pessimist image emphasized the idea of return as failure and, more specifically, as the impossibility of gaining access to land, which would have
been a principal motive for peasants. Even now, the historiography on the
Paulista case focuses on the debate regarding the possibilities that the
coffee economy offered workers the chance to acquire land. The data presented in the census of 1920 (showing that this possibility was real for
many people) are important on this point but less decisive than what has
been maintained. In this finding the issue is not so much about access to
the land but about how much land, when individuals would get it, and
where and what kind of land it was.[12]

In any case, the scheme rested on a disputable fact: that the migrants
had made a definitive decision when they emigrated, and that any determination to change this decision (such as returning) was a drastic example of the impossibility of being successful in America. It was also
seen as irrefutable proof of the shortcomings or the limits of the economic development model implemented by the South American countries
at the end of the nineteenth century. However, any observer who today
goes around the Asturo-Galician littoral in Spain or that of Liguria in
Italy would immediately find the houses, or the vestiges of them, of the
Americans (migrants returning from the New World) who were called—
in the Spanish literature of that period and with satirical purposes—Indians. This discovery should make us ponder whether at least some of those
who returned were not failures but successes. Furthermore, the great
movement of money for the purpose of investment in lands, in urban properties, or in debt redemption is an indicator of the degree to which the
structural investments of many immigrants were tied to the society of
origin and not to the receiving society. In reality the opposite idea demonstrates the point to which preconceptions have dominated scholarly studies instead of the investigation of the attitudes of the migrants themselves.

Finally, many immigrants could expect to be landowners in the country of origin but not in the receiving country. Moreover, the idea that in economic terms it was preferable to be an owner of a smaller parcel than a tenant on a bigger one (where a more-or-less dynamic land market existed as in Argentina) has been recently challenged with persuasive evidence.[13] Besides, to think that for strictly economic reasons property at destination was preferable to property at origin is simplistic; this argument does not consider the plans of the immigrants that could be linked to issues of prestige and social status. According to many emigrants, to be successful in America—*hacer la América*—was to make their fortune there but to show it off where it mattered socially, that is to say, in their home country in Europe.

It is obvious that a counterimage without nuances should not be substituted for what we have described as a homogeneous image. It is clear that the migratory experience embraced, in relation to the linearity or circularity of the process, migrants of different kinds whose decisions to return or to go permanently abroad were hardly definitive. What we have reconstructed about the temporary or definitive commitment of a migrant (as the contemporaries who suppressed this distinction from migratory statistics knew) was that it was the product of uncertainties, marches, and countermarches and many times more the result of circumstances than the product of a firm original decision. In any case, our interest is in pointing out the heterogeneity of situations that do not imply either irreversibility or any uniform sequence of stages in the transatlantic migrations to South America.

The third assumption we have pointed out was the "short" chronological framework in which the process takes place, be it in Marxian, Malthusian, or neoclassic interpretations—and in the narrow nexus between capitalism and migrations. We have observed above that the image of the *ancien régime* European societies that were without mobility except for marginal groups has not withstood the scrutiny of more recent investigations. Mobility in the old societies was very high, even if it generally represented movements of less distance and duration than the ones at the end of the nineteenth century.[14] This latter point is of great importance because the lack of trustworthy data made it necessary to calculate movement on the basis of the comparison between the different population measurements (before official censuses were taken), and this led to the underestimation of migratory movement that occurred between those measurements.

The importance of detaching human mobility from capitalism has many argumentative implications. Certainly, the great period of expansion of a new economic system or a new mode of production implied a very radical expansion of overseas migrations to certain destinies. However, capitalism cannot be considered as the cause of international migrations, but rather as a decisive factor of its expansion from its preceding basis. All this forces us to reject those arguments that correlate migrations and capitalism in a causal sequence, and to introduce again other kinds of notions such as culture or migratory tradition that place the problem far from all determinism and narrow economic issues. But the difficulty of establishing a causal sequence affects not only the initial stages of the migratory movement but also the whole process. A scarcely superficial observation of aggregate national data of transatlantic migrations shows that, during the first decade of this century, the percentage of emigrants per inhabitant is equivalent in both early English and late Spanish emigration.[15]

In the case we are studying, the limited chronology necessitates considering migrations during the colonial period as different from those of the late nineteenth and early twentieth centuries. This involves repeating the rhetoric of the progressive South American elites, when they insisted that European migration might play a significant modernizing role. However, the Spanish migratory movement to many areas of Hispanic America may be seen as continuous from the eighteenth to the twentieth century, interrupted only by the episodes of the wars for independence. This fact does not mean that only similar reasons motivated migrants of both periods, but that upon occasion it was the very same immigrants or families of these immigrants. Data from the 1855 census in the city of Buenos Aires show that some families of Spanish immigrants had members who had arrived at the end of the eighteenth century and the early nineteenth century, and others who had come in the early 1830s when relationships between Spain and America started to be normalized.[16]

For immigrants coming from the Italian peninsula the periodization has other implications. The process of settlement in the Plata regions by Ligurian migrants from the 1830s onward is already well known, and how the initial flow (in a manner similar to the Spanish case) fed the later movement. What this last example shows, however, is that immigrants were beginning to arrive in the Rio de la Plata in large numbers in the period of Juan Manuel de Rosas's xenophobic dictatorship (1829–1852). They were certainly not attracted by his rhetoric. Rather, they were attracted by the opportunities created by the decimation of the working-age population brought about by the wars of independence and by forced recruitment of native men to supply the armies fighting in civil wars. Regarding long-term migratory patterns, no meaningful break can be made between the period before 1852, when Rosas prohibited any pro-immigration inititatives, and afterward, when a liberal elite under the slogan "To govern is to populate" encouraged immigration. Furthermore, the Athens of the Plata, which Montevideo had become for many years during the Rosas period, was not a more appealing destination for those early migrants than was reactionary Buenos Aires. In fact, many immigrants circulated between the two cities.[17]

If we accept North American historiographical classifications, Spanish and Italians in the Rio de la Plata are chronologically part of the old emigration. Moreover, Spanish migration dates back further than any other European migration. As for the rest, this South American example seems to confirm that the success of these earlier groups had less to do with their specific characteristics (religious, cultural, industrial) than with their earlier arrival within the receiving country in relation to other migratory groups.

The next assumption is that migration should be studied at the national level. National scale analysis rests on the conviction that the unifying elements of economic markets and public policy are more important than other factors. This involves the overvaluation of the state's role in the judicial, administrative, and economic spheres. Furthermore, it involves the overvaluation of the homogenizing capability of the market in the allocation of the factors of production. In our cases it seems evident that the public policies had a limited role before 1930, except in the very few specific cases concerning restrictions imposed by the countries of origin. In this sense the Prinetti Decree (1902) limited Italian emigration to Brazil. The Spanish decree of 1910 restricting emigration to Brazil was much less effective. Public land policies also had a limited impact in facilitating the settlement process, except in a few specific cases of the earlier period. Also the constitutional and judicial guarantees were irrelevant because they were not supported by concrete administrative practices.

Actually, public policies seem to have been most influential in two areas: propaganda and subsidized passages. Regarding the first point, we must determine if the immigrants believed and trusted the propaganda of the agents of foreign governments. Undoubtedly, these agents were numerous; an estimate for Galicia shows the presence of over twenty consuls and vice consuls both in La Coruna and in Vigo around 1914.[18] The problem lies in whether we consider these agents as key actors in the decision of individuals to emigrate or simply as instruments at their disposal to help solve migrants' practical problems. Enrico Ferri noticed that the real agents for migrants were the letters of those who had already gone abroad. These letters were read on Sundays in church after Mass. If they discouraged migration, there was not an agent who could persuade people from the village to do so.[19] Within the structural limits imposed on them, we can argue that the immigrants were surely not children and could develop their own strategies.

Nevertheless, there is little doubt that their information was limited. For example, the source of information the migrants considered most trustworthy was that provided by their primary social group and secondarily by those people with whom they had face-to-face contact. This explains the role of the migration chains in orientating with precision the migratory flow. In those cases in which we find different migratory flows from the same town, it might be due to the possible linkages among diversified social networks in the form of a "spider web." These different flows might be based on occupational skills, the requirements of the external labor market, or even on different neighborhoods within the village (a different/complementary view of what has been called the village-outward approach[20]) the uneven circulation of information. In effect, if the information is selected by the receiver on the basis of the credibility of the sender, it is probably also distributed selectively by the sender. We are not only dealing with general information regarding the economic situation of the American nations, salaries, or the possibility of finding jobs but also in many cases with specific information about specific employment opportunities.[21] For this reason, the migratory chains are not only a source of information but also a source of assistance in obtaining a job in the new society as well as financial aid for the cost of the passage. Only a few new studies on the Spanish case range beyond approximations; they suggest that residence clusters of immigrants are not based on the whole village but on different areas within the village,[22] or on kinship obligations that led to the emergence of an intermediate level of compromise between the nuclear family and the town.

The second area in which the influence of public policy is undeniable is that of subsidized fares. For a short time (1887–1889) in the Argentine case, where government policy was initially oriented toward diversifying the flow of immigrants and only secondarily to increasing it, this government policy had a considerable impact; it successfully attracted Spaniards and limited the influx of Italians. In the case of São Paulo, the effect was always very significant for the rural areas.[23] As a whole, we should not forget those immigrants who did not use official government services, and neither should we underestimate the "spontaneous" flow to southern Brazil and to the city of São Paulo.

The subject of subsidized fares introduces the issue of the sources to finance migration, which in turn introduces the social groups involved in it. The possibilities for an individual migrant or a migrant family to set out for an overseas destination were tied, in the first place, to the possibility of the family group financing the cost of the move. This cost included the fare as well as the likelihood that one or more members of the same family would be without a job for a certain amount of time. In that case not all the family would move. These costs generally placed the poorer families outside the transatlantic migration experience. Nevertheless, some of those with lower incomes could take advantage of the second source of financial aid—the savings of those who had already emigrated and who often paid the fares for their families, relatives, and even friends.

In any case, those who did not have the resources to migrate had three ways to increase the possibilities of improving their situation. First, there was the option of protest and open social conflict in the same place where they lived. Second, there was the option of internal or intra-European migration to an urban area. And third, the potential migrant might solicit subsidized fares offered by foreign governments such as that of São Paulo or by labor agents. The latter, well known in the North American case, were less visible and probably less important in the Argentine and Uruguayan cases. Therefore, government policies regarding subsidized fares were important in promoting the emigration of social groups that otherwise would not have been able to afford it, but they were of limited impact among the traditional migratory social groups.

The other major argument focusing on the nation-state as the unit of analysis is the homogenizing capability of the market. Studies of economic history produced in the last twenty years have emphasized the regional disparities of economic development.[24] It does not take too much imagination to perceive, for example, the differences in the pace of industrialization in Liguria or Cataluna (rapid) on the one hand and in Basilicata or Extremadura (slow) on the other. These differences are not only economic but also demographic. For example, the demographic transition in the Piedmont is not only earlier but much shorter than that in Sicily.[25]

Actually, how can we not admit that in so many cases national data distort the reality? The larger the regional disparities, as in Spain and Italy as well as in the great receiving countries, the more arbitrary are the aggregate data. The situation is artificially homogenized by the manipulation of the quantitative public sources.

If there are differences in most demographic and economic variables, it is not surprising that disparities exist in the different regional migratory flows. Graph 2 shows the Italian case, in which we can easily observe that the disparities are huge. What system of causes can explain simultaneously migrations from Sicily, Liguria, and the Veneto? Let us commence with the case of emigration from Liguria. Clearly it constitutes a regional movement that reaches its peak before the emigration produced by the integration of the peninsula into the world market and by the great depression of agricultural prices. In spite of the early and successful settlement of Ligurian immigrants in the regions of the Rio de la Plata, the stock of established immigrants maintained only a weak movement between Italy and the South American countries. In this case, higher wages in Argentina first and in the United States second were not enough to sustain and increase migration toward these countries. It is well known that the industrialization in Genoa was remarkable and served to attract migrants from other regions of Italy, thus turning it into an area of simultaneous emigration and immigration. The problem of generalization is thus made even more difficult.

Graph 2. International Emigration from Three Italian Regions, 1876–1924

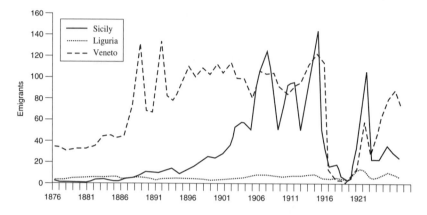

Source: Ministero Agricoltura, Industria e Commercio, Direzione della Statistica.

Sicily presents the opposite case. It responds to the demand for immigrants quite late, after the end of what is known as the great depression of European agricultural prices (1873–1896). Its migratory movements seem to be influenced by the irresistible appeal of existing conditions in countries overseas during the decade before World War I. Undoubtedly we could argue that it was due to the late beginning of the demographic transition, or to the fact that farm production in Sicily suffered less from the foreign competition that earlier affected grain production in the Po Valley. It would also be due to the late impact on Sicily of the economic transformations that affected other parts of Italy and delayed its economic integration into the rest of the nation. The point is that it is necessary to construct specific regional models of interaction among the different variables, because it is the regional space that permits us to see the simultaneous operation of distinct variables and to develop typologies of immigration that are less arbitrary.

The third case, the Veneto, certainly follows more closely the explanations given for the rest of Italy than do the other two. This finding suggests that in many cases national types are simply a projection of a regional case that may be numerically dominant or that may have received the earliest and most attention from historians.

Regional disparities also influence arguments about receiving countries. A good example is the idea that the Argentine case is an exception among the receiving countries in the Atlantic context. Using the percentage of immigrants in the total population as a point of comparison, some note that Argentine immigration was double or triple that of other nations such as the United States or Brazil. On this basis they have drawn various conclusions about transformations in the respective societies.[26] This comparison was certainly arbitrary. What perhaps should have been compared was the percentage of European immigrants in the total population in states such as São Paulo or New York or in the province of Buenos Aires rather than in entire countries. This procedure is important because the immigrants were not evenly distributed throughout the receiving countries.

Regional analyses present a number of problems. Do the regions to be studied coincide with historical regions, with intra- or transnational entities, or with smaller, more restricted units such as provinces? Studies of the Galician case show a provincial rather than a regional specialization in the flow to Cuba, Brazil, or Buenos Aires.[27] On the other hand, after analyzing Italian historical regions more globally we can discern a major orientation toward certain national destinations. For example, during the 1880s most Venetians went to Brazil, whereas most from the Piedmont went to Argentina and Lombards dominated the flow to Uruguay.[28] These regions, however, were not static. The River Plate region, for example, changed radically during the midnineteenth century when the configuration of the economy was structured around the circulation of men and goods along the area's rivers to later, when new political divisions and the railroad restructured economic activity. The problem, as we mentioned above, is that all these models presuppose one migrant type who reacts in the same way to similar stimuli.

International migrations included very diverse social types, and this fact posed a problem to contemporary experts of mass emigration regarding who should be considered an emigrant. The various national laws did not agree on this point. Thus, Italian legislation in 1901 and Spanish legislation in 1907 considered an emigrant a person who traveled in third class; Argentine legislation in 1876 and Uruguayan legislation in 1891 considered an immigrant someone who traveled in second and third class. Nevertheless, it is clear that those who traveled in second class were very different socially from those we generally imagine to be an indistinct mass of peasants and farm laborers in third class. However, there was among third-class passengers a variety of occupations. The percentages among the different occupations varied significantly, as did the relative proportion between the sexes. In any case, the migrant stereotype—a young male adult of rural origin—does little to help us understand the phenomenon. Two points have been made. They concern, first, the variety of occupations that individuals perform throughout their lifetime, making it arbitrary to assign a label at any one specific time; and second, the same occupational definition implies or may imply extraordinary differences in skills according to the specific context of the region of origin. If immigrants are so diverse or to a certain degree show diversity, how can we consider that all the causes of immigration operate uniformly? Consequently, a farm crisis may affect in a different way a small landowner, a tenant, or a settler from the same region.

However, rather than explore these diversities in this paper, let us focus on another point. It is said that migrants are not individuals who decide to emigrate by themselves. They find themselves tied with or compromised by other persons. In the first place they belong to a family that greatly influences all emigrant decisions. This decision making is also oriented by custom, for lack of a better word; by a specific migratory culture that is no more than the reproduction of certain social relationships over time; and/or by the specific economic situation in which migration takes place.

More schematically, we might argue that migrations can present themselves in three kinds of movements: migration of families that do so together, migration of families step by step, or migration of adult male individuals alone. The first two presume potentially greater permanence, while the third may be more temporary. The following table is part of a preliminary investigation of family types in regional Spanish migrations to Argentina (the data are based on passenger lists from 1910).[29] We can observe how these variables present themselves in a regional context. Emigrants from Pontevedra, Salamanca, and Vizcaya are certainly very different, and this finding suggests that they can respond flexibly to the situation. It also suggests that the three migratory movements occur at different points in the respective regional cycles. And, finally, we see that they have different traditions and are influenced in different ways by the changes in the macro-structural conditions.

First, let us look at a Galician provincial example (Pontevedra): it is mainly about males who emigrate alone (although it could be the first phase of a migration chain) who might have high expectations of returning. They were oriented in the manner of "birds of passage" to give priority to such conditions as salary differentials in order to earn as much as possible and to channel their savings to their society of origin. The reasons that allow us to presume that this is a migration of male members of a family group are backed up by qualitative sources that point to a long-term migratory cycle rooted in the colonial period; for some regions of Galicia as well as for the neighboring region in northern Portugal, it was the "men who emigrated and the women who stayed behind."[30] Undoubtedly, we might remember that this does not mean that the temporary migration of men alone could not later become family emigration. But we can assume it to be a typical supplementary immigration of insufficient structural resources and therefore more inelastic to the economic cycle.

Family Characteristics of Migrant Groups from Pontevedra, Salamanca, and Vizcaya (1910)

	Pontevedra		*Salamanca*		*Vizcaya*	
With or Without Family						
Migrants without families	77%		46%		44%	
Migrants with primary family	23%		54%		56%	
Total	**100%**		**100%**		**100%**	
	(N=241)		(N=197)		(N=176)	
Of Those With Family	23%		54%		56%	
Married	3%		28%		18%	
Married without children		(2)		(9)		(7)
Married with children		(5)		(33)		(16)
Married with children and other relatives		(0)		(14)		(9)
Single Parent with Child(ren)	17%		20%		35%	
Father with child(ren)		(12)		(10)		(2)
Father with child(ren) and other relatives		(0)		(0)		(0)
Mother with child(ren)		(23)		(24)		(58)
Mother with child(ren) and other relatives		(6)		(5)		(0)
Brothers	3%		6%		3%	

Source: Archivo Dirección de Migraciones (Argentina), Partes Consulares (1910).

A second example, opposite to the first one, is Salamanca. Here we do not have a long migratory tradition. Because of the lack of a long migratory tradition, the period in which it happens, and the dominant type of agricultural production, and because of the drastic change it implies for a family group to launch itself into such a radical adventure as to expatriate itself completely, we infer that the causes at work are of another type. This radical emigration of whole families combined with the characteristics of this grain-producing region imply that these groups were being pushed off the land as a consequence of the agricultural crisis brought about by the fall of the protective barrier of Spanish agriculture.

The third case, Vizcaya, an area of long-standing emigration to Argentina, is a more classic model. It is a deferred-family emigration in which the migrants find themselves in the third phase of the chain migration conceptualized by the MacDonalds, which is to say the women and children are reunited in the foreign destination with the male members of the family who had previously migrated.[31] The migrants of the third case, however, chose their destination, giving priority to the existence of factors in the country of destination other than salary differentials—such as the presence of relatives or villagers, communal institutions, greater similarities of social and linguistic forms, or the types of available jobs.

The variation in family types as well as in occupations and regions makes it impossible to talk about a single migrant, subject to the same set of causes and capable of responding unmistakably in the same manner in all cases. This aspect as well as the others previously discussed should serve to definitively challenge the usefulness of those models that decades of historical scholarship have produced. The more negative balance proposed here may seem insufficient. However, to individualize the problems, schemes, and arbitrary statements of many social science constructs is the necessary path to go down in order to arrive at a new history of the Americas—one in which European migrants both old and new become relevant actors.

Notes

1. For an up-to-date evaluation of the different optimist positions, see D. Baines, "European Emigration, 1815–1930: Looking at the Emigration Decision Again," *Economic History Review* 47 (1994): 525–44. For the pessimists, see F. Devoto, *Le migrazioni italiane in Argentina: Un saggio interpretativo* (Naples: Istituto Italiano per gli Studi Filosofici, 1994). A summary can be found in M. I. B. Baganha, *Portuguese Emigration to the United States, 1820–1930* (New York: Garland, 1990).

2. For classical Marxist model, see E. Sereni, *Il capitalismo nelle campagne* (Turin: Einaudi, 1968); E. Franzina, *La grande emigrazione* (Padua: Marsilio, 1976); and A. Trento, *Là dov'è la racolta del café: L'emigrazione italiana in Brasile* (Padua: Antenore, 1984).

3. J. Nadal, *La población española* (Barcelona: Ariel, 1984). Mixed visions are in G. Galasso, *Mezzogiorno medievale e moderno* (Turin: Einaudi, 1965).

4. A classic salary-costs model in emigration is suggested by G. Tapinos, *L'économie des migrations internationales* (Paris: A. Colin, 1974). Examples for the Italian migrations to Argentina and Uruguay are: R. Cortés Conde, *El progeso argentino* (Buenos Aires: Sudamericana, 1979); S. Rodríguez Villamil and G. Sapriza, *La inmigración europea en el Uruguay: Los italianos* (Montevideo: Banda Oriental, 1982), 91–100. For the Spanish case: B. Sánchez Alonso, *Las causas de la emigración española, 1880–1930* (Madrid: Alianza Editorial, 1995).

5. G. Maier, "The Economics of Information in the Context of Migration," in J. H. Johnson and J. Salt (eds.), *Labour Migration: The Internal Geographical Mobility of Labour in the Developed World* (London: David Fulton, 1990). For an application of the idea of stock and information flow as a key variable in transatlantic migrations, see D. Baines, *Migration in a Mature Economy: Emigration and Internal Migration in England and Wales, 1861–1900* (Cambridge: Cambridge University Press, 1985). Linked with the influence of information are the works based on the idea of "chain migration." See C. Yáñez Gallardo, *Saltar con red: La emigración catalana a América* (Madrid: Alianza, 1994).

6. R. Cortés Conde, "Migración, cambio agrícola y políticas de protección: El caso argentino," in N. Sánchez Albornoz (ed.), *Españoles hacia América: La emigración de masas* (Madrid: Alianza Editorial, 1988), 235–48.

7. M. I. B. Baganha, *Portuguese Emigration to the United States.*

8. M. S. Ospital, "La inmigración subsidiada y la oficinas de información, 1887–1890," in various authors, *Jornadas de Inmigración* (Buenos Aires: Ministerio de Cultura y Educación, 1985), 441–56; F. Devoto, "Políticas migratorias argentinas y flujo de población europea, 1876–1925," *Estudios Migratorios Latinoamericanos* 4 (1989): 135–58.

9. Statistica Generale del Regno d'Italia, *Censimento degli italiani all'estero (31 dicembre 1871)* (Rome: Stamperia Reale, 1874); F. Devoto, "La emigración italiana a Argentina y Uruguay en el siglo XIX: Un enfoque comparado," in Devoto, *Estudios sobre la emigración italiana a la Argentina en la segunda mitad del siglo XIX* (Naples: Edizioni Scientifiche Italiane, 1991), 7–43.

10. Argentina, Dirección General de Inmigración, *Resumen estadístico del movimiento migratorio en la República Argentina, 1857–1924* (Buenos Aires: Talleres del Ministerio de Agricultura, 1925); Instituto Geográfico y Estadístico, *Estadística de la emigración e inmigración de España (1882–1911)*, transcripts by C. Yañez Gallardo, *La emigración española a América (siglos XIX y XX)* (Colombres: Fundación Archivo de Indianos, 1994), 85–88.

11. M. J. Piore, *Birds of Passage: Migrant Labor and Industrial Society* (Cambridge: Cambridge University Press, 1970).

12. T. Holloway, *Immigrants on the Land: Coffee and Society in São Paulo, 1886–1934* (Chapel Hill: University of North Carolina Press, 1980); V. Stolcke, *Cafeicultura, homens, mulheres e capital (1850–1980)* (São Paulo: Brasiliense, 1986). See also C. Vangelista, *Le braccia per la fazenda* (Milan: F. Angeli, 1982); and J. de Souza Martins, "Del esclavo al asalariado en las haciendas de café, 1880–1914," in N. Sánchez Albornoz (ed.), *Población y mano de obra en América Latina* (Madrid: Alianza, 1985), 229–57. See the debate in the *Latin American Research Review* concerning the article of M. Font, "Coffee, Planters, Politics, and Development in São Paulo," in *LARR* 22 (1987): 69–90 and the comments by V. Stolcke and J. Love.

13. E. Gallo, *La pampa gringa* (Buenos Aires: Sudamericana, 1983).

14. Several examples of the Spanish and Italian cases are found in J. Nadal and E. Giralt, *La population catalane de 1553 a 1717* (Paris: SEVPEN, 1960). About the movements to America: C. Martínez Shaw, *La emigración española a América (1492–1824)* (Colombres: Fundación Archivo de Indianos, 1994). For the other peninsula: G. Levi, *Centro e periferia di uno stato assoluto* (Turin: Rosenberg & Sellier, 1985); and various authors, *Migrazioni attraverso le Alpi Occidentali* (Turin: Regione Piemonte, 1988).

15. The rate of emigrants per 1,000 inhabitants between 1901 and 1910 was 5.5 for England and Wales and 5.7 for Spain. See also D. Baines, *Migration.*

16. J. Moya, *Cousins and Strangers: Spanish Immigrants in Buenos Aires, 1852–1930* (Berkeley and Los Angeles: University of California Press, 1998), 68–72.

17. F. J. Devoto, "Liguri dell'America Australe: Reti sociali, immagini, identità," in A. Gibelli and P. Rugafiori (eds.), *Storia d'Italia: Le regioni dall'Unità a oggi. La Liguria* (Turin: Einaudi, 1994).

18. J. Moya, *Cousins and Strangers*, Chapter 3.

19. E. Ferri, *Camera dei Deputati, Discussione* 23 (Rome, 1909): 2833–34.

20. S. Baily, "The Village-Outward Approach to the Study of Social Networks: A Case Study of the Agnonesi Diaspora Abroad," *Studi Emigrazione* 105 (1992): 43–67; R. Gandolfo, "Del Alto Molise al centro de Buenos Aires: Las mujeres

agnonesas y la primera emigración transatlántica (1870-1900)," *Estudios Migratorios Latinoamericanos* 7 (1992): 71–99.

21. For the way information circulates in interpersonal networks, see the observations of M. Grieco, *Keeping It in the Family: Social Networks and Employment Chance* (London: Tavistock, 1987). In any case the situation may differ according to the moment of expatriation in the local or regional migratory cycle and according to the greater or lesser fluidity in the labor market in the countries of arrival. The role of strong family or kinship ties seems more evident in the initial migration and when competition to obtain a job is such that only close social relationships can provide employment. In the South American context during the consolidating migratory periods with high demand and rotating labor, weaker ties (friends of friends) seem to have played an important role as well, differentiating themselves from the classical chain pattern and ethnic neighborhood created in the North American examples. On "weaker ties" as a concept see M. Granovetter, "The Strength of Weak Ties: A Network Theory Revisited," in P. Marsden and N. Lin, *Social Structure and Network Analysis* (Beverly Hills: Sage, 1982), 105–30.

22. M. L. Da Orden, "Fuentes en España y Argentina para un estudio social de la migración española: El ejemplo de las pautas matrimoniales." Presentation in II Ecuentros Castropolenses de Historia, "Fuentes para la Historia de las Migraciones Regionales y Locales a Iberoamérica," Castropol, 1995.

23. T. Holloway, *Immigrants on the Land*. About the context of Paulist subsidies, see T. Holloway, "Creating the Reserve Army? The Immigration Program of São Paulo, 1886–1930," *International Migration Review* 12 (1978): 187–209. Also M. T. Schorer Petrone, "Política immigratoria e interesses económicos (1824–1930)," in G. Rosoli (ed.), *Emigrazione europea e popolo brasiliano* (Rome: CSER, 1987), 257–70.

24. S. Pollard, *Peaceful Conquest: The Industrialization of Europe, 1760–1970* (Oxford: Oxford University Press, 1981).

25. A. M. Birindelli, "Emigrazione e transizione demográfica," in M. R. Ostuni (ed.), *Studi sull'emigrazione: Un analisi comparata* (Milan: Electa-Fondazione Sella, 1991) 353–67.

26. G. Germani, *Política y sociedad en una época de transición* (Buenos Aires: Paidos, 1965), chapter 7; T. S. Di Tella, "Argentina una Australia italiana? L'impatto dell'emigrazione sul sistema politico argentino," in B. Bezza (ed.), *Gli italiani fuori d'Italia* (Milan: Franco Angeli, 1983), 211–30.

27. A. Vázquez González, "La emigración gallega: Migrantes, transportes y remesas," in N. Sánchez Albornoz (ed.), *Españoles hacia América*, 87.

28. Ministero Agricoltura, Industria e Commercio, *Statistica dell'emigrazione italiana nell'anno . . .* (Rome: Tip. Camera dei Deputati and others, 1880–1891).

29. We have used passenger lists to be found in documents in Consular Reports and available in the archives of the Direccion Nacional de Migraciones de la Argentina (temporarily in the Files of the Centro de Estudios Migratorios Latinoamericanos). About the nature of the sample and characteristics of sources please see F. Devoto, "Las migraciones españolas a la Argentina desde la perspectiva de los partes consulares (1910): Un ejercicio de tipología regional," *Estudios Migratorios Latinoamericanos* 34 (1996): 479–506.

30. R. Rowland, "La emigración a grandes distancias y sus contextos: Portugal y Brasil," *Estudios Migratorios Latinoamericanos* 7 (1992): 225–74; C. B. Brettell, *Men Who Migrate, Women Who Wait: Population and History in a Portuguese Parish* (Princeton: Princeton University Press, 1986).

31. J. S. MacDonald and L. MacDonald, "Chain Migration, Ethnic Neighborhood Formation, and Social Networks," *Milbank Memorial Fund Quarterly* 42 (1964): 82–96.

3

Portuguese Transatlantic Migration

Maria Ioannis B. Baganha

The overwhelming majority of Portuguese emigrants who left their country between 1880 and 1930 went primarily to Brazil (80 percent) but also to some extent to the United States. Maria Ioannis Baganha examines both the characteristics of the emigrants and those of the receiving societies and in so doing is able to shed light on which individuals were drawn to the respective destinations and why. She shows how the economies of the receiving societies and migrant social networks were crucial to defining the distinctive characteristics of each of these areas.

B etween 1815 and 1930 more than 50 million Europeans crossed the Atlantic to work or to join relatives already established in the United States, Argentina, Canada, Brazil, and other overseas destinations. All European nations of the period were involved in this mass transfer of population to the New World, but both the timing and the degree of involvement varied significantly from country to country. Thus, while the contribution of France, Belgium, and the Netherlands to this mass redistribution of people never surpassed overall more than 200,000 migrants, the contribution of countries such as Italy and Ireland was on the order of millions.[1]

The spread of railroads, the systematic replacement of sailing ships by steamships after the 1860s, and, at least until World War I, a seemingly infinite capacity of the New World labor markets to absorb newcomers help to explain the size of the transatlantic migration at the end of the nineteenth century.[2] The differential timing in Europe can be attributed to several disruptions in the labor market, changes in the structure of the population, and alterations in landholding patterns. These changes, brought about by processes of industrialization, demographic growth, and land fragmentation in rural areas, also help to explain why until the 1880s the Atlantic crossing was essentially dominated by migrants from northern and western Europe, and why after that date it became essentially an eastern and southern European phenomenon. Portugal followed this regional migratory pattern; it only became, relative to its demographic base, a high-emigration country during the 1890s.

From 1855 to the end of the 1930s, close to 2 million Portuguese left the country[3]; 90 percent of all departures occurred after 1880, and more than 95 percent of the migratory out-flow went either in the direction of Brazil or the United States.[4] Why did they leave? From where did they depart? What were their demographic characteristics and their socio-economic profiles? And what were their patterns of integration in the New World? These are the questions guiding the synthetic overview presented in this chapter. This overview is both a discussion of the principal determinants of the Portuguese transatlantic migration at the end of the nineteenth century and a description of the main characteristics of this migration.

Determinants of the Migratory Flow at the Turn of the Century

Several years ago, Votorino Magalhães Godinho concluded in one of his most influential works that, in the Portuguese case, migration must be considered a historical structural factor, deeply embedded in the country's way of life and in its people's mentality.[5] This contention can be interpreted as meaning that migratory pressure was, in Portugal, an endemic phenomenon rooted in an extremely biased redistribution of resources among its people. For centuries this situation pushed a substantial part of the population to look outside their place of origin for the extra resources that would enable the kin group and the community to maintain their patterns of life and to reproduce themselves. Obviously, the contexts in which this migratory pressure translated into an individual's actual migration varied over time.

Until the independence of Brazil in the early 1820s, the overwhelming majority of the migrants went to areas within the Portuguese empire. After independence, migration became essentially part of the transatlantic international flow of labor from Europe to the New World. Except for unusual circumstances in Portugal that temporarily increased migratory pressure, the main dynamics of the Portuguese migratory process from the 1820s onward were essentially determined by the needs of the receiving labor markets, by the political sanctioning of the countries involved, and by the strength of migratory networks active at both ends of the trajectory.

Given that both the cultural and the economic preconditions to spur migration were already present, the interesting question in the Portuguese case is why emigration became a mass phenomenon only in the last decades of the nineteenth century. Was it because a drastic increase in the needs of the receiving labor markets occurred during this period or because of a marked rise in the level of the migratory pressure within the country coupled with a favorable international situation that allowed sustained emigration? Although it can be convincingly claimed that from the 1880s onward the labor markets of both the United States and Brazil increasingly demanded unskilled workers—a situation particularly favorable to potential migrants from Portugal—the fact is that the major peaks of the Portuguese outflow do not coincide with the major peaks in transatlantic migration. This finding suggests that domestic causes must also be considered when trying to explain the mass migration that took place from the end of the nineteenth century to the unilateral closing of the doors by the main receiving countries in the early twentieth century.

The already existent asymmetries in Portuguese society, in fact, were further aggravated during this period. These changes, coupled with the new conditions of the international labor market, drove an increasing number of Portuguese abroad. Portugal's economic structure, characterized around the 1890s by an uneven distribution of natural resources and by an even more uneven distribution of the country's wealth, presented by 1930 an even darker scenario. The rich regions of the 1890s had grown richer; the poor regions had become more impoverished. Five factors were largely responsible for the widening gap between the developing regions and the stagnating areas. The first was the disproportionate economic and political weight of the capital, Lisbon. The second was that, except in agriculture, all economic development during this period was centered in two districts, Lisbon and Oporto. The third was the lack of a dynamic urban network, and the fourth was the lack of internal mobility. Finally, the fifth factor was the lack of a national labor market sufficiently dynamic and integrated to make people move from the pauperized regions to the developing areas. Obviously, these three last factors were as much a result of as well as a reinforcement of the two first factors.

The regional distribution of the migratory areas reflected the economic disequilibrium that characterized the Portuguese economy at the turn of the century. In other words, migratory areas corresponded to the economically stagnant regions, that is, the northern part of the country and the islands. The severe decrease of job opportunities for women in the northern regions of the mainland and in the Azore Islands helps to explain increasing female participation in the migratory flow after the 1900s. Moreover, as conditions in the domestic labor market deteriorated over a larger part of the country, the number of regions sending out emigrants expanded, encompassing almost the whole country by the 1920s. As the country's welfare went down between 1890 and 1930, reducing the availability of jobs, emigration went up. Confirming Joaquim de Oliveira Martins's insightful remark of 1891, "Portuguese emigration is the barometer of the country's life, marking in its ups and downs the welfare pressure of the nation."[6] In fact, as the country's welfare went down between 1890 and 1930, reducing the availability of jobs, emigration went up.

What is being said can be reinforced by briefly looking at some features of the Portuguese labor market evolution between 1890 and 1930. In fact, between these two dates the labor force decreased at an annual growth rate of .1 percent, while the population at risk for migration (here considered to be those age 10 and above) showed a positive annual growth rate of .76 percent. Labor force participation rates indicate that the decrease in the gainfully employed population was constant and marked throughout the whole period (see Table 1).

Table 1. Portuguese Labor Force, 1890–1930

Population	1890	1900	1911	1930
Economically active (No.)	2,530,450	2,457,253	2,544,964	2,516,693
Working age (No.)	3,905,426	4,175,972	4,550,597	5,294,048
Work participation rate (%)	65	59	56	48
Rate of economically active relative to 1890 (1890=100)	100	97	101	99
Rate of working age relative to 1890 (1890=100)	100	107	117	136

Sources: Census for the given year. Adapted from Maria Ioannis B. Baganha, *Portuguese Emigration to the United States* (New York: Garland, 1990); and Maria Ioannis B. Baganha, "A emigração atlántica e as migrações internas em Portugal," *Los 98 Ibéricos y el mar*, vol. 4, *La sociedad y la economía en la Peninsula Ibérica* (Salamanca: Fundación Tabacalera, 1998), 215–28.

Furthermore, between 1890 and 1930 the labor force participation rate for both males and females combined dropped 17 percentage points. The decline was particularly marked between 1890 and 1900 (6 percentage points) and even more so between 1911 and 1930 when it dropped 8 percentage points. Moreover, in every enumeration year, except 1911, the absolute size of the labor force fell below that of 1890. This contraction of the labor force can be attributed to dropouts from the job market, since the size of the population at risk was increasing. These values clearly point to a deterioration of labor market conditions between 1890 and 1930, the exact period of transatlantic mass emigration. In fact, during this period what was scarce were job opportunities, not labor supply.

Given that the country's population grew at annual rates that could not be absorbed by the job market, we can reasonably presume that the Portuguese emigrants at the turn of the century were departing not primarily because they had places to go, but essentially because they had no place to stay! Furthermore, we can also reasonably presume that if the "safety valve" mechanism had not been at work during this period, the retention in the country of more than 1.5 million persons plus their offspring might well have disrupted the Portuguese social fabric and have created a serious threat to the domination of the elites.

The demand for labor in the international market—especially from the American continents—partially solved this potentially dangerous situation. The regulation of emigration by the dominant social groups in Portugal through legal and social controls produced a selective migratory flow that postponed changes in the socioeconomic structure.

In sum, the removal of much of the surplus male population and the flow of remittances from the New World reduced the pressure on the Portuguese elites to favor policies that might have led to economic development and perhaps to their own displacement from power. As Magalhães Godinho notes, "emigration maintained archaic structures, [and] these archaic structures explain and sustain emigration through the centuries."[7]

Flows, Directions, and Regions of Departure

Portuguese statistics on emigration are flawed in many respects. Recording was unsystematic and poor until the 1900s; information for the period before 1866 is largely limited to the total number of emigrants per year. The records are often inconsistent, and there are temporal gaps in the information registered as well as changes in the recorded population. Finally, we lack information on the conceptual basis for compilation and aggregation.

Although missing or inconsistent information is common in nineteenth- and early twentieth-century statistics, lacunae in the Portuguese statistics on emigration are particularly serious in periods of heavy clandestine migration. Official statistics only recorded legal emigrants, that is, emigrants leaving the country with a passport. Considering these limitations, we now turn to some of the main features of the evolution of the Portuguese migratory flow.

Between 1855 and 1930 close to 2 million Portuguese left the country, with somewhere around 9 percent departing in a clandestine manner. The annual average number of departures was between 23,000 and 26,000, and the overwhelming majority went to Brazil. In fact, overall more than 80 percent of the migratory flow was to this destination. The second choice of the Portuguese was the United States, where 18 percent of the emigrants went until World War I, and 26 percent after that until the end of the 1920s (see graph).[8]

Portuguese Total and Legal Emigration, 1855–1930

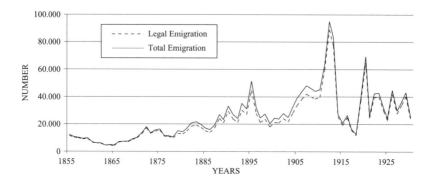

Sources: Maria Ioannis B. Baganha, *Portuguese Emigration to the United States* (New York: Garland, 1990); Maria Ioannis B. Baganha, "Social Mobility in the Receiving Society: Portuguese Immigrants in the United States," *International Migration Review* 25 (1991): 277–302; Miriam Halpern Pereira, "Liberdade e contenção na emigração portuguesa (1850–1930)," in Maria Beatriz Nizza da Silva et al. (eds.), *Emigração/imigração em Portugal* (Lisbon: Fragmentos, 1993), 9–16.

These synthetic descriptive features can begin to be broken up by looking at the evolution of the migratory outflow presented in the above graph. The data indicate that Portuguese emigration registered an average number of departures of 11,000 per year until the 1870s. During this period the curve of the emigration shows a phase of expansion during the 1850s followed by a phase of contraction until 1865. Thereafter, the curve presents an exponential trend up through 1912, when departures reached 95,000. In 1913, when the beginning of World War I brought about difficulties in transportation across the Atlantic, a sudden and marked drop followed this long phase of expansion. This decline in emigration continued until 1918. From 1919 to 1930, with the exception of 1920 when 65,000 emigrants left the country, the curve shows well-defined cycles of three to four years, with an annual average of 35,000 departures.

The marked increase in the migratory stream at the turn of the century can be illustrated by contrasting the early emigration rates with later ones. From an emigration rate of two emigrants per 1,000 inhabitants between 1855 and 1864, the Portuguese emigration rate rose continuously to a peak of seven per 1,000 during the 1910s. The rate dropped during the next decade to a slightly higher level than the 6 per 1,000 registered during the 1890s.[9]

Emigrants departed from all regions of Portugal, but there were some areas where emigration was systematically greater than in other parts of the country. In the Portuguese case, the regional selectivity of the migratory phenomenon is the direct result of the interplay of a set of factors, among which three were of particular relevance during this period: a widespread conviction that economic hardship could be surmounted by migrating abroad; a societal perception that migration was a legitimate option at certain phases of a person's life cycle; and channels of support and of information on the available opportunities in the receiving areas.[10] Until after World War II these three conditions were met consistently in only some areas of Portugal. The main migratory areas were the northern regions of the mainland, namely, the districts of Viana, Braga, Porto, Vila Real, and Bragança, and the region of Beira Alta (districts of Aveiro, Coimbra, and Viseu), and the islands of the Azores and Madeira. Maps 1 and 2 summarize the regional distribution of the Portuguese emigration for the periods of 1886–1910 and 1911–1930.

Prior to the 1920s the share of these main migratory areas never fell below 80 percent of the total number of emigrants. From 1920 to 1930 the relative size of emigration from the islands dropped markedly. Anti-immigration legislation passed by the United States during this period (particularly the Immigration Acts of the 1920s) helps to explain the change. Azorean emigrants—who tended to choose the United States as their destination—were seriously affected by the closing of the North American door, while their counterparts from the mainland—who favored emigration to Brazil—were much less affected.[11]

A second change in the source of emigrants was the steady rise after 1890 in the proportion from the province of Beira Baixa, particularly the district of Castelo Branco. This change can be attributed to worsening economic conditions in the area, most notably the progressive collapse of the artisan textile industry.

Based on information for 588,000 passport holders who left the country between 1897 and 1927, we may refine our analysis of regional behavior by country of destination. Of these 588,000 emigrants, 84 percent left from the mainland and 16 percent from the islands of the Azores and Madeira. Of the 495,000 departures from the mainland, 81 percent went to Brazil and 4 percent to the United States, while of the 67,000 departures from the Azores Islands, 85 percent headed for the United States and only 13 percent went to Brazil. The emigrants departing from Madeira were much more evenly divided between these two destinations. In fact, roughly one-half went to Brazil, while 34 percent departed for the United States.[12]

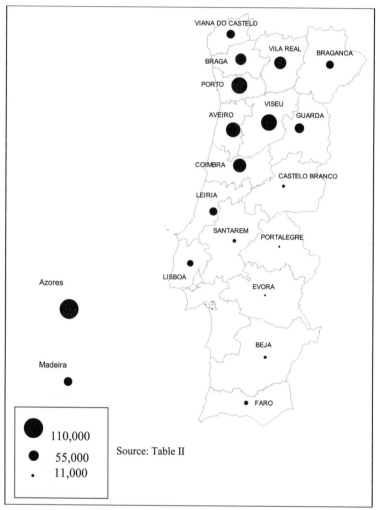

Map 1. Portuguese Emigration by District, 1886–1910

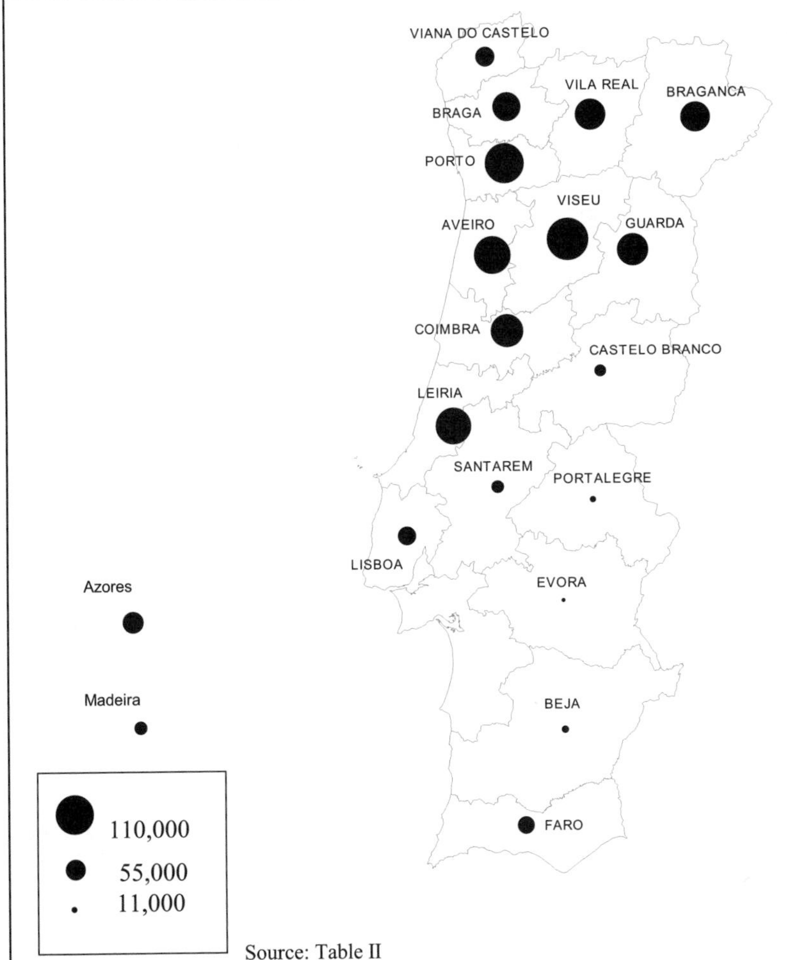
VIANA DO CASTELO
VILA REAL
BRAGANCA
BRAGA
PORTO
VISEU
AVEIRO
GUARDA
COIMBRA
CASTELO BRANCO
LEIRIA
SANTAREM
PORTALEGRE
LISBOA
EVORA
BEJA
FARO
Azores
Madeira
110,000
55,000
11,000

Source: Table II

Note: In 1926 a new district (Setúbal) was formed from the partition of the district of Lisbon (Lisboa). But for the purpose of this study we maintain this new district as part of Lisbon district.

Map 2. Portuguese Emigration by District, 1911–1930

As these figures clearly indicate, migration was not an overall national phenomenon, neither in terms of the regions involved nor in terms of the choice of destination. These facts not only indicate the existence of marked regional asymmetries within Portugal, but they also suggest the influence on the direction of the migratory flow of social networks active at both ends of the trajectory.[13]

Socio-demographic Characteristics

The typical migrant of this period was a single young adult male from a rural background who lacked any specific occupational skills. Although this was the predominant profile of most emigrants, several changes can be observed over time. Table 2 shows the demographic profile of the Portuguese emigrant during the period of mass migration.

Table 2. Demographic Characteristics of Legal Emigrants, 1886–1930

Characteristics	1886– 1890	1891– 1900	1901– 1910	1911– 1920	1921– 1930	Total 1886– 1930
Sex						
Males	80,466	199,205	247,021	288,161	250,462	1,065,315
Females	24,486	70,812	79,246	137,614	74,290	386,448
Age						
< 14 years	20,406	59,690	60,954	80,293	18,910	240,253
> 14 years	84,546	210,327	265,313	345,482	305,842	1,211,510
Marital Status						
Single	57,680	147,371	171,493	236,240	153,542	766,326
Married	44,062	113,695	144,075	177,857	162,051	641,740
Other	3,204	8,951	10,699	11,678	9,159	43,691
Total	**104,952**	**270,017**	**326,267**	**425,775**	**324,752**	**1,451,763**

Sources: For Portuguese official statistics on emigration, see Maria Ioannis B. Baganha, *Portuguese Emigration to the United States* (New York: Garland, 1990); Maria Ioannis B. Baganha, "A emigração atlántica e as migrações internas em Portugal," *Los 98 Ibéricos y el mar*, vol. 4, *La sociedad y la economía en la Peninsula Ibérica* (Salamanca: Fundación Tabacalera, 1998), 215–28.
NOTE: The marital status for the period 1886–1890 is different for the same period because in 1890 the official statistics presented numbers for the different marital statuses that did not sum up to the total that is presented in the same official statistics.

As should be expected, the extremely biased gender composition of the migratory flow revealed in Table 2 markedly affected the country's demographic structure. From the 1890s onward, Portugal had one of the highest rates of net emigration in western Europe. This fact, coupled with the demographic selectivity of emigration noted above, produced an anomalous population structure compared to that of other European countries. Portugal had an exceptionally high proportion of females in its population. As it should be expected in these circumstances, in terms of age, males under 15 were overrepresented, and males between 15 and 60 years of age were underrepresented. Indeed, this last group (males 15 to 60) comprised a smaller proportion of the population in Portugal than it did in other European countries.

That Portuguese emigration was individual (rather than familial) and male-dominated seems beyond discussion. The systematic lack of cash among the rural peasantry together with Portugal's emigration policy favored and perpetuated this outcome. After 1900, however, contemporaries noticed that these traditional characteristics were changing. Emigration was going "from temporary to permanent and from individual to familial," wrote Afonso Costa in 1911.[14] More recent writers subscribe to the same idea of a marked change in the composition of the migratory stream after the turn of the century. Although Table 2 lends some support to this contention, this statement is misleading because it lumps together two different types of emigration going on simultaneously. The first outflow departed from the mainland, the second from the islands of the Azores and Madeira.

Even without correcting for clandestine migration,[15] when we examine the differences in the sex, age, and marital status of the migratory flows from the two separate regions, the figures speak eloquently. Between the 1860s and the 1920s, the female share of the migratory flow was 21 percent for the mainland, compared to 44 percent for the Azores and 35 percent for Madeira. The share of minors (those under age 14) represented only 15 percent of the migratory stream from the mainland, versus 26 and 25 percent for the Azores and Madeira. Furthermore, for each one hundred married men leaving between 1897 and 1906, there were twenty-one married females departing from the mainland and sixty-seven from the islands.

In sum, Portuguese emigration from the mainland was consistently a much more individual and male-dominated phenomenon, and was initially sought as a "temporary" move, than out-migration from the islands, which from the beginning included a much higher share of women and children. Not only was the mainland flow dominated by young adult males departing alone when compared to the migratory stream from the islands, but what is probably more interesting is that compared to the other southern European migratory flows of this period, the Portuguese migratory flow registered the highest proportion of males, of adults, and of persons travelling alone.

In two respects, however, the migratory flows from the mainland and the islands were almost identical. Regardless of their region of origin,

Portuguese emigrants were overwhelmingly illiterate and unskilled. As Lisbon's consul in Boston noted in 1874, "Almost all [Portuguese immigrants] are laborers. Very few have a craft before they arrive in this country. The majority do not know how to read or write."[16] Thirty years later the situation had not improved much. Between 1901 and 1908 more than one-half of the Portuguese emigrants who legally departed were either unskilled or without an occupation, and more than 60 percent were illiterate.

If the Portuguese migratory flow showed a remarkable homogeneity in its composition, the same cannot be said of the migratory experiences of the Portuguese immigrants in Brazil and the United States. In fact, these experiences were considerably different, according to the country of destination.

Emigration to the United States

Portuguese migration to the United States was first spurred by the needs of the American whaling and merchant fleets that, since the late eighteenth century, had stopped at Faial harbor in the Azores in search of supplies and crew members. It was further strengthened by the establishment of American mercantile houses on that same Azorean island. After the midnineteenth century gold rush, a second wave of emigrants headed to California, first for the mining camps and soon afterward for the rural and fishing areas.

The stock of Portuguese residents in the United States was relatively small before 1870; in 1850 there were only 1,274 Portuguese immigrants in the United States. Between 1870 and 1910, however, the Portuguese resident population grew at an average rate of 5.6 percent per year. In 1910 the 78,000 Portuguese-born residents in the United States represented a demographic base eight times larger than the base registered in 1870 and sixty-one times larger than that in existence in 1850.

As had their predecessors, the Portuguese arriving in the United States at the turn of the century settled overwhelmingly in specific communities in the states of Massachusetts and California. The tendency for new arrivals to flock to these two main areas of previous settlement became even greater from the 1870s onward. In fact, while the Portuguese residents in these two states in 1870 accounted for 68 percent of the total number of their countrymen in the United States, by 1890 they represented 80 percent of the total, and by 1910 they corresponded to 83 percent.

The mobility paths of the Portuguese immigrants in California and in Massachusetts were significantly different, regardless of their similar characteristics at entry,[17] as can be seen by the review of a study of Portuguese communities in the United States based on the 1910 manuscript census.[18] The database of the study contains a 10 percent random sample of the households headed by Portuguese-born residents in the textile city of Taunton in Bristol County (Massachusetts) and all the households headed by the Portuguese-born in Milpitas in the rural region of Santa Clara County (California). Overall the sample contains 155 households, sixty-one for Taunton and ninety-four for Milpitas.

Although the Portuguese initially came to Massachusetts as crewmen for the Boston whaling and merchant fleets, by the 1880s they were profiting like other "new" immigrant groups from the opening of low-skill job opportunities in the textile mills of the region. The occupations and the economic sectors of activity of the Portuguese male household heads in Taunton were restricted and clearly determined by the labor market of the receiving community. Ninety-one percent of the Portuguese male heads in the city were wage earners, and of those 79 percent were unskilled industrial laborers.

In California the Portuguese soon became farmers. But the available land, even at low prices, was not immediately affordable for the majority of these immigrants. Still, through a process of renting followed by buying, the Portuguese succeeded in making a niche for themselves in two branches of agriculture: market gardening and dairy production. In Milpitas the Portuguese were involved in market gardening, and, as in Taunton, the market economy of the receiving region determined their place in the occupational structure. Ninety-five percent of the Portuguese household heads were connected to agricultural activities. Of these 95 percent, 87 percent were either employers or self-employed.

The mean size and the type of Portuguese immigrant households in Milpitas were, relative to those in Taunton, larger and less dominated by nuclear families. The high proportion of households with employees and of extended family households indicates that the immigrant households in Milpitas relied on both extended family members and wage earners to satisfy their labor demands. The fact that all the employees in Portuguese households were themselves Portuguese and that a substantial number of the extended family members were males who had arrived after the household head indicates that Portuguese employers in Milpitas relied on kinship and informal migrant networks active at both ends of the trajectory (in this case, the Azores and California) to supply their labor demands. In Taunton the high proportion of households with boarders suggests that a significant share of immigrant households in that city took in lodgers to supplement their incomes. Boarders in the Taunton sample were all first-generation Portuguese, indicating that this strategy to supplement household earnings could be managed within the Portuguese migrant network active in the region.

In sum, the Portuguese migrant network was crucial in both areas. In California it offered readily available work in a setting where the spoken language was mainly Portuguese. Networking between California and the

Azores seems to have been an effective "informal" information system able to support a labor market based on both sides of the Atlantic. In Massachusetts it offered logistical and cultural support, substantially reducing the costs of displacement for the new arrivals. Furthermore, the Portuguese who went to California performed far better economically than those who chose or were directed to Massachusetts. In fact, the temporal pattern of ownership indicates that in Milpitas the Portuguese immigrants in time would acquire some kind of property, while in Taunton only 25 percent of each wave of newcomers could expect to become property owners.

Emigration to Brazil

Brazil's declaration of independence from Lisbon in 1822 was followed by anti-Portuguese sentiment that sometimes was expressed in the form of open violence against the Portuguese community. Such demonstrations deterred other emigration to Brazil and even promoted a significant number of returns to the mother country. After the midnineteenth century, nationalistic spirits in the former colony had calmed somewhat and the flow to Brazil began to regain strength. This flow of immigrants was pulled by the growing labor needs of the Brazilian economy and was further increased by the de facto end of the slave traffic and, in 1888, by the end of slavery itself. In addition, two other contributing factors were the Brazilian government's need to populate the country, and the potential emigrants' awareness of the economic opportunities to be found in Brazil. This information was spread by *engajadores* (agents) and by successful returnees.

An array of sources notes that artisans, craftsmen, and young adult males from northern Portugal who went to join relatives or "family acquaintances" to work in retail trade in the cities were part of the migratory stream to Brazil until the late 1870s. At midcentury (1856–57), Portuguese immigrants owned more than one-third (35 percent) of all commercial houses in the country. This characteristic of the early Portuguese emigration to Brazil changed markedly during the last decades of the nineteenth century.[19] In fact, during the period of highest migration, when the numbers more than tripled—going from 121,246 in the Census of 1872 to 433,577 in the Census of 1920—a remarkable change in the economic incorporation of the Portuguese took place. This change had been under way since midcentury, when growing numbers of migrants came from Portugal under contract to work in the coffee plantations or in the undifferentiated urban activities of Rio de Janeiro and São Paulo. By the turn of the century this paradigmatic change was already highly visible in the occupations of the Portuguese immigrant population in Brazil, as Table 3 demonstrates. By 1900 agricultural work for men and domestic service for women had clearly become the two dominant occupations of the Portuguese immigrants.

Taking into consideration the migrants' characteristics and their respective insertion into the labor market, migrants to Brazil may be divided into three groups. The first was composed of adolescents and young adults who went to join relatives or "friends" to work in the trades. This group departed almost exclusively from the northern regions of Portugal. The second group was somewhat older, and, with some sort of property or skill, they could easily find a niche in the expanding Brazilian urban economy.[20] The third group was made up of those with no skills who entered the unskilled labor market. It has been estimated that at the end of the nineteenth century the first group represented 8 to 11 percent of the total legal flow, while the second group accounted for a maximum of 10 percent.[21] Thus, the last group corresponded to close to 80 percent of the flow. The occupational categories of the Portuguese immigrants in Brazil in 1900 do not contradict these assessments because they include the cumulative effect of previous migratory waves, which, as we know, included a higher share of migrants destined to trades.

Table 3. Main Occupations of the Portuguese Population in 1900 (Percent)

	Male	*Female*
Agriculture	42	21
Crafts	16	7
Trade	29	2
Capitalists	3	0.7
Transportation	4	—
Domestic Service	—	66
Other	6	3.3
Total	**100**	**100**
	(N=57,378)	(N=18,490)

Source: Brazilian Census for 1900, Instituto Brasileiro de Geografia e Estatística do Rio do Janeiro.

In light of the evidence presented, it seems reasonable to assume that, relative to the United States, the first two groups chose the destination that maximized their skills or assets, since their transference was not blocked by the use of an unknown language and was eased by the existence of a large Portuguese community well established in Brazil. The choice of Brazil does not seem as reasonable for the last group, not only because unskilled wages were higher in the United States but also because insertion in this segment of the labor market did not necessarily require knowledge of the English language. In addition, need for fluency in English lessened particularly after 1870, when the Portuguese migratory flow to the United States had become a sustained movement and was backed by a growing Portuguese immigrant community.

Although accurate and comparable figures are hard to come by, the group that made up at least three-quarters of the Portuguese emigration to Brazil at the turn of the century seems to have performed far worse economically than the Portuguese immigrants in the United States with similar occupational profiles. In fact, while for Brazil extremely high rates of mortality and subsidized returns due to indigence or extreme sickness are repeatedly referred to in contemporary sources, no such statements were made regarding the Portuguese immigrants in the United States.

Conclusion

At the end of the nineteenth century, Oliveira Martins noted that the distributions by sex, age, and marital status of the Portuguese emigration differed markedly between regions.[22] In fact, as far back as the records extend, the mainland and the islands were points of departure for different types of emigration that persisted into the twentieth century. Adult males overwhelmingly dominated emigration from the mainland. Emigration from the islands, although also dominated by adult males, incorporated a sizeable number of children and women. This situation was partially due to the existence of different regionally based emigrant labor contracts.[23]

Regardless of these differences the economic profile of the migrants departing from both regions was still extremely similar. As a rule they were of rural origin and extremely poor in human capital, particularly during early phases of their life cycle; even more so if they were unskilled laborers and were heavily dependent on the migratory network active in their region of origin.[24] These factors not only greatly determined the migrants' country of destination but also partially affected their economic mobility path in the receiving country.

In sum, those migrants with some sort of skill or property, generally older than the rest of the flow and probably with a lesser need to rely on the established channels of support, enhanced their chances for betterment by going to Brazil. Young unskilled migrants, who usually lacked the necessary means to depart on their own, relied on family support and on the migrant network active in their region to boost their probabilities of success in the receiving area.

In the Azores, that network directed these migrants to the United States, where the chances for upward economic mobility were far greater than in Brazil. As a rule these migrants did not return; rather, they called upon their family, kin, and neighbors and provided the solid grounding for the development of the Luso-American communities in California and New England. On the mainland the existent migratory networks essentially directed emigrants toward Brazil. Of those who succeeded, some returned and built mansions, often of yellow and green bricks, the colors of the flag of the land that had given them a fortune. These "Brazilian houses" that still dot the Portuguese landscape are more than historical evidence of the transatlantic migratory cycle; they are, in fact, one of the few remaining symbols of the dreamed *el dorado* that drove abroad a significant share of the Portuguese population at the turn of the century.

Notes

1. Dudley Baines, *Migration in a Mature Economy* (Cambridge: Cambridge University Press, 1985); idem, *Emigration from Europe, 1815–1930* (Cambridge: Cambridge University Press, 1995).
2. The present overview draws essentially on the author's previous works. For the sources used in this essay and for a list of further readings on Portuguese migration, see the notes and bibliographies of the works listed below: Maria Ioannis B. Baganha, *Portuguese Emigration to the United States* (New York: Garland, 1990); idem, "Social Mobility in the Receiving Society: Portuguese Immigrants in the United States," *International Migration Review* 25 (1991): 277–302; idem, "Uma imagem desfocada—a emigração portuguesa e as fontes sobre a emigração," *Análise Social* 26 (1991): 723–39; idem, "Portuguese Emigration to the United States," in R. Cohen, ed., *The Cambridge Survey of World Migration* (Cambridge: Cambridge University Press, 1995), 91–96; idem, "Registos de pasaportes: Sus limitaciones y sus posibilidades para el estudio de la emigracion," *Estudios Migratorios Latinoamericanos* 11 (1996): 303–11; and idem, "A emigração atlântica e as migrações internas em Portugal," *Los 98 Ibéricos y el mar*, vol. 4, *La sociedad y la economía en la Peninsula Ibérica* (Salamanca: Fundación Tabacalera, 1998), 215–28.
3. Only from 1855 onward do Portuguese sources systematically register yearly information on emigration.
4. Although numerically much smaller and much more ephemeral than these two major migratory destinations, the Portuguese did leave during the period for other overseas destinations such as Hawaii, British Guiana, and Venezuela.
5. Vitorino Magalhães Godinho, "L'Èmigration Portuguaise (XVe-XXe)—Une constant structurale et les réponses au changement du monde," *Revista de História Económica e Social* 1 (1978): 5–32.
6. Joaquim P. de Oliveira Martins, *Fomento rural e emigração* [1st edition 1891] (Lisbon: Guimarães Editores, 1956).
7. Victorino Magalhães Godinho, L'Èmigration portugaise: Histoire d'une constant structurale. Conjuncture Èconomique, structures sociales (Paris: Mouton, 1974).
8. Baganha, "Uma imagem desfocada"; idem, "A emigração atlântica."
9. The yearly average emigration rate per thousand between decennial censuses was 1855–1864: 2.01; 1865–1874: 2.54; 1875–1884: 4.23; 1885–1894: 5.62; 1895–1904: 6.90; 1905–1914: 7.06; and 1915–1930: 5.25.

10. In other words, the Portuguese case exemplifies paradigmatically that it is not enough for a community to face economic hardships for emigration to occur; these hardships have to be combined with the popular perception that emigration is an acceptable alternative, and the necessary channels must be open for migration to take place.

11. Only in 1929 did Brazilian authorities bar illiterate immigrants from entering the country, and only in 1934 did Brazil establish a quota system that drastically reduced the annual number of entries.

12. Earlier in the nineteenth century, regional disparities were even more pronounced. Of the 5,010 emigrants who left for the United States between 1855 and 1865, 5,008 departed from the Azores and the remaining two from Madeira.

13. The concept of migrant networks is used in a broad sense. The term here refers to both kin/community-based networks and to impersonal structures of information and support. The evidence on the Portuguese emigration of this period strongly suggests that kin/community migrant networks were more relevant than impersonal structures of information and support.

14. Afonso Costa, *Estudos de economia nacional: O problema da emigração* (Lisbon: Imprensa Nacional, 1911), 84.

15. Since clandestine departures were essentially done by males, the female share in the total migratory flow, depending on the period considered, may be considerably lower than the value suggested by the legal flow. In fact, data coming from Portuguese representatives in Brazil indicate that the male share in the migratory flow must have been much larger than that suggested by the official Portuguese statistics, and that the share of married females must have been much smaller.

16. Ministério dos Negócios Externos, *Documentos apresentados às cortes—Emigração* (Lisbon: Imprensa Nacional, 1874, 1885), 248.

17. The Portuguese arriving in the United States at the turn of the nineteenth century (from 1899 to 1910) were a very homogeneous group. More than 90 percent of them came from the Azores; 68 percent were illiterate, 88 percent were unskilled, and they were overwhelmingly single and between 16 and 25 years of age. Their financial resources at entry were extremely low: 88 percent declared themselves to be carrying less than thirty dollars, and 46 percent stated that their passage was paid by others.

18. Baganha, "Social Mobility"; idem, "Portuguese Emigration to the United States" (1995).

19. Herbert S. Klein, "Imigrantes portugueses no Brasil," *Análise Social* 28: 244; Tania P. Monteiro, *Portugueses na Bahia na segunda metade do séc.XIX: Emigração* (Porto: SEE, 1985); Boris Fausto (ed.), *Fazer a América* (São Paulo: EDUSP, 1999).

20. In the 1872 Census of Rio de Janeiro three in every four foreign craftsmen were Portuguese. During the late nineteenth and early twentieth centuries the Portuguese were the largest foreign group connected to manual unskilled jobs in the urban industries such as textiles and tobacco.

21. Oliveira Martins, *Fomento rural*, 231; J. Evangelista, *Um século de população portuguesa* (Lisbon: INE, 1971), 130.

22. Oliveira Martins, *Fomento rural*, 228, 229.

23. The bilateral treaty on emigration and trade signed in 1882 with Hawaii, for example, specifically stated that labor recruitment for the plantations (by rule including the whole family unit) could not be done on the mainland. Baganha, *Portuguese Emigration*.

24. A high percentage of the emigrants had their passage paid by someone else.

4

Italian Immigrants in Buenos Aires and New York City, 1870–1914: A Comparative Analysis of Adjustment*

Samuel L. Baily

Samuel Baily describes and explains the settlement and adjustment of the Italians who went to Buenos Aires and New York during the half century preceding World War I. He argues that those who went to Buenos Aires adjusted more rapidly, effectively, and successfully than did their counterparts in New York City—that is, they were more effective in getting jobs and finding housing, recreating a social life, fighting for better working and living conditions, and increasing their economic resources. By systematically evaluating the Italian experiences in these two cultural settings, Baily shows the power of the comparative method to explain the differing outcomes. In addition, he examines in each society such variables as the pace of migration, the opportunity structure, and the various strategies employed by immigrants to make their way.

Italian international mass migration began in the decades following the final unification of the country in 1870 and continued uninterrupted until temporarily curtailed by World War I in 1914. Although 15 million Italians went back and forth to multiple destinations on five continents during this period, the greatest number chose the United States and Argentina as their destinations—4.1 million or 29 percent chose the United States, and 2.3 million or 16 percent chose Argentina. Within both countries the immigrants concentrated in certain areas and especially in the

---

*This essay is based on Samuel L. Baily, *Immigrants in the Lands of Promise: Italians in Buenos Aires and New York City, 1870 to 1914* (Ithaca, NY: Cornell University Press, 1999). For the citations of the sources used in this essay and for a list of further reading on Italian migration, please consult the notes and bibliography in the above-mentioned book.

major economic centers of Buenos Aires and New York City (see Table 1). By 1914 the Italian colonies in New York and Buenos Aires were by far the largest such concentrations of Italians anywhere in the world outside their homeland. New York had 370,000 Italians; Buenos Aires, 312,000; and São Paulo, a distant third with 110,000. In the United States, cities such as Boston, Philadelphia, and Chicago all had substantially less than 100,000 Italians.

Table 1. Italian Population of Buenos Aires and New York City

	Buenos Aires				*New York City*		
Year	*Total Population*	*Italian born (No.)*	*Italian born (%)*	*Year*	*Total Population*	*Italian born (No.)*	*Italian born (%)*
1855	91,395	10,279	11	1860	813,669	1,464	0.1
1869	177,787	44,0001	25	1870	942,292	2,794	0.3
1887	433,375	138,000	32	1880	1,206,999	12,223	1.0
1895	663,854	182,000	27	1890	1,515,301	39,951	2.6
1904	950,891	228,000	24	1900*	3,437,202	145,433	4.2
1909	1,231,698	277,000	23	1910	4,766,833	340,765	7.2
1914	1,576,597	312,000	20	1920	5,620,048	390,832	7.0

Sources: República Argentina, *Segundo censo de la República Argentina, mayo 10 de 1895*, 3 vols. (Buenos Aires, 1898), 2:163, and *Tercero censo nacional: Levantado el 1 de junio de 1914*, 10 vols. (Buenos Aires, 1916–1919), 2:148, 219, 237, 248, 278, 395–96; U.S. Department of Commerce, Bureau of the Census, *Thirteenth Census of the United States Taken in the Year 1910* (Washington, DC, 1913), 1:804, and *Fourteenth Census of the United States Taken in the Year 1920* (Washington, DC, 1922), 2:698, 928.

*In 1898, New York City, which until that time had comprised only Manhattan and part of the Bronx, incorporated its neighboring counties to assume its current boundaries: Manhattan, Brooklyn (King's County), Queens (Queen's County), Richmond (Staten Island), and the Bronx. Thus, the pre- and post-1900 figures refer to different geographical boundaries in the city.

The exceptional size and preeminence of the Italian colonies of Buenos Aires and New York make them an excellent laboratory for researching the lives of migrants who resided abroad. A multinational comparison of immigrants enables us to understand what was unique to the experiences of the Italians in one city and what was common to both. It will thus help us to develop generalizations and explanations that we could not as reliably make on the basis of one case. Such an analysis will enable those who have studied Italians in different destinations abroad to compare the results here with theirs, to confirm or modify these findings, and to increase in this way our confidence in the explanations set forth.

The primary goal for most Italian migrants was to do better economically abroad than they had been able to do in Italy. To achieve this goal they needed to adjust to some extent to their new environment. Adjustment, as the word is used here, refers to a long-term, open-ended process of interaction that began when immigrants first came into contact with a new environment and the people living there. It is the process during which the immigrants gained the experience, developed the knowledge, and created and/or participated in the organizations that enabled them to function effectively and protect their interests in the new society.

The collective effort of the individual Italians in the two cities to adjust to their new environments created patterns that can be measured and compared. I will attempt to determine the relative speed, effectiveness, and completeness of adjustment by comparing the outcomes of their collective efforts to obtain jobs and housing, to make a new social life, to fight for better working and living conditions, and to increase their economic resources. The first section of this essay compares the patterns of adjustment of Italians in the two cities. The second section explains why these patterns differed.

The Adjustment Patterns of Italians in
Buenos Aires and New York City

A great deal of data demonstrates that the Italians in Buenos Aires adjusted more rapidly, effectively, and completely than did the Italians in New York. Let me briefly summarize this evidence in the important areas of economic activity, residence patterns and living conditions, and organizational activity.

Economic Activity. Although there was intermittent unemployment, Italians in the two cities were able to find jobs with relative ease and were remarkably successful at earning money. In both locations approximately one-half of the Italians managed to earn a surplus in good years and another quarter at least broke even. Most were blue-collar workers—many in construction—but a higher proportion in Buenos Aires were skilled and white-collar workers and owners of small industrial and commercial establishments. In fact, Italians in Buenos Aires dominated the vital commercial and industrial sectors of this rapidly growing city throughout the period under consideration. As early as 1887 the Italians in Buenos Aires, who constituted one-third of the population, made up one-half of the workers and more than one-half of the owners of industrial establishments. In commerce they represented a little less than one-half of the employees and somewhat less than one-quarter of the owners. These percentages gradually decreased due to the growth of a second generation of Italian Argentines who were no longer counted as Italians. Nevertheless, in

Buenos Aires the Italians were significantly higher up in the labor skills and business ownership hierarchies than in New York.

In addition, Italians in both cities were able to achieve some upward occupational mobility. Many of those who began as unskilled workers were able to move up into semiskilled and skilled occupations. This progress was especially true of the second generation of immigrants. In New York, however, this mobility was restricted to the blue-collar sector, from unskilled to semiskilled to skilled. In Buenos Aires, the mobility extended into and within the white-collar sector. More Italians in Buenos Aires moved up from blue-collar to commercial jobs and from commercial jobs to ownership.

Italians in Buenos Aires also played a more significant role in organizations of workers (labor unions) and employers than they did in New York. Italians in Buenos Aires made up the majority of the members and leaders of the newly organizing labor movement. They were also significant contributors to the development of the Argentine major industrial businessmen's association, the Argentine Industrial Union. By contrast, Italians in New York at the turn of the century were not part of the leadership of the National Association of Manufacturers nor were they a major presence within the mainstream labor unions.

Residence Patterns and Living Conditions. Residence patterns and living conditions provide another measure of the process of adjustment. In both cities, Italians settled in the crowded and often unhealthy low-rent districts in the center areas. In Buenos Aires the Italians were more evenly dispersed, while in New York they were highly concentrated in the Bowery district of Lower Manhattan and in East Harlem.

Living conditions were miserable in both places. Immigrants for the most part lived in overcrowded and poorly ventilated apartments that often lacked adequate running water and sanitary facilities. In Buenos Aires, however, conditions were relatively better if only because immigrants were less crowded there. In New York three times as many Italians lived in highly congested tenements as they did in Buenos Aires. Moreover, the population density in New York's Italian neighborhoods was twice as high as it was in the most thickly settled districts in Buenos Aires. In New York most immigrant housing was six or more stories high whereas in Buenos Aires it was usually only three or less.

Per capita home ownership was considerably higher among Italians in Buenos Aires than in New York. In Buenos Aires between 1887 and 1904 the percentage of Italians among all homeowners increased from one-third to just under one-half, while that of Argentines declined from just under one-half to one-third. At the same time the number of Italians who owned homes increased from 9 to 16 percent and that of Argentines dropped from 7.5 to under 5 percent. In New York the data are not as complete but nevertheless indicate that the most optimistic approximation is that less than one-half of Italians owned homes as they did in Buenos Aires.

Finally, there was considerably greater residential mobility among Italians in Buenos Aires before World War I than there was among their counterparts in New York. In 1900 two-thirds of New York's Italians lived in Manhattan, and ten years later three-fifths still resided there. In contrast, in 1895 only one-third of the Italian population of Buenos Aires lived in the equivalent core area, and by 1914 this number had declined to less than one-fifth. In other words, by 1914 more than four-fifths of the Italian population of Buenos Aires had moved out of the core area of the center city compared to two-fifths of the Italian population of New York. Movement to the outlying areas was an important indicator of adjustment because these outer areas were less congested, living conditions were better, and opportunities were greater to buy a home.

Organizational Activity. All Italian immigrants were active to a greater or lesser degree in a number of organizations that helped them meet their daily needs, protect their interests, and achieve their various goals. These institutions included mutual aid societies, schools, churches, labor unions, newspapers, banks, chambers of commerce, recreational and social clubs, and hospitals. What is significant is the extent and strength of these organizations. The difference between our two cases in this area is another important measure of the respective patterns of adjustment.

In Buenos Aires the Italians developed an extensive, wealthy, and powerful immigrant institutional structure around less than a dozen large (1,000+ members) mutual aid societies. These societies, which were open to all Italians, provided many essential services (schools, hospitals, medical clinics, job placement, unemployment and death benefits). By 1910, the membership in these larger societies, combined with that of many other smaller ones, represented nearly one-third of adult Italian males in Buenos Aires and about 10 percent of the women.

The leaders of these societies were part of an elite that created Italian-language newspapers, the Italian hospital, Italo-Argentine banks, the Italian Chamber of Commerce, and the prestigious Club Italiano. *La Patria degli Italiani*, the leading newspaper of the period, was read by perhaps one-half of the Italian population, and the Italian Hospital was one of the leading health-care institutions of any kind in the city.

Although the Italians of Buenos Aires initially participated primarily in ethnic immigrant institutions, they gradually became more involved in the host society. During the first decade of the twentieth century, labor organizations provided Italian immigrants with a working-class alternative to the multiclass mutual aid societies. Tens of thousands of Italians became both members and leaders of the developing labor organizations and were perhaps the most important single group within this movement. Italians were never very active in politics before World War I primarily because the Argentine elites who controlled the political system discouraged their participation and because elections were usually fraudulent.

The pattern of Italian institutional participation was very different in New York. The primary focus of activity was the mutual aid societies, as it was in Buenos Aires, but the New York mutual aid societies were smaller, commanded fewer resources, and were less powerful. These societies' combined membership in New York did not represent anything near the percentage of the Italian population that it did in Buenos Aires. They did not provide the extensive range of services (schools, hospitals, pharmacies, etc.) that their counterparts in Buenos Aires did. Furthermore, the Italian elites who ran these societies differed significantly from those in Buenos Aires. In New York the elites were more self-serving and did not seek to represent all the sectors of the Italian community. In Buenos Aires the elites certainly acted on self-interest but defined it in a much broader and inclusive way. They were, therefore, able to provide more effective leadership for the whole community.

Italians in New York before World War I participated in host society institutions even less than did those in Buenos Aires. In New York those who controlled these institutions discouraged the Italians from taking part. The Irish-dominated Catholic Church was slow in creating Italian-speaking parishes and in making the Italian immigrants feel generally welcome. The same was true with politics and organized labor; Irish and other earlier immigrants controlled both and did not seek to incorporate Italians. In all three institutions there were serious efforts in the years before World War I to create niches of Italian-speaking leaders and members, but these efforts did not result in substantial Italian immigrant participation until after the war.

Most Italian immigrants in New York relied more on informal rather than formal institutions, in particular in the very small and often nonregistered (licensed) mutual aid societies made up of members from their own town or province in Italy. They also participated in informal local clubs that met in cafés.

Thus, the combined evidence on economic activity, residential patterns and living conditions, and organizational activity presented above indicates two very distinct patterns of adjustment: the Italians in Buenos Aires adjusted more rapidly, effectively, and completely than did those in New York. We now turn to the important question of why this was so.

The Explanation of the Patterns of Adjustment

A large number of frequently interrelated variables explain why Italians in Buenos Aires at the turn of the past century adjusted differently than did those in New York. To facilitate an understanding of how these variables influenced adjustment, I have arranged them in three clusters: those things—both mental and material—that the immigrants brought with them to the New World; those things that they found in their new environment when they arrived; and the subsequent developments that resulted from the interaction of the first two over time. Each of these clusters of variables and the relative outcomes are presented in Table 2.

Table 2. Key Variables Associated with Respective Patterns of Adjustment

	More Rapid, Effective, and Complete	Less Rapid, Effective, and Complete
Variable	*Buenos Aires*	*New York City*
What They Brought with Them		
Expectations of permanency	Higher	Lower
Social and economic skills and resources	Greater	Lesser
What They Found		
Opportunities in skilled and white-collar jobs and in small business	Greater	Lesser
Italian community	More developed	Less developed
Language and religion	Similar	Dissimilar
Host attitude	More positive	Negative
Subsequent Developments		
Pace of migration	Spread out	Concentrated
Time of critical mass	Early	Middle
Absolute size	Large	Large
Relative size	Large	Small
Resulting strategy	Long term	Short term

Source: Adapted from Samuel L. Baily, *Immigrants in the Lands of Promise: Italians in Buenos Aires and New York City, 1870 to 1914* (Ithaca, NY: Cornell University Press, 1999).

Although the immigrants brought a number of things with them, perhaps none was more important than their economic resources, occupational qualifications, and organizational skills. The migrants did not come from the very poorest sectors of society. They needed money to pay for their passage as well as information and assistance in finding a job and housing. Both were often provided by members of a family or by kin and/or *paisani* (countrymen) networks that existed in their village of origin and generally extended to their new community abroad. Financial resources not only paid for the passage but also bought the tools and equipment necessary to work at a job or to invest in an artisanal shop or small business.

Occupational and organizational skills also proved to be an advantage in making money and protecting one's interest. Skilled and white-collar workers were paid substantially more than unskilled and semiskilled workers. Owners of small commercial and industrial establishments had greater opportunities than salaried workers. Similarly, those with management skills were better off. They had experience in organizing labor unions, cooperatives, or small businesses that would help them protect their interests.

And finally the expectations of permanency influenced adjustment. If the immigrant assumed he would stay in Buenos Aires or New York a long time or even permanently, he was more likely to adjust rapidly and effectively than his countryman who saw the stay abroad as temporary. The more permanent immigrant was more likely to support protective organizations and to strive for better living and working conditions. The temporary immigrant was anxious to make as much money as possible in the shortest amount of time and to return home with his savings. He had little interest in protective organizations or in improving his working and living conditions in the new land. He saw no reason to pay dues to unions or mutual aid societies, to engage in struggles that might jeopardize his job and his earnings, or to fight to improve his living conditions.

The Italians who went to Buenos Aires had, as a group, greater economic and social resources. A greater percentage of them were skilled workers and artisans than those who went to New York. Although in both cases there were not many white-collar workers and professionals, more of them went to Buenos Aires, and those who did had greater organizational skills. A significantly greater percentage of them came from Italy's industrialized north and were therefore more familiar with various forms of labor organization.

Expectations of permanency are difficult to determine since, with the exception of scattered letters, we have no direct way of knowing what emigrants thought when they left their homeland. Nevertheless, indirect evidence suggests that more of those Italians who went to Buenos Aires intended to stay for a long time or permanently than did those who went to New York. More of them actually returned to Italy from New York (50 percent) than from Buenos Aires (40 percent). In addition, although the large majority of Italian immigrants in both cities were of working age, there were more families, children, and older people among those who went to Buenos Aires than to New York. To be with your family meant a greater commitment to and permanency in the new society than was the case with the single male migrants. Families generally were more permanent migrants than were individuals.

Thus the Italians arrived at the docks in Buenos Aires with greater occupation and organization skills, greater financial resources, and greater expectations of permanency than their counterparts who landed at Ellis

Island in New York. All of these factors would give them an advantage as they sought to adjust to their new environment.

What the Italians found when they arrived at their respective New World destinations is the second cluster of variables that helps to explain the respective patterns of adjustment. Most important, the available economic opportunities differed significantly in the two cities. The United States had by 1900 become one of the leading industrial powers in the world and New York was a major port, financial center, and industrial center. The vast majority of opportunities that were available to the Italian immigrants were unskilled jobs in construction and the service sector. Most of the skilled and artisanal jobs were already filled by the members of earlier immigrants group (English, Germans, Irish et al.). Similarly, jobs in the white-collar and professional sectors were already taken.

Argentina, on the other hand, was still primarily an agricultural and meat-exporting economy with a substantial service sector. Industry, and especially heavy industry, was in its infancy. Furthermore, there were no other large earlier groups of immigrants. The Italians who entered this economy thus found skilled and artisanal employment, some room in the white-collar sector, and even some professional jobs as engineers and architects. They entered the job market at a higher level than their counterparts in New York in part because they had the skills to do so, but primarily because there was greater opportunity in the middle and at the top of the job hierarchy in Buenos Aires than in New York.

Immigrant institutions often played an important role in the adjustment of the Italians. If these organizations were well developed and had sufficient resources, they could provide services, defend the interests of the Italians, and strengthen the community. The nature of the respective Italian communities in Buenos Aires and New York at the time of mass migration thus is important in explaining the patterns of adjustment. When mass migration began in the early 1880s, the Italian community of some 90,000 individuals in Buenos Aires had established institutions capable of helping the newcomers adjust to life in the city. In New York, on the other hand, when mass migration began in the early 1890s, the Italian community of some 40,000 had not developed a sufficiently effective organizational infrastructure capable of helping the new immigrants adjust.

The differences in the cultures of the respective host societies also affected adjustment. In Buenos Aires, the Italians entered a society whose Latin culture, values, language, and religion were more similar to their own than were those of the Italians who entered the predominantly English-speaking, Protestant, Anglo culture of New York. In New York the Italians had problems with language and had greater difficulty understanding some of the values of the host society.

Host society perceptions of and attitudes toward the Italians also significantly influenced the patterns of adjustment. Italians in Buenos Aires were perceived in more positive terms than were those in New York. In Buenos Aires the elites not only wanted the labor of the Italians but also believed that the newcomers would intermingle with the so-called inferior and backward native population and thus over time create a more progressive people. In this sense the Italians were seen as the bearers of civilization.

In New York, on the other hand, Italians were viewed in rather negative terms. The host society needed their labor, but many viewed the great mass of southern Italians as an inferior race that threatened the purity of the northern European stock. The native-born elites demanded that the Italians adapt to the "superior culture" of the United States if they were to succeed. The negative perception of southern Italians in New York resulted in discrimination against them and limited their economic opportunities.

The third cluster of explanatory variables is related to the subsequent developments over time. Perhaps the most important of these variables was the respective pace of the two migrations. The Italian migration to Buenos Aires was spread out more evenly than was that to New York City. In 1869–70, a decade or so before mass migration began in either country, 44,000 Italians lived in Buenos Aires and less than 3,000 in New York. The Buenos Aires community developed gradually over the next four decades. The annual average increase between 1887 and 1914 was a moderate 4.3 percent. New York's Italian community started with a much smaller base in 1870, but from about 1890 onward grew at a much more rapid pace than its counterpart in Buenos Aires. More than three-quarters (77 percent) of all Italians who arrived in New York between 1860 and 1914 did so during the fifteen years preceding World War I. In Buenos Aires just one-half of the Italians arrived during the same fifteen-year period.

The more gradual pace of Italian migration to Buenos Aires combined with the larger initial size of the Italian population there and the greater wealth and effectiveness of the Italian immigrant organizations enabled the existing Italian community to help the newcomers adjust to their new environment. The arrival of massive numbers of Italians in New York in a comparatively shorter period of time overwhelmed the existing Italian community and kept it from providing much support to the newcomers.

The relative concentration and numerical strength of the Italians in Buenos Aires further eased their adjustment. In 1910, Italians represented 12.5 percent of the total population of Argentina, but only 1.5 percent of the total population of the United States. Perhaps more important, one-third of all Italians who lived in Argentina resided in Buenos Aires and more than 20 percent of the city's total population between 1869 and 1914 was Italian-born (see Table 1). One-quarter of all Italians who lived in the United States lived in New York, and at no time were more than 7 percent of the city's population Italian-born. This concentration and numerical strength increased the opportunity to form organizations and build a strong community. It also served to give the Italians a greater say in Argentine society.

The differences between the Italian elites in the two cities also help to explain the respective patterns of adjustment. In New York the Italians developed two basic social strata within the larger multiclass host society. At the top was the tiny group of successful businessmen and professionals called the *prominenti*; the other was the mass of blue-collar workers. There was no coherent or effective group in the middle that could mediate between the two or press for reform. In Buenos Aires, however, the occupational structure of Italians provided the basis for the development of a middle class. The middle groups—the skilled and white-collar workers and the owners of small businesses—were an important influence in the community and as such were able to articulate a broader agenda to serve the interests of all Italians.

Because of the differences between the two Italian elites, the mutual aid societies and the leading Italian-language newspapers in Buenos Aires were more likely to defend the interests of the blue-collar workers as well as those of the rest of the community than they were in New York. Furthermore, in Buenos Aires, Italians from different regions of their homeland were more likely to cooperate with each other than those living in New York. In New York the small group of northern Italians distanced themselves from the frequently scorned southern Italians, whereas in Buenos Aires those from all parts of Italy, despite any regional hostility, joined the same organizations and worked together. This distinctive pattern of interaction among the Italian social groups in the two communities is an important part of the explanation of the differing patterns of adjustment.

Finally, over time the Italian immigrants developed different strategies for responding to the host societies that in turn influenced the patterns of adjustment. When they left Italy, almost all of the migrants assumed they would return home with their savings. This short-term strategy meant that they did not invest their savings abroad or improve their living standards there. In response to changing circumstances, some immigrants modified their initial objectives. Consequently, those who decided to stay abroad for a longer period or even permanently generally developed a long-term strategy of improving their lives abroad.

Most Italians in New York pursued a short-term strategy of saving to invest back home in Italy, while more of those in Buenos Aires followed a long-term strategy of investing in homes, education, and immigrant institutions there. This long-term strategy encouraged the building of an immigrant community with the necessary resources and influence to help its members adjust to their new environment.

In conclusion, the Italians in Buenos Aires adjusted more rapidly, effectively, and completely than did those in New York because of the specific interactions of what they brought with them, what they found abroad, and what developed over time. One way to link these explanatory variables is to focus on the nature of the opportunity the immigrants encountered in their new environments and how the other variables impacted on this opportunity. Italians adjusted more rapidly, effectively, and completely where there were certain kinds of opportunities. In Buenos Aires there were more skilled and white-collar jobs and opportunities in small business. The immigrants there, more of whom were from the north of Italy and had greater social and economic skills and resources, were able to take advantage of these opportunities. In addition, they faced less competition and less discrimination from native Argentines and other immigrant groups. The established Italian community was wealthy and able to help the immigrants articulate and defend their interests. The gradual pace of migration enabled the community to absorb and assist the newcomers, many of whom adopted the long-term strategy of investing most of their savings where they were. Slower, less effective, and less complete adjustment occurred in New York and other places where employment was limited primarily to unskilled labor. The host society's negative perceptions, competition with immigrant groups who had arrived earlier, discrimination, ineffective immigrant organization, a concentrated pace of migration, and adoption of a short-term financial strategy all contributed to limiting the opportunity of New York's Italians.

In each situation the Italians responded to the unique opportunities in the new environments with different resources and skills and with different results. Each pattern responded to the needs of the particular group of Italians and served their interests effectively. This approach can also be applied to other cities where Italians have settled and will help us understand the patterns of adjustment there.

5

Sharing the City: Residence Patterns and Immigrant Integration in Buenos Aires and Montevideo

Hernán Otero and Adela Pellegrino

Settlement patterns and their impact on immigrant integration into the receiving society is an important but neglected issue in migration studies. In this selection, the authors compare the relative spatial segregation (as measured by indexes of concentration and dissimilarity) in the large metropolises of Buenos Aires and Montevideo of immigrants from various European nations, immigrants from nearby Latin American countries, and internal migrants. The respective settlement patterns in Argentina and Uruguay are explained by such variables as the time of arrival of an immigrant group, the nature of pre-migration networks, the job and housing markets, and the cultural and social makeup of the specific group. Hernán Otero and Adela Pellegrino argue that the spatial concentration of immigrants of all types was relatively low in Buenos Aires and Montevideo compared to cities in other countries, that there were different patterns of integration in the various areas within each city, and that the similarities in the concentration levels of Europeans, Latin Americans, and internal migrants suggest, among other factors, the common influence of social networks.

The considerable developments that have taken place in River Plate migration studies in the last two decades have concentrated upon a variety of themes of unquestionable historiographic interest; moreover, they have substantially revised our understanding of European mass-migration and of those societies that migration helped form.[1] While some experiences such as matrimonial integration, ethnic associations, social mobility, the political participation of foreigners, and pre-migration chains and social networks have been analyzed with greater intensity and with progressively revised approaches, other themes have received little attention or have been the objects of simplified treatment. Among the latter,

the spatial segregation of immigrants stands out for its relative underdevelopment. This is so not only because of the lack of attention in an historiographical tradition that, like the River Plate's, has developed with few
contacts with geographers, but also because of its underdevelopment in
absolute terms. Thus the spatial integration of the immigrants has occupied, with few notable exceptions, a marginal place in migration studies,
constituting in the best of cases a contextual section in studies of greater
breadth oriented primarily toward other topics.[2]

As in many other aspects of migration studies, it was Samuel Baily
who first called attention to this problem in a remarkable study about the
spatial integration of Italians in Buenos Aires and in New York.[3] This
study combined a significant methodological preoccupation with structural variables appropriate to all studies with a desire to frame the case of
Buenos Aires in a suggestive comparative analysis. As with other works
by this author, the settlement of immigrants was placed within the context of a larger inquiry into the modes of integration that characterized
the River Plate case with other societies of massive immigration. At the
risk of oversimplifying a complex debate, we could summarize the argument as a conflict between dichotomous associations that tend to identify
spatial segregation with the concept of Cultural Pluralism and the absence of the concept of spatial segregation with the Melting Pot theory or,
in its Creole translation, *el crisol de razas*.[4]

In spite of the simplicity of our summary, we will use this debate as
the starting point of our analysis, and, subsequently, we will attempt to
unearth some of its complexities. As a consequence, the topic of our study,
as the title suggests, will be an examination of the relative spatial segregation of various immigrant groups in Buenos Aires and Montevideo during the period of mass migration. We will focus our presentation upon the
following objectives: 1) to incorporate social actors, particularly internal
migrants and immigrants from bordering nations, who in migration studies have been artificially isolated from the flow of Europeans to the Americas despite the significant role they played; 2) to give equal consideration
to other dimensions that influenced spatial segregation such as religion;
and 3) to reflect upon the interrelationship of patterns of spatial settlement and other variables (such as marriage markets, state action, etc.) in
the process of migratory integration and especially upon the influence
that urban space and the forms of immigrant settlement exerted in creating new multi-ethnic social networks. At this point, we will give priority
to the *behavioral dimension*—the readily observable behavior of immigrants—rather than the *symbolic dimension*—the more general process
of the formation of ethnic identities.

Two interrelated concerns underlie the outlined objectives. First, we
proceed with a comparative analysis of the two principal cities of the River

Plate—Buenos Aires and Montevideo—a task that until now has few antecedents;[5] and second, we intend to go beyond the methodological and historiographical limitation that sees ethnicity and ethnic identity as the primordial dimensions in the study of immigrant integration. What has been said so far is not an attempt to negate the evident theoretical usefulness of identity in such processes, but it does question the a priori assumption that identity is an independent variable. This work tries to place the immigrant in broader social contexts that would allow us to break with what H. Sábato has called "the ethnic capsule."[6]

Methodology and Sources

The proposed objectives impose a macro-analytic methodological perspective as much for the nature of measurement as for the comparative reach among groups and large-scale environments. In addition, the sources used (national and municipal censuses of population and housing), by setting forth the basic macro-structural characteristics of the nineteenth-century statistical paradigm, induce an approach of this type. At the same time, this approach imposes limits upon any attempt to go beyond the information gathered by the state in each census.[7] For this same reason, here we will study the residential patterns of immigrants without including the spatial and social mobility that accompanied the forms of settlement even though they may constitute, as has been demonstrated by Baily, fundamental aspects of the process.[8]

Rather than focusing on the well-known limits of the macro-analytic paradigm, we wish to point out some of its fundamental advantages. Such advantages relate to four basic concerns. First, the inclusion of the total population in our analysis permits us to see more clearly the experience of various groups of immigrants in the urban space. As such, it will allow us to avoid the upward mobility bias of the micro-perspective, which is usually confined to the experience of the more stable and generally more successful immigrants. Second, it allows us to juxtapose, in a single frame, different groups and situations that the microanalytic perspective, by focusing on specific ethnic groups, is forced to isolate in an artificial way. Third, while the selection of the scale of analysis favors and hinders the putting into play of some explanations, the scale of analysis and the explanatory model do not correspond directly. Thus, as we will see, it is possible to think in a micro way about the results obtained from a macro perspective.[9] Finally, the micro-analytic criticism of the macro-analytic models only acquires some relevance when those macro models have previously reached their explanatory and heuristic limits. Given the dearth of studies on the subject, this situation is far from being the rule in River Plate historiography. In sum, representativeness, the comparative analysis of multiple situations, the possibility of interpreting macro results in micro terms, and the relative historiographical underdevelopment all justify the strategy adopted here.

The sources used are the national and municipal population and housing censuses of Argentina (first, second, third national censuses of 1869, 1895, 1914, respectively, and municipal censuses of the city of Buenos Aires of 1887, 1904, 1909) and of Uruguay (the Montevideo census list of 1858–59, first, second, and third national censuses of 1852, 1860, 1908, and the municipal census of 1889). The series thus established presents the classic problem of census sources: variation from one census to another in the questions asked and the tabulations developed, intercensus intervals of irregular duration, and, without a doubt the biggest problem for our purposes, significant changes in the number and boundaries of the sections into which the cities were divided. This last problem makes a systematic comparison from one census to another impossible (except for Buenos Aires between 1869 and 1887 and for the period 1904–1914), but it does not impede the specific analysis of synchronic cross sections (see Map 1).

The forms of measurement for the study of spatial segregation are many and cover everything from some simple measures, such as absolute or proportional stocks of various groups or the relative proportions of the migrants present in each section of the cities, to more elaborate summary indexes. Much like any structural analysis, the main problem is that of utilizing an index that would represent the presence of a migrant group in relation to the presence that that group would have had in the total absence of segregation, in other words, in the supposed case of random distribution. The index of concentration (Ic) that we use satisfies this requirement and allows comparisons between groups of different sizes. The index of concentration is the result of dividing the percentage of a group of people within each section of the city by the percentage of people of the same group in the city as a whole. When both are the same, the index will have the value of 1 (equal distribution); values smaller than 1 indicate that the presence of the group is smaller than the expected amount and those bigger than 1 indicate growing degrees of concentration. The index of concentration is used to measure the concentration observed of a group in *each chosen section* of a city, but it does not give us information about the degree of segregation of a given group in the respective cities *as a whole* (see Map 2).

To do this we need a measurement that summarizes the whole series, a requirement covered by the index of dissimilarity (Id), which, given its generalized use, allows results that are comparable to other studies. This index is calculated for each migratory group by summing up the differences between the percentages of the total population in each section of the city and the percentages of the population of that migratory group in each

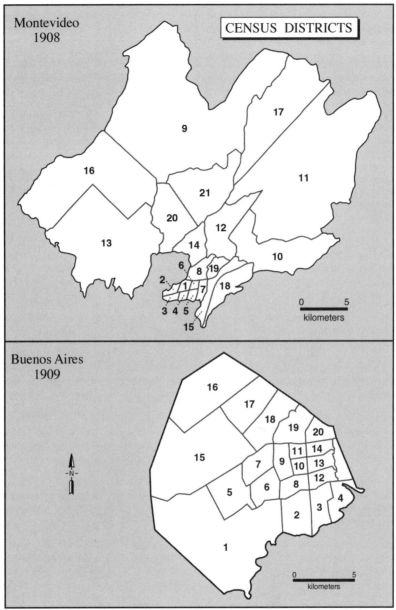

Map 1. Census districts, Montevideo (1908) and Buenos Aires (1909). NOTE: This map and the subsequent maps in this chapter are based on information from the following sources: the national and municipal population and housing censuses of Argentina (first, second, and third national censuses of 1869, 1895, and 1914, respectively, and municipal censuses of the city of Buenos Aires of 1887, 1904, and 1909) and of Uruguay (the Montevideo census list of 1858–59; first, second, and third national censuses of 1852, 1860, and 1908; and the municipal census of 1889).

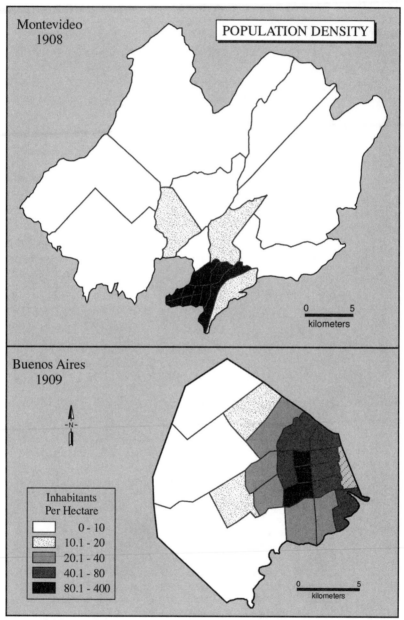

Map 2. Population density, Montevideo (1908) and Buenos Aires (1909). *Sources*:
See note, Map 1.

section. These results are then divided by 2. The index moves between zero (absence of segregation) and 100 (maximum level of segregation).[10]

Overview of the Cities

Foreigners

The analysis of the European presence in the city of Buenos Aires (Map 3) shows that the three main immigrant groups—Italians, Spaniards, and French—have since 1887 presented a pattern of spatial settlement characterized by a greater immigrant concentration in specific sections of the city. In spite of the possible artificial variations produced by changes in the definitions of specific sections of the city, these three groups tended to concentrate in a considerably stable distribution pattern throughout this period. Stability is in fact relative and shows up mostly in those sections where the index of concentration is highest. However, this pattern does not happen in sections of intermediate concentration that change more easily. From a wider perspective, the concentration patterns are as follows: the Italians clustered in section 20 from 1887 to 1895, where we can find the well-known neighborhood of La Boca, and, to a lesser extent, in the central sections—central in a geographical sense of the city (sections 8 to 11 in 1904.) Spaniards dominated the central sections, which are the oldest areas of the capital city, and occupied a strip parallel to the Rio de la Plata (sections 3, 12, 13, 14, and 20) and, within these, had a major concentration in section 13—Monserrat. Last, the French show an equally stable distribution that coincides in part with that of the Spaniards, but they moved toward sections 14 and 20—San Nicolás and Socorro—as the period advances. As G. Bourdé observes, this pattern of stable distribution was mostly the same for the German and English immigrants as well.[11]

These three cases show distinctive features of temporal stability and, in strictly spatial terms, the nonoverlapping of groups with a higher index-of-concentration numbers in the same sections. Within each immigrant group, the spatial contiguity of those sections with the greater concentration of each group is a feature that testifies to the partially artificial character of these sections as well as to the validity of the indicators used. If we create a scaled comparison regarding concentration levels, French groups with the greatest concentration and Italians with a more even distribution would be the two ideal types at each extreme, and the Spaniards would be in a position between the other two. The more even distribution of Italians is especially interesting because in no section is the index-of-concentration level higher than 2—a fact that is accentuated after 1914 when only section 4 had an index-of-concentration level higher than 1.1. In the three immigrant groups of interest, the most significant

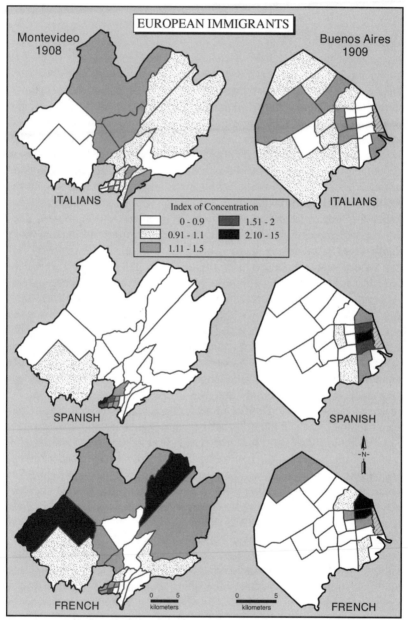

Map 3. Concentration of European immigrants, Montevideo (1908) and Buenos Aires (1909). *Sources*: See note, Map 1.

development over time in Buenos Aires is the decrease in concentration levels. The indexes of dissimilarity changes between 1887 and 1914 are as follows: Italians (11.6 to 9), Spaniards (26.5 to 15.1), and French (28.9 to 19.5).

The Montevideo case presents some significant differences. Compared with the Buenos Aires municipal census of 1909, the Uruguayan census of 1908 highlights three interesting features. First, a lesser concentration of the three European groups—except in the case of the Spaniards, who show the same index of dissimilarity in both cities, less spatial proximity in their settlement patterns, and a different relative ranking of groups. Thus, even though the Italians were again the least concentrated with a very low 6.3 index of dissimilarity, unlike in Buenos Aires the French were an intermediate group (14.9), and the group with the highest concentration was the Spanish (18.6). In the same way as the case in Buenos Aires, the Spaniards in Montevideo concentrated in significant numbers in the oldest sections of the city (in the port and sections 1 to 6 and 8, reaching the highest concentration levels in section 2). Italians were less homogeneous in their distribution because they concentrated less and because there was no spatial proximity. The French concentrated in the city's northeast (section 17), northwest (section 16), and to a lesser extent in section 4 in the central area. The relative position of the groups varied in this city according to the evolution of migratory flows (although always in low concentration). This finding is implied by partial data from the Montevideo census register of 1858–59 in which the French, who were the biggest group during the first half of the nineteenth century, show the highest index of concentration among the groups analyzed.

The inclusion of bordering-country immigrants (Map 4) is particularly illuminating because, even though there is practically no cultural distance that separates them from the local population, they showed almost identical concentration levels as the European immigrants. Chileans settled in Buenos Aires in sections 11, 13, and 14 and the Paraguayans in section 4. Thus, they settled in the same areas as Spaniards and Italians, respectively. We may also find a significant stability in settlement areas because the zones they preferred in 1914 were the same zones as in 1895. The Paraguayan presence in La Boca in section 29 in 1895 and the population along the river suggest the existence of professional networks linked to seafaring. On the Uruguayan side, index-of-dissimilarity levels are similar but the concentration is less prominent, particularly with regard to spatial proximity in those sections with a greater presence of the respective immigrant groups. As could be foreseen, the Uruguayans in Buenos Aires and the Argentines in Montevideo made up groups from border countries that were closer to being evenly distributed than were those from countries farther away.[12]

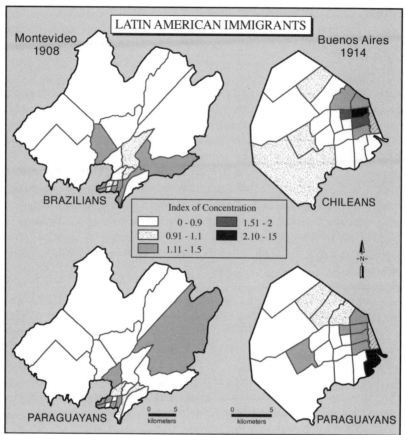

Map 4. Concentration of Latin American immigrants, Montevideo (1908) and Buenos Aires (1914). *Sources*: See note, Map 1.

Internal Migration

Argentine censuses of 1869, 1895, and 1909 and those of 1889 and 1908 in Uruguay permit us to analyze the presence of internal migrants in the respective capitals (see Map 5). By 1910, we can see in Buenos Aires a general pattern characterized by the greater concentration of internal migrants in certain sections of the city's northwest (Belgrano) and northeast (Balvanera Norte, San Nicolás, Pilar, and Socorro). This pattern does not include internal migrants from the province of Buenos Aires, who, like Uruguayans, were close to equal distribution. As was the case with foreigners, these patterns continue those of 1895. As in the celebrated gravitational model of G. K. Zipf, the presence of migrants of four different provincial origins decreases with the geographic distance that separates the points of departure and arrival.[13] What is most interesting is that index-

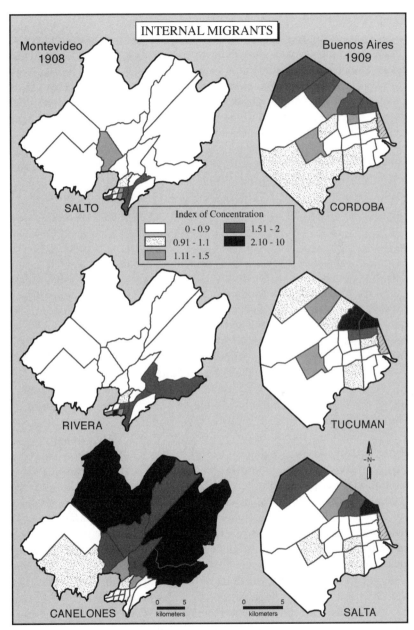

Map 5. Concentration of internal migrants, Montevideo (1908) and Buenos Aires (1909). *Sources*: See note, Map 1.

of-dissimilarity rates increase as the distance increases that separates the provinces of origin from the city of Buenos Aires (Entre Ríos, Córdoba, Tucumán, and Salta, respectively). All of this occurs as if the migratory difficulties brought about by the greater distances were part of a greater reliance on migratory chains and networks and by a greater propensity to establish concentrated settlements.

This relationship did not happen as systematically in the case of Uruguayans—unsurprising because the distances are smaller in Uruguay than in Argentina. Those groups of the most distant provincial origin (Artigas in the northernmost part of the country) had an index of dissimilarity of a high of 23.2. People who came from Salto, Rivera, Soriano, and Artigas present a pattern of settlement that was very similar (sections 6, 7, and 15), while those coming from Canelones (an area adjacent to the city) settled in a completely different pattern—they occupied the outskirts of the capital and were practically absent from the center of the city.[14]

Religion

The data about religion constitutes a dimension distinct from that previously set forth for two reasons. First, there is a difference between belonging to a group in more or less vague terms such as a legally defined nationality, and the greater level of cohesion and closeness implied in belonging to a religious denomination—even more so when we are dealing with religious minorities within countries with a Catholic majority.[15] Second, there are differences in the population that has been included in each case; in the category of nationality, only foreigners were included, but in the case of religion, both foreigners and natives (the majority of whom were descendants of foreigners) were included.

The index of concentration presented in Map 6 illustrates patterns of Protestant and Jewish residence in 1909 in the city of Buenos Aires. This map shows clearly some important patterns: 1) the very high spatial concentration according to religious beliefs—the index-of-concentration figures were among the highest observed, with values over 9 in some sections for Jews as well as for Protestants. When we turn to look at their overall measure of dissimilarity, Jews had the highest dissimilarity levels observed;[16] 2) spatial contiguity among sections with high indices and in sections where groups did not overlap—except in section 14. Finally, over time the stability of these areas of settlement according to religion was less than that observed for groups of different nationalities.[17]

In the case of Montevideo we cannot measure levels of segregation according to religious beliefs because the census did not include such questions. The bulk of Jewish immigrants to Uruguay arrived after the period under consideration. T. Porzecanski's work implies that this group tended to settle initially in the center of the old city but later, as a result of

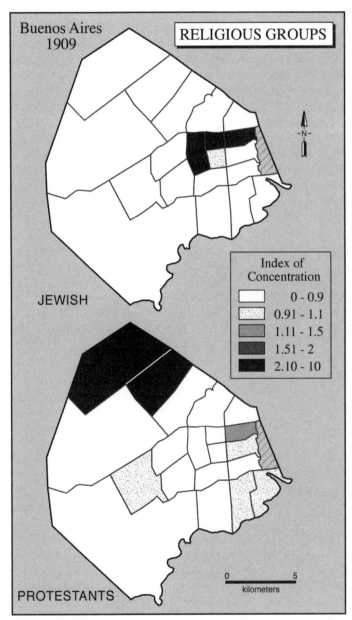

Map 6. Concentration of religious groups, Buenos Aires (1909).
Sources: See note, Map 1.

social mobility, moved to other neighborhoods.[18] Census data (1909) confirms this impression by permitting the identification of "Polish" and "Russian" concentrations (nationalities with a high proportion of Jews) in areas that historically were Jewish neighborhoods. This situation contrasts with what was observed for the rest of the migratory groups. High levels of Jewish concentration in both cities of the River Plate make up, together with the Italians in La Boca, the only situations close to fulfilling the ethnic enclave model.[19]

Residency and Home Ownership

The settlement of immigrants in urban space may take two basic forms: general residency (whatever the legal relationship with the dwelling), and settlement by ownership. The latter is particularly relevant because it is a clear indicator of one level of integration. Access to real estate requires a significant level of income and employment stability, factors that in general are associated with greater success and with longer residency in the receiving society. To these economic factors we should undoubtedly add expectations and specific cultural values because home ownership was not an objective of equal importance for all immigrants. Rather, home ownership was one more aspect of general strategies that could be oriented in various directions. Thus, the accumulation of capital, the obtaining of savings for future activities or for sending to the family of origin, or the expectation of return could have made the purchase of real estate unnecessary or economically unfeasible.

Seen together, the settlement of homeowners in Buenos Aires is characterized by a model that is *peripheral and homogeneous in regards to contiguous space*. As evidenced by Map 7, immigrants of all nationalities who owned their homes settled in a compact manner and with high indices of concentration in the west of the city. If we compare this situation with that of 1887, we note that although the model of settlement remained essentially stable, between 1887 and 1904 there was a progressive movement to the west. As always, it is easier to measure this phenomenon than to interpret it. Moving to the periphery may have been the consequence of the upward economic mobility of more successful immigrants. In contrast, the explanation may be found in the fact that more recent immigrants who found the central zone saturated generally settled on the outskirts of the city. The few studies we have on interurban mobility tend to contradict rather than corroborate the first hypothesis; they suggest that migrant mobility was characterized by being of short distance, although we should keep in mind that these results could be influenced by the upward mobility bias inherent in the sources used.[20]

Whatever the answer to the last point may be, there are at least two features that are of unquestionable importance. In the first place, the dis-

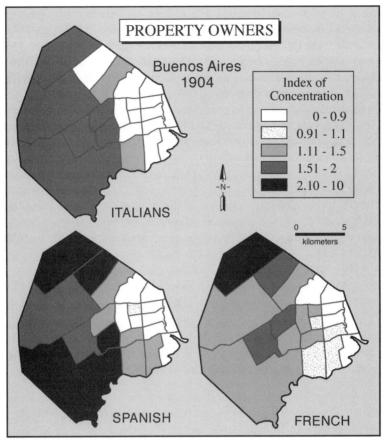

Map 7. Concentration of European property owners, Buenos Aires (1904).
Sources: See note, Map 1.

crepancy between the main areas of settlement according to whether we
are dealing with resident immigrants in general or with property-owning
immigrants is clear; for the three analyzed groups, property-owning immigrants were consistently more concentrated than residential immigrants
in general. In the second place, there was a significant correlation between the distribution of property owners and the price of land; the high
indexes of concentration of property-owning immigrants—over 1.5—can
be found without exception from 1887 onward in the sections with purchase prices lower than $10 per square meter.[21] This pattern shows un-
equivocally the importance of the housing market and the ability of
immigrants to maximize their incomes and guide their strategies according to the possibilities of that market. If this explanation does not necessarily contradict the relational model of migratory settlement (migrants

settling near kin and co-nationals), it does suggest that we should not forsake the more impersonal factors of a macro-economic nature.

Finally, the relatively low frequency of access to property of different groups—about 10 percent of all immigrants had property in 1904—reminds us that as a rule in Buenos Aires at the turn of the century people rented rather than owned their dwelling. At the same time, similar levels of property ownership between natives and foreigners, which fluctuated between a low of 8 percent for Spaniards to 11 percent for native Argentines with other immigrant groups in between, allow us to conclude that, at least in this dimension, we can talk of a particularly successful integration—even more so if we remember that we count children of immigrants within the Argentine population.

For Montevideo, although we do not have such precise quantitative data, we can also observe a model analogous to that of Buenos Aires. In Montevideo the expansion toward the area surrounding the Ciudad Vieja and the Ciudad Nueva allowed better access to individual dwellings for the middle sectors, the artisans, and the small merchants, most of whom were immigrants. Home ownership was, in its turn, more extensive in the newer areas of the city, while in the old urban core more than 80 percent of all housing units were rentals.

Spatial Insertion and Integration: Constructing the Macro through the Micro or the Micro through the Macro?

It is clear that no simple model provides a general explanation of settlement patterns for all groups and that the spatial settlement of the different migrant groups in Buenos Aires and Montevideo appears as a complex framework of overlapping factors. The time of arrival, the nature of pre-migration networks, the housing market, and the social makeup of the different groups, among others, influence in difficult-to-determine proportions the observed distribution. From the methodical perspective, the nature of the data and the fact that the units of analysis are spatial add supplemental difficulties, particularly in regard to the well-known ecological fallacy—much more because the level of disaggregation in the published census data differs from one variable to the other.

It is evident that the patterns observed respond to factors of the three basic orders of social explanation: structural, categorical, and personal or relational.[22] Immigrants settle in an urban setting by taking advantage of certain ecological niches determined by economic variables as would presuppose a structural explanation. The explanation once advanced by Bourdé, based on the differential social composition of each group, moved in the same direction.[23] We can also identify specific characteristics in the settlement of each nationality, a fact that suggests the validity of a categorical explanation. Finally, we can state in personal or relational terms that the effect of pre-migratory bonds, starting with the original nuclei of immigrants, would explain the future settlement of people originating in the same social space of origin. As is already suggested by C. Mitchell's theoretical blueprint, and as has been shown by Baily and J. Moya, none of these explanations is enough by itself to define the causes of the observed settlement patterns.

If we admit that the instantaneous results captured by the macro vision are the product of the micro-social mechanisms developed by the participating actors, it can be argued that the general structures observed would shed some explanatory light upon the micro-mechanisms that produced them. Of course, the whole is not conceived as merely being the sum of its parts but, as in systems theory, as the complex *output* of a multiplicity of factors of different weight. The relationship between the macro and micro levels, which we understand as two possible scales of analysis without necessarily claiming the epistemological superiority of either one, can take two basic directions: to explain the macro by means of the micro; or, taking off from macro observations, to explain how these condition micro aspects.

In the case of spatial segregation, it carried with it an interpretative model, well known due to the excellent works of Baily and Moya that consider the pre-migratory social networks in their different types—chains as well as friendship, village, and kinship networks—as the main predictive element of the settlement patterns of migrants in the urban space.[24] Thus, the settlement of migrants in a given area of the city appears as the result of the information and/or help given by previously settled immigrants.[25] Some well-documented cases, such as that of the Agnonesi in the barrio Del Carmen and that of numerous Spanish regional groups or the Italo-Albanians in the barrio Santa Elena in the Buenos Aires metropolitan area, are paradigmatic examples of this explanatory relational model of urban settlement.[26]

It is in the clarity and explanatory power of this model where we see without doubt one of the major advances in River Plate migration studies during recent years. Without denying its validity we could, nevertheless, set forth some questions about its more general applicability, linked to three basic although not novel questions of migration studies: How do we explain the spatial settlement of the first immigrants of a given pre-migratory social network? To what degree does the relational mechanism detected represent the total migratory experience of the group? And what is the validity of extrapolating on the basis of the detected micro-mechanisms to postulate them as a universal explanation for a large-scale space?

The first question refers to one of those notorious blind spots in a theory such as that of networks. Networks have been particularly apt in explaining the nature of migratory strategies in the receiving countries on the basis of the framework created by pre-established migrants. The theory, however, was less capable of explaining the origin of these networks. Emphasizing the influence of the structural variables—work, housing, etc.—over the settlement of the pioneers, and of the cultural ones— migration chains—for the subsequent migrants, Baily has given an intelligent explanation of this problem.[27] It certainly is a convincing one, but it cannot be generalized if, as we believe, the model of chain migration does not constitute the only possible mechanism.

The second question refers to a more general doubt about one of the basic assumptions of the relational model in its migratory version, that is, the idea according to which strong ties (family, *paesani*) would have predominated over other more impersonal relations or over mechanisms of access to goods and to more impersonal information such as the market. This second observation is not independent of the first because the generation of social networks based on strong ties does not happen in a vacuum in which other alternative possibilities do not operate. On this point, there is enough empirical evidence[28] to affirm that a significant portion of the migratory flow was not necessarily part of the relational mechanisms based on strong personal ties as was the case in North America or Australia. As F. Devoto has convincingly argued in a recent text, countries such as Spain and Italy that sent migrants to the River Plate area were characterized by an emigration context in which individuals were very familiar with the possibilities and the limits of emigration and had multiple sources of information.[29] The emigrants therefore did not have to depend so greatly on the news provided by their extended families to decide where to migrate.

On the other hand, and in distinction from today's world, the nineteenth-century River Plate region was characterized by a great capability for economic expansion, by the existence of high-demand and fluid labor markets, by notable legal freedom of movement to enter and exit, and by the absence of strong discriminatory prejudices toward a foreign workforce. These factors made the strong relational ties less necessary for individuals to emigrate and to gain access to the labor market than was the case in North America. These arguments are good explanations, from our perspective, both for the processes of getting a job and for access to other goods and services such as housing, which were fundamental to the spatial integration of any group.

If we accept the preceding observations, we could doubt the usefulness of extending the relational model of strong personal ties to the whole of the migratory experience. On a higher level of abstraction, we could doubt the possibility of understanding the macro exclusively from a generalization of evidence—certainly important—but methodologically limited to the micro scale of analysis. More clearly, the predictive character of elements such as belonging to a pre-migratory social network is only valid in the universe of reconstructed networks but, perhaps, not for the whole of the migratory experience if, as it has been affirmed, those networks of strong personal ties do not represent the enormous plurality of possible networks that we supposed. On the other hand, regarding prediction, the macro and micro levels are not necessarily compatible in logical terms; in terms of relational analysis, belonging to one network can predict more or less adequately the settlement of its members in places close to the pioneers. However, the spatial distribution of the whole ethnic collective, the macro distribution, cannot be logically derived from the prediction of an innumerable, complex, and very diverse ensemble of micro networks.[30] Last, belonging to networks is not necessarily the most relevant aspect of the problem because equally important is the type of capital (economic, social, cultural, and informational) linked by these networks.[31]

Because of all of this, more than explaining in depth the observed settlement patterns, we will try to analyze the macro/micro relation, having as a research objective seeing to what extent and in which way the macro results obtained allow us to discuss micro-analytic aspects. In this second direction, the residential patterns would be seen not so much as something to be explained but, above all, as potentially conditioning factors and therefore in some measure as explanatory of other migratory patterns. In other words, we will seek to utilize the macro configurations detected in the maps as triggers of the *conditions of possibility* of the social networks of migrants already settled in the receiving society, in particular the networks established after settlement that condition and define migratory integration. Following this logic, in the following section we shall see, always in spatial terms, three basic conditioning factors of the formation of new social networks: marriage markets, density and frequency of contacts, and the action of the state through public education.

Marriage Markets as Integration Vectors

Endogamous marriages (marriage within one's group) have been one of the most widespread interpretative keys of immigrant integration not only because they are relatively easy to measure, but also because of the evident social importance that the formation of couples has in the social and cultural reproduction of a given society. Generally models of analysis of matrimonial integration have resulted systematically in the notion of a marriage market and in its operative translation through the index of masculinity, an index that represents the relative presence of men and women in a specific group in the matrimonial marketplace. Numerous research studies have clearly indicated the dangers of a model that is based exclusively on these parameters.[32] They have also unmistakably exposed the unavoidable limits that the unbalanced gender composition in the immigration flow imposed on endogamy, and how this effectively determined that a portion of foreign men would marry Argentine women, accelerating in this way the process of integration. Although some authors (especially M. Szchuman in his 1977 study about the city of Córdoba) have called our attention to the need to include space as a conditioning factor in the formation of couples, studies have had to identify the marriage market within the total space of the regions examined, a risky operation for studies of major cities.[33]

Map 8 of the masculinity indexes of the main migratory groups effectively shows the existence of spatially segmented marriage markets in Buenos Aires in 1909 and Montevideo in 1908. It presents significant variations in the distribution of men and women of each nationality within the urban space. In the general context of the overabundance of male immigrants, specific sections of the city were characterized by particularly high masculinity rates. Even more notable—since it contradicts the traditional images to which we are accustomed—is the fact that some sections present balanced masculinity rates or even had a shortage of men (the paradigmatic case here is the Spaniards from the north of Buenos Aires and sections 5, 11, and 19, respectively, and the French in the central-south of Montevideo). In this last case, the overabundance of men increases toward the periphery of the city. The absence of men in some sections was generalized among the native population.

There is little doubt that pre-migration social networks were used to expand a marriage market particularly scarce of potential spouses by means of well-known practices such as the *llamado* (the calling) for kin and *paesani* (of which high levels of micro-regional endogamy would be a good indicator of these practices). It is equally clear that when analyzed spatially the effectiveness of such strategies must have been quite varied. On this point, the most salient conclusion is that the settlement in certain urban spaces, whatever the initial causes, conditioned in good measure the limits of action for the realization of endogamous marriage. Thus, there were spaces that more clearly than others fit the conditions for greater and more rapid matrimonial integration, both with other groups and with natives. What has been argued thus far is, of course, also applicable to immigrants from neighboring countries and to internal migrants.

This logic can also be detected in other kinds of analysis, as is suggested by the 1887 Buenos Aires data about people who reside in *conventillos* (tenements). Even if the municipal census of that year does not offer detailed information for each national group, the contrast between Argentines and foreigners shows that, although foreigners (especially men) were the majority of residents in a typical *conventillo*, Argentines (mainly women) were also a significant portion of the *conventillo* population. If we take these dwellings and living spaces as a social universe that conditioned the formation of couples, it would be difficult not to admit that these environments constituted channels of more

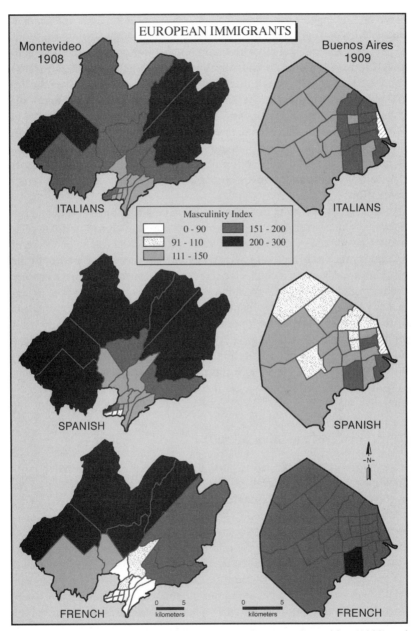

Map 8. Masculinity of indexes of European immigrants, Montevideo (1908) and Buenos Aires (1909). *Sources*: See note, Map 1.

rapid and intense urban integration than other urban locations, more so because exogamy (marriage outside one's group) in terms of nationality could be accompanied by social homogamy (similar incomes and occupations). Clearly segregated along social lines (not only for including the structurally defined poorer population but also for concentrating the new arrivals) but without clear and strong evidence of ethnic segregation, the *conventillos* encouraged a kind of "melting pot" at the bottom of the social pyramid. This point is not trivial if we consider that 40 percent of the population that resided in Buenos Aires lived in *conventillos* in 1887.[34] In Montevideo, on the other hand, the sum of the people who lived in boardinghouses and *conventillos* (without any apparent family nucleus), in addition to those who lived in other homes as domestic help, or renters or in dwellings with nonrelatives constituted 66 percent of the immigrant population.

We cannot give to these matrimonial submarkets an absolute and deterministic character because *conventillos* were not closed units. A relatively modern and extensive public transportation network helped expand an immigrant's matrimonial horizon beyond the immediate market of the neighborhood because it connected individuals to dances, parties, and other events organized by the immigrant communities. It would nevertheless be equally difficult to deny that the more openly multi-ethnic interaction of these spaces did not condition the formation of new social and matrimonial relationships. Similarly, it would be daring to suppose that the internal mobility of the population of the cities in the River Plate at the turn of the last century was more significant than at the present time when, in spite of easy transportation, the formation of couples is strongly conditioned by distance.

Density and Postmigration Networks

A key point of network theory, particularly regarding the so-called morphological criteria,[35] concerns the quantity of contacts that the actors weave in their social lives. These contacts contribute to the formation of new relations and as a consequence to the modification (and eventual suppression) of pre-existing networks. Among the multiple factors that condition the quantity of emerging relations we find, of course, geographic space. Any linear relationship between the forms of urban settlement and the resulting relational configuration of the migrants would be inappropriate. Nevertheless, we cannot either postulate a situation in which networks were totally autonomous from spatial conditions. Geographic space is always a socially articulated space and not a Euclidian isomorphic space. This way of visualizing the problem is not extraneous to the concept, frequently found in the French sociological tradition, of social space, whose success in explaining the existence of specific emigration areas is well known in the Riverplatine historiography of migration movements.[36] Given the fact that the pre-migration social space was, above all, a rural space, it may seem that the extension of this concept to a large urban metropolis such as Buenos Aires or Montevideo is a risky idea. However, the opposite hypothesis, according to which the large metropolis completely suppresses the forms of interaction and the spatial limitations characteristic of smaller environments, should also be discarded given the current state of our knowledge of the subject.[37]

Independently of other interacting factors, one of the basic elements in the development of interpersonal relations constructed in the places of arrival (no doubt with co-nationals but also with the remaining native population and those of other national origins) was physical proximity. Even after discarding the traditional perspective of the "uprooted" in the migratory process (where individuals sever ties to their former lives), it is undeniable that migration introduces a spectacular modification in the social spaces of the individuals. In their new setting, migrants insert themselves into new environments requiring the development of new relationships that, in some way, can be reduced to the simple continuity of the pre-migration social ties or to their amplification within the institutional framework of the ethnic community. If this is so, we have abundant qualitative evidence that the "postmigratory social space" (the neighborhood, the job, etc.) brought together components of all the different ethnic groups. While censuses are structured around the individual as the unit of analysis, we can use population density as a way to enrich our analysis of migrants' social space.

Map 2 offers information about the per-hectare density of Montevideo and Buenos Aires and enables us to understand the influence of population density as a condition for the formation of new multi-ethnic social networks. Both cities show around 1908–09 a radial model with a high-density center (sections 8, 10, and 11 in the Buenos Aires case, and southwest of the bay in Montevideo) from which the density of the remaining sections decreases as the distance between them and the center increases. Beyond highlighting the model itself, it is important to consider the extraordinary variation in the median densities of the different zones. Although we cannot answer the question as to what was the influence that density had over the intensity and shape of emerging social relationships, we can affirm that those variations did constitute differential conditions for social urban integration. In particular, we can consider the periphery as a kind of internal frontier of the city, analogous to the rural frontier with respect to the urban centers.

The interpretation thus set forth suggests that the different areas of the city exercised conditioning standards that favored or hindered the process of integration of the immigrants by providing the context for the development of networks of multiethnic interaction of varied character and density. Density appears as a possible vector of the formation of new spaces and networks. The application of the concept requires new refinements: we must examine neighborhood, work, and socializing spaces, characterized by different densities and implying different geographic distances.

Public Education, Spatial Segregation, and Integration

Second-generation integration—the true Gordian knot of any debate about Cultural Pluralism or the Melting Pot—depended on another decisive dimension, that of the level of state policies guaranteeing the socialization of the children of immigrants through public schooling. This dimension was also uneven according to the different sections of the urban space (see Map 9). Regrettably, governmental sources do not allow us to examine the problem for each national group, but they give us some basic data sufficient for a cursory analysis. Taken as a whole, the school age Buenos Aires population—from 6 to 15 years of age—in 1904 shows a high level of attendance at public school that almost completely monopolized the offerings of educational services.[38] With the exception of the west side of the city (sections 1 and 15), all of the Buenos Aires sections could count on classroom attendance of more than 60 percent of the children, reaching levels of over 70 percent in the north side of the city. The spatial distribution in the case of Montevideo is similar, even though the levels are much lower, especially on the west side.

These numbers are eloquent testimony to the importance of the action of the state. The state was a fundamental actor in the process of integration of the foreign-born population in the River Plate model, thanks to the integrating role of an extensive public school system imbued with patriotic rituals and a significant capacity for cultural homogenization.[39] State action thus reinforced the integrative tendencies that from a behavioral perspective were played by mixed marriages (especially because in these marriages the main socializing agent, the mother, was in the majority of cases native) and by the more or less fluid residential patterns observed.

Even though there were ethnic schools (mainly Italian) that cautiously rivaled the monopolistic will of the state in the socialization and instruction of the children of foreigners, they enrolled only a small part of the school-age foreign-born population. Similarly, the mutual aid societies did not seem to have exercised great influence in this area, given that of the 214 societies polled in the Argentine capital in 1913 only twenty-one had schools. These numbers are questionable in part because they refer only to the ethnic schools supported by mutual aid societies and not to the total educational experience undertaken by immigrants.[40] On the other hand, it is very probable that the official data, produced in a context of

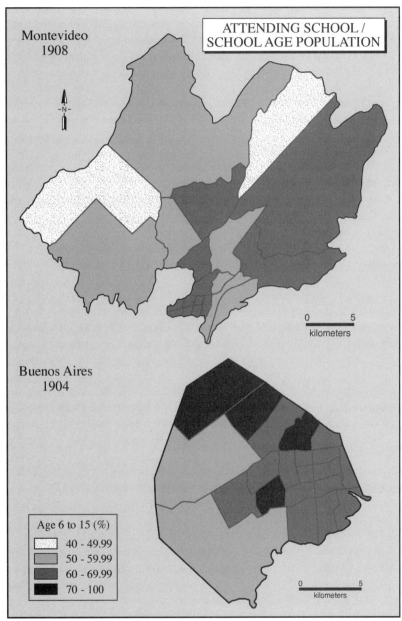

Map 9. Percentage of school-age population (six to fifteen years) attending public school, Montevideo (1908) and Buenos Aires (1904). *Sources*: See note, Map 1.

statistical euphoria designed to show precisely the ability of the state to act in this manner, underestimate the real impact of the ethnic schools. Even so, the overall image we can reconstruct eloquently shows the educational activities undertaken by the public schools and allows us to imagine its real integrative effects on the new society.

If we set aside the formal instruction and refer to the more general socializing stamp of the ethnic institutions, the view does not change fundamentally because children only made up 5 percent of the total membership of the mutual aid societies and, in an overwhelming 69 percent of the cases, were members of a cosmopolitan or multiethnic association. Given the fact that more than one-half of the mutual aid societies were established between 1901 and 1913, the described situation had to be even more overwhelming still for the period before the beginning of the twentieth century. Membership in mutual aid societies (the most important but not the only ethnic institution) was important, but none of the three immigrant groups analyzed brought together more than 17 percent of their conationals in the city.

Conclusion

Two implicit questions can be derived from this article. First, can pre-migratory social relationships and the settlement patterns derived from them, detected on a micro level, be generalized to the whole migratory experience? Or, putting it differently, can we reduce the patterns of sociability and the relational universe of the immigrants to the networks based on strong personal ties and to their institutional prolongation in the context of community organizations? And second, can the levels of spatial concentration of the immigrants adequately characterize their relations with the urban space and, by extension, their forms of integration into the host society? We believe that with some variations both questions require a negative answer.

In the first case, the characterization of urban spaces starting from the broadest set of variables and dimensions—matrimonial markets, population density, and presence of public schools—and our proposed inversion in the sense of thinking of the micro as an effect of macro conditions, we can show that each urban space created different possible conditions for the formation of new social networks and for the weakening of the relative importance of the pre-migration personal networks. On this point, even though we believe that one of the major advances in Riverplatine migratory historiography of the last decade has been the discovery of existing continuities between immigrant departure and arrival areas, we believe also that this emphasis has perhaps led us to an exaggerated image of persistence in the migratory process that overlooks the extraordinary transformations that overseas migration imposed on its actors.

If this is so, the future historiographical tasks should be to follow a more eclectic vision that combines the search for continuities as well as capturing the disruptions in the process and, among the latter, the mechanisms, the intervening factors, the resulting types, and the intensity obtained by the process of formation of new pluralist social networks. With his usual sharpness, A. MacFarlane has pointed out that with regard to the concept of community, the studies devoted to the subject run the risk of systematically finding it; to put it in his own words: "expecting to find 'communities,' the prophecy fulfilled itself and communities were found."[41] Similarly, our efforts to find networks and strong ties has led us to reduce the investigation to the micro level, forgetting that at the broader level it is possible to detect other mechanisms and other ties that are not as strong as those of the family and *paesani*, although equally significant. The influence of the urban market and the action of the state are undoubtedly aspects that require more of our attention.

In the second case, we have tried to demonstrate that even though it has great value as an indicator, the existence of variable levels of immigrant concentration cannot be read directly as an unmistakable base for the resulting integration processes. As we have seen, spaces with a greater concentration of immigrants can be characterized as well by the presence of other factors favorable to integration, such as very unequal marriage markets, a greater density of people for possible relationships, or a high incidence of attendance in the public school system. In the methodological key, what we have already said does not make us consider any particular dimension (segregation, endogamy, aid to ethnic schools, etc.) as a direct or excluding indicator of pluralist or integrationist characteristics until they are integrated into more comprehensive visions that discriminate more clearly the specific influence of each factor. Some scholars note that the utilization of polythetic categories could be of great benefit for migration studies because the determined levels of settlement in a social space could acquire very different meanings—even opposite meanings—according to the combination of variables present in each case.[42]

In spite of its limitations, the argumentative line we have followed permits us to show the extremely complex and in considerable measure the ambiguous character of the spatial segregation of immigrants in both capital cities of the Rio de la Plata. In addition, it has set forth some propositions with considerable empirical support:

1) Both Buenos Aires and Montevideo share common features in the spatial concentration of immigrants, especially the existence of areas of settlement for each group set in an overall context of low levels of spatial segregation. Placed in a wider comparative setting, we can see that such levels position both cities of the River Plate among the least ethnically segregated in the world.

Moreover, as the historiography of the topic has shown, regional
and family micro-concentrations are significant but not of sufficient intensity to be considered as ghettos or ethnic enclaves.
The Italians in La Boca and the Jewish population are probably
the only exceptions where people can be considered as living in
ethnic enclaves. This statement has greater weight if we argue
that the existence of even a minimum level of segregation (ethnic, racial, class, etc.) is a normal fact, statistically speaking, of
every social space and if we remember the notable tendency to
low levels of spatial concentration in both cities, according to
ethnic criteria. On the other hand, the extraordinary and massive
quantitative influence the immigrants and their descendants had
on both capitals makes it unnecessary to resort to mechanisms of
spatial concentration. This evidence suggests that in the classic
but not yet exhausted cultural Pluralism-Melting Pot debate, the
cases studied bear witness, at the macro level of segregation, to a
model much closer to the minimum level of pluralism expected.

2) Similarities in the concentration levels of the residential patterns
of Europeans, Latin Americans, and internal migrants suggest
that the existence of relational mechanisms (networks, chains)
often used to explain the transfer and insertion of the first migrants should be generalized in a much wider sense to other migration experiences. This proof, certainly not new, might in some
sense permit us to contextualize the common knowledge in such
mechanisms that translate directly into a search for cultural affinity, because they are present independently of the cultural distance that separates the immigrants from the host society. As we
have already stated about endogamy, we can see in the existence
and effects of such networks more continuity of the pre-migratory relational mechanisms (that which makes these networks an
evident fact of an explicative character more than a variable to
be explained) than a search for the preservation of ethnic values.[43] Following this path, the relational model, initially associated with the very important contributions of Cultural Pluralism,
can contribute new evidence in favor of the traditional model of
the Melting Pot as articulated by G. Germani without embracing
its initial methodological and interpretative limits.[44] Thus, we can
conjecture that in the evident dimensions of Cultural Pluralism
that characterized River Plate society of this period (press, ethnic leadership, and ethnic associations, among others), space
would not have had such a significant role as in classic models
of the Chicago School of communities in the United States. The
explanation of unequivocal signs of pluralism would belong more

to the symbolic and the political sphere and, above all, as Devoto suggests, to the predominance of a language or the capability of the ethnic *leadership* to control specific environments more than to the existence of space and behavioral bases.

3) Spatial analysis of key variables (marriage markets, density, and public school activity) shows a map of areas that interact in a different way in the integration process. Generally speaking (a finished model should be undoubtedly more complex), the periphery of the city was characterized by a matrimonial market more propitious for exogamous integration and by a real estate market equally favorable to the acquisition of land. On the other hand, the periphery offered a more dispersed space in which to live, a lower population density, and fewer public schools, and these factors must have played the opposite role. The city center was the opposite of this peripheral image in all the mentioned variables. Conditions for the possibility of forming new multiethnic networks were clearly dissimilar in different urban spaces, as we have implied by our way of thinking in macro terms about micro mechanisms. The conclusions of this model constitute suggestions and working hypotheses more than effective proofs, but they back up the historiographical necessity of studying how, by what means, thanks to which possibilities, and in spite of which limits, immigrants constructed networks with other groups and with the local society. Research on the formation of these new multiethnic networks, and not only those that existed among immigrants, is the historiographical task for the coming years—a task that requires us to return to the uprooting process and to give to the continuities a less important role than we have given them up to now.

Notes

1. The River Plate region includes the countries that border the River Plate, that is, Argentina and Uruguay.

2. For an up-to-date study of migration historiography see for the Argentine case, F. Devoto, *Movimientos migratorios: Historiografía y problemas* (Buenos Aires: CEAL, 1992); and for the Uruguayan case, C. Zubillaga, "La historiografía sobre el proceso de inmigración masiva en Uruguay: Un acercamiento crítico," in *Jornadas Interescuelas y Departamentos de Historia* (Montevideo, 1995).

3. S. Baily, "Patrones de residencia de los italianos en Buenos Aires y Nueva York: 1880–1914," *Estudios Migratorios Latinoamericanos* 1 (1985). See also Chapter 4 in this volume.

4. The Melting Pot theory posits that immigrants rapidly assimilated into the host culture, thus losing their culture of origin. Cultural Pluralism, on the other hand, suggests that immigrants often maintain much of their culture of origin.

5. We will proceed with a comparison that alternates two of the types suggested by N. Green: convergent comparison (between two ethnic groups in the same space) and divergent comparison (the same groups in different spaces). See N. Green, "L'histoire comparative et le champ des Ètudes migratoires," *Annales Economies, Sociétés, Civilisations* 6 (1990).

6. H. Sábato, "El pluralismo cultural en la Argentina: Un balance crítico," *Historiografía argentina (1958–1988)* (Buenos Aires: Comité Internacional de Ciencias Históricas, Comité Argentino, 1989).

7. About the Argentine census paradigm see H. Otero, "Estadística censal y construcción de la nación: El caso argentino, 1869–1914," *Boletín del Instituto de Historia Argentina y Americana "Dr. Emilio Ravignani"* 16–17 (1998); and idem, "Hombres ávidos de bienestar: Espacios, ciudades y migrantes en la estadística censal argentina, 1869–1914," *Studi Emigrazione* 35 (Rome: CSER, 1998).

8. Baily, "Patrones de residencia."

9. See the terminology of the classic text of C. Mitchell, ed., *Social Networks in Urban Situations: Analysis of Personal Relationships in Central Africa Towns* (Manchester, Eng.: Manchester University Press, 1969).

10. Given the changes that took place in the division of the urban space, the numbers of the sections mentioned in the text correspond to the number assigned to the section at each specific census date. When this is not mentioned, we are referring to the enumeration of the last period (see Map 1): 1908 for Montevideo and 1904–1914 for Buenos Aires. For reasons of space we only adjust those maps that are most significant for this last period.

11. G. Bourdé, *Buenos Aires: Urbanización e inmigración* (Buenos Aires: Ed. Huemul, 1977).

12. Index-of-dissimilarity rates in bordering immigration in Buenos Aires (1909) are as follows: Uruguayans (5), Chileans (18), Paraguayans (15). For Montevideo (1908) the range was: Argentines (8), Brazilians (12), Paraguayans (19).

13. G. K. Zipf, "The P1*P2/D Hypothesis: On the Intercity Movement of Persons," *American Sociological Review* 11 (1946).

14. Provincial index-of-dissimilarity rates (1869 and 1909) in Buenos Aires were as follows: Entre Ríos (15.7 and 10.8), Córdoba (23 and 16.9), Tucumán (17.8 and 19.6), Salta (35.5 and 24). For Montevideo (1908): Canelones (22.8), Soriano (14.7), Rivera (22.7), Salto (18.4), Artigas (23.2).

15. The proportions according to the Municipal Census of 1904 were as follows: Catholics (86.6 percent), Protestants (2.6 percent), Jews (0.6 percent), without a religion (1.4 percent), and without specifying (7.8 percent) (Note that the percentages do not total one hundred due to roundings.).

16. The index-of-dissimilarity figures according to religion for 1887, 1904, and 1909 were respectively as follows: Jews (39.6, 45.8, and 47.2); Protestants (25.5, 17.7, and 19).

17. Protestants, who made up an elite model of immigration, concentrated in 1887 in the center and in the southern part of the city (sections 1 and 19) and later occupied the north (sections 16 and 17) in 1909. Jews moved in the opposite direction but became closer in distance.

18. T. Porzecanski, *Historias de vida de inmigrantes judíos al Uruguay* (Montevideo: Kehila, 1988); idem, *El universo cultural del Idisch: Inmigrantes judíos de Europa oriental en el Uruguay* (Montevideo: Kehila-American Joint Distribution Committee, 1992).

19. A. Portes and R. Manning's work is an important reference here. According to these authors the prerequisites for the emergence of an ethnic enclave (for example, the Jewish population in Manhattan) are the presence of a significant

number of immigrants with experience in business, which was acquired in the country of origin, and sources of capital and hand labor, which came from family labor as well as from the continual arrival of members to the community. See A. Portes and R. Manning, "The Immigrant Enclave: Theory and Empirical Examples," in S. Olzak and J. Nagel, eds., *Competitive Ethnic Relations* (Orlando, FL: Academic Press, 1986).

20. S. Baily, "La cadena migratoria de los italianos en la Argentina: Los casos de los agnoneses y siroleses," in F. Devoto and G. Rosoli, *La inmigración italiana en la Argentina* (Buenos Aires: Biblos, 1985); J. Moya, *Cousins and Strangers: Spanish Immigrants in Buenos Aires, 1850–1930* (Berkeley: University of California Press, 1998). Mutual societies, which often include the community of migrants according to origin, refer to the more stable and most successful members of the community. On the other hand, if mutual societies cover specific spatial areas, their use for research on the residential patterns of migrants can have in some cases a tautological result.

21. Regarding land values, see M. Jalikis, *Historia de los medios de transporte y de su influencia en el desarrollo urbano de la ciudad de Buenos Aires* (Buenos Aires: Companía de Tranvías Anglo Argentina, 1925).

22. Mitchell, *Social Networks*.

23. Bourdé, *Buenos Aires*.

24. Baily, "Patrones de residencia"; Moya, *Cousins and Strangers*.

25. As Moya argues, "the combination of socioeconomic status and local origin clearly represented the most powerful predictor of residential choice; when the variables are separated, the latter always proved a better predictor than the former." Moya, *Cousins and Strangers*, 147.

26. Baily, "La cadena migratoria"; Moya, *Cousins and Strangers*; D. N. Marquiegui, *El barrio de los italianos: Los Italo-albanenses de Luján y los orígenes de Santa Elena* (Luján: Librería de Mayo, 1995).

27. Baily, "La cadena migratoria."

28. In the last few years a considerable effort has been mobilized to sort out more precisely the proportions of immigrants who arrived as part of family and *paesani* chains. See, for example, the analysis about Basques, French, and Danes included in M. Bjerg and H. Otero, eds., *Migración y redes sociales en la Argentina moderna* (Tandil: CEMLA-IEHS, 1995).

29. Fernando Devoto, "Información, cadenas y redes. El papel de los fuertes y débiles en el movimiento migratorio de los españoles e italianos a la Argentina," IUSSP international seminar, "Cambios y continuidades en los comportamientos demográficos en América," Cordoba, October 27–29, 1978.

30. See Moya's data reconstruction regarding the residency of Spanish immigrants in the period 1902–1930 in *Cousins and Strangers*, 191.

31. For a discussion of the important relation between belonging to networks and access to social and cultural capital, see D. Massey, R. Alarcon, J. Durand, and H. González, *Return to Axtlán: The Social Process of International Migration from Western Mexico* (Berkeley: University of California Press, 1987); and P. Fernandez Kelly, "Social and Cultural Capital in the Urban Ghetto: Implications for the Economic Sociology of Immigration," in A. Portes, ed., *The Economic Sociology of Immigration: Essays on Networks, Ethnicity, and Entrepreneurship* (New York: Russell Sage Foundation, 1995).

32. The scholarly production regarding endogamy is abundant for the Argentine case. A synthesis of this issue can be found in E. J. Míguez, "Il comportamento matrimoniale degli italiani in Argentina: Un bilancio," in G. Rosoli, Ed., *Identita degli italiani in Argentina: Reti sociali, famiglia, lavoro* (Rome: Centro Studi Emigrazione, Edizione Studina, 1993).

33. M. Szuchman, "The Limits of the Melting Pot in Urban Argentina: Marriage and Integration in Córdoba, 1869–1909," *Hispanic American Historical Review* 57 (1977).

34. This average includes noteworthy variations that go from 8 percent in section 17 to almost all the population (97 percent) in section 13.

35. Mitchell, *Social Networks*.

36. See A. Morel, "L'espace social d'un village picard," *Etudes Rurales* 45 (1972): 73.

37. For actual Latin American examples of the workings of networks in big cities see L. Adler de Lomnitz, *Redes sociales, cultura y poder: Ensayos de antropología latinoamericana* (Mexico City: FLACSO, 1994).

38. The alternative forms of education in the public schools (in factories or workshops, in the home, etc.) have very little importance (5 percent) in both cities in the first decade of the twentieth century.

39. L. Bertoni, "Construir la nacionalidad: Héroes, estatuas y fiestas patrias, 1887–1891," *Boletín del Instituto Ravignani* 5 (1992); idem, "Nacionalidad o cosmopolitismo: La cuestión de las escuelas de las colectividades extranjeras a fines del siglo XIX," *Anuario del IEHS* 11 (1996).

40. By 1905, for instance, the Danish consulate in Buenos Aires counted forty-six ethnic schools of all nationalities (data supplied by M. Berg).

41. A. MacFarlane, "History, Anthropology, and the Study of Communities," *Social History* 5 (1977): 632.

42. P. A. Rosental, "Maintien/Rupture: Un nouveau couple pour l'analyse des migrations," *Annales Economies, Sociétés, Civilisations* 6 (1990); R. Needham, "Polythetic Classification: Convergence and Consequences," *Man*, New Series, 10 (1975).

43. E. Míguez, M. Argeri, M. Bjerg, and H. Otero, "Hasta que la Argentina nos una: Reconsiderando las pautas matrimoniales de los inmigrantes, el crisol de razas y el pluralismo cultural," *Hispanic American Historical Review* 71 (1991).

44. Gino Germani, *Política y sociedad en una época de transición: De la sociedad tradicional a la sociedad de masas* (Buenos Aires: Paidos, 1962).

6

The Japanese in Peru and Brazil: A Comparative Perspective*

Daniel M. Masterson and Sayaka Funada

The Japanese were latecomers to Latin America, but they proved impor-tant to the development of Peru and especially to that of Brazil. In this essay, Daniel Masterson and Sayaka Funada compare the trajectories of the Japanese in these two countries. Among the issues they discuss are the role of the Tokyo government in encouraging emigration to Latin America, the painful story of anti-Japanese sentiment and legislation during the late 1930s and especially during World War II, and the con-flicts between the older generation's ties to their homeland and the younger generation's commitments to life in Brazil. Since World War II the Japa-nese in both Peru and Brazil have made a remarkable recovery; they have reestablished their institutions and prospered.

The great Atlantic migrations of Europeans who settled mainly in Ar-gentina and Brazil were largely over when most of the Japanese im-migrants began arriving in Peru and Brazil after World War I. Indeed, less than 800 Japanese migrated to Latin America before the twentieth cen-tury began. A closed society during the Tokugawa Shogunate (1603–1867), Japan's modernization program during the Meiji Restoration (1868–1912) encouraged emigration in an effort to alleviate severe problems of over-population and poverty in the rural sector.

The population of Japan increased by nearly one-third from 35.9 mil-lion in 1879 to 50.6 million at the beginning of World War I. The peas-antry suffered significantly during this era. In the words of one Japanese reformer, they "are falling into deeper poverty and have reached a point where they cannot maintain life."[1] The rural masses were being forced to

---

*This article is based on Daniel M. Masterson with Sayaka Funada, *The Japa-nese in Latin America: Immigration, Settlement, and the Sojourner Tradition* (Ur-bana: University of Illinois Press, 2003). For a more comprehensive treatment of the Japanese in Latin America and more information on sources and a bibliogra-phy, please consult the above-mentioned book.

finance Japan's rapid industrialization through higher land taxes. When they could not meet these tax burdens, they encouraged their sons, and less frequently their daughters, to emigrate temporarily. The young emigrants, mostly from the southern prefectures and Okinawa, hoped to earn money to secure their family's future and to return home after four or five years "dressed in golden brocade" to lead more prosperous lives. Militarization and the initiation of the so-called blood tax or national conscription also encouraged many young Japanese males to emigrate to avoid the draft.

Lacking suitable opportunities in its newly acquired territories of Taiwan and Korea, the Tokyo government responded to calls for cheap labor in the West by developing an overseas emigration policy that sent the first Japanese to Peru in 1899 and to Brazil in 1908. Before traveling to Latin America, Japan's emigrants in the 1870s first were directed to the northern island of Hokkaido. Later in that decade they journeyed to Hawaii to toil in the sugarcane fields. After 1890, many of these sojourners in the Hawaiian Islands were drawn to the west coasts of Canada and the United States, and in smaller numbers to Mexico, by higher wages in the fields, mines, fishing villages, and lumber and railroad camps of North America after 1890. But economic rivalry and racial antagonism soon led to a campaign to exclude Japanese immigration to North America. Theodore Roosevelt's Gentlemen's Agreement of 1908 and Canada's Lemieux Accord of 1907 initiated the exclusionist campaign. California's Alien Land Laws further deprived first-generation immigrants of their economic gains.

Eventually, all Japanese immigration to the United States was prohibited by the 1924 Immigration Act. Canada allowed only a few hundred to enter after 1925. When at the end of the first decade of the twentieth century the Porfirio Díaz government in Mexico City cooperated with Washington in imposing restrictions, Peru and Brazil became the primary "safety valves" for Japanese immigration to the Americas. Above all else, it must be understood that very few Japanese who migrated to Peru and Brazil before World War II ever intended to leave their homeland permanently. They had what may be called the "sojourner mentality," that is, the idea that they would make their fortune abroad and then return home. One naive carpenter from Kunamoto Prefecture in southern Japan who was among the first 781 immigrants to arrive in Brazil boasted on his departure from the port of Kobe that he planned to return with "a suitcase full of yen bills." Even most of the young men who left Japan to avoid conscription on "emigrant deferments" had intentions of someday returning.

Of those with the sojourner mentality, very few ever went back to Japan. The repatriation rate for the Brazilian Japanese, for example, was less than 7 percent, far less than the return rates for the European immigrants who had arrived earlier in the southern states of São Paulo, Paraná, and Rio Grande do Sul. The reasons are many, but a distinct pattern can be discerned among the Japanese who reluctantly made new lives in Peru and Brazil. The first-generation Japanese in these two nations generally enjoyed economic success before World War II.

Most important, the emergence of the Japanese immigrant family kept the first generation in Peru and Brazil after they accepted the reality that they very likely would not go home again. By this time, they had transferred their hopes and dreams to their children who, despite the best efforts of the parents, often identified as much with the culture of South America as with that of distant and unknown Japan.

Today, more ethnic Japanese live in these two nations than anywhere else in Latin America. At present, Brazil is home to 1.2 million ethnic Japanese, and Peru to more than 50,000. They are the legacy of courageous early immigrants who sought to create better lives for themselves. Ironically, as the Latin American economies declined in the 1980s, many third- and fourth-generation Japanese would become temporary migrants to Japan to earn enough to improve their situations when they returned to Latin America.

Peru's Japanese, 1899–1941

Before Japanese immigrants arrived in 1899 to harvest sugarcane on Peru's coastal plantations, a failed attempt to establish a colony near the junction of the Perené and Ucayali rivers had been made six years earlier by Ikaturo Aoyagi, a prominent Japanese businessman and University of California graduate. He hoped to have the immigrants grow coffee in a "magnet" colony that would draw a substantial number of Japanese to Peru. Such a colonization effort had been made with mixed success in the state of Chiapas in Mexico in 1897. The Peruvian venture, however, never moved beyond the planning stages as the internal political troubles that would eventually plunge the country into civil war in 1895 prevented officials from taking any substantive action. Still, the demand for sugar workers remained constant.

Two individuals, one Japanese and the other Peruvian, were primarily responsible for initiating Japanese immigration under the contract labor system in 1899. Teikichi Tanaka, an official of the Japan-based Morioka Emigration Company, and Augusto B. Leguía, a prominent sugar planter and future president of Peru, negotiated the first four-year contract that brought 790 immigrants to Callao on the Japanese Mail Line vessel *Sakuru-maru* in April 1899. The contract called for the overwhelmingly male workforce to be paid twenty-five yen or about U.S. $12 per month. Expenses for housing, food, and transportation were to be deducted from their wages at the rate of ten yen per month. The workers hoped to save fifteen yen every month, thus having the substantial sum of 720 yen or over $300 at the end of their four-year obligation. Since the average agricultural worker in Japan was paid only one-half the wages in one year that the sugar workers in Peru were contracted to earn in one month, the uncertainty and hardships of leaving home for a strange land seemed worth the risks. However, few of these immigrant workers, who came predominantly from the southern prefectures of Nigata, Yamaguchi, and Hiroshima, ever earned even a fraction of the illusory 720 yen or stayed on the plantations where they were originally sent.[2]

From the first difficult days in Peru, the pioneers confronted the legacy of a plantation system that was based on centuries of coerced labor. Sugarcane planters were not willing or prepared to deal with workers who demanded adherence to labor agreements and readily sought the assistance of their home government to redress their grievances. Violations of the terms of the contracts drove many of the laborers to flee the plantations. Language difficulties, misunderstandings over work assignments, and disagreements over the obligation to purchase food and supplies at plantation stores were the main points of contention between the Japanese and the plantation managers. In a revealing memorandum by Tanaka to his superiors in the Morioka Emigration Company in Tokyo, he lamented the conditions on the Cayalti plantation and concluded: "It is clear that when the plantation tried to force the laborers by threats to do more work, they banded together to do average work. I tried to negotiate with both sides, but it is clear that the employers would not abandon their slave master habits. The plantation is a country unto itself into which the national law does not enter; the owner is a potentate, and punishment a matter of course. Even life and death are at the will of the plantation."[3]

Adding to the misery of the first immigrants was disease. The initial group of contract laborers was devastated by malaria, typhoid, yellow fever, and dysentery. As many as 149 of the original 790 immigrants who had sailed on the *Sakuru-maru* died of these illnesses during their first year in Peru.

Within less than six months of their arrival, 321 contract workers left the plantations for the port of Callao to await passage back to Japan. However, a lack of shipping and the inability to pay the return passage kept the vast majority of them in Peru. During the next ten years, Japanese immigrants met with continuing harsh conditions on the coastal sugarcane plantations either from the *hacendados* (owners of large estates) or from native workers angry at the initial willingness of the Japanese to work for lower wages.

During the first decade of the twentieth century more than 6,000 Japanese migrated to Peru. Only 230 of these migrants were women, mainly the wives of contract laborers brought to Peru before 1906. Unlike the Brazilian coffee planters in São Paulo who favored the migration of entire Japanese families to work in their fields, Peruvian *hacendados* preferred single male contract laborers. Indeed, only 184 of the migrants before 1910 were free immigrants not obliged by contract to work on the plantations. At the end of the decade nearly 80 percent of these 6,000 Japanese were still living in Peru. Death had claimed 481 of them, and 414 were able to return to their homeland. Only 242 transmigrated to other Latin America countries, mainly to Bolivia and Mexico.

It is clear that most of the original immigrants who arrived before 1910 stayed in Peru more out of necessity than by choice. Low wage scales kept most of them from saving enough for the return fare to Japan. Ships were also rarely available since Peru's trade with Japan was still limited. The first-generation Japanese continued to express their dislike for contract labor by leaving the plantations, often before their contracts expired. Most migrated to Lima or to its port city of Callao; indeed, by 1910 one in five Japanese migrants was living in the Lima-Callao area. They were employed as barbers, café operators, small traders, grocers, carpenters, waiters, masons, fishermen, and common laborers. The Japanese barbers formed an association as early as 1907, presaging many such economic unions among the immigrants in the decades to come.

Some of the early sugarcane workers made attempts to stay on the land by creating informal laborers' associations and by negotiating terms as tenant farmers on the plantations. Such efforts were unusual, however, before the 1920s when Japanese immigrants began reclaiming nonirrigated land for cotton production. The lack of arable land and Peru's rigid landholding system largely prevented the transition from agricultural laborer to tenant farmer and finally to independent landholder that would occur among the Brazilian Japanese after 1908. Thus, most of Peru's Japanese immigrants who arrived before the 1930s made new lives outside of agriculture.

Among the immigrants before 1910 was a small contingent from the Ryukyu Islands. Primarily from the main island of Okinawa, these Ryukyuans would become an increasingly large component of the Japanese stream to Peru and Brazil before World War II. Migrating from the overpopulated Ryukyu, these immigrants, in search of arable land, would constitute one-third of Peru's Japanese before 1941. The Okinawans generally were not accepted by the *naichi-jin* (home island Japanese) in the immigrant community in Peru. The Okinawans organized their own cultural associations similar to their *naichi-jin* counterparts.

One of the most remarkable examples of success among the group of pioneers was the career of Nikumatsu Okada. He rose from contract sugar worker to the leading cotton grower in the Huaral district in the Chancay Valley north of Lima. Okada's cotton empire started with a hacienda he purchased after serving as its manager. He worked with the cooperation and hard labor of other Japanese migrants whom he hired to clear land, dig or repair irrigation canals, and rebuild the hacienda's main house. Only nine years after arriving in Callao to cut cane, Okada became Peru's largest Japanese landholder. He served as the example for other Japanese migrants to venture into cotton production in the Chancay Valley, where a significant number found success. Okada eventually was elected president of the Sociedad Central de Japonesa del Valle de Chancay (Central Japanese Society of the Chancay Valley) and in 1924 was instrumental in founding a Japanese school in the valley. Sadly, his status as a leading member of Peru's Japanese community prompted Okada's deportation to the United States during World War II when many Peruvian Japanese were interned there.

Very few first-generation Japanese were as successful as Okada. Yet despite continuing anti-Japanese sentiment during the three decades after 1910, Peru attracted nearly 30,000 Japanese before World War II. Many of these people would transmigrate to Brazil or Argentina for better opportunities in agriculture or urban commerce. By the second decade of the twentieth century, the trend of Japanese leaving plantation agriculture for urban commerce was well established. The most notable was in the river valleys adjacent to Lima. The growing Japanese community in Lima-Callao organized itself more diligently than any other ethnic group in Peru. Following the pattern of the Nihonjin Doshikai (Japanese Brotherhood Association) formed in 1909, the first generation in Lima soon organized the Japanese Chamber of Commerce, the Lima Restaurant Association, the Household Goods Association, and the Central Market Association. These groups and numerous others established before World War II provided economic assistance, ensured the perpetuation of traditional Japanese culture, protected the community against anti-Japanese agitation, and served as liaisons with Tokyo's diplomatic representatives in Peru. Seeking to coordinate the activities of these diverse associations, Japanese community leaders formed the umbrella organization known as Perú Chūō Nihonjinkai (Central Japanese Association of Peru) in October 1917. Perú Chūō Nihonjinkai quickly became a powerful force. All "called" immigrants (*yobiyose*) or those who were sponsored by their first-generation relatives, for example, had to be first approved by Perú Chūō Nihonjinkai before their names could be submitted to the Japanese consul in Lima.

Perú Chūō Nihonjinkai and similar local agencies outside of Lima assumed a predominant role in the education of the second-generation immigrants before 1941. The vast majority of the instructors in the Japanese schools in Peru have been hired in Japan or drawn from the ranks of the better-educated male first generation soon after they arrived. These schools were patterned closely after those in Japan. The model for Peru's elementary schools was the one founded by Perú Chūō Nihonjinkai in Lima in 1920. By 1930 this educational institution had enrolled nearly 1,000 second-generation boys and girls who studied in both Spanish and Japanese. Ultimately, the Japanese community operated fifty schools in Peru at various times during the interwar years. Most of these were small, enrolling no more than fifty students, and all were closed after World War II began.

The Japanese-language press in Peru played an integral role in fostering community solidarity as well as in enhancing the immigrants' cultural bond with Japan. The biweekly *Andeseu Jihō* (Andean Times), the first Japanese-language newspaper published in South America, appeared in 1913. By the early 1920s a second newspaper, the *Nippi Shimpo* (Japan-Peru News) was being circulated to more than 1,200 readers on a triweekly basis. Thereafter, Japanese- and Spanish-language newspapers, catering to the second generation who did not read Japanese well, proliferated.

Unquestionably, these schools and the press facilitated the settlement of the first Japanese in Peru. Paradoxically, however, these institutions also reinforced the separation of the Japanese community from the mainstream. Thus the immigrants became suspect and vulnerable to the increasing anti-Japanese sentiment that was inflamed by Tokyo's militaristic policies after the takeover of Manchuria in 1931.

Seiichi Higashide accurately referred to the Japanese immigrants in Peru as a "closely linked community that interacted with an intimacy that was even stronger than between brother and sister in Japan."[4] Most first-generation males still faced a serious dilemma when they wanted to marry, since until the mid-1930s men outnumbered women in the Japanese community by two to one. Very few men could afford to return to Japan to choose a wife. Immigration restrictions also effectively ended the "picture bride" system by the late 1920s. As confirmed by Higashide, cultural notions prevented male immigrants from marrying native Peruvian women. "Moreover," Higashide recalled, "first-generation immigrants harbored a strong sense of discrimination" against native Peruvians. These cultural notions were so pervasive that a significant number of older immigrant men decided not to marry after their arrival in Peru. Thus, younger immigrants such as Higashide sometimes married second-generation women or delayed marriage until the proper partner could be found. Consequently, the Japanese immigrant family in Peru grew slowly.

The unwillingness of the first immigrants to assimilate produced deep suspicions of these immigrants' motives that grew more intense as World War II approached. Widespread violence and looting were directed against the Japanese community in August 1930 during the revolution of Lieutenant Colonel Luis M. Sánchez Cerro. The revolution toppled the autocrat Augusto Leguía, who had promoted Japanese immigration during his eleven-year dictatorship (1919–1930). Tokyo's consul in Lima, Saburu Karusu, pressured Sánchez Cerro's government to allow the Japanese community leaders to form "vigilance committees," which quelled the disturbances. Nevertheless, Tokyo, recognizing that the high concentration of Japanese in Lima-Callao contributed to the violence, sought to direct further emigration to the rural sierra by subsidizing the creation of the Peru-Takushoku Kumai (Peruvian Colonization Association) in March 1931. Purchasing 2,450 acres in the remote Chanchamayo Valley on the eastern slopes of the Andes, the association sought to attract new immigrants to pioneering agricultural cooperatives. Such ventures were proving successful in Brazil at that time. Since the land was of marginal quality and the Peruvian government was not prepared to build the infrastructure needed to connect the new colony with its markets, the initiative failed. This project was the only effort to establish Japanese agricultural colonies in Peru during the twentieth century.

After Sánchez Cerro's assassination in April 1933, the succeeding administration of General Oscar R. Benavides bowed to increasing nationalist sentiment and issued a series of decrees that limited the rights of the Peruvian Japanese. As a consequence, Japanese immigration was reduced to less than 600 per year by the end of the 1930s. Employing the 1924 U.S. Immigration Act and the Brazilian immigration legislation of 1934 as models, Benavides closed Peru's door to substantive Japanese immigration after 1936. Thereafter, Peru prohibited immigration by "racial groups," which effectively denied the return of Japanese nationals after they left the country, and limited the ownership of businesses by foreigners to 20 percent of the nation's total. Moreover, foreigners could only sell or transfer their businesses within the stated quotas. To survive economically, Peru's Japanese followed the lead of their counterparts in the United States after the passage of the Alien Land Laws in the western states. Denied ownership of their property, first-generation Japanese in the United States and later in Peru were able to transfer the ownership of their businesses to their sons. A substantial number in Peru would, however, be confiscated by the Prado government during World War II. In the face of these oppressive measures, it is understandable that after 1936 more Japanese were transmigrating to other Latin American nations or were returning to their homeland than were entering Peru.

Following the restrictive legislation of 1936, the Japanese immigrant family evolved without a significant influx of new migrants. As the second generation began to come of age, familiar generational conflicts began to emerge. In his perceptive memoir, Higashide observed, "From the time we had been in Peru, I noticed a wide gap between the first-generation immigrants and their children who had been born and raised in Peru." The second generation was influenced by Peru's unpressured life-style and tended to be easygoing. That attitude seemed irresponsible and lazy to their quick-tempered and hard-working parents.

With Japan's invasion of China in 1937, the situation for Peru's Japanese became even more difficult. A persistent theme in the Peruvian press was the danger from a "fifth column" of spies within the ranks of the Japanese community. These false allegations were made by nearly all the political elements in Peru, from the conservative regimes of Benavides and his successor, Manuel Prado y Ugarteche, to the outlawed populist Alianza Popular Revolucionaria Americana (APRA) of Víctor Raul Haya de la Torre. Eighteen months before Pearl Harbor, anti-Japanese feeling exploded into the worst violence against any immigrant community in twentieth-century Peru. Two days of rioting and looting in mid-May 1940 left ten Japanese dead and hundreds injured. More than 600 Japanese businesses were damaged at a cost later estimated at $1.6 million. Brought on by rumors of espionage and military activity within the Japanese community, these riots escalated while the police refused to intercede. One second-generation Japanese, 18 years old at the time, later vividly remembered the looting of her parent's business: "They stole everything, even the toilet out of our house."[5] Clearly, more than four decades of Japanese settlement in Peru had not quieted the same resentment that confronted the original *Sakuru-maru* immigrants when they left their ship in 1899.

The census of 1940, completed only one month after these riots, enumerated 17,598 Japanese in Peru. This count very likely was the most accurate of the Japanese community by the Peruvian government. Lima needed reliable statistics to deal with its highly "suspect" Japanese population. Interestingly, the 1940 census figures were far below the grossly inflated estimates of most rumor-prone journalists and politicians. And sadly, this census data would soon be used to bring even more trouble to the Japanese community during World War II. The concentration of Peruvian Japanese in Lima-Callao made them particularly vulnerable. This demographic reality stood in sharp contrast to the rural-based Brazilian Japanese before World War II.

Brazil's Japanese before World War II

During the three decades after 1908, more Japanese immigrants were drawn to Brazil than any other country except Manchuria. Boasting the most dynamic economy in Latin America, large tracts of arable and affordable land in the southern states of São Paulo and Paraná, favorable immigration legislation (until 1934), and most of all a continuing need for labor on the coffee plantations, Brazil admitted 182,268 Japanese migrants through the entry port of Santos during this era. These Brazilian Japanese arriving at this time comprised 75 percent of all Japanese immigration to Latin America before World War II. Indeed, the period from World War I to 1934 was known in Japan as the epoch of "Brazilian Immigration." The Japanese thus became the final component of Brazil's complex multiracial mosaic created by immigration after the abolition of slavery in 1888. Like Japanese immigrants everywhere before World War II, most of Brazil's newcomers saw themselves as temporary migrants and were unwilling to admit that they would never return permanently to Japan. Further complicating the attitudes of Brazil's Japanese was the continuing arrival of large numbers of new immigrants through 1937. The Brazilian Japanese were thus divided between the pioneers, who arrived before 1925 to pick coffee in the south's vast *fazendas*, and the nearly 150,000 *Shinimin* (new immigrants), who migrated with substantial financial support from Tokyo.

Brazil's Japanese were welcomed as *colonos* or coffee workers to replace the Italian immigrants who had labored on the *fazendas* following the abolition of slavery until the first decade of the twentieth century. Poor labor conditions on the *fazendas* finally prompted the Italian government to cancel their immigration contract with the Brazilian government in 1902. These same problems would ensure that relatively few immigrants of any nationality would remain in the coffee fields as laborers after their arrival.

After prolonged negotiations between Tokyo and the state government of São Paulo, the first group of 781 Japanese arrived at the port of Santos on the ship *Kasato-maru* in June 1908. Nearly half of the *Kasato-maru* passengers were from Okinawa and 165 were members of families. Few, however, were the experienced farmers they claimed to be when they applied for the immigrant subsidies offered by the Paulista government. The *fazenda* owners, continuing the pattern they had established with the earlier Italian migrants, strongly favored the importation of Japanese families. The planters hoped to avoid the transient nature characteristic of single Japanese male migrants to Hawaii and North America before 1908. Many of the *Kasato-maru* "families"were "falsely constituted," however, having been assembled from close relatives or even neighbors before leaving Japan. Some were even joined on the ship after its departure for Brazil. This pattern would continue while the Brazilian government was subsidizing Japanese immigration throughout the early 1920s.

Badly financed and poorly planned, the experience of the *Kasato-maru* immigrants closely resembled the dreary circumstances of Peru's first Japanese. The more than 200 assigned to Fazenda Dumont, São Paulo's largest coffee plantation, for example, found their wage scales to be far below what had been promised them, housing to be unavailable or unsanitary, and working conditions to be harsh. Eventually, most of the *Kasato-maru* immigrants scattered throughout São Paulo state to work on other coffee plantations, on the Northeast Railroad construction gangs, or on the docks in Santos. Argentina was the destination of 160 of the *Kasato-maru* Japanese.

Just as initial failure did not deter future immigration to Peru, the same circumstances prevailed in Brazil after the disastrous experience of the *Kasato-maru* immigrants. For the most part, *colono* contracts were more closely honored by the *fazendeiros* over the course of the next twenty years as their need for Japanese labor remained constant. Paulista legislators continued to subsidize Japanese immigration in response to the labor needs of the coffee planters. An unstable Japanese economy following World War I and the highly destructive Kanto earthquake of 1923, which left thousands of people homeless, prompted the Tokyo government to view Brazilian emigration as an important safety valve for its growing population.

The era of the Japanese immigrant pioneers (1908–1925) saw 35,000 migrants arrive in Brazil. The pioneers generally left *colono* labor as soon as possible in their effort to become independent landowners. This process generally took two to five years while the first generation worked as sharecroppers or lease farmers. When the Japanese government subsidized the successful agricultural colony at Iguape on São Paulo's southern coast before World War I, opportunities for the pioneers in rice farming, produce farming, and coffee production increased significantly. Nearly 90 percent of all Japanese immigrants before 1925 migrated to São Paulo state. Unlike the ill-fated *Kasato-maru* immigrants, most were experienced farmers from Japan's southern prefectures. Their independent farming experience explains their disdain for the financial limitations of wage labor.

Many of these first-generation immigrants quickly realized the potential for earning substantially more if intensive farming was practiced on their own land. Furthermore, the Japanese were willing to produce crops such as rice and vegetables that were in demand but were of no interest to the status-conscious coffee *fazendeiros*. Even while they were serving as *colono* laborers, the Japanese planted cash crops between the rows of coffee trees. A *colono* family could earn as much as 1,200 *milreis* (U.S.$150) per year from the sale of these cash crops. Moreover, these plantings made their food costs minimal. These savings were frequently used to lease or purchase new land in undeveloped areas of São Paulo.

The life of the Japanese *colono* family was difficult, but, unlike in Peru, these contract immigrants frequently had the option of leaving the coffee *fazenda* and settling on one of the growing number of subsidized colonies known in Brazil as *colonias*. These *colonias* were established in the states of São Paulo, Paraná, and Amazonas between World War I and the mid-1930s. Earlier *colonias* of this type had been created by small groups of Swiss, German, and Italian immigrants in São Paulo and Rio

Grande do Sul between 1895 and 1911. These *colonias* never achieved the scale or the level of financial support that the Japanese government-backed *colonias* enjoyed. Seeing the Japanese as both contract laborers and potential middle-class agriculturalists who could develop São Paulo's southern coast and western frontier, Paulista political leaders continued to welcome the second generation until the Great Depression years of the mid-1930s. Paulista leaders greatly admired the Japanese immigrant work ethic and thus supported the colonization effort. In 1924, for example, federal congressman Francisco Chávez de Oliveira Botelho, while commenting on the practices of Japanese rice farmers in the new Registro Colony on São Paulo's southern coast, marveled at their work habits: "How admirable their farming is."[6]

After 1920 the Tokyo government facilitated Brazilian colonization by combining all of its overseas emigration companies into one major firm, the Kaigai Kogyo Kabushiki Kaisha (Overseas Development Corporation, or KKKK). This corporation recruited and transported contract workers, extended loans to colonists, and invested in colonization projects abroad, most particularly in Brazil. In 1927 the KKKK opened the Emigrant Training Center in Kobe where prospective immigrants were given free housing while taking a short course in rudimentary Portuguese and Western customs before departing for Brazil. Based upon decisions arrived at during Japan's Imperial Congress for the Economy, held between April and June 1924, its political leaders decided not only to subsidize Brazilian immigration aggressively but also to encourage the immigrants to settle there permanently. Thus, the Burajiru Takushoku Kumiai (BRATAC), the agency administering the colonies in southern Brazil, launched a campaign with slogans such as "Love the (Brazilian) land," "Enjoy the Work," "Be rooted for the children."

The Japanese government wanted desperately to avoid the abject failure of its immigration policy in the United States as reflected in the radically exclusionist Immigration Act of 1924. Tokyo considered the problems of its nationals in the United States to be the result of the unwillingness of the immigrants to attempt cultural adaptation and to accept foreign citizenship. It clearly wanted to establish permanent "Japanese villages in Brazil" with new immigrants directly from Japan, but if these villages remained isolated from the Brazilian mainstream, the same cultural and racial animosity that had been the case in the United States, Canada, and Peru would result. Thus, Tokyo launched its "Prosperous Coexistence" policy that was founded upon close cooperation between the Brazilian and Japanese governments in the areas of frontier colonization, infrastructure development, and subsidized immigration. In sum, the Japanese would be the rural middle class that Brazilian positivists had been calling for since the late nineteenth century.

The early success of the Iguape Colony on São Paulo's southern coast was assured not by new colonists recruited from Japan but rather by *colono* "vagabonds" who drifted into the settlement from local *fazendas*. Attracted by reasonably priced land subsidized by the Japanese government, these *colonos* comprised a significant majority of the settlers at Iguape and on later *colonias* established in Brazil through the mid-1930s. Administrators for the Japanese colonization project were rarely able to fill their quota of immigrants from the home islands because of the persistence of the sojourner mentality. Still, these successful *colonias* did serve as magnets for more than 132,000 in the decade after 1924. During 1933, the high point of "Brazilian Immigration," 23,299 Japanese arrived at the port of Santos.

Eventually, highly successful *colonias* were created at Registro, Sete Barros, and Katsura in the Iguape Valley; at Bastos Lins, Bauru, Araçatuba, Andradina, and Alianca in western São Paulo state; and at Londrina and Tres Barras in the state of Paraná. Less successful colonization efforts were made in the northern state of Amazonas. All of these *colonias* were situated in frontier areas where cheap land was readily available. Most of these settlements grew quickly. By the mid-1930s the population of Bastos, for example, exceeded 10,000, including the native Brazilian workers who located there to work as agricultural laborers for the Japanese proprietors. The original settlers of Bastos purchased sixty-acre plots for $718 with full payment deferred for four years. These immigrants, coming directly from Japan, were required to hold more than the purchase price of the property in transferable capital before they arrived in the *colonia*. This requirement kept the poorest from settling in Bastos, but, since transportation costs were subsidized by the Japanese government, migrants of moderate means could begin a new life in this *colonia*. Within less than a decade, Japanese farmers owned most of their operations and were farming in a diversified manner, even including raising dairy cattle.

From the early beginnings of the settlement in the *colonias*, the migrants met the need for schools for their children by creating so-called *terakoya* schools. The schools were so named because they were often held in *teras*, or temples, during the Edo Period in Japan. The *terakoya* schools gave way to strictly Japanese-language schools that often existed side by side with the public school system of São Paulo in more populated areas. In these areas the second generation would attend a Japanese-language school for part of the day and the Brazilian one for the remainder of the session. In the remote frontier areas where no Brazilian public schools existed, Japanese-administered schools provided courses in Japanese and Brazilian culture. The schooling of the Nisei (second-generation Japanese) was coordinated by the Zaihaku Nihonjin Kyoikukai

(Association for the Education of the Japanese in Brazil) after 1927. The guiding principle of this coordinating body was that the Japanese schools in Brazil would be administered as extensions of the schools in Japan and would thus emphasize Japanese culture and values. While this principle conflicted with Tokyo's effort to weaken the immigrants' sojourner mentality in Brazil, it was a logical outgrowth of the militant nationalism that pervaded Japanese government policy during the decade prior to World War II.

By 1932 the Brazilian Japanese operated 187 schools enrolling 9,178 students. Only nine of these schools were located outside the state of São Paulo, with eight in Paraná and one in Mato Grosso. During the 1930s the "Japanese first" educational approach was challenged by the highly nationalistic government of Brazilian President Getúlio Vargas. When Vargas in 1938 established his corporatist dictatorship, known as the Estado Nôvo, the Japanese schools were ordered closed. Nevertheless, many of them continued to operate clandestinely until World War II, and many first-generation parents returned to the earlier practice of home schooling. Even during the troubled 1930s, many second-generation students were being prepared for secondary schooling in Japan. Others attending the dualistic educational system in São Paulo's more populated areas were experiencing the cultural dilemma of the second-generation Japanese everywhere in the Americas.

Like most first-generation immigrants, Brazil's Japanese steadfastly identified with their native culture and wanted their children to have a deep appreciation of its central values. The Vargas government's restrictive policies seemed to strengthen their resolve to bind themselves spiritually and psychologically to their homeland. One first-generation colonist from Tietó, the father of two children, lamented in the midst of the Vargas government's nationalization campaign, "We did not come to Brazil to live permanently, but for attaining material well-being. Japan is the country we love and returning home with success is what our heart desires. Our immigration will mean something only if our blood purifies the Brazilian impurity with our superior tradition."[7] Despite these sentiments, in the end nearly all the Japanese remained in Brazil. Among the many reasons that kept them from returning to their homeland was their responsibility to their families.

The Japanese family in Brazil prospered in the intensely ethnic setting of the *colonias*. Unlike anywhere else in the Americas, entire Japanese families migrated to Brazil because of the immigration policy of the São Paulo *fazendeiros*. As already noted, some of these "families" were artificially constituted to conform to immigration requirements. Indeed, nearly one in six first-generation families during the pre-World War II years was classified as *kosek-kasoku* (incorporated family members).

Adopted children comprised the largest share of this group among the early arrivals before 1925. The Brazilian Japanese also enjoyed a more favorable gender ratio than the Japanese elsewhere in Latin America, since a greater number of females migrated to Brazil during the *colono* labor and colonization eras.

As the Japanese immigrant family evolved in Brazil, it confronted the familiar dilemma of how it would sustain its ethnic identity in a foreign environment. Takashi Maeyama and Christopher Reichl, among others, have carefully studied the stages in the evolution of ethnicity among the Brazilian Japanese. Reichl concludes that when native Japanese household or *ie* bonds were broken with immigration, they were frequently replaced in Brazil with fictive relationships created for both administrative and social purposes. The numerous clubs, youth groups, and fraternal societies that were quickly created in Brazil were merely a logical attempt to replicate the egalitarian neighborhood relationships known in Japan as *kumi*.

Holding equally important implications for the Brazilian Japanese were their religious views. The social construct of religious expression in Japan involved the household, the village, and the nation. Maeyama and Reichl contend that once the Japanese left the home islands, their religious expression underwent a profound change. In Brazil, having broken ties with the household, the immigrants had little reason to practice the Shinto rituals that were based primarily upon memorialism and ancestor worship. All that was left in a tangible sense when the Japanese arrived in Brazil was the symbol of national unity, the emperor. Reichl concludes, "When the Japanese communities in Brazil were formed, the relationship between each Japanese national and [the] emperor was the common thread that provided the basis for ethnic expression."[8]

Emperor worship thus replaced ancestor worship and became the single most important mode of ethnic and religious behavior. As the Japanese nation grew in military strength and prestige, this change was reflected in increased nationalism among the first generation in Brazil and elsewhere. As discreet as the Brazilian Japanese were in their demonstrations of nationalism and emperor worship, this form of cultural expression still aroused suspicion. The second-generation Japanese were caught in the middle of this cultural dilemma. Their parents had tenaciously struggled to raise them to identify with Japan and its culture. Still, some of the second generation coming of age in Brazil in the late 1930s resented their parents' efforts. A member of São Paulo's Japanese Student League typified the frustration of his peers when he asserted in the League's newsletter: "We are proud and happy of being born in Brazil. Even though the blood of the Japanese nation runs in our veins, our heart throbs with patriotism for Brazil. . . . How can we have patriotism for a country that is so far away and unknown? We respect the home country for our fathers, but we love Brazil. It is a big contradiction to force us to have patriotism toward an imaginary country."[9]

The children of the first immigrants may have identified more with Brazil than Japan, but they and their parents were facing increasingly difficult times after 1933. Motivated by Tokyo's militarism, the cultural insularity of the Japanese community, the economic ramifications of the Great Depression, and the Vargas regime's xenophobic nationalism, Brazil finally adopted an exclusionist immigration policy in 1934. The immigration legislation of 1934 mirrored similar policies in North America a decade earlier.

The virulent racism that marked the exclusionist campaign in the United States and Canada, however, was less evident in Brazil. It was raised as an issue, however, by a few leading anti-Japanese legislators from Rio de Janeiro, although Paulista deputies defended the Japanese as hardworking and respectful of government authority. What the Paulista deputies could not overcome were allegations of Tokyo's militaristic intentions as well as economic arguments that the influx of Japanese immigrants was causing hardship for Brazilian workers during the depression. In the end the Brazilian government did not prohibit Japanese immigration, as did the United States. Instead, Article 121 of the Constitution of 1934 established a yearly entry quota that limited the Japanese to 2 percent of the total number of their nationals residing in Brazil in 1933. Effectively, this article reduced Japan's immigrant quota to less than 3,000, down from nearly 24,000 in 1933. Paulista *fazendeiros* were able to obtain waivers from these quotas, and for a few years the number of entering Japanese was one-half of the 1933 levels.

By 1938, however, the era of "Brazilian Immigration" was over; that year little more than 2,500 Japanese arrived in Santos. This figure dropped to less than 2,000 in 1941. Future Brazilian immigration probably would have declined anyway, as Manchuria and later Eastern China and Formosa were being rapidly capitalized and settled by thousands of Japanese immigrants. Although post-World War II immigration would be significant, never again would Brazil see the large influx of Japanese migrants that totaled more than one-half of the nation's immigrant arrivals in the 1930s. Still, by 1941, the Japanese community in Brazil was larger, more autonomous, and more financially secure than anywhere else in the world. These advantages would be critically important as the Brazilian Japanese confronted the difficult years of World War II.

The Trauma of World War II

Japan's defeat in the Pacific War ended the fleeting hopes of the Peruvian and Brazilian first generation that they would ever return to lead secure lives in their homeland. After the world conflict, with Japan in ruins, they were forced to rebuild their lives in Latin America. No immigration occurred from Japan during the seven years following the war, and when it resumed after 1952, the number of Japanese migrating to Peru and Brazil never approached pre-World War II levels. The sojourner mentality, however, was not forsaken easily. Militantly nationalistic Japanese in Brazil refused to accept the reality of Tokyo's surrender and formed the Shindō Renmei (Way of the Subjects of the Emperor's League) to resist, often violently, "defeatism" among the country's Japanese community. Both the Japanese communities of Peru and Brazil were also divided between a *kachigumi* (victory) group that refused to acknowledge the military failure of their homeland, and the *makegumi* (defeatist) faction. Influenced by Brazil's Shindō Renmei, Peru's militantly nationalistic Japanese formed the Aikoku Doshi-Kai (Society of the Japanese Patriots of Peru) to perpetuate the myth of Japan's invincibility. This society did not engage in the extremist tactics associated with Shindō Renmei in Brazil, but its very existence was used by the Peruvian government to justify its restrictive measures against the Japanese following World War II.

Peru's Japanese suffered the worst fate during the war. Of the 2,118 Latin American Japanese interned in the United States, more than 1,800 were Peruvian. Initially, the U.S. government had plans to "exchange" these interned Latin American Japanese for its own nationals caught in Japanese-occupied territory after Pearl Harbor, but this swap never materialized.[10] These Japanese were held in internment camps in the southwestern United States, some until 1948. Japanese males were the first to be deported during the period from early 1942 until mid-1944, when the deportations terminated. The males were joined by their wives and children at the Crystal City "family" detention camp in Texas later when it became clear that these families would not be otherwise reunited. Those deported were supposedly leaders of the Japanese community who were the most likely to be a security threat. In reality, many were simply randomly detained and deported by the Peruvian authorities to fill their arrest quotas. Some leaders of the Japanese community were able to avoid deportation by going into hiding or by bribing Peruvian officials. These strategies became increasingly difficult, however, as the war progressed and the U.S. intelligence presence in Peru became more pronounced. Peru refused to readmit these deportees after the war and eventually less than one hundred ever returned to Peru.

The majority of the Peruvian deportees were "repatriated" to Japan after the war as "enemy aliens" by the U.S. government. Among the Latin American Japanese internees, little more than 300 were able to remain in the United States following the war as a result of the efforts of a crusading American Civil Liberties Union attorney, Wayne Collins. A significant number of internees from the Crystal City group who remained in the United States made the transition from the camp to new lives in the United States. First-generation immigrant Seiichi Higashide offers a vivid account of the struggles of his family to regain control of their lives during and after the internment years at Seabrook Farms, New Jersey, and later in Chicago. In his autobiography, Higashide lamented, "I still feel that I am spiritually Japanese. At the same time, I believe if the war had not intervened, my roots would have remained planted in Peru . . . and I would have had my bones buried in its soil. Such was my love for Peru."[11]

For the majority of the Peruvian Japanese who were able to avoid deportation during the war, many lost their property in a process very similar to what the Japanese in the United States endured. Rather than intern its remaining Japanese in domestic detention camps, Peru chose to restrict sharply the scope of their activity. Gatherings of more than three (other than families) were prohibited, telephones and radios were confiscated, and Japanese schools and newspapers were closed. The Japanese community was closely monitored by the Peruvian and Brazilian police and later by agents of the Federal Bureau of Investigation assigned to the U.S. embassy in Lima.

The mandate for the anti-Japanese campaign was established at the January 1942 Conference of American Republics at Rio de Janeiro. Approved at the Rio Conference was a resolution calling for the "Detention and Expulsion of Dangerous Axis Nationals from Latin America." Used against Italians and German nationals as well as the Japanese, this mandate allowed various U.S. organizations, the Federal Bureau of Investigation, the Department of State, and the Immigration and Naturalization Service to work hand in hand with Peru's wartime government of President Prado y Ugarteche to implement the deportation program.

Politically vulnerable during most of his early presidency (1939–1945), Prado saw the internment program as a means of gaining the economic and political support of the United States and ridding his nation of the unpopular Japanese. Indeed, after the deportation program began to bog down in mid-1944 primarily because of a lack of shipping, Peru's ambassador to Washington, Pedro Beltrán, personally requested President Franklin Roosevelt's support in facilitating the removal of all people of Japanese ancestry from Peru.[12] That only 10 percent of Peru's Japanese were deported and interned in the United States was not due to the lack of resolve on the part of the Prado government to relocate the entire Japanese community. Instead, logistical problems, particularly the lack of shipping, and shifting U.S. war priorities after 1943 were responsible.

In the end, charges of espionage, the primary reason for deporting Peru's Japanese, proved to be without justification. John K. Emerson, the State Department officer who headed the counterespionage and deportation program through the U.S. embassy in Lima, later concluded that the

Peruvian Japanese posed no threat to hemispheric security. In his memoirs, Emerson later wrote of Peru's deportees: "I looked into the faces of these humble and bewildered people—shopkeepers, farmers, carpenters, barbers, and fishermen—starting on a voyage to an unknown future. These were not spies, saboteurs, bomb throwers, or plotters against the state."[13] Brazil's Japanese immigrant community at the beginning of World War II was second in size only to the militarized colony in Manchuria. Its sheer number made large-scale internment or deportation an impossibility. The relatively remote nature of many of the *colonias* also reduced the "perceived" security risk. Like the Hawaiian Japanese, the Brazilian Japanese had become an integral component of the nation's agricultural economy. Therefore, their contributions to cotton, rice, sugar, and vegetable production were considered critical to Brazil's wartime economy.

Still, as a wartime ally of the United States and a leader of the hemispheric defense campaign, the Vargas government cooperated in the security effort by adopting measures similar to those taken against the Japanese community in Peru. Leaders of the Japanese community were at times arrested and interrogated, but they were generally not detained for extended periods. Interviews by Sayaka Funada in the early 1990s indicate that the treatment by the Brazilian police of the Japanese was frequently harsh. Reports of rape and abuse were not uncommon. Significantly, for the Japanese community, its newspapers were closed and the Japanese schools remained under a ban. The use of the language was technically forbidden, but this edict was impossible to enforce in many of the remote *colonias* where only Japanese was spoken. Without their newspapers and their ability to meet in their familiar associations, many Brazilian first-generation Japanese became isolated completely from the homeland.

After the war, as in Peru, the Japanese were divided into the *kachigumi* (victory) and the *makegumi* (defeatist) factions with the latter being in the distinct minority immediately after Tokyo's surrender. Shindō Renmei included former Japanese army veterans among its leaders; this league stressed the need for enhancing patriotism in order to prepare for Brazil's occupation by Japan and perhaps the eventual mass return of the Brazilian Japanese to their homeland. Shindō Renmei terrorized the Japanese community in Brazil by threats and assassinations for many months after the war until the organization was finally broken up by the police in 1947.[14]

With Japan's defeat, the Brazilian Japanese faced a painful reckoning, made all the more difficult by the fanatical resistance to the reality of their homeland's military collapse by the leaders of Shindō Renmei. Nevertheless, the cultural solidarity created by years of mutual hardship and success in both Peru and Brazil would ensure that the Japanese of both nations would overcome the trauma of World War II to rebuild their lives in nations where they now knew they would remain.

From First to Fifth Generations in Peru and Brazil

During the half-century following World War II, the Japanese communities in Peru and Brazil have made remarkable recoveries from the dislocation of the war and have grown and prospered. The mutual aid associations, schools, and newspapers that were the backbone of the Japanese community's cultural solidarity before the war were reestablished. In Peru, Japanese cotton farmers in the Chancay Valley, for example, regrouped in January 1961 to form the Associacíon Fraternal Japonesa de Valle de Chancay (Japanese Fraternal Association of the Chancay Valley). As a cultural, recreational, and scholarly focus for the Japanese community, the Centro Cultural Peruano Japonés (Peruvian Japanese Cultural Center) in Lima has been an integral resource since the early 1960s for aging Japanese who regularly meet to socialize. Since the election of a second-generation Japanese, Alberto Fujimori, to Peru's presidency in 1990, the Centro has grown in size and political importance.

The data for the meticulously conducted 1989 self-census of the Japanese community in Peru, directed by sociologist Amelia Morimoto, are housed at the Centro. This census counted 45,644 "ethnic" Japanese. Projections through the year 2000 estimate the community will grow to over 56,000. In the early 1990s the second, third, and fourth generation-Peruvian Japanese comprised nearly half of the community, while the fifth generation began to appear in Japanese households. The aging first generation, who had endured so much during the early years of settlement and World War II, were now mostly in their 70s and 80s and represented only 5 percent of the community.[15]

The legacy of Peru's anti-Japanese policies during World War II together with the continuing appeal of Brazil and new colonization prospects in Bolivia and Paraguay after 1952 meant that no substantive new immigration emerged from Japan following the war. After 1963, Japan's dynamic economy obviated the need for future immigration. Thus, Peru's Japanese colony experienced modest growth from an estimated 32,000 counted during the first self-census in 1966. The Japanese community is still heavily concentrated in the Lima metropolitan area.

In the midst of Peru's terrible troubles with rebels in the mountains in the late 1980s and early 1990s, Japan's prosperity and the continuing image of Peru's Japanese as capable and successful was clearly an element in the political rise of Fujimori from obscurity to the presidency. Given the destructive riots of May 1940 and the deportation of one in every ten Japanese during World War II, few Peruvians, most particularly the Japanese community, could have ever envisioned a Japanese in the Pizarro Palace. Such a scenario would have seemed far more likely in Brazil, where the Japanese attained substantial economic and social status in the half-century after World War II.

Understandably, when immigration from Japan resumed in 1952, Brazil once again received the vast majority of the migrants. Other Asian nations were closed to Japanese immigration, and thus Latin America once again became attractive. Brazil still claimed 81 percent of all Japanese during the period 1952–1963. These years saw 45,650 new migrants settle mainly in southern Brazil but also in significant numbers for the first time in northern Brazil. The two decades following World War II were the last substantive period of Japanese immigration before the century-old Japanese diaspora came to an end during the late 1960s. By the early 1980s, after Japan experienced the economic boom that continued until the recession of 1993, only an additional 15,000 Japanese settled in Brazil. For the Japanese there after World War II, the key trend was the migration of many members of the second and third generations to metropolitan São Paulo. This movement was a component of the massive exodus of rural Brazilians to São Paulo and Rio de Janeiro after 1950. By the 1980s, Brazil's Japanese were primarily urban-based.

While in both Peru and Brazil the Japanese communities were reestablished after the war, a more contemporary phenomenon has also emerged. In the past few decades following Japan's new prosperity, Japanese from both Peru and Brazil by the tens of thousands have returned to their homeland to work. Statistics for the number of these Latin American Japanese traveling to Japan as "guest workers" are still questionable, but at least 300,000 Japanese Brazilians are now living in Japan, and the number for Peru may exceed 20,000. Complicating the issue are the relatively large number of Peruvian "false Japanese" who have forged identity papers and altered their facial features by plastic surgery in a desperate attempt to flee what was a failing country. By 1992, Japan's Ministry of Justice calculated that more than 200,000 Latin American Japanese were living in Japan as guest workers. During Daniel Masterson's October 1998 research visit to Japan, some estimates were as high as 400,000. The vast majority of these people were from Brazil. They certainly hoped to benefit from Japan's high wages, but the high cost of living left many of them dismayed. Some referred to their Japanese hosts as "severe and cold" or openly "racist." One Brazilian Japanese sadly remarked to a Japanese interviewer that in Brazil she was Japanese, but in Japan she was Brazilian. Recent research indicates now, however, that many Japanese from Latin America are staying for longer periods and adjusting to life in Japan. Thus the future of the younger Japanese in Latin America is very uncertain.[16]

Conclusion

It is difficult to draw accurate comparisons of the Japanese communities in Peru and Brazil because of their disparate size. More than twenty times larger than its counterpart in Peru, the Japanese community in Brazil has assumed a cultural and economic influence that in many ways exceeds that of other immigrant groups in southern Brazil. The Japanese Brazilians have come to dominate the growing of produce in the environs of São Paulo city; they are heavily represented in all phases of industry, commerce, and the services sector; and, as previously indicated, they are well represented in the educational community, the arts, and the professions.

Far smaller in numbers, the Peruvian Japanese maintained barely visible but successful lives in many of the same economic activities that the first-generation pioneers entered after fleeing the plantations in the early twentieth century. It is still possible, for example, to walk the streets of Lima's suburbs of Miraflores and San Isidro and see many small Japanese-owned shops that have been in business for decades.

Because of the dislocation of World War II and Peru's chronically faltering economy, Peru's Japanese never attained the level of economic success of the Brazilian Japanese. Primarily urban-based from the first years of their settlement in the Andean nation, the Japanese of Peru did not experience the rapid adjustment from *colonia* to city life that many of the second- and third-generation Japanese of Brazil have successfully completed. Still, the grandchildren and the fourth generation of both nations are now undergoing the common experience of temporary immigration to Japan. Many young Brazilian Japanese have traveled to Japan so many times to seek temporary work that they are no longer considered reliable employment risks for Japanese-owned companies in Brazil.

Where, then, is the future for the third and fourth generations of Japanese of Peru and Brazil? They cannot continue to be torn between cultures that are similar yet very different. The future of the economies of Peru, Brazil, and Japan may well determine the choice of which culture to embrace. Thus, the sojourner mentality may persist. Such is the dilemma that faces the two largest Japanese communities in Latin America as they enter the second century of the Japanese presence on the continent.

Notes

1. Tetsuji Kada, "Meiji shoki shakai keizai shiso shi" (A history of economic and social thought during the early Meiji period), quoted in Thomas C. Smith, *Political Change and Industrial Development in Japan: Government Enterprise, 1868–1880* (Stanford: Stanford University Press, 1955), 84.

2. Amelia Morimoto, *Fuerza de trabajo inmigrante japonese y su desarrollo en el Perú* (Lima: Universidad Nacional de Agraria, 1979), 6–11.

3. Toraji Irie, "History of Japanese Immigration to Peru," A translation of *Hojin Kagai Hattenshi*, by William Himel, Part I, *Hispanic American Historical Review* 31 (August 1951): 447.

4. Seiichi Higashide, *Adios to Tears: The Memoirs of a Japanese-Peruvian Internee in a U.S. Concentration Camp* (Seattle: University of Washington Press, 2000), 51.

5. Response of Masao Kishi to "Questionnaire of the Peruvian Japanese of the Crystal City Internment Camp," December 1993. This questionnaire was submitted by the authors to the former internees of the camp at Crystal City, Texas. Kishi was responding to: "How would you describe your treatment by the Peruvian people before World War II?"

6. Nabuya Tschuida, "The Japanese in Brazil, 1908–1941" (Ph.D. diss., UCLA, 1978), 193.

7. Ibid., 194.

8. Christopher Reichl, "Stages in the Historical Process of Ethnicity: The Japanese in Brazil, 1908–1988," *Ethnohistory* 42 (Winter 1995): 41; Takashi Mayema, *Ethnicity to Burajiru Nikkeijin* (Ethnicity and Brazilian Nikkei) (Tokyo: Ochanomizu-shobo, 1996).

9. Tschuida, "The Japanese in Brazil," 195.

10. See C. Harvey Gardiner, *Pawns in a Triangle of Hate: The Peruvian Japanese and the United States* (Seattle: University of Washington Press, 1981) for the internment of Peruvian Japanese in the United States; and D. Scott Corbett, *Quiet Passages: The Exchange of Civilians between the United States and Japan during the Second World War* (Kent, OH: Kent State University Press, 1987), for the exchange program.

11. Higashide, *Adios to Tears*, 8.

12. Corbett, *Quiet Passages*, 163.

13. John K. Emerson, *The Japanese Thread: A Life in the Foreign Service* (New York: Holt, Rinehart and Winston, 1978), 144.

14. James L. Tigner, "Shindō Renmei: Japanese Nationalism in Brazil," *Hispanic American Historical Review* 41 (1961): 515–32.

15. Amelia Morimoto, ed., *Población de origen japones en el Perú: Perfil actual* (Lima: Comisión Conmemorativa del 90 Aniversario del Inmigración Japonesa al Perú, 1991).

16. Takeyai Tsuda, "The Permanence of 'Temporary Migration': The Structural Embeddedness of Japanese-Brazilian Immigrant Workers in Japan," *Journal of Asian Studies* 58 (1999): 687–723.

II

Argentina

Manuel Suárez Martínez (1845–1917), a Galician Migrant to Argentina

Eduardo José Míguez[1]

This section on the Rio de la Plata opens with the story of a migrant from the Galician region in northwestern Spain who in the midnineteenth century went first to the port of Cádiz in southern Spain and then overseas to Buenos Aires and Tandil in Argentina. Manuelillo's life gives us insight into a number of significant aspects of the migration process: the reasons why people left home; the precarious nature of sailing across the Atlantic in 1864; how a migrant could work his way up the occupational ladder from peon in a general store to owner; and the difficult life on the Argentine frontier before the native Americans were driven out in 1879. Most important, the story illustrates the crucial role that social networks of family, friends, and fellow Galicians—both in Spain and Argentina—played in the survival and advancement of the migrants. At every step of the way, Manuelillo relied on these networks; they determined where he would go, where he would live, how he would travel, what jobs he would get, whether he would advance, and with whom he would associate.

I n July 1916, at the age of seventy-one, Manuel Suárez Martínez began to write his memoirs. His son, the minister José Manuel Suárez García, had asked him to recall his adventurous past. The old Galician peasant, with the help of a few letters and other documents and in remarkable prose—compact, succinct, and fresh—produced a notable text. But before he had finished the manuscript, the death of his younger son, Miguel Angel, took away his will to complete the task. A few months later, he himself died.

The manuscript, which covers the period up to 1880, tells a story of progress and success but also of incidents and adventures. Many of these took place on the southern frontier of the province of Buenos Aires and remind the reader of stories of the American West—with Indians, sometimes friendly, sometimes hostile, and with savage bandits. As far as we can judge by contrasting Suárez Martínez's story with other documentary evidence, it is an accurate account with few mistakes in spite of the lapse of many years between the time when the events took place and when the story was written.

Years after Manuelillo—as he called himself and as we shall call him in this story—had died, his son the minister, who was an amateur historian, added a few notes, documents, and photographs to the brief autobiography and published a limited edition for members of the family.[2] It is from this text that I have based this short story of this immigrant's life. Because of the limits of space, I have left out many of the picturesque details of his experiences as frontier storekeeper and itinerant trader, to concentrate on the network of social relations that guided his progress from a poor and nearly illiterate peasant boy to a respectable storeowner and county bailiff. This story, I believe, illustrates the way in which many immigrants met their expectations of progress as they left their family and land in search of a more promising future.

Manuel Suárez Martínez was born in January 1845 in a small hamlet, La Peregrina, two miles away from Santiago de Compostela, Galicia's main city. When he was only eight years of age, he began to do his share of the chores of the peasant family into which he had been born. He was in charge of looking after the household's few cows, oxen, and sheep while they were grazing in the common meadows. At eleven, he started school in Santiago. But only a few months later his father died, and he had to quit school. His mother remarried, but Manuelillo and his brothers did not get along well with their stepfather, and at fourteen years of age his mother allowed Manuelillo to leave home.

Manuelillo's mother had relatives in Cádiz. Francisco Botana, a Galician from La Peregrina who had moved to Cádiz many years ago, had returned to his home to visit his relatives after ten years of hard work in Andalucía. Manuelillo's mother sent her son to him in Cádiz and included a letter of recommendation for her relatives. Francisco was employed by Manuel Nieto, another Galician immigrant, who had first worked in a shipping company and later became rich as an owner of confectionery shops.[3] Nieto employed Manuelillo with the approval of the relatives, who ran a simple fruit stand, to whom the boy had been recommended.

In turn, Nieto sent Manuelillo to work with Antonio Burgos, who was in charge of one of his confectioneries. Manuelillo spent several years there, sleeping on the premises with the other employees and putting in long hours from before dawn to night, and sometimes even after midnight. Burgos, who became fond of the boy, taught him how to read, write and do basic arithmetic. Later on, when Nieto decided to sell his businesses, he found another job for Manuelillo as the principal clerk in a smaller confectionery that belonged to one of his friends.

In 1864, when Manuelillo approached his twentieth birthday—the age at which Spanish men were drafted for five years into the army—he decided to emigrate to America. At that age emigration was illegal, since young male Spaniards could not leave the country until they had ful-filled their military obligations. But many embarked secretly, as Manuelillo did, to avoid the long years of service. Thus, with his small savings (he had sent part of his earnings to his mother in Galicia) and with the help of Manuel Nieto and his old bosses at the shipping com-pany, Manuelillo managed to board a ship to Buenos Aires.

The difficulties and fears of that first Atlantic crossing in a sailing ship represented one of the significant obstacles to migration to South America at that time. Several youngsters had boarded the ship secretly to escape the draft. The constant rocking of the boat made the travelers seasick for several days. Moreover, the food was bad, and drinking wa-ter was in short supply, particularly when the lack of winds prolonged the crossing. The blazing sun of the tropics and the gales of the South Atlantic also had to be endured by the emigrants. And the captain and crew showed little concern for these poor and unrecorded passengers. In the end, however, Manuelillo, his friend Santos Otero (another young-ster who went to Buenos Aires with him), and the other migrants arrived safely in Buenos Aires.

Traveling conditions would begin to change shortly thereafter. A little over ten years later, Manuelillo returned to Spain for a visit to his mother and his old Galician homeland. Even though his memories of that trip on board the steamboat *Potosí* of the British Royal Mail Line still reflect certain discomforts of the Atlantic crossing, the conditions were much better. The trip took less than a month, and the ship no longer had to depend on the wind. Thus, it was easier to predict accurately the provi-sions of food and water needed for the duration of the voyage. These improvements in traveling conditions help to explain why migration to South America became more common in the later years of the nine-teenth century, when steam navigation all but displaced the old sailing ships.

Let us return to Manuelillo and his friend. Upon arrival in Buenos Aires, Otero, who was also Galician and had been employed in Cádiz by Nieto, would establish himself as a clerk (*dependiente*) in the store of another Spaniard in Buenos Aires, where he would work for many years. Manuelillo was more fortunate. When he decided to emigrate to Buenos Aires, his mother sent him a letter of recommendation to José María Blanco and his brothers Ramón and Marcelino, the relatives whom Manuelillo was to meet in Buenos Aires. Once there, and after spending a few days with his relatives, Manuelillo was sent upriver some 200 miles to the town of Concepción in Uruguay, where he was to work as a peon in the store of another Spanish friend of Blanco. Manuelillo's recollec-tions of his trip by riverboat to Concepción, with the Genovese sailors and their food and habits—so strange to him at the time and so common in present-day Argentina—reflect the problems of integration in a multiethnic society. The creole society and the large black population of Entre Ríos at the time did not suit Manuelillo any better, so he decided to return to Buenos Aires.

His cousin Blanco was not pleased with Manuelillo for leaving the job he had found for him, so Manuelillo had to look for his next job in the advertisements of the Buenos Aires newspaper, *La España*. He was hired by another Spanish storeowner, who had been the founder of the Spanish Society (Sociedad Española[4]) together with Blanco, and for whom the fact that Manuelillo was Blanco's cousin served as reference. Blanco later took Manuelillo again under his protection and sent him to work at a store he had bought in Tandil[5] with a Uruguayan partner (*habilitado*[6]), Iñiguez. In November 1864, Manuelillo left Buenos Aires for his new job, together with a Spanish youth, José Martínez, who would later become his partner and one of his best friends. In the years that followed, despite the difficulties of adapting to a new and strange land, he made considerable progress in his work—first as a general hand, then as a clerk, and finally as an assistant manager.[7]

An interesting aspect of this stage of the life of Manuelillo was his relation to the family of Colonel Antonio Machado, a political boss in Tandil allied with General Bartolomé Mitre, the first president of the unified Argentine nation (1862–1868). While Manuelillo always kept a strong Spanish identity, he also built a political one in Argentina as a Mitrista.[8] He explained his loyalty to Mitre on two grounds. First, when the conflict arose between Spain and the South American countries of the Pacific (Peru and Chile) in 1866, Mitre kept Argentina strictly neutral in spite of pressures to align with the two Latin American nations. Second, Manuelillo's relationship to the Machados would prove significant. The fact is that together with the social network of Spanish traders, a resource that would help him throughout his entire social and economic life, Manuelillo would also count on the patronage of the Machado family, for whom he would do personal and political favors.

Manuelillo's affinity with the Mitristas brought him into conflict with his Uruguayan boss, Iñiguez, who preferred the rival Alsinistas. It is important to note that most of the storekeepers and partners of whom Manuelillo speaks well in his memoirs were Spaniards, mainly Basques or Galicians. The conflict would finally end when Blanco, Manuelillo's relative, dissolved his partnership with Iñiguez and installed his two Spanish clerks (José Martínez and Manuelillo) as *habilitados* in a new store.

Before that, however, Iñiguez, trying to avoid the dispute with Blanco, offered to give Manuelillo merchandise as a *habilitado*. Manuelillo would go out in a wagon and sell his wares in the frontier territory to the south.[9] In the company of a young peon and Señor Bueno, an older Galician who knew the frontier well and who would act as guide as well as take charge of the wagons and the animals, Manuelillo spent three months traveling and peddling his goods on the frontier. Always armed, he had to face outlaws, Indian raids, burned-out lands with no water or grass for the horses and oxen, and the other hazards of a still wild territory.[10] On his return to Tandil, Manuelillo was able to show a substantial profit. In an area with no permanent stores, his goods could be sold at very high prices.

Finally, at twenty-four years of age but already with a hazardous life behind him, Manuelillo together with his friend and partner Martínez were in charge of a store. His cousin Blanco was the principal backer. A year later, with the advice (and very likely the financial support) of Blanco and other prosperous Spanish traders, he bought his own *esquina* (corner store), "La Providencia," in a rural area near Tandil, in the county of Lobería. He placed a Basque, Julián Izaguirre, as *habilitado* and divided his time between the store in Tandil, where he was a minor partner, and the one in Lobería, where he was the main owner. Finally, in 1872 he dissolved his partnership with Martínez and Blanco. He then concentrated on his activities as a storeowner and also as a rancher on the *estancia* on which the *esquina* was located, which Manuelillo rented.

In January 1872, when the "Tata Dios" incident in Tandil occurred,[11] Manuelillo, together with other foreigners, helped to reestablish peace and calm in the region. Later, as a respectable storeowner and a man of character—and also, perhaps, because of his political connections—he would serve as bailiff of the area where his store was located. Three years later, in 1875, he made a trip to visit his mother and his homeland, where he also called on his old boss and protector, Manuel Nieto, in Cádiz. During this trip he traveled with two of his cousins, Ramón and Marcelino Blanco. The older of the two, Ramón, would find a fiancée in his hometown (the young woman later traveled to Buenos Aires, where they married). The three men spent nearly a year in Spain—in part because Ramón did not want to leave before formalizing his new relationship—and they returned to Buenos Aires by mid-1876.

Once home, Manuelillo worried about the Indian raids that took place that same year, fortified his *esquina*. But these rebellions were the last markers of a time about to end. Three years later the Native Americans would be defeated and subdued or expelled from the province of Buenos Aires. On a trip to Buenos Aires in 1877, Manuelillo met Michaela García, whom he would marry in 1879.[12] He then proceeded to liquidate his ties to Izaguirre and established himself with his new wife at "La Providencia" as a storeowner and rancher.

Here ends Manuelillo's account of his life. It shows the progress achieved though his firm personality, his will to improve, and his broad network of kin, countrymen, and friends. In his first move to Cádiz, he obtained an education as a storekeeper and a certain familiarity with a world far more complex than his simple Galician hamlet. Later, emigrating to Argentina, he became a prosperous storeowner and an *estanciero* on rented land. This pattern is sometimes called stage-migration: the migrant first becomes acquainted with the urban world and more modern economic structures and later looks for better opportunities through a longer-distance migration. But it is obvious that a network of kin and friendship as well as ethnic solidarity were significant parts of the foundation on which he built his material progress.

Though far more sketchy, the notes and documents included by his son, José María Suárez García, in the printed version of the memoirs allow us to follow the later stages of Manuelillo's life. He remained at "La Providencia" until 1889, when he sold the store and livestock and passed on the lease of the *estancia* to Andrés Piñeiro, a Galician who had worked as a clerk and then a *habilitado* at the store and who had married a sister of Micaela, Manuelillo's wife. The new operation would be underwritten by Ramón Santamarina, a Galician *estanciero* from Tandil, who had built a proverbial fortune in Argentina.

This decision, however, does not seem to have been a good financial one for Manuelillo. In spite of the overall prosperity of the 1880s, his business did not seem to flourish, and Argentina underwent a profound economic crisis in the very year of the sale, a crisis that would last until the mid-1890s. The family, already with several children—Manuelillo and Micaela would have eleven—went to live in Buenos Aires. According to Manuelillo's son José María, they wanted their youngsters to get a better education in the city than they could in the countryside. Once in Buenos Aires, Manuelillo started a nail factory, but without success, perhaps because of the crisis. After this failure, he decided to return to Tandil, where he tried his luck at several businesses. Always with the help of his friends and countrymen, including his old partners Izaguirre, Piñeiro, and Santamarina, he established a flour mill, a bakery (where he would be in perpetual conflict with the anarchist workers), and later on a bleach factory.

His son's notes complain about Manuelillo's financial problems. He also mentions on several occasions the sale of real estate, and in 1912 both Manuelillo and José María traveled to Spain. That he was able to afford the passage suggests that while Manuelillo kept working all his life, his family never had to face real hardships. His former Basque partner, Julián Izaguirre, however, seems to have been more fortunate. In 1912, Piñeiro (who had traveled to Spain together with Manuelillo and his son) and José María visited Izaguirre in the comfortable mansion he had built near Bilbao in the Basque country, where he enjoyed the fortune he had made in Argentina.

Even though Manuelillo could not, or did not want to, return to his homeland, he had made solid progress. A measure of this success is shown in an incident that took place during his first visit to his native land. Even though his mother had repeatedly summoned him, arguing that she was seriously ill, Manuelillo had not told her that he was coming. When he arrived in Santiago, he found that his mother's illness was nothing more than a trick to force him to come home. In reprisal, when he went to his mother's house after being away for seventeen years, he did not reveal his identity. When the old peasant woman found on her doorstep a well-dressed gentleman, she invited him to come in because he said he had news of her son in Argentina. She warned him that she did not have any chairs, so he would have to sit on a stool. Later, after he had made himself known to her and spent a long time visiting his friends and relatives in the hamlet, he stayed at night at an inn in the city. The inn was over an hour's walk away, but he was no longer used to the hardships of peasant life. He gave to his brothers, who needed it badly, the money he had brought with him to travel through Spain.

Ultimately, the peasant migrant boy Manuelillo managed to create a solid middle-class life in Tandil. His daughters married well-to-do men, his sons studied at the university in Buenos Aires, and his grandsons and great-grandsons are now respected members of the local society.

Notes

1. I would like to dedicate this story to the memory of another Galician immigrant, with a life in several ways not unlike that of Suárez Martínez: José Míguez Gandara, my grandfather.

2. *Memorias de Manuel Suárez Martínez, seguidas de los apuntes biográficos de D. Manuel Suárez Martìnez por José María Suárez García*, Tandil, published by the author, 1942. The memoirs have been used by several researchers, among them M. Bjerg and H. Otero, "Inmigración y liderazgo en comunidades rurales: Un análisis desde las biografías y las redes sociales," unpublished.

3. In Spain, as in many places in Latin America, confectioneries are also coffee houses that sell sweets, sodas, and beverages for consumption at tables on the premises.

4. A sort of Spanish social club in Buenos Aires whose members were the better-off immigrants.

5. Tandil, a small city on the southern frontier of the province of Buenos Aires, was some 200 miles south of the capital. For more information, see Chapters 7 and 8 in this volume.

6. A *habilitado* is a minor partner in a commercial business. Instead of a salary, the *habilitado* usually shares in the profits but may also provide some of the capital. Frequently, he is in full charge of running the business.

7. Frontier stores at the time covered a wide range. The *almacén* was a general supply store, the *tienda* offered clothing with a section for ladies and customers "of a better sort," and the *despacho de bebidas* was a section for buying drinks and playing cards. In the more modest grocery stores, the *pulperías*, all activities coexisted in the same room. In the better *esquinas*—literally street corners, but the term at the time also referred to important stores, even if they were not located at a crossroads—there were several rooms for the different "departments."

8. There were two main political parties in the province of Buenos Aires at the time: Nacionalistas or Mitristas, the followers of Mitre; and Autonomistas or Alsinistas, the followers of the Alsina family.

9. These *pulperías ambulantes*, or mobile stores, were not uncommon on the frontier.

10. Due to lack of space, I cannot narrate here many interesting episodes in the life of Manuelillo, both on this trip and in the rest of his frontier experience. Several times he had to defend himself or draw his guns—although he never

actually shot anybody—to get out of difficult situations. After the expulsion of Native Americans from the province of Buenos Aires in 1879 and with the increase in settlers in the territory in the following decade, life would become much calmer.

11. The so-called Tata Dios Massacre took place in Tandil on January 1, 1872. A group of gauchos, inspired by Tata Dios, a healer, raided the country to the shout of "Death to Foreigners and Masons" and killed nearly fifty immigrants. They were then pursued by the local militia. Some of the gauchos were killed, others caught, and the rest disbanded. This was the most important xenophobic incident in the history of mass migration to Argentina; no other incidents of this sort have been recorded. A full account may be found in John Lynch, *Massacre in the Pampas, 1872* (Norman: Oklahoma University Press, 1998).

12. On the wedding of Micaela and Manuelillo, who was already thirty-two years old, see Chapter 8 in this volume on marriage and household.

7

The Danes in the Argentine Pampa: The Role of Ethnic Leaders in the Creation of an Ethnic Community, 1848–1930

María Bjerg

This study of Danish immigrants in the province of Buenos Aires during the second half of the nineteenth century offers valuable insights into the formation and development of ethnic communities. The information on Hans Fugl, the Danish farmer who was the first of his countrymen to settle in the Argentine Pampa, gives us a rare glimpse into the life of an immigrant pioneer around whom a social network emerged. María Bjerg explores the changing relations between the Danish ethnic community and the host society. The early Danish migrants integrated themselves into the political and cultural life of Argentina, whereas the later community eschewed Argentine politics and focused instead on the preservation of Danish culture and religion.

When an immigrant arrives in a new land, he or she is often unfamiliar with the life patterns of the new environment—the customs, the language, the economic opportunities and barriers, the power structure. Leaders emerge within the immigrant group to help newer arrivals make their way under trying circumstances. These leaders are often a bridge to the native world and as such interpret that world to the newcomers. If they are successful, the leaders can benefit immensely from the power generated by their positions and by the dependency of the new immigrants. Nevertheless, while leaders of immigrant groups are given power over their members, they are also confined by the circumstances in which they find themselves.

The experience of the Danes in the Argentine Pampa in the second half of the nineteenth century illustrates the ways in which a fairly small immigrant group without many common ties to the dominant society could flourish in the New World. The story of the Danes in Tandil and other communities southeast of the province of Buenos Aires in Argentina and the varied efforts of their leaders to organize them makes visible the multifaceted relationship between immigrants and their community's leaders.

Throughout the decades of 1860 and 1870 the early Danish leaders participated actively in the municipal government of Tandil. The ethnic and the political leaders were two faces of the same coin that by being joined together reinforced their influence. However, this situation would change in the last decades of the nineteenth century when the Danish leaders—withdrawing from the local government—would focus their energy on the complex challenges imposed by the organization of an ethnic community. These changes were the response to both the transformations experienced by nineteenth- and early twentieth-century Argentine society and to the new social arrangements and internal reconfiguration of the Danish community in the pampa.

The Power of the Pioneer

The first group of Danish immigrants arrived in Tandil in 1860 from the parish of Magleby on the island of Mön in southeastern Denmark. These people had been lured to Tandil by Hans Fugl, a Danish farmer who had settled on the frontier in 1848. The group that originally comprised around twenty members grew relatively fast throughout the decades of the 1860s and 1870s due to the spread of accurate information about prospects in Argentina through village and kinship networks that connected Tandil with the islands of Mön and Lolland-Falster. These networks helped spread emigration fever from the original source to the rest of the islands and later to the peninsula of Jutland.

These networks began to develop in 1858 when Hans Fugl returned from Argentina to visit his place of origin in Denmark. Planning to build a flour mill in his new home in Tandil, Fugl went back to Denmark in search of materials, technology, and skilled labor scarce in the pampa. In Mön, Fugl persuaded his old friends and acquaintances to move to Tandil where, he argued, a remarkable unexploited economic opportunity was waiting. The lure of prosperity, the availability of virgin land, and the need for labor convinced the first group of Danes to follow Fugl across the Atlantic. When the immigrants finally arrived in the hot summer of 1860, Fugl helped them get jobs either by employing them himself or by recommending them to the affluent landowners who controlled the municipal government where he already had carved out his own political niche.

This contingent was the origin of a social network that, in the near future, would attract an increasing number of Danish immigrants—first to Tandil and later to the counties of Tres Arroyos, Necochea, and Coronel

Dorrego in the south of the province of Buenos Aires.[1] The tacit internal hierarchy established during the migration would influence both the personal and institutional relationships fostered among the members of the Danish group throughout the process of creation of an ethnic community. Between 1860 and 1875 the Danes did not have many chances to challenge the monopoly of Fugl's leadership even if they had wanted to. He had organized the migration from Mön and had helped with the settlement of the first Danes in Tandil. Through his social relationships with some of his powerful Argentine neighbors, he also had arranged lodging and jobs for those compatriots he was unable to hire. Fugl's leadership was rooted in the bonds he had fostered with the local society's elite during the time he was the sole Dane settled in Tandil. Soon after the arrival of the first immigrants, Fugl became the "patriarch of the Danes" (as he portrayed himself in his memoirs). He gained a power that would be enhanced by his compatriots' material and symbolic acknowledgment of his position as he maintained his ability to open doors into the local society for an ever-increasing number of new immigrants.

In the decade between his arrival in Tandil and his first return to Denmark in 1858, Fugl's political power in the municipal government improved substantially. The promise of fertile farmland had attracted him to a frontier where the economic potential was sometimes obstructed by the local landowners' hostile attitudes toward foreigners. In his early days in Tandil, the voracious appetite of the free-ranging cattle in an open area mostly devoted to cattle raising constituted a permanent threat to Fugl's wheatfields. Repeatedly he argued with the justice of the peace and wealthy landowners, insisting that the agricultural protective laws be put into practice. Ironically, his bitter quarrels with the local authorities brought Fugl into close contact with municipal politics, fostered networks with the local elite, and helped him carve a niche in a society where European immigrants gradually began to share political power that had traditionally been the privilege and monopoly of wealthy Argentine landowner families.

By the time he decided to build the flour mill, Fugl was cultivating ten farms in Tandil's countryside and had built several houses in the village. Parallel to the improvement in his economic situation, his participation in municipal politics increased. Eight years after his arrival, Fugl was elected director of the municipal board of education and entrusted with the task of drawing the council's first cadastral map (the public land register for tax purposes) and organizing the distribution of public land among native and foreign claimants. The improvement in his economic situation along with the fact that he had obtained a teacher's degree in Denmark in the early 1840s favored his incorporation into local political circles. From the host society's standpoint, his education made Fugl a symbol of "civilization" in a frontier society in close contact with "barbarism," an evil that in the opinion of the romantic promoters of "Modern"

Argentina hindered the country's progress. Fugl was seen as a representative of modernity and civilization because, to his advantage, he came from the world of the Northern European Protestant farmers who at the time epitomized the best characteristics to be transplanted, as Juan Bautista Alberdi put it, "like vine stocks" to the new nation.

As time went by, Fugl moved from the disadvantageous position of being a foreign farmer in permanent conflict with the local authorities to having an intricate network of relations with powerful landowners. One such landowner was the Spaniard Ramón Santamarina, one of the wealthiest *estancieros* (large landowners) in the province of Buenos Aires who joined with Fugl in a political venture.[2] In the municipal election of 1873, Santamarina, Fugl, and Manuel Eigler (a Danish grocer who had arrived in Tandil along with the first group of Danes in 1860) ran for the municipal council as the representatives of the provincial political party called Alsinismo. Although the victory was based on a narrow margin—350 to 317 votes for the opposition representing the Mitrismo—the Alsinismo won the election.[3] As one of the more powerful landowners of the province, Santamarina presumably attracted the majority of the voters; however, Fugl also played an important part in the candidates' success. None of the fifty-five Danes who went to the polls voted for the Mitrismo candidate. Fugl's political supporters decided the final outcome of the election.[4]

From 1860 until 1875, when Fugl returned to Denmark for good, his ties to the political power structure grew stronger. His ethnic leadership played an important role in his successful career in local politics. The years spent in Tandil helped Fugl understand the economic, political, and social codes of the frontier world. In 1860, when his compatriots arrived, Fugl was able to decipher those codes for them. He had jobs and housing to offer, money to lend; in addition, he was the only one who spoke Spanish and understood the local cultural symbols. Fugl could guide the new arrivals in an uncertain and sometimes hostile world. For example, in January 1872 a messianic character known in the region as Tata Dios organized a group of fifty gauchos and led a horrible massacre of foreigners. More than thirty persons including Spanish, French, Italian, and English men, women, and children were murdered by this "messiah," savior of Indians and "criollos." Although the massacre was just an isolated sample of extreme hostility, more subtle xenophobic attitudes frequently permeated the daily life of Danes in the rural society of nineteenth-century Argentina. For example, the Catholic priests steadfastly refused to bury Protestant immigrants in the cemetery of Tandil.

In spite of his Lutheran faith and as long as there was no Danish congregation in Tandil, Fugl and his family found it reasonable to attend services at the Catholic church. However, this attitude was not prevalent among the Danish immigrants, most of whom clung to Lutheranism. In the 1870s, Fugl participated in the municipal commission in charge of raising funds and obtaining financial aid from the national government to build a new Catholic church in Tandil. These efforts helped him establish an amicable relationship with the Catholic priests that his compatriots could hardly dream of ever having.

Seeking to satisfy the Danes' religious needs, Fugl used to serve as a lay priest by celebrating weddings, baptizing children, burying the dead on his farm, and providing Sunday services in his house. Throughout the decades of the 1860s and 1870s as the Danish community of Tandil grew, Fugl's farm turned into a gathering place where an increasing number of Danes shared a social and religious life. A decade after the arrival of the first group, Fugl had reached the pinnacle of ethnic leadership.[5] His farm was a reference point for almost every Dane—a place where uncertainties could be resolved, and material or spiritual needs could be met. Somehow every Dane in Tandil was indebted to Fugl: the first job, a place to stay, a loan of money, a farmland deed, the baptism of a child, or the burial of a family member. Gradually, Fugl surrounded himself with a clientele who allowed him to develop both unquestionable leadership within the Danish community as well as the image of a powerful man in the local society.

His political participation grew with the enhancement of his ethnic leadership. Between 1860 and 1875, Fugl was elected a member of the municipal council and president of the board of public education twice; he participated in meetings with the interior minister and succeeded in getting financial support for the Catholic church of Tandil. He was elected president of the Foreigners' Society, a civilian post aimed at protecting Tandil's immigrants during upheavals brought about by the revolution of 1874.[6] When Bartolomé Mitre—a former president of Argentina who led the revolution—arrived in Tandil with part of the revolutionary forces, Fugl was among the immigrants who met with him seeking guarantees and security for the foreign population.

Fugl's ethnic leadership gave him an aura of power that originated in his Danish clientele and resulted in the enhancement of his power in the municipal government and in the local society. In the local Danish society only one of his compatriots, Manuel Eigler, had a position of power comparable to Fugl's. His grocery store was a gathering place both for Danes who had long been settled in Tandil as well as for those recently arrived from Denmark. In spite of the fact that Eigler had not obtained a higher degree, he had pursued formal education in Denmark, was able to speak many languages (French and German, among others), and had learned Spanish with amazing rapidity. In his store, Eigler informally taught Spanish to new Danish immigrants and read the local newspapers aloud to his compatriots who still had difficulties with the language. As the years passed, Eigler's grocery store, patronized mostly by Danish customers, prospered, and he began to travel to Buenos Aires to buy goods imported from Denmark to satisfy the needs of the ethnic segment of the market he controlled. In the capital city he fostered a strong link with the Danish consul, Christian Sommer, to whom Fugl had introduced him. In the late 1860s, Eigler married Sommer's niece, and his bonds with the consul grew even stronger. Gradually, those newly arrived immigrants whom Sommer used to recommend to Fugl were sent to Eigler, who was finally appointed Danish royal vice consul of Tandil in 1885 ten years after his mentor, Hans Fugl, had resettled in Denmark.

Although Eigler had participated in Tandil's public and political sphere in the 1860s and 1870s (he was elected to the municipal council in 1873 and was appointed military commander by the Foreigners' Society during the revolution of 1874), his economic position and political career were still in their beginnings in comparison with Fugl's. Moreover, Eigler seemed to depend a great deal on Fugl's will to carve his niche in the political and ethnic leadership. Most Danes still preferred to seek the "patriarch's" advice.

In his seminal work on ethnic leadership, John Higham asserted that by creating the ethnic group's institutional structures aimed at reproducing and transmitting values and symbolic expressions, ethnic leaders help the immigrants focus their ethnic consciousness, make the group's identity visible, and ease its adaptation to the host society.[7] Among the first Danes in the Argentine Pampa, the early leaders did not seem concerned with the reconstitution of the group's beliefs brought with them from the homeland. Fugl's ties to his compatriots in Tandil were restricted to the fact that he shared a national origin with them; he was not interested in the creation of an institutional structure that endeavored to reproduce in Argentina what the Danes had had in Denmark.

The low degree of ethnic identification among the first Danish immigrants in Tandil had to do with the circumstances of the pioneers' settlement. The possibility of recreating an ethnic culture in a new society partly depends on the size of the group, on the existence of an incipient institutional structure, and on the availability of economic means to support the ethnic institutions. Except for Fugl and a handful of Danish pioneers who came with the first group, throughout the decades of the 1860s and 1870s most Danes were just beginning their integration into the Argentine labor and land markets. Few of them had even earned enough to donate part of their income to build a Lutheran church or a Danish school. For example, in the years between the first meeting of the Protestant Society and the dedication of the church in 1877, more than a decade had passed.

However, the circumstances would change drastically by the turn of the century in the other Danish settlements at Tres Arroyos, Necochea, and Coronel Dorrego in the southern Buenos Aires province. An increasing Danish population, the availability of vast tracts of inexpensive farmland, and the community's firm resolution to reconstitute their Danish culture in Argentina made fundraising much easier and helped the Danish leaders build community churches and schools with remarkable speed. That had not been the case with Tandil in the first decades of the Danish settlement. Living in a reality with inscrutable codes, latent xenophobia, and virtual hostility had led the Danes to sacrifice an important part of their bonds to the Old World and its culture.

In 1875, Fugl returned to Denmark for good. New leaders, some of the Danes who had followed him in 1860, took the place he left vacant. In Tandil, Manuel Eigler was soon regarded as Fugl's natural heir. However, changes would occur both in the local political arena and within the Danish community that would make it impossible either for Eigler or for any other Dane to monopolize the ethnic leadership as Fugl had. The new leaders would have to share power with the new protagonists of the community life: the Lutheran pastors, the Danish teachers, and the immigrants who began to arrive in the late 1880s from the peninsula of Jutland. These new immigrants brought with them new ideas about the importance of recreating a Danish identity in the settlements of the province of Buenos Aires.

Fugl's leadership in the frontier society could be characterized as traditional and patriarchal. The legitimacy of his power originated in the fact that the leadership took place among peers. However, this patriarchalism could develop only in a society with a low degree of social diversification, where the absence of the state and its bureaucratic structures made persons such as Fugl or Eigler, with their wide knowledge of the new reality and the means of access to power, a necessity.

The social and political role of the immigrants in the society of the frontier was characterized by the intense involvement in public sphere activities that were nonethnically based during the decades of the 1860s and 1870s, while led by pioneers such as Fugl. More than Italians, Spaniards, French, Basques, or Danes, individuals of different nationalities would define themselves not so much by their ethnicity but as *neighbors* in charge of creating the institutions and infrastructure of a society that was growing more complex and diversified. Constructing roads, building churches, opening the first common public school, drawing a cadastral map, organizing the distribution of land, and maintaining relations with the Indians were all responsibilities the immigrants would have to assume as long as they were granted a share of power in the muncipal government and in the public sphere.

This intense activity in public affairs involving both the institutions of the political system and the organizations of the civil society would change in 1880 with the advent of a new national regime. The Argentine state undertook centralization and sought to merge local communities into a larger whole under the aegis of the provincial and national governments,

thereby modifying the relations between rulers and governed. Centralization weakened the influence in municipal affairs that the neighbors had
enjoyed in the decades before 1880, when both Creoles and immigrants—
using the interstices left by the the the legal system—took responsibility for
the construction of the community where they lived.[8]

In the first half of the 1880s, editorials in the local newspaper, *El Eco
de Tandil*, often complained about the loss of municipal autonomy and
political participation that state centralization had caused in the rural society of the province of Buenos Aires. In the early 1880s, with the reform
of the Constitution of the Province of Buenos Aires on the horizon, the
newspaper constantly espoused the idea of decentralization, which would
allow the neighbors in the municipalities to elect freely justices of the
peace, members of the school board, and military commanders of the
Guardia Nacional. Given the apathy shown by the residents who by the
end of 1882 did not vote as massively as the newspaper had expected in
the election of deputies to the Constitutional Provincial Assembly, one
might assume that the editorials exaggerated the eagerness for municipal
autonomy. Nevertheless, the sources reveal a high degree of participation
of both natives and foreigners in the political and public spheres throughout the decades of the 1860s and 1870s. Beyond the bias of *El Eco de
Tandil*, the editorials might have been a response to the slow and erratic
penetration of the Argentine state into the rural world, and the imposition
of a bureaucratic system still unfamiliar to the frontier population where
custom and law had been separated for decades by a blurred line. At the
end of the nineteenth century, in the society ruled by a new political regime, the Danish leaders' focus no longer would be the institutions of the
municipal government, but those they would have to create in their ethnic
community.

Turning Inward: The Development of a
Danish Ethnic Community, 1875–1930

Although Fugl returned to Denmark in 1875, he maintained his influence
on the internal life of the Tandil Danish community for a long time. Ernesto
Pedersen, a Danish farmer who had arrived in Tandil in 1867, was elected
president of the Protestant Society and Manuel Eigler its treasurer and
secretary. In 1876 the Society came back to the original project of building a church, while in Denmark Fugl tried to find a pastor for Tandil. He
soon contacted Oscar Meulengracht, who, after being ordained in Aarhus
Cathedral, moved to the Danish congregation of Tandil. In the future, the
pastors would play an important role as spiritual and ethnic leaders of the
community; however, it took them some time to attain this position. They
initially had to gain the sympathy and confidence of many immigrants
who were not used to participating in church !ife and who had been living

for a long time in a community without Lutheran ministers, churches, or a religious life.

The first decade of the Protestant congregation was rather erratic. After staying six years in Tandil, Meulengracht returned to Denmark. The church remained without a minister for three years. Although little information is available about the time the first pastor served in Tandil, sources reveal that Meulengracht tried his best to gain new members for the congregation, either by holding services on the farms of Danes who were settled too far away from the church or by convincing those who showed little interest in religious life to join the church for Sunday services. Because the Danes were used to a leadership system rooted in reciprocity and exchange of gifts and favors, finding new parishioners and gaining a place among the community's leadership were daunting challenges. The idea of going to church every Sunday in exchange for spiritual solace was not as attractive as gathering at Fugl's farm to listen to his tedious reading of the Bible in exchange for a job or a farmland property deed.

By the time the first pastor took charge of the congregation, the community was divided into two groups of parishioners—or potential parishioners. On one side were the believers who congregated in the Protestant Society; on the other were those who had little time for religious concerns since they were focused on the hardships of their first years in Argentina. Adjustments and time were needed to attract these potential parishioners. The ethnic leaders had to find a way to transform the church into something that could help satisfy the material, social, and educational needs of the community.

In 1886, when the second pastor, Niels Dael, took over, the situation was gradually changing. The first important change was the arrival of immigrants from different parts of Denmark. The majority no longer came from the islands of Mön and Lolland-Falster in the southeast but from central and northern Jutland. In these latter areas the religious philosophy of the nationalist bishop, N. S. F. Grundtvig, had spread widely since the late 1840s and particularly after Denmark, defeated by Prussia in 1864, lost the territories of Schleswig in the south of Jutland. According to Grundtvig, Lutheranism should devote itself to a national crusade focused on the revindication and preservation of the Danish culture. Grundtvigians believed a person could leave Denmark but never abandon the Danish language, heritage, and traditions. In the United States the nationalist ideas of the Grundtvigians found both adherents and enemies and brought about a great deal of internal upheaval in Danish settlements. The church's internal battles in the midwestern sectarian landscape caused the split of many congregations along religious and ideological lines.[9] Although in Argentina the congregations were never involved in as great a conflict as those that shook the congregations in the United States, the arrival by the turn of the century of pastors and teachers who shared the principles of

Grundtvig's nationalist philosophy had a strong impact on the definition of the community's ethnic identity and on the meaning of being Danish in the midst of the Argentine Pampa.

Educated in Askov School, a *Grundtvigian* institution, Pastor Dael believed the church had to work toward the preservation of Danishness among immigrants settled in foreign countries. In Tandil he found both a tiny group of parishioners eager to revive the congregation that had been without a pastor for three years as well as a majority of Danes who lacked a religious life and group cohesiveness. In many letters addressed to his colleagues and friends in Denmark, the pastor described the difficulties faced by the few members of the Protestant Society in keeping the church alive. He also told about the preference of many rural workers and newly arrived Danes to socialize with outsiders in the village pubs. From the pastor's standpoint these individuals risked not only their morals but also, more seriously, the continuity of the Danish cultural codes of conduct when exposed to such contact with the new society.[10]

During the decade he served in Argentina, Dael helped create a model church that was concerned not only with preaching and theological work but also, above all, with the construction of a communal social fabric based on Danish values and symbols. The church was seen as a bastion for the defense of these values and entrusted with the Danish cultural formation of the generations born in Argentina. After three decades of settlement, the community comprised an important number of families with children of school age.[11] After reaching an agreement with the authorities of a divided Protestant Society (where some members still favored the rapid integration of the Danes into the host society), Dael hired Danish teachers whom he had met during his stay in Askov and attracted to Tandil a considerable number of Grundtvigian families from the congregation of Mors in northern Jutland, where he had preached before moving to Argentina.

The minister and the teachers continued to redefine the cultural and religious boundaries of the group by focusing on the education of the Danish-Argentine children and on attracting to the church those habitués of the local pubs who were more inclined to share their free time with strangers than going to church and meeting their compatriots. To accomplish these goals the church had to focus on the creation of an array of ethnic institutions aimed at promoting new activities and to offer a wide range of services beyond the religious ones.

By the turn of the century the Danish community was growing; new settlements in the Tres Arroyos, Necochea, and Coronel Dorrego areas flourished and attracted new immigrants lured by the availability of farmland at low prices.[12] Compared to the pioneer era, the internal structure of the community was becoming more complex and diversified. Many rural workers and small farmers, Jutlanders, big landowners, and affluent farmers burst onto the community's scene: Adolf Petersen was the son of one of the Danish pioneers who had arrived in Tandil as an adolescent along with his family in the 1860s and by the end of the century was farming thousands of hectares; Niels Peter Larsen was a dynamic farmer who often employed recently arrived Danes; the Jutlanders Niels and Blas Ambrosius, Carl Anderberg, Christian Skov, and Christian Albeck began their life in Argentina as rural laborers on Niels Peter Larsen's farm. By the end of the 1880s the last five moved southward to Tres Arroyos and Necochea where, after about a decade of residence, they were found among the most prosperous landowners of the region.

Compared to these wealthier Danes, Fugl, the owner of small farms and a flour mill, seemed not to have gained much economically by moving from Denmark to the Argentine Pampa. Nevertheless, the financial success of the new immigrants would not necessarily translate into the political power and social relations that Fugl had fostered on the frontier. From the end of the nineteenth century onward, the Danish community would have an existence that ran parallel to the host society. In this process of turning inward, the new community leaders would focus almost exclusively on the ethnic domain. Even when the tradition of immigrant participation in the public sphere did not fade away completely, the few Danes who participated in local politics (both in Tandil and in the new settlements) did not reach any particular heights in the ethnic leadership.[13] The time was seemingly over when leaders such as Fugl were entrusted with the task of opening the door of the host society to the new immigrants.

As time went by, more Danes settled in the southern province of Buenos Aires; the community there grew, and new religious congregations were created that emulated the internal organization of the "mother church" of Tandil. In those churches, schools for the immigrants' children were promptly opened along with mutual aid societies, labor and employment agencies, clubs, libraries, Danish folk groups, and theater associations. These institutions had a strong impact on community life and helped develop a profound sociability that tied the people together and assured their social and cultural reproduction.

The committees regularly formed by a handful of affluent farmers together with the pastor and schoolteacher organized the community's institutions, while the majority of Danes provided the economic resources to support them. Going through the membership records that list the name and amount of contributions to either churches, schools, mutual aid societies, or libraries, a striking difference is seen between the time the Danes of Tandil took the first steps toward the organization of the Protestant Society and the bonanza years at the beginning of the twentieth century. Unlike the experiences of frustration and difficulty faced by the pioneers when trying to organize a first congregation in the late 1860s, the one set up by the new leaders was less traumatic. The existence of a critical number of immigrants able to contribute economically to the common interest of the community eased the task of creating an ethnic institutional structure.

Although the majority of immigrants contributed to the creation and support of the community's institutions, the amount of their contributions differed. By giving amounts of money substantially larger than the average, landowners and prosperous farmers probably tried to secure a place on the committees that controlled the institutions and, hence, could dominate the community's leadership. The target of the fundraising seemed to have been mostly the farmers, since the contributions asked were generally a percentage of harvest yields. However, the collaboration of those with lower incomes—as poor farmers, rural laborers, and recently arrived immigrants—was also requested. This social sector helped with small amounts of money or by buying a ticket to attend the festivals, the bazaars, and the dances organized by the community's institutions. These events were aimed at raising funds, but they also served to strengthen ethnic sociability by including Danes with a long residence in the community along with those recently arrived.

At this point, one might ask: Why did the rural laborers and poor farmers give their money to support the community institutions? The continuation of some of the practices that characterized Fugl's traditional leadership suggests a possible answer. The Danish landowners and affluent farmers who controlled the community's leadership were the same people who had employed the new immigrant, had helped a trusty rural laborer take his first step as an independent farmer by offering him a share-crop contract, or had lent him money to rent a piece of land.

Often the pastors of the Danish churches were early and helpful contacts for new immigrants. Since an important part of the Danish population was either scattered in big areas of the southern counties or settled too far way from church, the pastors used to visit the parishioners and gather Danish neighbors at a given farm to hold religious services. These gatherings were an opportunity for the immigrants to socialize and exchange information and gossip. The pastor took part in the male parishioners' conversations and knew all about land prices, harvest yields, shortage of rain, and needs of labor. As the new immigrants arrived in the Danish areas, one of the first places they customarily went was to the church, where the pastor would put them in contact with farmers who needed hands.

Along with this informal means of obtaining laborers and jobs, the community organized more formal associations. In 1892 the Danish consulate in Buenos Aires founded a mutual aid association called Dansk Hjaelpeforening (hereafter DHF). In addition to the various aid programs DHF offered to its members—health insurance, hospital services, burial funds, etc.—its major efforts were devoted, at least between the early 1890s and 1930, to helping newly arrived Danes without kin or acquaintances in Argentina to get their first job. Although the headquarters of the association was located in the city of Buenos Aires, more than one-half of the membership came from the rural settlements of southeastern Buenos Aires province, and these members provided part of the association's leadership. These rural settlers regularly paid their dues and eventually made generous donations of money, generally by the wealthiest farmers of the community. In exchange, these wealthy landowners had at their disposal a growing pool of cheap labor for their farms. Urged to find a place to work, many of the Danes who arrived without the usual immigrant social networks went directly to DHF. Before leaving their homeland the new immigrants had been made aware of DHF by a brochure handed out by agents when the emigrants purchased their tickets.

Unlike the idea of ethnicity prevailing in the early days, which only went as far as supporting an informal sociability among compatriots, the new leaders regarded the goal of an ethnic community as comprising an umbrella of institutions that formally regulated the community's social life and aimed at recreating among the Danes "webs of significance" in Argentina. The leaders believed the recreation of the past and the maintenance of the Danish value system would be beneficial for the whole community. It would help the new immigrants avoid being lost in a world of unfamiliar habits and cultural codes. The church leadership feared the repetition of the scene of many Danes in unguarded association with outsiders in the pubs of Tandil as described by Pastor Dael in the 1880s.

Entrusted with the social control of the community, the Lutheran church would create the means to incorporate as many immigrants as possible into a life that would take place within the ethnic community. Providing immigrants with a wide array of services, the ethnic institutions allowed Danes to solve their problems and socialize with their peers in an alternative environment to that offered by the host society. However, not every Dane would participate. On the one hand, the poor farmers and rural laborers were often more concerned with finding a job, saving money, or getting a convenient share-crop contract with their landlord. On the other hand, there were those immigrants who had not been active in their churches in Denmark. For one reason or another, these people chose not to take part in the development of the ethnic institutions, either because they were spurred by economic interests rather than cultural and religious ones or because they did not share the concerns of their compatriots about the importance of preserving a Danish identity in the new society. Therefore, the undertaking fell by default to an ethnic elite with economic resources, organizational abilities, and the intellectual and educational skills to handle the two most important institutions of the community—the church and the school.

By the end of the nineteenth century, the ethnic leadership was composed of a combination of wealthy immigrants and intellectual ones, combining farmers who had the economic means to support the projects along with the pastors and the teachers. Often the wealthy farmers undertook the search for pastors for the congregation. Karen Sunesen, the wife of one of the first ministers of the Tres Arroyos congregation, recalled: ". . . Blas [Ambrosius] convinced my husband to be the pastor in Tres Arroyos when Vimtrup moved away. In spite of the fact that my husband had studied theology, he had come to Argentina with the intention of being a farmer. . . . Don Blas convinced my husband, saying the Danes needed him in the church rather than in the fields. Don Blas talked to the other farmers who were church leaders about my husband's salary and obligations and made him a satisfactory offer."[14]

By taking part in the leadership of the community organizations, both pastors and teachers were in a vulnerable position, since the rest of the leaders hired them and determined their salaries. On the one hand, pastors and teachers were allowed to give their viewpoints and participate in the decision-making process about the destiny of the community's internal life, even when neither group could vote in the annual meetings of the congregation. On the other hand, they were also employees, dependent on the will of the wealthy members who controlled the ethnic institutions.

The rest of the community had different reasons to be aligned with the ethnic elite. Some considered it necessary to sacrifice part of their income to support a church and preserve the Lutheran faith and social bonds with their compatriots. Others judged it important to give money to build Danish schools to educate their children, given the shortage of public schools in the rural areas where the Danish settlements were located. Those who were less concerned about nurturing the spirit or securing elementary instruction for their children found that a good reason to contribute their support was in the extensive social life organized by the community's institutions. Finally, there were Danes who did not agree with a life confined within close ethnic boundaries but still paid their contributions to the congregations or the schools. Some Danes enrolled voluntarily as members because they were persuaded of the importance and necessity of the association's goals; others felt forced to back the leaders' initiatives and contributed only because they felt indebted to the leaders. How could a rural laborer whose pastor had found him a job in hard times refuse to support the church? How could a farmer resist the subtle pressure to help build a new school from the same landlord who once had lent him money or offered him a share-crop contract?

The growth of the Danish communities both in terms of numbers and prosperity meant the development of a more institutionalized community. The personalized leadership of Fugl gave way to a broader base of leadership among the economic elite, the pastors, and the teachers. The development and expansion of Danish ethnic institutions helped them to consolidate their power and at the same time strengthened the ties of the immigrants to each other.

The Conflict over the Preservation of Danish Culture

When the pioneer era was over, a conflict erupted that was part of the tension that permeated the Danish rural settlements as they experienced a redefinition of their ethnic identity. By the end of the century, the insistence among part of the Danish leadership on the importance of preserving their culture and religion was a controversial issue that divided the elite and, through it, the community. The conflict between those who wish to preserve the immigrant culture in a new society and those who are more focused on the host society is a perennial one. The experience of the Danes in Argentina shows how the elites managed to maintain their power even while they were divided over these issues.

In an earlier day, Fugl had been able to smooth over conflicts that had arisen during his tenure as de facto leader of the community. In his memoirs he describes the arguments he had with his neighbors or with members of the political elite with whom he shared the municipal government. At times, Fugl's political disagreements and frequent discord with his traditional enemies—the justice of the peace, Figueroa; the military commander, Machado; or the local bank president, Moisés Jurado—made his public life turbulent. With his compatriots he argued about personal problems, mostly related to money (loans that were not paid back, or land and house rents not received on time), or to the emphatic religious tone of the social gatherings on his farm. More secular Danes disliked these gatherings and left to try an alternative sociability with the host society, an attitude that made the "patriarch" indignant. Nevertheless, none of these controversial issues seemed to undermine Fugl's leadership either in municipal politics or within the Danish community.

In 1889, after Fugl had long returned to his homeland, the first sign of friction arose when Pastor Dael hired in Jutland a Grundtvigian teacher for the Danish school. In accordance with the ideology that the Grundtvigians espoused, the teacher believed that the instruction of the second generation should revolve around the transmission of Danish values, national iconography, history, and culture. In a community where, since the midnineteenth century, parents believed in the necessity of sending their children to the public school where they could rapidly learn Spanish, the pastor's initiative and the teacher's ideas were not welcome.

The controversy was recorded by the Danish newspaper, *Tandils' Tidende*, and in the minutes of the congregation's meetings. The majority of the community disagreed with the pastor's stand on the importance of giving the children a Danish education. They regarded hiring schoolteachers in Denmark both as the intrusion of a group of recently arrived Jutlanders in a community used to sending their children to the public Argentine school and as a hindrance to the integration of the Danish immigrants into the host society.[15] The news of the confrontation attracted the attention not only of the leaders but also of the community membership, and it was thoroughly reported by the *Tandils' Tidende* during the first two months. Finally, the editor of the newspaper stopped writing about the "byzantine" discussion of the future of the Danish past in Argentina since he saw no hope for resolution.

In the first decade of the twentieth century the differing viewpoints on the importance of the Danish past again provoked internal disputes. However, the power relations within the community had changed. In 1907 and 1908 the issue dividing the ethnic elite was a proposal presented by the new pastor, Thorvald Andresen, to hold the Lutheran services in Spanish. Even the more apathetic members of the community became involved in the controversy. The Grundtvigian ideas about the importance of preserving Danish culture had permeated the settlements that had been experiencing a process of internal redefinition since the last decades of the nineteenth century.

The long controversy led to a profound revision of the role of the Danish language and culture in Argentina. During the two first decades of the twentieth century the Danish ethnic newspapers and the "Danish School Annals" (published both in Tandil and Tres Arroyos) focused on the issue. Editorials and articles on whether it was important or futile to attempt the reconstitution of former beliefs in a new society were written by pastors, teachers, ethnic leaders, and parents of children attending the Danish school. One of the supporters of rerooting the old social, cultural, and theological practices in the New World was the teacher at the Danish school of Tandil, Lars Baekhöj, a Jutlander who had been trained in the Grundtvigian school of Askov. Baekhöj expressed his views through his articles in the *Tandils' Tidende* and in the annals of the Danish School in Argentina, an institution formed in 1908. The creation of this association at the height of the controversy was not only a means of fundraising for the building of Danish schools in the rural settlements but also a way to measure the level of sympathy that the preservationist ideals awoke in the community. In his articles, Baekhöj was principally concerned with determining the weight that should be placed on the Danish and Argentine value systems in the instruction of children, given that both seemed to find themselves in continued conflict. He believed that education had to emphasize the language and culture of Denmark that were at risk of being lost by the overwhelming weight of the new cultural reality of the Danes' daily life.

What is without question is the different role that the Lutheran church played in the new society relative to its role in Denmark. As a source of solidarity for its members and as an institution concerned with the schooling and economic activities of its members, the church and its pastors helped the immigrant community preserve the traditions of the past and reinvent a new role for the church on the Argentine Pampa.[16] Coming from the reality in Denmark where the church was perceived as a place to attend only a few times during one's life, by the beginning of the new century religion—through the *Grundtvigian* perspective—was transformed into an ideology that made legitimate the new Danish identity in Argentina. Oluf Johansen described the church services held in Necochea in the early 1920s:

> When on Sundays the old pastor celebrated Mass in the small Danish church of Necochea . . . we met almost every member of the colony, first, second, and third generation Danes. That was the occasion to met compatriots . . . we have never before had the habit of going to church but suddenly we found ourselves singing enthusiastically beautiful religious hymns, and being wholly assimilated to a community where the religious life was so crucial. During our life in Denmark we had never experienced such a profound sense of identity and belonging as we did in Necochea.[17]

Other than the controversial issue over the preservation of Danish culture that erupted at certain points after fairly long periods of dormancy, the community's institutional life was peaceful and the leaders seemed to enjoy the support of the majority of the membership. When the Danish settlement had comprised no more than a hundred immigrants, personalized relationships had prevailed. By the beginning of the twentieth century more formal institutions represented a substitute for what had been Fugl's informal protection of the society on the frontier. Although the leadership rooted in the ethnic elite's relations with the political circle of the host society had been replaced by a new configuration, the old mechanisms were still present.

Few immigrants could avoid the influence that the wealthy farmer-leaders had on their lives. These grower-brokers controlled a segment of the labor market and hence most of the new immigrants' and rural laborers' opportunities for economic independence and upward mobility. Embodying new features, the patron-client relationship and the initial vulnerability of the new immigrant continued to be the foundation on which the ethnic leadership was based.[18] The mutual aid association DHF, the Danish pastors, and in particular the landowners helped to mitigate the economic vulnerability of newcomers, rural workers, or poor farmers. Initial aid in getting a job along with the widespread practice among affluent farmers and landowners of signing share-crop contracts with trusted rural laborers seemed to have had an impact on the development of patron-client relationships that consequently led to the redefinition and enhancement of the leaders' ethnic power.

These relations were made visible not only at the material but also at the symbolic level. The close personal contact held by those unequal partners, who shared work, leisure, social life, the pastor, and the same teachers for their children helped to maintain the fiction of equality. The patron, turned into a community leader, supposedly worked for the benefit of his peers. He strengthened the bonds with his clients by lending them money and by finding work for them during times of economic adversity. In addition he helped the clients' newly arrived relatives find a place to stay, or he gave grants to the children of rural workers and poor farmers toward the cost of their education in the ethnic schools. In exchange the clients endorsed the patron's opinions, decisions, and status in the ethnic elite and blocked any challenge to his legitimacy.

Conclusion

Reconstituting former beliefs, upholding values, and preserving the continuity with the Danish past were not always the focus of the Danish community leaders in Tandil. The leadership that had originated with the arrival of the pioneers from Mön and Lolland-Falster turned more complex as time passed and the host society, the Danish society, and the Danish ethnic community in Argentina went through profound changes. These new circumstances influenced the leaders' viewpoints concerning the importance of rerooting former ethnocultural loyalties in the settlements of the pampa. Departing from an original community demarcated by somewhat blurred ethnic boundaries, Danes in Tandil ended up forging a strong ethnic identity by inventing or reinventing traditions and by slowing down the pace of the immigrants' adjustment to the Argentine society.

The close community, fostered in part by an ethnic elite whose discourse highlighted the importance of Danishness, seemed to be, beyond some periods of conflict, the best soil in which to transplant cultural roots brought from Denmark. A second generation, able to understand the language and cultural codes of their parents, pastors, and teachers, may be called the fruit grown from the old Grundtvigian roots.

Although the leaders displayed differing viewpoints regarding the Danish past and its recreation in the New World, their experience revealed continuities in the nature of the their relationship with the rest of the community members. Both during the pioneers' or the Grundtvigians' leadership, the common trait seems to have been the asymmetrical ties established between vulnerable newly arrived Danes and those who could pave the way for them. The leaders could maintain their hegemony either because they were part of an established political network or because they controlled a niche in the labor and land markets. The preservation of the Danish culture was a means by which those in power could maintain their status by creating a strong community spirit among those who were tied to the leaders by more basic asymmetries of power.

Notes

1. A more detailed analysis of Danish immigration in Argentina and the sources with which to study it can be found in María Bjerg, *Entre Sofie y Tovelille: Una historia de la inmigración danesa en la Argentina, 1848–1930* (Buenos Aires, 2001). On social networks and the formation of Danish settlements see idem, "Sabiendo el camino o navegando en las dudas: Las redes sociales y las relaciones impersonales en la inmigración danesa a la Argentina, 1848–1930," in M. Bjerg and H. Otero, eds., *Inmigración y redes sociales en la Argentina moderna* (Tandil, 1995). See also Hans Fugl, *Memorias de Juan Fugl: La vida de un pionero durante treinta años en Tandil, 1844–1875* (translated by Alice Larsen Rabal) (Tandil, 1989), 380.

2. Ramón Santamarina, who had arrived in Argentina in 1840, had left for his descendants by the end of the century 200,000 hectares spread over thirty-three landed estates in the province of Buenos Aires as well as an export trade company with branches both in the capital city and in the province.

3. Nacionalistas, also called Mitristas, and Autonomistas, or Alsinistas, were the political parties that since 1862 had traditionally vied against each other in the elections of the province of Buenos Aires as well as in the national ones. The Nacionalistas owed their name to their favorable attitude toward the nationalization of the province of Buenos Aires. On the other hand, the Autonomistas opposed federalization and sought to defend the province's political and territorial autonomy.

4. The ballot was not cast individually and in secret; on the contrary, people voted in public by raising their hands. Therefore, it is possible to trace the kinds of voters and the candidates whom they backed.

5. The first national population census of Argentina in 1869 records forty adult Danes settled in Tandil. Taking into account children of Danish parentage born both in Denmark and in Argentina, the community comprised about 100 persons.

6. In 1874, Nicolás Avellaneda was elected president of Argentina. His victory was the result of a coalition between Avellaneda's supporters of the Partido Nacional, which represented a variety of provincial interests, and Adolfo Alsina from the Partido Autonomista. This coalition defeated the Partido Nacionalista led by former president Bartolomé Mitre, who, in an attempt to reverse the election outcome, headed a revolution that was defeated by government forces.

7. John Higham, *Ethnic Leadership in America* (Baltimore and London, 1978).

8. In 1854 a law that regulated the municipal governments of the province of Buenos Aires was passed. Among other provisions the law allowed only Argentine citizens to vote in municipal elections. At the end of the 1850s immigrants were granted the passive vote (they had the right to vote but not to be elected to office). Finally, in 1876, foreigners meeting certain conditions of property and age could vote both passively and actively. However, in 1878 the governor of the province of Buenos Aires, Carlos Tejedor, derogated the right by decree. In spite of the legal constraints, the sources reveal intense participation by the immigrants in the local government.

9. On Grundtvig's influence in the United States and the Danish congregation cleavages see Henrik Bredsome Simonsen, *Kampen om Danskheden: Tro og*

Nationalitet i det danske Samfund i America (Aarhus, 1990); Thorvald Hansen, "Church Divided: Lutheranism among the Danish Immigrants in America," in Birgit F. Larsen et al., eds., *On Distant Shores: Proceedings of the Marcus Lee Hansen Immigrant Conference* (Aalborg, 1992); Jette Mackintosh, "Little Denmark on the Prairie: A Study of the Towns Elk Horn and Kimballton in Iowa," in *Journal of Ethnic History*, vol. 7, no. 2, 1988; Paul Nyholm, *The Americanization of Danish Lutheran Churches in America*, Kirkehistorie Studier Nr 16 (Minneapolis, 1963).

10. Some of those letters were published by Oluf Johansen, *Johannes og Katrine: En sanfaertig fortaelling fra Danmark og* (Buenos Aires, 1944).

11. According to the records of Argentina's Second National Census of Population of 1895, 270 adult Danes lived in Tandil. In Tres Arroyos, Necochea, and Coronel Dorrego, where the settlements were in their infancy, 140 Danish immigrants were recorded.

12. The Danish census by the consulate in Buenos Aires recorded 470 Danes in Tandil in 1902 and 500 Danes in the southern counties of the province (Tres Arroyos, Necochea, and Coronel Dorrego). In the Third National Census of Population of 1914 the Danish population of Tandil was stagnated at 230, while 1,000 Danes lived in the new settlements in the south.

13. For example, Blas Grothe, the owner and editor of *Tandils' Tidende*. Until his death in 1938, Grothe was an active participant in the local society: school board director; treasurer of the multiethnic mutual aid society, *La Cosmopolita*; member of the municipal council representing the Radical Party; vice president of the local bank, Comercial del Tandil; and member of the board of trustees of the insurance company La Tandilense. In spite of his remarkable presence in the political and public spheres, Grothe took little part in the ethnic leadership. He was a member of the commission that founded the Scandinavia Society in 1886 and three times treasurer of the Protestant Society in the 1880s and 1890s.

14. Interview with Karen Sunesen, wife of the pastor who served in the church of Tres Arroyos between 1901 and 1935, Tres Arroyos, November 1988.

15. *Tandils' Tidende*, October 5 and 15, 1889.

16. Eric Hobsbawm and Terence Ranger, *The Invention of Tradition* (Cambridge, 1983); Kathleen Neils Conzen et al., "The Invention of Ethnicity: A Perspective from the USA," *Altreitalie* 3 (1990).

17. Oluf Johansen, *Nybygger* (Copenhagen, 1934), 187.

18. "Patron-client relationship" means a link established between individuals who are clearly unequal in economic and political power. The link is based on personal loyalty, obligations, and exchange of material and symbolic gifts and favors. See Alan Zuckermann, "La política de clientes en Italia," in Ernest Gellner et al., *Patrones y Clientes* (Madrid, 1985).

8

Marriage, Household, and Integration in Mass Migration to Argentina: The Case of Tandil

Eduardo José Míguez

To better understand the process of immigrant integration into Argentine society, Eduardo José Míguez examines the marriage patterns of immigrants in Tandil. Endogamy (intermarriage) is highest among most immigrant groups in the first generation, but it drops off significantly in the second generation. The important factor that determines marriage partners is what the author calls the "context of sociability"—that is, the social networks that define the immigrants' daily lives. He compares his findings on Tandil with other studies of rural Argentina and with the large cities of Buenos Aires, Córdoba, and Rosario and suggests that integration as measured by marriage patterns seems to take place more rapidly in rural areas. Whether the "Tandil model" of rapid integration represents the basic model for all of Argentina is still an open question.

Tandil is a small city in the center of the province of Buenos Aires, some 220 miles southwest of the city of Buenos Aires.[1] It began as a military outpost on the frontier in 1823, and in the next forty years Indian invasions and civil strife hampered its development. But after 1860, Tandil finally began a process of sustained growth that transformed it by the 1870s into a commercial center of regional importance. As almost everywhere else in the pampas, this period of growth was marked by the arrival of numerous European immigrants.

In 1854, 1,207 women and 1,692 men lived in Tandil. Of them, only seventeen women and 162 men were foreigners. By 1869, 9 percent of the 2,190 women and 22 percent of the 2,680 men had been born outside Argentina, mainly in Europe. This trend continued at least up to the 1920s. By 1895 there were 15,000 inhabitants in Tandil, with 41 percent of the men and 23 percent of the women foreign born. By the Third National Census in 1914, of the 34,000 people who lived in Tandil, 37 percent had been born abroad. This figure translates into 44 percent of the men and 26 percent of the women being foreign born.

Two facts become apparent from these data. First was the growing importance of foreign immigration and its impact on population growth. In this respect, it must be remembered that, as in the United States, children born to immigrants in Argentina are considered citizens, and that these data include population of all ages. Thus, as there were a small number of children among immigrants, if we consider only the adult population, the proportion of foreigners was much higher. The second fact to be considered is the strong masculinity rate of the immigrant population. In spite of Tandil's being a frontier town, natives showed a considerable balance between the sexes, but the masculinity rate for immigrants (the number of males per 100 females) fluctuated above 230 during this period.

Where did these immigrants come from? The main countries of origin were the same as in Argentina as a whole, though not the rhythm of arrivals. The largest number came from Spain up to 1870, but between that date and the turn of the century, Italians were the most numerous group. In the 1900s, Spain again provided the greater contingent of immigrants. The third largest group consisted of the French, to a large extent Basques, but this migration declined after 1890. One particularity of Tandil was the small influx of Danish migrants. Even though their numbers were modest, their presence in the region was clearly felt, since they behaved as a distinct community.[2] Table 1 shows the distribution of European immigrants to Tandil by their sex and nationality of birth.

Table 1. European Population by Sex and Origin, Tandil (1869, 1881, 1895, and 1914)

| | *Number of Persons* | | | | | | | |
| | *1869* | | *1881* | | *1895* | | *1914* | |
	Male	*Female*	*Male*	*Female*	*Male*	*Female*	*Male*	*Female*
Italian	84	24	517	174	1443	599	3,006	1,290
Spanish	197	56	552	222	929	411	3,886	1,708
French	159	59	357	93	478	231	403	236
Others	94	33	325	133	641	283	1,022	333

Sources: 1869, 1895, and 1914 National Censuses and 1881 Provincial Census.

Beyond these numbers, what was this frontier community really like? Leaving aside the language, clothing, and local customs, its evolution was not unlike that of many frontier towns of the nineteenth century in other regions of the world, including the United States a few decades earlier. In the small town, we find merchants, services (transport, primitive financial institutions, education, health), artisans, and specialized workers. Near the town small farmers produced for the local market. The state bureau-cracy was minimal. Small businessmen met local demands (flour millers, brick makers, cigarette makers, liquor distillers). After 1890 a stone quarry industry grew that served wider markets. This and other developments were made possible, as in many frontier areas, by the arrival of the rail-way in 1882.

There are two important differences between the settlement of Tandil and the settlement of the American West. On the one hand, in Tandil the agrarian structure was such that the concentration of property in a few hands was higher than in North America (except, perhaps, in regions such as Texas or other southwestern states), creating conditions for a higher proportion of salaried workers (peons and day workers) among the popu-lation. On the other hand, immigrants had a more prominent position in the social structure of Tandil than would be expected in a North American frontier town. Natives were a majority among the peons and day workers in Tandil as well as among the large landholders; foreigners predomi-nated as specialized workers, artisans, merchants, and farmers. In other words, Italians, Spaniards, French, Danes, and other small groups of Eu-ropean immigrants made up most of the middle class.

This fact does not imply that there were no poor Europeans in Tandil. By 1895, almost half the peons and day workers were immigrants. In the stone quarries, Italians and Austrians (many of the latter also Italian-speaking) worked long, hard hours for low wages, but these wages were still higher than those back home and allowed them to save money. Fig-ures from the 1895 census show, however, that while more than 60 per-cent of male workers in Tandil were foreign born, natives accounted for less than 20 percent in some of the typical middle-class occupations. Na-tives predominated at each end of the social hierarchy, being over 50 per-cent of the wealthier landowners and of the less fortunate classes.[3]

In present-day Tandil there are nearly 100,000 persons living in the city, almost all of them native born. Even though there has been consider-able movement of population, we may easily identify surnames that have been there from the late nineteenth century. It would be useless, however, to look for an ethnic element. Even families who have persisted in the city for several generations and whose surnames are ostensibly immigrant maintain only a blurred memory of their relation to an immigrant com-munity. All of them, except perhaps for a few Danish descendants, would define themselves as "unhyphenated" Argentines—not Italian-Argentines, or Hispano-Argentines, but simply Argentines. Material traces of the im-migrant communities may still be found: the Spanish Theater, the Italian Hospital, or streets with several old buildings of Basque stores and ho-tels—El Bilbaino, El Viscayno, the Kaiku Hotel. But those same places (which are slowly disappearing, the victims of urban modernization) are now used by Argentines of varied origin.

What has happened? In contrast to immigrants arriving in other areas of the world, did those who went to Tandil abandon their previous identity to blend into the culture of their new homeland? Evidence of the existence of ethnic institutions and neighborhoods suggests that it has not been that simple. Rather, it seems that at some moment during the twentieth century, a process of fusion took place, which transformed the variegated mass of immigrants into present-day Argentines.[4]

In the following pages we shall try to take a closer look at some aspects of this process. The formation of couples and households is only one aspect of the complex phenomenon of ethnic interrelations between immigrants of different origins and Argentines of older stock, but it is an important one. First, it is important because the formation of a couple, or even the choice of a temporary house partner, is the result of a decision that implies a certain ethnic stance. To what degree did the immigrants in Tandil marry within their own group (endogamy) or outside it (exogamy)? Did they marry Argentines or immigrants from other countries? What factors influenced their decisions—the numbers available of the opposite sex? Old World traditions? Their new community life? Second, whatever the reasons, these decisions have important consequences for the integration process. If foreigners generally married within their own group, their integration into the Argentine society might have been less than if they had married natives. And it is more likely that their children will be brought up within their Old World ethnic heritage.

We will center our analysis of marriages and households on Tandil. Although we do not imply that Tandil is an adequate representative of the varied situations that we may find in Argentina, it is a good point of reference for comparisons. The early students of immigration to Argentina, based on the modernization theory, had supposed that integration began in the larger cities, particularly in Buenos Aires.[5] Later research has shown that the problem is more complex. Perhaps smaller, newer, more open areas, such as the frontier regions that were fully incorporated into the life of the nation only in the second half of the nineteenth century, fostered a more rapid process of social and cultural syncretism. In any case, at the end of this chapter we will compare the information we have on Tandil with that of other regions of Argentina. Similarities and contrasts will suggest some possible explanations for the process of integration in Tandil in particular and in Argentina in general.

To close this introduction, a few words on the historiography on this subject are necessary. Scholars writing the pioneer works of the 1960s, based on the evidence of what seemed to them the syncretic culture of their time, assumed a rapid integration of the immigrants. North American scholars, and particularly Samuel Baily, based on the experience of U.S. historiography on ethnicity in immigration to North America, began to reassess the importance of this phenomenon in mass migration to Argentina. Since then, much progress has been made on the subject. But, as frequently happens in social research, we are far from reaching unanimous agreement. As we shall see, the web of social relations in which new couples were formed was far more complex than the simple relationship between immigrants and natives.

Marriage Patterns in Tandil

As we have noted, one of the characteristics of the population of Tandil was a high masculinity rate, mainly due to the high adult male component in the European migrations. In our earlier work on marriage patterns in Tandil we have argued that we could reasonably expect immigrants to prefer to form couples with persons of their same stock. And in general, most studies of marriage patterns for Argentina and other places in the world tend to confirm this view. The high masculinity rate and these preferences are the starting point in explaining the information found in Table 2.

Table 2. Endogamy in Tandil, 1865–1914

	1865–1879	*1880–1895*	*1896–1914*
Argentines (index)	0.62	0.57	0.40
Male endogamy (%)	97	93	89
Female endogamy (%)	81	65	56
Italians (index)	0.66	0.70	0.51
Male endogamy (%)	52	59	44
Female endogamy (%)	90	94	74
Spaniards (index)	0.59	0.46	0.49
Male endogamy (%)	44	48	45
Female endogamy (%)	76	62	74
French (index)	0.53	0.46	0.30
Male endogamy (%)	43	41	25
Female endogamy (%)	71	63	43

Source: Based on marriages registered in the Parishes and Civil Register of Tandil between 1864 and 1895, a total of 2,885 cases, and a random sample of 1,331 cases between that year and 1914. For more detail see E. Míguez, M. Argeri, H. Otero, and M. Bjerg, "Hasta que la Argentina nos una: Reconsiderando las pautas matrimoniales de los inmigrantes, el crisol de razas y el pluralismo cultural," *Hispanic American Historical Review* 71 (1991): 794.

Let us elaborate on these statistics. The endogamy index is a measure built by demographers that expresses the proportion between certain types of marriages and the possibilities of these marriages happening by mere chance. Zero indicates a totally accidental distribution, and, as we come closer to the number 1, a higher endogamy rate is indicated. The problem with this index, leaving aside its statistical limitations,[6] is that it presents in a single measure the behavior of both males and females, which, as may be seen in the percentages described in the table, was quite different. Therefore, we offer both the index and simple percentages in Table 2. Percentages have the problem that they obscure the possibilities of endogamy taking place by mere chance, due to the size of immigrant communities. In large immigrant groups a sizable number of endogamous marriages is to be expected by mere chance and thus is less meaningful than in a small immigrant group. We have to keep this warning in mind to interpret the statistics.

Exogamy by Argentine males was rare (see Table 2). In contrast, it was frequent and became increasingly so among Argentine females, and it was not oriented toward any particular immigrant community. In fact, this exogamy by Argentine women was only the other side of the coin of the existence of a large population of foreign men of different nationalities. In the vast majority of cases, when foreign men married women outside their own nationality, they married Argentines. There were some exceptions, such as some Frenchmen who married Spanish females. But in these cases, nationality masked the cultural continuity across European borders. For example, Basques were marrying individuals from either side of the French-Spanish border.[7] The exogamy of immigrants with those of a different national origin (say, French Basques with non-Basque Spaniards or, the most frequent case due to the size of immigrant communities, Spaniards and Italians) was very small and similar to the exogamy of native men (less than 10 percent). Although they were not very frequent, these would be the more meaningful exogamic behaviors because they are not explained by the composition of the population. Marriages between foreign men and native women may be attributed to a large extent, at least from the male point of view, to the scarcity of females of the same origin.

The strong downward trend of the endogamy *index* among Argentines reflects, apart from some statistical problems, their relative loss of weight in the local population. If we look at endogamy *percentages*, these also tended to fall, but mostly because of the behavior of the Argentine women. Among Argentine men, endogamy remained high, but it was very low among Argentine women, particularly after 1880. (It must be remembered that a high percentage should be expected by the mere composition of population: there was a high percentage of Argentine men).

For Italians, we start with a high endogamy rate, which became even higher with the increase in the migrant flow from Italy. It decreased significantly when the current of Italian immigration lost ground in favor of Spaniards. Among the latter, the general trend was somewhat lower, but it also paralleled the intensity of immigrant arrivals: endogamy was higher when immigration from that particular origin was at its peak. The French were the least endogamic group, partly because they were the smallest of the communities under scrutiny. Moreover, endogamy tended to fall with the decrease of new arrivals from France.

These analyses allow us to draw certain conclusions about the marriage patterns of the larger immigrant communities. First, endogamy was high, having as its main limitation the demographic structure of the communities. Second, the larger the immigrant group, the stronger its endogamy (sometimes called the *stock effect*). Third, endogamy was stronger in the communities in which the arrival of new immigrants was still strong, and less so when the flow became weaker. Obviously, the recent arrivals kept a closer relationship to their nation of origin and had weaker links with the local society. We must, however, be careful about these generalizations, for each migrant community had its own peculiarities.

Our table does not include information on the marriage pattern of the Danes because the available data are not fully comparable with those of the larger ethnic groups. But this group shows very interesting behavior and introduces another element that affects endogamy. Even though it was a relatively small community, in the nineteenth century, Danes in Tandil were almost absolutely endogamous, independent of variations in the immigrant flow. And even though the masculinity rate of Danes was high, endogamy was prevalent not only for women but also for men. Thus, many Danish men never married rather than choose a woman with a different ethnic background. Out of seventy-seven Danish women who married in Tandil between 1867 and 1895, seventy-one did so with Danish men, five with other northern Europeans, and the remaining one with an Argentine of Danish origin. Out of eighty-eight men who married in that period, one married a Frenchwoman, another an Argentine daughter of Argentines, twelve married Argentine daughters of Danes, seventy-one married Danish folk, and three did so with other northern Europeans.[8]

Two factors must be pointed out in this case. One, obviously, was religion. The Danes were a small Protestant community in the midst of a vast Catholic population. The other, in a way related to the first, was the weight of community life. There was strong sociability among the Danes centered on the Lutheran church.[9] After 1910, there was a small increase in the number of marriages outside the community, but at least up to the 1930s the marriage patterns were very different from those of the other immigrant groups.

The Formation of New Couples

To proceed with our analysis, there is another question we need to consider. How were new couples formed in Tandil in that period? We tend to suppose that marriages originated in the free choice of the spouses—a choice based on "love" or convenience. Was this actually the case in Tandil a century ago? We do not have enough knowledge to give a definitive answer to this question, but it was more complex than we may suppose. Even though romantic love played an increasingly important role in the selection of a partner, it was far from always being the determining factor.[10] Various questions suggest themselves. What was the relation between the immigrants and the old society when it came time to choose a mate? What role did those in the new community play? What were the roles of the family and friends? Did the act of migration change the outlook of the immigrants with regard to the selection of a mate?

Among the elite until well into the twentieth century, marriage was decided on the grounds of social strategy and the preservation of family wealth. The choice of a spouse was based on the preservation of the social position and patrimony of the family. But these considerations hardly ever affected immigrants, who rarely arrived at these social heights. At the other end of the social scale, life for the poorer and less educated was more spontaneous. Couples were formed according to the will and necessity of the partners at the moment, most frequently without formal sanctions from the Church or the Civil Register. The duration of these "consensual unions," as they were called, was very variable.[11] However, consensual unions were not the most frequent pattern for immigrants and their descendants. Since there was no registration of these informal unions, the only way to measure them is through their offspring, who were considered "illegitimate." We know that almost all children declared "illegitimate" by their mothers had been born to creole (native Argentine) women. It is not the same with fathers, since informal unions were not uncommon for immigrant males. On occasion, the marriage of an immigrant with an Argentine woman was the legitimization of a consensual union and was succeeded by the recognition of several children.

The following, written and published in the 1890s, sums up what some families were experiencing:

> "But Eleuterio, Susanita is the fifth of your daughters to get married, and you are still touchy about it! . . . What is it that you want?"
>
> "Heavens, Ramona, what do you mean? Do you think that I, of pure creole stock, will be happy when my daughters marry in this way? . . . First began Julia with a German boy [. . .] Petrona with an Italian, Antonia with a Portuguese, Eulogia with an English boy, and now Susana brings a Frenchman." [12]

The text suggests that its author, José Alvarez, a genre writer sensitive to social situations, considered it reasonable for the daughters of an Argentine of old stock to choose their husbands without their father's advice and also, even allowing for satiric exaggeration, to choose immigrants. Given the social and demographic structure of the time, these choices were hardly surprising. For native women, marrying a foreigner could well mean social advancement. Given the unbalanced distribution of population by sex, even transcultural unions could be attractive to men who had been in the country for several years and who otherwise would remain bachelors.

Statistics show that these cases of intermarriage were frequent, though not the majority. The experience of a Gallego immigrant living in Tandil, Manuel Suárez Martínez, follows a different path (see Story 2, this volume). The social network through which Manuel met his wife shows another pattern. Suárez Martínez was a storekeeper. Having gone to Buenos Aires on business, he paid a visit to Andrea Machado, the daughter of Benito Machado, an army officer and strongman in Tandil, who was living in Buenos Aires. Andrea was married to José Puente, whose brother Gumercindo was married to a Spanish woman, Concepción García. On the occasion, Manuel met Concepción's father, Don Miguel, and his daughters, Concepción's sisters. One of them, Michaela, would become Manuel's wife.

There are some other interesting details. Both Suárez Martínez and Don Miguel García had been born in Galicia and had lived in Cádiz for a long time before emigrating. In fact, all of Don Miguel's daughters were from Andalucía. Moreover, Gumercindo Puente and Francisco Correa (married to another of the García sisters) were both merchants as was Manuel; it is also very likely that Don Miguel himself was a merchant.[13] Another of the García sisters was married to a certain Mairini, the captain of a merchant ship; and the younger of the sisters, Pepa, wed years later an old business partner of Suárez Martínez, Andrés Piñero, also a Spaniard. This was obviously a network of merchants. While there was a strong cultural affinity between Manuel and his father-in-law, both Gallegos who had emigrated to Argentina through Cádiz, the contact between them actually took place through their connection to a creole woman, Andrea Machado.[14]

Another case, this time of immigrants living in Buenos Aires, shows a certain parallel to Manuel's. Oreste Sola arrived in Argentina in 1901 from Valdengo, a small town near Biella, in the Piedmont in Italy (see Story 1, this volume). In 1908 he married Corinna Chiocchetti from Gaglianico, also near Biella. From the correspondence between Oreste and his parents we know that his family had no role in the formation of the couple. We do not know whether Corinna's family had any part, but her parents still lived in Gaglianico. There was a certain tension in the correspondence of that period regarding whether Oreste's parents would approve of the match. Their attitude, however, seems "modern": they declared that they accepted Corinna as their daughter, even though they never got to meet her. On the other hand, when Oreste first told his parents that he planned to get married, he did not tell them the name of the girl—probably as a self-conscious affirmation of his independence. However, the social networks across the Atlantic allowed the parents to find out who the girl was before Oreste was prepared to tell them. This lapse upset Oreste. After the wedding, the parents got together in Biella, but they would never see their son and daughter again. Unfortunately, due to Oreste's reticence, we do not know how the couple met. However, we may suppose that they met each other in the context of the social relations that Oreste regularly kept with other immigrants from the Biella area.[15]

Returning to Tandil, on this occasion with a Danish example, we find a different situation. A successful immigrant, Juan Fugl, returned for a visit to Denmark where he met Dorothy, who was to become his wife. The couple married and went back to Argentina. Dorothy was actually Fugl's niece, but it seems that the family played no part in the formation of the couple, other than being the context in which the two met. In fact, Fugl's brother and sister-in-law seemed to have opposed the marriage, not primarily because of the couple's blood ties but because Dorothy was the younger daughter. According to Danish custom, she was supposed to remain single to look after her parents in their old age.[16]

Thus, endogamic marriages could take place in the framework of the immigrants' continuing social relations across the Atlantic. In Fugl's case, it was due to his own initiative. On other occasions, when the immigrant decided to wed, he would tell his family back home, and they would arrange the marriage in the local village. If possible, he would return to see his family, meet his future partner, and marry her before going back to his adopted land. More commonly, the bride traveled to meet her husband, usually under the oversight of friends of her family who had migrated earlier to the same region. A frequent pattern was one where the marriage had been arranged before the departure of the male emigrant from his country of origin; the woman would join her future husband once he was well established in his new country. This pattern is sometimes called migration by stages.

An important question regarding how immigrant couples were formed concerns the issue of what we call "regional endogamy." To what degree did immigrants from the same region in the country of origin marry each other? There are really two sources. First, transatlantic relations linked immigrants to their community or to a larger region of origin. Most likely, a high proportion of marriages of migrants from the same area was due to a family strategy of migration by stages, as mentioned above. This stage migration was also frequent with marriages that had taken place in Europe, on occasion with several children migrating in the second stage together with their mother (family reunions).

A second source of regional endogamy was the formation of couples in the context of communities in the New World of migrants from the same region in the country of origin, as in the case of the Solas. We know that immigrants who came from the same "social space"[17] tended to group together in neighborhoods and maintain an intense social life among themselves, as shown by the case of Agnonese studied by R. Gandolfo.[18] Thus, they built a social space even in the heart of a large city, or even of a small town such as Tandil.[19] We also know that a high proportion of brides and grooms lived within a short distance in their new country.[20] Thus, the social space of a local ethnic community was frequently the context in which new couples were formed.

Although these situations were not unusual, it is difficult to determine exactly how frequent or representative they were. The data in Table 3 provide some insight into how couples were formed by examining the closeness of the marriage partners with regard to place of origin. Were the partners from the same town, the same province, the same region of the country, or were they just fellow countrymen? The data in Table 3 show that over half of the marriages between immigrants from the same country of origin came from the same community or communities very close to each other, that is, town and province. This finding is relevant because it allows us to distinguish different situations in couple formation. First, we find in the new area very strong rebuilding of the primary

Table 3. Regional Endogamy, Tandil, 1896–1914 (Danes 1889–1930)

	Town* %	Province %	Region %	Area %	Country %	Cases No.
Foreigners	22.4	34.9	13.5	n.a.	29.2	281
Spanish	23.1	36.6	16.0	n.a.	28.0	109
Italians	21.1	25.7	19.3	25.7	8.3	134
Danish	21.9	36.5	17.0	24.3	0	82

Source: E. Míguez, M. Argeri, H. Otero, and M. Bjerg, "Hasta que la Argentina nos una: Reconsiderando las pautas matrimoniales de los inmigrantes, el crisol de razas y el pluralismo cultural," *Hispanic American Historical Review* 71 (1991): 801, except for the Danes, taken from María Mónica Bjerg, "Dinamarca bajo la Cruz del Sur: Asentamientos daneses en el centro-sur de la provincia de Buenos Aires, 1850–1930" (Ph.D., Universidad de Buenos Aires, 1994), 264.

*"Town" refers to marriages of people coming from the same town, "Province" from the same province, and so forth. "Area" refers to the great cultural areas such as north, central, and southern Italy. Data are organized to indicate the closest possible propinquity of the two marriage partners. Thus, those included in "Town" are not included in "Province," etc. "Foreigners" refers to a combined total of all foreigners.

communities of origin. Marriages between those from the same community or close communities testify to this fact. Second, we find marriages between partners based on a new social reference point: their national or regional identity. Unlike that in their country of origin, immigrants in the New World were surrounded by immigrants from other nations as well as by those from different regions of their own country of origin. Many of them thus formed new ethnic social links, based on a national (for example, Italian) or regional (north Italian or more, likely, Ligurian or Piedmontese) identity. Considered in this way, the data suggest that over half of nationally endogamous marriages were due to the continuity of primary social links, whereas a little more than 40 percent suggest the construction of new relationships based on national or regional identity.

Research carried out by Hernán Otero permits us a closer look at this question. Otero has studied the effect of chain migration on the life of the immigrant in his new country, including the formation of a couple. He concludes that those who migrated together with other members of the family tend to be more endogamous than those who migrate in a more solitary way. Moreover, his study shows the persistence of practices of family alliances after migration. Among the Basques in France, multiple marriages (say, the marriage of two sisters with two brothers) were frequent. This practice may also be found among French-Basque immigrants in Tandil.[21]

Marriage and Integration

At this point, there is another question we have to tackle. How did these different ways in which couples were formed relate to the process of social integration of immigrants? The two classical models on this question tend to oversimplify the problem. One model assumes the continuity in the new society of the immigrant's cultural identity developed in his place of origin. This model predicts the formation of a multicultural society in the new land. The other theory, frequently called the "melting pot," assumes the integration of immigrants into a dominant local culture—or an Argentine variation of this theory: the fusion of the different cultures of immigrants into a syncretic local culture, which also resulted in a greater homogeneity in the emerging local culture. In these views, endogamy was a sign of the prevalence of cultural continuity, and exogamy was a mark of integration or syncretism. Our analysis suggests that the situation was more complex than that.

For the vast majority of immigrants, with the exception of some of the members of the ethnic elite, there is no evidence that the definition of their own ethnic social territory was something that worried them. Most likely, their problems were more real and concrete. Were they actually achieving the economic goals that had brought them to Argentina? Were they comfortable, surrounded by strangers (or new acquaintances), or had they found a group of kin and fellow countrymen in their new setting? Were men looking forward to returning home some day? In this case, could they endure a life of relative solitude, an occasional visit to a brothel, letters to the family, and substantial savings? Or did they prefer to look for a consort and raise a family, realizing that this act drove them farther away from their homeland?

The drama for the immigrant was not a choice between cultural preservation and integration but rather one of smaller, more trivial, and daily decisions. On Saturday night, would he visit with his relatives or go to a dance with his workmates? Very often, the decisions were easy. If relatives and *paesani*[22] surrounded him, he would spend his free time with them. If not, he would have to look for new friends and other forms of sociability, either with people from the same country of origin or Argentines or immigrants from other countries. Finally, if a couple fell in love, it was likely that they would form a family in spite of other considerations.[23]

Thus, marriages did not emerge from strategies oriented toward preservation or cultural integration but were rather the result of the situation in which the immigrant lived. And, of course, marriage affected these conditions. For example, immigrants who wed and had children in Argentina were less likely to return home than those who remained single or who were already married when they migrated. What our information reflects, therefore, is primarily the context of sociability in which the immigrant lived—that is, whether his daily relations involved mainly his *paesani* or a different and new cultural context.

Recent sociology and anthropology findings have taught us to think of human beings not only as the intersections of great macro-social categories—class, nationality, religion—but also of concrete networks of interpersonal relationships. In most cases, these networks played a significant role in marital selection. They must have also played a fundamental role in the definition of social identity, which is our ultimate concern. The data we have presented suggest in an overly simplified way that nearly one-third of the immigrants who arrived in Tandil kept a significant part of their social life within the network of *paesani*, and an additional one-quarter built new relations with people of the same national origin. For the 40 percent who married Argentine women, we would overestimate integration if we argued that they did so because they had built new links of sociability with the local population. It is obvious that many of them, in spite of an exogamic marriage, largely due to the scarcity of women from their own cultural background, would preserve their identity and continue to socialize with *paesani* and other people from their own nation. However, the decision to marry an Argentine shows a certain openness toward integration. Those who drastically opposed it—

such as the Danes—excluded marriage with natives as an alternative, even though the composition of the Danish population by sex was not more favorable than in other communities. On the other hand, sharing daily life with an Argentine woman certainly favored the adaptation of both spouses to the emerging syncretic society, an authentic plural culture.[24] Fortunately, there was also room for the behavior of immigrants who did not conform to any of these typical patterns.

The Second Generation

The marital behavior of immigrants is a rather limited indicator in the study of the process of social integration. It may well be assumed that for someone who was born and raised in a particular cultural context, it is only natural to look for a companion with the same or similar background. What occurs with the second generation is far more revealing of relations between immigrants and the host society. If the network of local ethnic relations or the construction of national or regional ethnic relations in the new society predominates, the second generation will be raised in a social and cultural milieu that will favor endogamic marriages. Alternatively, if the social bonds and the cultural identities of the second generation develop in the context of the new syncretic culture, their marital choice may not correspond to the ethnicity of their parents.

Another factor that has a strong effect on this situation is the ethnic character of neighborhoods. We know that it is very likely that couples will form in a very limited spatial context. It is easy to imagine that the son of an Italian immigrant brought up in a Little Italy in San Francisco or New York would most likely become engaged to marry the daughter of another Italian immigrant.[25] However, it is enough to take a quick look at the Manuscript Census Schedule of Tandil to realize that, with the exception of the granite quarries—mostly worked by northern Italians and Montenegros from mining regions in Europe—there were no neighborhoods in Tandil where immigrants from a certain region predominated. Overall, Tandil followed a general pattern in Argentina where immigrant concentrations with this degree of density were not frequent.

Hernán Otero and Adela Pellegrino's chapter in this book, and other work by Samuel Baily and José Moya on Buenos Aires, tend to show that there were ethnic neighborhoods, but these neighborhoods were defined by the residence of a certain number of *paesani* in the same quarter rather than by the prevalence of any immigrant group in one part of the city.[26] In fact, immigrant groups were rarely more than a relatively small percentage of the total population of any neighborhood. Thus, the descendants of immigrants had as neighbors other young people of varied origin as well as the sons and daughters of their parents' *paesani*.

How did this and other factors influence the choice of spouses in the second generation? It is difficult to know, but we do have some data on the marriage pattern of the second generation for Tandil for the late nineteenth and early twentieth centuries. The information on the nineteenth century (1876–1895) is not very rich, for the number of Argentines with foreign parents who were married in that period was too small to allow a useful analysis. The data for the twentieth century begin in 1913 and are included in Tables 4 and 5, which explore the degree to which second-generation Argentines of foreign descent married partners from the same nationality as at least one of their parents.

Table 4. Marriage Patterns of Argentines of Foreign Descent, According to Partner's Ethnic Heritage, Tandil, 1913–1920

| | *Second-Generation Argentine Husbands* | | |
	Wife Same Heritage	*Wife Not Same Heritage*	
Husband's Ethnic Heritage			**Total**
Italian	44.8	55.3	100%* (N=172)
Spanish	41.5	58.4	100% (N=154)
Foreign	43.8	56.2	100% (N=416)
	Second-Generation Argentine Wives		
	Husband Same Heritage	*Husband Not Same Heritage*	
Wife's Ethnic Heritage			**Total**
Italian	48.8	51.1	100%* (N=272)
Spanish	51.6	48.4	100% (N=260)
Foreign	44.8	55.2	100% (N=726)

Source: E. Míguez, M. Argeri, H. Otero, and M. Bjerg, "Hasta que la Argentina nos una: Reconsiderando las pautas matrimoniales de los inmigrantes, el crisol de razas y el pluralismo cultural," *Hispanic American Historical Review* 71 (1991): 805.

NOTE: Argentine children of immigrants (second-generation Argentines) are grouped in three categories according to their ethnic heritage: Italian, Spanish, and Foreign (the latter includes Argentines of any other foreign descent). "Foreign" includes any second-generation husband (for the first half of the table) and second-generation wife (for the second half) who had at least one parent of foreign origin, including those of mixed origin, or who had a foreign father and a native mother. To discriminate between Argentines with one or both foreign parents made no significant difference in the outcomes (see table source). *Totals may not add to 100 percent due to rounding.

We find in Table 4 that for both sexes, marrying outside one's heritage ranged from 48.4 percent to 58.4 percent, with women marrying slightly more frequently within their own ethnic group than the men. For men, Italians were more likely to marry a partner of Italian descent, while among women, husbands of Spanish descent were more favored. However, endogamy does not seem particularly meaningful if we take into account the relatively high percentages that were to be expected because of the large number of Argentines of foreign descent who formed the young population of Tandil. By then, 60 percent of Argentine male grooms and 80 percent of the brides in Tandil had at least one foreign parent.

Table 5. Marriage Patterns of Argentines of Foreign Descent, According to Partner's Ethnic Heritage and Whether Partner was Argentine or Foreign, Tandil, 1913–1920

	Second-Generation Argentine Husbands				
	Argentine Wife		*Foreign Wife*		
Husband's Ethnic Heritage	*Same Ethnic Heritage*	*Not Same Heritage*	*Same Ethnic Heritage*	*Not Same Heritage*	*Total*
Italian	40.1	48.3	4.7	7.0	100% (N=172)
Spanish	34.4	55.2	7.1	3.2	100% (N=154)
Foreign	37.3	49.0	6.5	7.2	100% (N=416)
	Second-Generation Argentine Wives				
	Argentine Husband		*Foreign Husband*		
Wife's Ethnic Heritage	*Same Ethnic Heritage*	*Not Same Heritage*	*Same Ethnic Heritage*	*Not Same Heritage*	*Total*
Italian	25.3	27.2	23.5	23.9	100% (N=272)
Spanish	20.4	36.5	31.2	11.9	100% (N=260)
Foreign	21.4	35.1	23.4	20.1	100% (N=726)

Source: E. Míguez, M. Argeri, H. Otero, and M. Bjerg, "Hasta que la Argentina nos una: Reconsiderando las pautas matrimoniales de los inmigrantes, el crisol de razas y el pluralismo cultural," *Hispanic American Historical Review* 71 (1991): 805.
NOTE: See Table 4.

However, when we separate out the marriages of the second-generation Argentines with foreign immigrants of the same or different heritage, we find an interesting phenomenon. There were few marriages between second-generation Argentine men of foreign descent and first-generation foreign women of the same nationality as the men's foreign parents. This pattern, by contrast, was much more frequent among the daughters of immigrants, that is, Argentine daughters would marry immigrant men of the same nationality as the women's parents. This finding for men reinforces the idea that nationality played a minimal role in the selection of spouse by this group.

On the female side, the situation is more varied. Considering only marriages between Argentines, second-generation endogamy is hardly more visible than among men and quite low when considering that a certain percentage was bound to take place by mere chance. By contrast, marriages with foreigners were quite frequent, be it with immigrants of the same nationality as the women's fathers or of a different national origin. In the first case, this may be attributed to the search for cultural homogeneity by the immigrant men and by the immigrant parents of the Argentine women and also to the persistence of pre-migration relations between the immigrant men—or their families—and their in-laws before migrating. But the marriages with foreigners of a different nationality show that unions between foreigners and natives cannot always be explained as masking cultural endogamy. Finally, the higher percentage of marriages of the daughters of Spaniards with Spanish men than in other groups of origin seems related to the size of Spanish migration in that period. In short, the general view derived from Table 5 is that endogamy related to the origin of parents was far less significant among the Argentine-born children than it had been for their parents' generation.

This information becomes more relevant when compared to what happened with some of the smaller immigrant groups. Otero's studies on the French show how in this relatively small community the second generation was more exogamic than in the immigrant population as a whole: 90 percent of males and 50 percent of females married Argentines, who in only 21 percent and 24 percent of the cases had French ancestors. Of the remaining 50 percent of women who married immigrants, less than one-half married Frenchmen.[27] At the opposite end, María Monica Bjerg's study of the Danes shows an authentic second-generation endogamy: 59 percent of Danish-Argentine men married Danish-Argentine women; and 15 percent, new Danish immigrants. For the women 51 percent of the Argentine daughters of Danish immigrants married Danish immigrants; and another 31 percent, Danish-Argentine men. These statistics mean that only 18 percent of the second-generation Danish-Argentine women and 26 percent of the men married outside their community in spite of its being small.[28]

If we return to our starting point, we begin to find certain answers. Among immigrants, the search for cultural continuity was very noticeable, but it seems to a large extent based on the continuity of the local social networks from before migration rather than on the construction of a new macro-social identity based on the nation of origin. It is not that this collective identity did not exist; the immigrant elite played an active role in trying to develop it. It seems, however, to have affected only a small part of the immigrant community. The second generation, which diverges considerably in its ethnic behavior, is witness to this process. Without doubt, Argentine public schools were an important factor that favored the formation of a syncretic culture. Beginning in the 1880s, but particularly from the beginning of the past century, the state sought to make public schools an instrument of "Argentinization."[29] Simultaneously, less consciously—but most likely, more effectively—forces were creating a new culture. Denuded from its ethnic content, this new syncretic atmosphere was favorable for the emergence of a new identity. It was in this context that the effort carried out by the state schools to implant the symbols of the new nation had a better chance to prosper.

This process was not free of obstructions. To mention only the most obvious one, the leaders of ethnic communities created their own schools. The language, history, and geography of the motherland were taught there in an effort to prolong the national identity of origin in the second generation. The Danish School, for example, seems to have succeeded in this goal. In the other communities of immigrants in Tandil, only a small minority attended ethnic schools. On the other hand, identity seems to have been based more often in the network of primary micro-social personal relationships than in the public and symbolic spheres in which the elite acted. For many members of the second generation, the reference to a local *paese* that they could not even imagine as the core of their identity was not a likely alternative. Some may have been rallied by the militant elites to adopt a "national" identity such as Italian-Argentine, Spanish-Argentine, or simply Danish. But judging by the selection of spouses of the second-generation Argentines of Tandil, most of them did not seem conditioned by their parents' ethnicity.

Households and Singles

In the process of integration of modern Argentina, the formation of a family plays a significant role in part because it is the matrix in which the new generation is molded. To understand turn-of-the-century Tandil it is also necessary to look at the vast number of people who did not marry. With this in mind, we have carried out a study of the single population of Tandil that provides some interesting information, which is presented in Table 6.[30]

The data in this table report on the characteristics of households in which single people lived. As may be seen, the larger group of Argentine single men resided together with other men who are similarly employed, particularly peons and day workers, but they also shared dwellings with single workers from other occupations. There were also many young people living with their parents as well as a significant number of consensual unions. What is notable is how many immigrants of the same nationality lived together in shared houses. In some cases, these groupings must have followed from the migration process. They were most likely cases of relatives or friends migrating together or following each other in chain migration.

Table 6. Number of Households Containing Single Persons Aged 15 or Older, Tandil, 1895 (Organized by Nationality of the Single Individual)

| | Males | | | | | |
	Argentine	Italian	Spanish	French	Danish	Total
Household Type						
Where Singles Lived						
No relation identified	21	3	4	1	1	30
Family	20	7	1	1	0	29
Ethnic context	n.r.**	20	11	5	4	40
Occupational context	27	4	8	4	0	43
Consensual couples*	9	1	2	2	0	14
Total	**77**	**35**	**26**	**13**	**5**	**156**

| | Females | | | | | |
	Argentine	Italian	Spanish	French	Danish	Total
Household Type						
Where Singles Lived						
No relation identified	23	1	0	0	0	24
Family	47	3	4	1	1	56
Ethnic context	n.r.**	0	3	1	1	5
Occupational context	9	2	1	1	0	13
Consensual couples*	42	4	0	0	0	46
Total	**121**	**10**	**8**	**3**	**2**	**144**

Source: Household reconstruction based on a sample of the 1895 National Census manuscript schedules.
*Consensual couples are not clearly registered as such in the schedules, but it is possible to infer them from the information on the schedules, through the sex and ages of people living together and through the number of consensual unions that is indicated in a summary at the end of each schedule leaflet.
**Not relevant.

In other cases, the households included people of a different origin. For example, Manuel Rodriguez, a 30-year-old Spaniard from La Coruña, lived together with Antonio Gonzales, a 20-year-old man from Burgos,[31] and a 32-year-old Italian, José Caroni. As may be seen, the ethnic behavior of the single men in the formation of their households was not so different from those who married. In this period, in which Italians were at the peak of their migration cycle, they were the most endogamous of the larger migration groups. At the same time, Italians lived together with other single men of the same origin more frequently than with any other group. Spaniards seemed somewhat more integrated at that moment, and the French even more so.

Single women generally lived with a family, including consensual unions. In the few cases where women of the same occupation lived together, it was always as a collection of housemaids. Generally the permanency of single women in their parents' household up to a considerable age was the norm. In one extreme situation, 50-year-old Josefa Rodríguez lived with some of her twelve children (the products of a long consensual union or of several successive couplings?) and her mother and father (aged 101 and 89 years, respectively). Consensual unions were more frequent between Argentine men and women, but there are also several cases of Argentine women living with foreign men.

Tandil and Argentina

The large number of studies of social behavior in Tandil allows us to analyze the process of integration of immigrants in this corner of the province of Buenos Aires. It may now be useful to see to what extent what took place in this small town and its surrounding rural area was similar to what occurred in other places on the Pampa, the central area of Argentina surrounding Buenos Aires. This comparison will show some very interesting results, although it is not always possible to draw a clear conclusion.

In general, endogamy was stronger in the larger communities of foreigners—Italian and Spanish—and less so in the smaller ones—French and British. It was also stronger when the migration flow from a particular area was at its peak; as migration subsided, so did endogamy. In all cases female endogamy was much higher than that of males, a fact that is hardly surprising given the high masculinity rate of immigrant populations. Necessarily, the Argentines behaved in the opposite way; women were particularly exogamic, whereas Argentine men rarely married foreign women. These findings are consistent with the sociological theory of endogamy, which is stronger in larger and growing communities and weaker in the smaller groups or in those that received fewer new immigrants. As we have seen for the Danes of Tandil and Necochea, there are other small communities with strong linguistic, cultural, and/or religious differences from the native society, such as the Albanian-speaking Italians of the city of Lujan or the German-speaking Russians of the province of La Pampa that seem to be closed communities.[32]

How strong was endogamy elsewhere? For Italians, for example, in the city of Buenos Aires, it was higher in the early period, before 1880 when Italian immigration increased, with percentages as high as 90 percent for females and 80 percent for men.[33] In the 1880s, when the Spanish community was growing in Buenos Aires, its male endogamy rate rose from 52 percent to 66 percent, whereas female endogamy remained near 75 percent, with the index growing from 0.5 to 0.7.[34]

For Italians, after the peak of 1871–1874 (84 percent for men, 93 percent for women), endogamy tended to fall consistently. It was 70 percent for men in the 1880s; 65 percent and 85 percent for men and women, respectively in the 1890s; 56 percent and 80 percent in the 1900s; and 50 percent and 75 percent in the 1910s. At the end of the period considered by both Ruth Seefeld and Samuel Baily (1918–1923), when the arrival of Italians was much lower than before World War I, endogamy was only 40 percent for men and 65 percent for women. Baily provides also the homogamy index that confirms the trend, from 0.7 in the 1880s to 0.44 by the 1920s. The trend for the Spaniards was quite different: it grew to reach 80 percent and 81 percent, respectively, for men and women in the 1910s, although it also began to fall after the war.

Although endogamy was quite strong among immigrants, there was, as we have seen, a certain number of foreign men, and a smaller number of women, who married women and men with an ethnic background different from their own. As in the case of Tandil, most of them were Argentine women and men, but exogamy between immigrants with different national origins was also growing. For Italian men, for example, it grew from 5 percent in 1882–1887 to 12.5 percent in 1918–1923, and for women it went from 6 percent to 10.5 percent during that same period.

Is it possible to draw conclusions from this comparison between Tandil and Buenos Aires? The relationship between the strength of the immigrant flow and the rates of endogamy are obvious in both cases. The importance of immigrant stock (the size of the immigrant community) is less clear. For example, whereas the percentage of Italians in the overall composition of the flow declined over time in Buenos Aires, the stock of the Italian population continued to increase in the city at least until 1910; and, in spite of this, endogamy was decreasing. This situation presents us with a different question. The growing trend of marriages between Italians and Argentines may be reflecting an increase of unions between foreigners and the Argentine descendants of immigrants of an older wave. One study tried to measure this for the Italian neighborhood of La Boca and found that it was so, but the results may not be generalized for the whole city, particularly because La Boca is probably the area of Buenos Aires with the strongest ethnic character.[35]

For Córdoba, the second largest city of Argentina, figures on Italians provided by Mark Szuchman do not diverge from those for Buenos Aires.[36] The results of Carina Silberstein's research on Italians and Spaniards in Rosario (the country's third most important city) are also not unlike those obtained for Buenos Aires.[37]

What happened in less populated areas more similar to Tandil? Sergio Maluendres has done some research in two rural areas, Guatrache and Trenel, of the province of La Pampa.[38] These areas include small towns and immigrant colonies. His study of Guatrache covers the period 1910–1939 and shows relatively low levels of endogamy, only partially compensated for by the marriage of Italian men with the Argentine daughters of their compatriots. "Real" endogamy (that is, including marriages with second-generation immigrants) is near 40 percent for Italians. At Trenel, Maluendres observes similar figures for Italian endogamy (40 percent for men and 65 percent for women) but higher ones for Spaniards. When he takes into consideration the second generation, endogamy at Trenel becomes much higher, since marriages of foreigners with the Argentine descendants of immigrants of the same nationality were very frequent.

In our study of Necochea, a rural area in the south of the province of Buenos Aires, Italian male endogamy was 54 percent in the 1890s and fell to 38 percent for 1904–1918. Female endogamy fell from 80 percent to 73 percent for that same period.[39] The endogamy index decreased from 0.58 in 1889–1903 to 0.46 for 1904–1918. In all these cases, as occurred also for the French and Spaniards, endogamy was less marked in Necochea than in the more "urban" area of Tandil. Another study of French and Spaniards, this time for the small city of Luján, near Buenos Aires, shows "real" endogamy growing among Spaniards from 31.9 percent in the 1880s to 52.8 percent in the 1910s, and decreasing from 62.3 percent to 38.1 percent for the French during the same years.[40] The overall level of endogamy for these groups as well as the trend, the difference between male and female endogamy, marriages of foreigners with sons and daughter of immigrants of the same origin, and regional endogamy are not unlike those of Tandil and Necochea.

Conclusion

We may conclude that endogamy was relatively strong everywhere for first-generation immigrants and that it became stronger when the immigration flow was at its peak. In Rosario, Tandil, and Necochea, for example, Italians arrived at a later date than they did to Buenos Aires; in the period when relatively more immigrants were arriving from Italy, endogamy was higher. After 1890–1900, the relative importance of the Italian inflow tended to decrease everywhere, and so did endogamy. In the case of the French, their endogamy in general was lower and tended to decrease everywhere as French immigration subsided. The opposite occurred with Spaniards. The Spanish inflow was a growing trend up to the 1910s, and the same occurred with endogamy. This relation between the number of arrivals and the rate of endogamy could be explained by a process of adaptation to the new society or, more likely, by the strong persistence during the early stages of immigration of traditional kin and folk relations of the old *paese*.[41] Part of it may also be explained by an age factor. Some of those marrying in an older migrant community may have arrived in Argentina as children, and, although they were formally foreigners, their situation was more similar to that of the second generation because they had been raised in their new country.

The evolution of endogamy in the larger cities does not seem to support the theory of "stock," that is, that the size of the immigrant community determined the endogamy of its members. Particularly in the case of Italians, we find that in spite of the growing numbers of immigrants of this origin almost everywhere, the percentages of endogamy tended to fall almost everywhere. But the comparison of rural and urban areas does support the stock theory. The results are particularly interesting, because the early studies, such as those of Mark Szuchman and Gino Germani based on modernization theory, assumed that the natural context for the melting pot would be large cities. It becomes clear now that in many smaller towns, integration was actually faster than in the larger urban centers. It is true that in other towns and rural areas, dominated by particular ethnic groups that formed separated colonies, integration was probably very slow, although little research has been carried out in these areas.[42] Overall, however, it seems safe to say that the research conducted up to the present suggests that small towns and rural areas fostered a higher rate of exogamy than the urban centers.

Were these rates of endogamy really high in relative terms? To begin, if we compare them with endogamy in the English-speaking nations of strong immigration (Australia, Canada, New Zealand, the United States), the Argentine rates seem somewhat lower,[43] but they were probably higher than in Brazil.[44] In another essay, we argued that for first-generation immigrants, endogamy could be considered natural and that only special circumstances, such as the masculinity rate or an exceptionally fast process of acculturation, could explain exogamy.[45] Undoubtedly, masculinity rates played an important role in determining marriage patterns in Argentina as they did in many other immigration nations.[46] Acculturation or, rather, as already argued, fusion, does not seem to have been as linear and fast as Germani and his followers thought. But it is quite likely that at least some of the exogamous marriages may be explained by the shortening of cultural distances between the main immigrant groups and the new Argentine generations.

Comparisons between Tandil and elsewhere are more difficult because less research has been done on this subject. Several works have analyzed marriages between foreign men and the daughters of their fellow immigrants (which were not infrequent).[47] But this pattern is different from that of the Argentine children of the immigrant generation. We do have some data, but they are far from conclusive. Mario Oporto and Nora Pagano show a 57 percent endogamy for La Boca in 1895, based only on thirty-five cases, and Maluendres shows 30 percent male and 59 percent female endogamy for Guatrache, but also with less than forty cases under scrutiny. These rates, as those we found for Tandil, are particularly low, especially if we consider that by the beginning of the twentieth century, the majority of Argentine children were born from foreign parents.[48] But other research has found higher second-generation endogamy rates that cannot be explained by mathematical probability. Silberstein shows an endogamy rate for sons and daughters of Italians and Spaniards in Rosario of over 80 percent, which is similar or even higher than that of the immigrants themselves.[49] In his work on Trenel, Maluendres also found much higher endogamy rates than those he had established for Guatrache.

As has been argued, much of the endogamy of immigrants is directly related to the social networks within which they led much of their daily social life. Other aspects of their lives, such as work, school, or commerce, were carried out in a broader context that fostered syncretism. But how strong was the construction of new identities related to the nation of origin? Second-generation endogamy may in some cases be the consequence of the prolongation of social networks into the second generation, but it also suggests the significance of national identities of origin for the second generation. Except for particular groups such as the Danes, Tandil seems to have been a world of strong integration, in which ethnic institutions tended to lose their ethnic character or disappear with the deaths of the first generation. There are similar situations in other places in Argentina, but there are also studies that show a very different behavior, particularly in the meaningful second generation. Thus, whether the "Tandil model" of integration with its variations[50] can be taken or not as the basic model for the whole of Argentina is still an open question.

Notes

1. In fact, the same name is used for the city and its surrounding *partido* (county). The data in this paper always refer to the *partido* unless stated otherwise. Throughout the period under consideration the population in the town was nearly one-half the total population of the *partido*.
2. See Chapter 7 in this volume.
3. Eduardo José Míguez, "La mobilidad social de nativos e inmigrantes en la frontera bonaerense en el siglo XIX: Datos, problemas, perspectivas," *Estudios Migratorios Latinoamericanos* 24 (1993): 139–70.
4. Scholars have used the terms "integration," "fusion," and "syncretism" to refer to this process. Although there are nuances in the definitions, in this essay we have used any of the three terms to refer to the process by which a new "local" identity emerges from the "fusion" of the local and the different immigrant heritages. See the discussion in the section "Marriage and Integration" in this chapter.
5. Franco Savorgnan, "Matrimonial Selection and the Amalgamation of Heterogeneous Groups," *Population Studies*, Supplement (1950): 59–67; Gino Germani, *Política y sociedad en una época de transición* (Buenos Aires: Paidós, 1962).

6. Mark Lathrop and Gilles Pison, "Méthode statistique d'étude de l'endogamie. Application à l'étude du choix du conjoint chez les Peul Bandé," *Population* 3 (1982): 513–42; Robert MacCaa, "Isolation or Assimilation? A Log Linear Interpretation of Australian Marriages, 1947–60, 1975, and 1986," *Population Studies* 43 (1989): 155–62; Robert MacCaa, "Gender in the Melting Pot: Ethnic Marriage Squeeze and Intermarriage in New York City, 1900–1980," Paper presented at the conference "El Poblamiento de las Américas," Veracruz, México, 1992.

7. Hernan Otero, "Una visión crítica de la endogamia: Reflexiones a partir de una reconstrucción de familias francesas (Tandil, 1850–1914)," *Estudios Migratorios Latinoamericanos* 15/16 (1990): 343–78; idem, "La inmigración francesa en Tandil: Un aporte metodológico para el estudio de las migraciones en Demografía Histórica," *Desarrollo Económico* 32 (1992): 79–106; Marcelino Iriani, "Inmigración vasca a la Argentina 1840/1920" (Ph.D. diss., Universidad Nacional de La Plata, 1998). Another case is that of northern Italians with Italian-speaking Swiss and Austrians.

8. María Argeri and Hernán Otero, "Pautas matrimoniales de la frontera interior: El caso de Tandil, Buenos Aires, en la segunda mitad del siglo XIX" (Unedited "tesis de licenciatura," Universidad Nacional del Centro de la Provincia de Buenos Aires, 1986).

9. María Monica Bjerg, "Dinamarca bajo la Cruz del Sur: La preservación de la herencia cultural danesa en la pampa Argentina," *Studi Emigracione* 102 (1991); idem, "Dinamarca bajo la Cruz del Sur: Asentamientos daneses en el centro-sur de la provincia de Buenos Aires, 1850–1930" (Ph.D. diss., Universidad de Buenos Aires, 1994).

10. David Kertzer and Caroline Brettell, "Advances in Italian and Iberian Family History," *Journal of Family History* 12 (1987): 87–120; Thomas Fox, " 'Traditional Marriage': An Image or Reality? A Look at Some Recent Work," *Journal of Family History* 10 (1985): 206–11; David Levine, " 'For Reasons of Their Own': Individual Marriage Decisions and Family Life," *Journal of Family History* 7 (1982): 255ff; Eduardo Mìguez, "Familias de clase media: La formación de un modelo," in F. Devoto and M. Madero, *Historia de la vida privada en la Argentina* (Buenos Aires: Taurus, 1999).

11. Míguez, "Familias de clase media."

12. Fray Mocho (José S. Alvarez), "En familia," *Cuadros de la Ciudad* (Buenos Aires: EUDEBA, 1961).

13. The successful social condition of these immigrants who arrived from Andalucía—even though they had been born in Galicia—coincides with what has been suggested by Moya on the relative success of immigrants from this part of Spain. See José Moya, *Cousins and Strangers* (Berkeley: University of California Press, 1998).

14. The information comes from the memoirs of Manuel Suárez Martínez. There is a private edition of one hundred copies of these memoirs that is kept by descendants of the author. I must thank Dr. José Luis Ortiz for allowing me access to this volume.

15. The Sola correspondence is in Samuel L. Baily and Franco Ramella, eds., *One Family, Two Worlds: An Italian Family's Correspondence across the Atlantic, 1901–1922* (New Brunswick, NJ: Rutgers University Press, 1988).

16. Fugl's case is taken from his memoirs, translated in Spanish by Alice Larsen Rabal in 1989. See also Chapter 7 in this volume.

17. The concept of "social space" refers to an area in which the people who live there have a strong chance of interacting in their daily lives. It has a close

parallel with what functionalist sociology called face-to-face relations. The concept is based on the small European rural communities in which the local residents may identify their neighbors (for instance, in an area between three and ten miles, according to geographic conditions and other factors). It is less meaningful when we refer to large cities where even close neighbors do not know each other. On the concept of social space used by many migration scholars, see Alain Morel, "L'espace social d'un village picard," *Etudes Rurales* 45 (1972): 62–80.

18. R. Gandolfo, "Un barrio de italianos meridionales a fines del siglo XIX," in F. Devoto and M. Madero, *Historia de la vida privada*, vol. 2.

19. Although it is impossible to reconstruct social networks for all immigrants in Tandil, there are two studies that provide some information. Hernán Otero has analyzed the local networks of the French and has found, for example, that almost 60 percent of marriages between migrants from the same province involve people who had come from villages less than twelve miles away from each other. See Otero, "La inmigración francesa en Tandil," María Monica Bjerg has shown the morphology of the Danish migration chains and their influence in matrimonial selection. See Bjerg, "Dinamarca bajo la Cruz del Sur" (1994).

20. Mark D. Szuchman, *Mobility and Integration in Urban Argentina: Córdoba in the Liberal Era* (Austin: University of Texas Press, 1980), chap. 7; Mario Oporto and Nora Pagano, "La conducta endog·mica de los grupos inmigrantes: Pautas matrimoniales de los italianos en el barrio de La Boca en 1895," *Estudios Migratorios Latinoamericanos* 4 (1986): 483–97.

21. Otero, "Una visión crítica," 359–68.

22. In Italian, people from the same *paese*, or small region.

23. Even if, as argued, romantic love was not the only factor in the formation of couples, it was certainly an important one. On the other hand, other factors such as solitude, convenience, sexual desire, or the desire for parenthood could encourage marriage, thereby creating favorable psychological conditions.

24. The term "Cultural Pluralism" has been used to refer to societies that contain, more or less harmoniously, different cultural traditions. Here I use the term "plural culture" to describe an attitude that incorporates diverse cultural behaviors into daily life, such as a family who drink maté, eat pizza, and go to the theater to see a *zarzuela* (Spanish light opera).

25. Dino Cinel, *From Italy to San Francisco* (Stanford: Stanford University Press, 1982); John Briggs, *An Italian Passage: Immigrants to Three American Cities* (New Haven: Yale University Press, 1978).

26. Samuel Baily, "Patrones de residencia de los italianos en Buenos Aires y New York, 1880–1914," *Estudios Migratorios Latinoamericanos* 1 (1985): 8–47; idem, *Immigrants in the Lands of Promise: Italians in Buenos Aires and New York City, 1870–1914* (Ithaca: Cornell University Press, 1999); Moya, *Cousins and Strangers*.

27. Otero, "Una visión crítica," 355–56.

28. Bjerg, "Dinamarca bajo la Cruz del Sur" (1994): 260–61.

29. Lilia Ana Bertoni, "Construir la nacionalidad: Héroes, estatuas y fiestas patrias, 1887–1891," *Boletín del Instituto Dr. E. Ravigani* 5 (1992): 5; idem, "Nacionalidad o cosmopolitismo: La cuestión de las escuelas de las colectividades extranjeras a fines del siglo XIX," *Anuario IEHS* 11 (1996): 179–202; idem, "Soldados, gimnastas y escolares: La escuela y la formación de la nacionalidad a fines del siglo XIX," *Boletín del Instituto Dr. E. Ravigani* 13 (1996).

30. For a discussion of the methodology and other aspects of this study, see Eduardo Míguez and Hernán Otero, "The Excluded from the Marriage Market: Migration and Celibacy in an Argentine Frontier Town," Paper presented at the meeting "Personal Sources and Research on Overseas Migration to the Ameri-

cas," Centro de Estudios Migratorios Latinoamericanos, Buenos Aires, September 1995.

31. The cities of La Coruña and Burgos are both in Spain, but not only are they very distant from one another but also Gallego is spoken in the first one and Spanish in the second.

32. Dedier Norberto Marquiegui, "Aproximación al estudio de la inmigración italo-albanesa en Luján," *Estudios Migratorios Latinoamericanos* 8 (1988): 51–82; Sergio Maluendres, "Los migrantes y sus hijos ante el matrimonio: Un estudio comparativo entre alemanes de Rusia, españoles e italianos en Guatrache (La Pampa, 1910–1939)," *Estudios Migratorios Latinoamericanos* 18 (1991): 191–222.

33. Ruth Freundlich de Seefeld, "La integración social de extranjeros en Buenos Aires según sus pautas matrimoniales: ¿Pluralismo cultural o crisol de razas? (1860–1920)," *Estudios Migratorios Latinoamericanos* 2 (1986): 222–23.

34. Seefeld, "La integración social de extranjeros"; Samuel L. Baily, "Marriage Patterns and Immigrant Assimilation in Buenos Aires, 1882–1923," *Hispanic American Historical Review* 60 (1980): 39–41.

35. Oporto and Pagano, "La conducta endogámica."

36. Mark Szuchman, "The Limits of the Melting Pot in Urban Argentina: Marriage and Integration in Córdoba, 1869–1909," *Hispanic American Historical Review* 57 (1977): 24–50.

37. Carina Silberstein, "Inmigración y selección matrimonial: El caso de los italianos en Rosario, 1870–1910," *Estudios Migratorios Latinoamericanos* 18 (1991): 161–90; idem, "Más allá del crisol: Matrimonios, estrategias familiares y redes sociales en dos generaciones de italianos y españoles (Rosario, 1895–1925)," *Estudios Migratorios Latinoamericanos* 28 (1994).

38. Maluendres, "Los migrantes y sus hijos ante el matrimonio;" idem, "De nuevo sobre las pautas matrimoniales de los migrantes y sus hijos: Piamonteses y leoneses en Trenel, territorio nacional de la pampa (1911–1940)," *Estudios Migratorios Latinoamericanos* 9, no. 28 (1994): 449–79.

39. E. Míguez, M. Argeri, H. Otero, and M. Bjerg, "Hasta que la Argentina nos una: Reconsiderando las pautas matrimoniales de los inmigrantes, el crisol de razas y el pluralismo cultural," *Hispanic American Historical Review* 71 (1991): 781–808.

40. Dedier Norberto Marquiegui, "Revisando el debate sobre la conducta matrimonial de los extranjeros. Un estudios a partir del caso de los españoles y franceses de Luján," *Estudios Migratorios Latinoamericanos* 20 (1992): 13–14.

41. Eduardo Míguez, "Il comportamiento matrimoniales degli italiani in Argentina," in Gianfausto Rosoli, ed., *Identita degli italiani in Argentina: Reti sociali, famiglia, lavoro* (Rome: Edizione Studium, 1993), 81–106.

42. The German-speaking Russians of La Pampa who lived in colonies could be an example of this situation, as could the Danes of Necochea. But the Danes of Tandil, who were not spatially segregated, maintained their strong ethnic identity. So it is not obvious in these cases if ethnicity depended on the formation of a colony or on a particular ethnic tradition. Unfortunately, we do not have studies of Italian colonies that would show us how the majority groups behaved under the conditions of an agricultural colony. For the Russians, see Maluendres, "Los migrantes y sus hijos ante el matrimonio"; and Olga Weyne, *El último puerto: Del Rhin al Volga y del Volga al Plata* (Buenos Aires: Instituto Torcuato Di Tella, 1986). For the Danes, see Bjerg, "Dinamarca bajo la Cruz del Sur" (1994).

43. Maureen Molloy, " 'No Inclination to Mix with Strangers': Marriage Patterns among Highland Scots Migrants to Cape Breton and New Zealand, 1800–1916," *Journal of Family History* 11 (1986): 221–43; MacCaa, "Isolation or Assimilation?"; MacCaa, "Gender in the Melting Pot"; John E. Zucchi, "Italian

Hometown Settlements and the Development of an Italian Community in Toronto, 1875–1935," in Robert Harney, ed., *Gathering Places: Peoples and Neighborhoods of Toronto* (Toronto: Multicultural History Society of Ontario, Toronto, 1985), 121–46; Baily, *Immigrants in the Lands of Promise*, 151–52.

44. Herbert Klein, "La integración social y económica de los españoles en Brasil," *Revista de Historia Económica* (Madrid) 7 (1989): 439–57.

45. Míguez et al., "Hasta que la Argentina nos una."

46. MacCaa, "Gender in the Melting Pot."

47. Szuchman, "The Limits of the Melting Pot in Urban Argentina"; Oporto and Pagano, "La conducta endogámica"; Maluendres, "Los migrantes y sus hijos ante el matrimonio"; Marquiegui, "Aproximación al estudio de la inmigración italo-albanesa."

48. Eduardo Míguez, "Migraciones y el repoblamiento del sudeste bonaerense a fines del siglo XIX," *Anuario IEHS* 6 (1991): 184–85; Seefeld, "La integración social de extranjeros en Buenos Aires," 210.

49. Silberstein, "Más allá del crisol."

50. For example, we may now come to expect higher endogamy and slower integration in the larger urban centers.

9

Immigrants and Female Work in Argentina: Questioning Gender Stereotypes and Constructing Images—The Case of the Italians, 1879–1900

Carina L. Frid de Silberstein

Women's roles in the migration process are an important but neglected topic in migration history. Using primary sources from Italy and Argentina, Carina Frid de Silberstein examines Italian women in Argentina's third largest city, Rosario. Although these women were an essential part of the world of work and made a significant contribution to the economic development of Rosario and Argentina, their role has been obscured by the lack of statistical data, the biases of male scholars, and the complexity of women's participation in the labor force. We need to revise the traditional images and models of immigrants and strive to include the crucial role of women.

The history of immigrations constitutes a privileged space for approaching the dynamic that maintains intergender relations. *Relational* perspectives allow us to construct a more precise analytical profile of the plurality of models in which migratory movements are inscribed, and of which statistical sources contemporary with the phenomena had suggested an homogeneous and oversimplified image.[1]

With substantial delay in relation to the vast literature that exists in the field of study of international migrations in Argentina, the treatment of the problematic of gender and women as active subjects of immigration is an area that has been scarcely approached to date.[2] This problematic offers the possibility of extending our gaze to both sides of the Atlantic. In one case, it enables us to construct a less fragmentary image of the social settings created by the migratory social configurations that were mobilized,[3] while on this side of the Atlantic it allows us to recognize the complexity of the urban universe of the River Plate during the second half of the 1800s. Europeans incorporated themselves into this social universe early on, participating in the process of transformation of the labor market that began with the development of agro-exportation in Argentina during the second half of the nineteenth century.

An examination of the structure of the transatlantic migratory movement will facilitate a revision of the traditional images that have been projected with regard to immigrants and work. Inspired by the numerical limitation of the public statistical summaries concerning the professions of female immigrants upon arrival at their destination, the image promulgated is of the inactive and subsidiary character of European women in relation to their male counterparts.[4] The phenomenon appears to have been reinforced, in turn, by the marked familial character of the migratory models adopted by the new arrivals (migration in families, a majority of married women). This family migration also dissuaded contemporaries from noticing the presence of more concrete indicators (the presence of single women and of women unaccompanied by family members) with regard to a potential integration of the immigrants into the local labor market.

This traditional view has persisted and subsequently been adopted by studies of immigrant behavior within the River Plate labor market.[5] The continuity of the image is evident in early research circumscribed by the framework of modernization, with stress placed on the role of male immigrants as the privileged agents of the process of transformation of Argentine society.[6] More recently, and based on other conceptual models, greater weight has been given to the underlying processes of social mobility and to the existence of cultural conditioners from the places of origin as arguments for justifying the low rates of labor participation observed in the case of Italian women.[7]

The study of female work activity, however, has not often been approached from the perspective of the structural dynamic of the population under study (patterns of geographic mobility, changes in the composition of age and sex groups of the active female population [native born and foreign], family typologies, etc.).[8] It is within this alternative framework that the norms of incorporation of European women immigrants into the world of work of the River Plate will be examined. To this end, the point of departure will be the analysis of the experience of Italian women, who constituted the largest female group to arrive in Argentina during the years of massive immigration. As such, the starting points for this analytical task are the ways in which socio-professional and family models of Italian women immigrants articulated with the River Plate urban labor market. Bearing in mind the plural nature of the Argentine female labor market in the second half of the nineteenth century, the examination of basic differential indicators (national and migratory origins, marital status, and socio-professional profile) has been given precedence. The particular case examined is the city of Rosario in the last three decades of the nineteenth century, at the time the second most important urban center in Argentina in terms of economic importance and the concentration of a population of migratory origin both from overseas and the interior.

Those Who Crossed the Atlantic: Itineraries and Migratory Models of the Female Italian Flow

On of February 22, 1889, the steamer *Nord America* docked in Buenos Aires with 907 Italians aboard. The third-class passengers included Clara De Bonis, single and twenty-three years old. Upon being questioned about her profession and job, De Bonis declared herself a "millionare." Leaving aside the irony displayed by this illustrious immigrant, we know that Clara formed a part of the contingent of more than 300,000 Italians who arrived on the River Plate littoral between 1882 and 1900. This was the time of the boom and development of the great Italian migratory movement that hit Argentina during the final decades of the nineteenth century.

Only relatively recently has it been possible to relate the analysis of the Italian women's movement to Argentina with transformations brought about in the structure and gender composition of the migratory groups from the peninsula. Readings of new records have enabled the identification of gendered patterns, as well as the presence of correlations between migratory trends and economic cycles in the spaces where the immigrants were received.[9] While male migratory mobility demonstrated a greater capacity to react in relation to the oscillations of the labor market, the female trend responded with less elasticity to local conditions. This outcome is exactly the tendency suggested by a reading of the trajectory of the Italian women who went to the River Plate between 1883 and 1910. The less elastic nature of the women's movement can also be inferred from a reading of Graph 1, which shows the spectacular rise of the flow of Italians to the River Plate area from 1884 to 1889 and the subsequent fall in numbers that accompanied the interruption of the Italian current during the Argentine economic crisis of 1890.

Female mobility models constitute a rich informative arsenal for explaining the links between migratory rhythms, family typologies, and relevant determining factors (agrarian crisis, inheritance systems, rights of land ownership, etc.) within the movement directed toward the River Plate. Although framed by its own rhythms, the emigration of women was an integral part of a far-reaching phenomenon inscribed within the migratory cycle (relational, familial, or provincial).[10] While the presence of women was almost nil or had little impact once provincial mobility was under way and during the seasonal or temporary movements, the female component did carry weight when the current was transformed by a trend toward greater permanence at the destination.

Graph 1. Italian Immigration: Distribution by Sex, 1882–1910

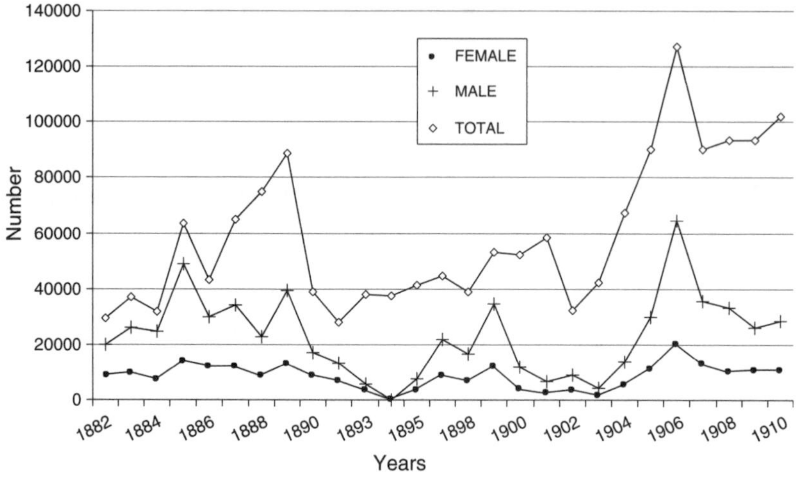

Source: Produced by the author. República Argentina, Dirección General de Migraciones Passenger Lists (1883–1910).
NOTE: There is no data available for 1894.

At this point in the migratory cycle a process of reunification of families began, continuing a sequence that started with the preemptive move of some male members of the family or relatives (father and sons, brothers, et al.). In contrast, when emigration constituted one of the responses to grave socio-economic crises in Italy, women's exodus was connected in a more direct way with the emigratory trend, whether in more established movements or those initiated in relatively recent periods.

From the analysis of two samples of the Italian women who arrived in 1883 and 1889, the representativeness of the models of family emigration for Italian women for this decade have been measured. Included in the analysis, therefore, are the takeoff point and the consolidation of the Italian trend during the 1880s, prior to the fall in emigratory numbers as a result of the financial crisis of 1890. The structural data (sex, age, marital status, profession, and type of family accompaniment) were obtained, in this case, from the Passenger Lists of arrivals at the port of Buenos Aires for both years (1883 and 1889).[11] The comparison of the two samples (see Table 1) relative to the forms of accompaniment is unequivocal evidence of the weight of the family model in Italian female emigration to Argentina, coinciding with the clearest signs of the entrance of farmers drawn by the offer of land in the open spaces of the Pampa region.[12]

Table 1. Italian Female Migratory Trend to Argentina: Typologies and Family Models (1883, 1889)

Family Models	1883 %	1889 %
With husband	8	4
With husband and children	17	13
With children	41	58
With father	4	4
Brothers/sisters	10	6
Single women	20	15
Total	**100**	**100**
	(N=538)	(N=604)

Source: For 1883—Produced by the author from sample. República Argentina, Dirección General de Migraciones, Passenger Lists (1883–1889), CEMLA database. Ships: *Braunschweig* (1/7/1883); *Lassel* (2/29/1883); *Río Grande* (3/4/1883); *Montevideo* (2/22/1883). For 1889—Produced by the author from sample. República Argentina, Dirección General de Migraciones, Passenger Lists, CEMLA database. Ships: *Nord America* (2/22/1889); *Napoli* (4/12/1889); *Amérique* (9/7/1889).

The main axes of female patterns inaugurated by the emigratory trend to Argentina in the 1880s show a significant presence of married Italian women (see Graph 2), who emigrated accompanied by their children subsequent to the departure of the adult males of the family group, and a smaller presence of postmarital emigrants (young adult couples without children), widows, and joint emigrants (married couples with children).

Graph 2. Italian Women Immigrants According to Marital Status

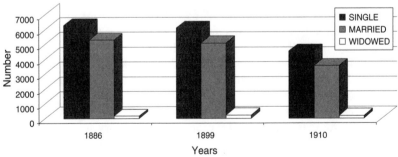

Source: Produced by the author. República Argentina, Dirección General de Migraciones, Passenger Lists (1886, 1899, 1910), CEMLA database.

The exodus of unaccompanied women is less represented (18.5 percent and 14.0 percent, respectively) but equally significant. The consultation of sources produced on a local scale at the places of origin (*nulla osta* [permission to emigrate] and passport records) reaffirms, however, the degree to which the emigration of women apparently unaccompanied by family also formed part of the strategies that emerged from personal networks.[13] A microanalysis of emigration from the Ligurian riviera—one of the most persistent regional flows to the River Plate throughout the nineteenth century—enables the phenomenon to be observed with greater precision. Ligurian immigration anticipated the massive influx of Italians into Argentina. Ligurians began their connection with the River Plate area extremely early on—from the third decade of the nineteenth century, when the navigation of coastal traffic and the craft activities linked to it opened up a significant space for economic investment. By 1855 the city of Buenos Aires and other urban centers located on the Paraná and Uruguay rivers already had a solid core of Ligurians dedicated to small business, crafts, and navigation. Data from passport applications by Italians preparing to leave the area of Chiavari for Argentina between 1870 and 1871 enable us to reconstruct the *relational* structure that is hidden behind the group of "single" women.[14] The samples obtained (see Table 2) suggest, in effect, a significant presence of women from Chiavari who traveled unaccompanied by family or relatives (38 percent of the total). However, the same source also informs us that this group was responding to the "summons" for reunification made by husbands, brothers, cousins, uncles, and boyfriends at their destination.

It is also possible to verify another set of links between marital status, family typologies, and migratory cycles. The subgroup of widows, for example, constitutes a precise indicator of the limits and the strategies involved in the female exodus. The minimum presence of widows in the flow (representing between approximately 1 percent and 2 percent of the total between 1882 and 1899[15]) and their age profiles, which are concentrated in the "older" cohorts (50–65 years old), demonstrates the wariness that was felt by women in charge of family groups when faced by an emigratory model that only appeared functional in relation to those productive family centers, which were capable of taking on the investment and risk involved in the migratory project on behalf of the entire group and not only for themselves.[16]

Recent, more discriminatory analyses of the Passenger Lists have also allowed us to revise the simplification in the migratory statistics that has led to an overly homogeneous image of the immigrant. This image was constructed through the annual statistical summaries in which only those women who stated that they practiced trades considered "feminine" (seamstress, dressmaker, laundress, ironer, weaver, etc.) were recorded as active. This practice not only excluded the overwhelming number of women in agricultural jobs (as neither the laborers, day laborers, nor farmers were

Table 2. Emigration of Italian Women: Professions According to the Nulla Osta Records for the District of Chiavari (1870–71)

Age	Marital Status	Profession	Husband's Profession	Summons/ Type of Accompaniment
29	M	No profession		Summoned by husband
19	S	Embroiderer		With brother
18	S	No profession		Summoned by male cousin
23	S	Spaghetti maker		Summoned by governess
34	S	Horticulturist		Summoned by brother
62	W	No profession		Summoned by children
28	S	No profession		Reunite with brother
19	S	Horticulturist		Reunite with brother
48	M	No profession		With children—Reunite with husband and son
42	M	No profession		Reunite with husband
24	S	Domestic servant		Summoned from Rosario
22	M	Silk worker		Reunite with husband and mother
28	M	No profession		With children—Reunite with husband
21	S	Landlady		Summoned by brother
17	S	Laundress		
32	M	Seamstress		With son—Reunite with husband
25	M	No profession		With consent of husband
28	S	Domestic servant		
22	M	Seamstress		With children—Reunite with husband
26	M	No profession		With children—Reunite with husband
12	S			With consent/accompanied by S. Frugoni
32	M	Horticulturist		Reunite with husband
21	M	No profession	Blacksmith	With husband
44	M	No profession	Shoemaker	With husband
31	M	No profession	Day laborer	With husband
49	M	No profession	Miller	With husband
25	M	No profession	Carpenter	With husband and children
40	M	No profession	Bricklayer	With husband and children
23	S	No profession		Summoned by fiancé
49	M	No profession	Draper	With husband and children
25	M	No profession	Confectioner	With husband and children
18	S	No profession		Summoned by male cousin
19	S	Domestic servant		To work in the house of employer

Source: Archivio Comunale di Chiavari, Stato Civile: Nulla Osta, 1870–71, Cartella 1.110.

recorded as women) but also the diverse list of professional positions in their places of origin.

These significant exclusions and simplifications are explained by the contemporary imagery of work and the place that identification and recognition of women's labor activities occupied within it. The record of female professions (and also, to a degree, the male ones) was an integral part of the social representations in European society of the second half of the 1800s. In this context the concrete professional label had a relative meaning when confronted by self-ascription in a specific social setting.[17] A declaration such as that of "peasant woman" refers to the world of origin—to the social world with which the protagonists identified themselves, whether from a position that they themselves were identified with by society or from one to which they wished to ascribe themselves. The frequent fusion of equivalent denotations such as *massaia/massaio*, *negoziante, cameriere, calzolaia/calzolaio* (housewife, shopkeeper, waiter, shoemaker), intensified by the absence of feminine adjectivization in the case of professions considered weightier and of greater importance in the flow toward Argentina such as *bracciante, giornaliere, agricoltore* (laborer, day laborer, farmer), indicates the existence of a marked interaction between these declarations and the assignation of marital and relational status.[18]

Furthermore, on the Argentine side a reading of the migratory movement records suggests a specific pattern in the information on immigrant professions. The greatest distortions are found in the first statistical series on immigrant entries through the port of Buenos Aires (1882–1887), a product of the systematic transcription of the lists provided by ship captains to the Argentine authorities.[19] Added to a defective implementation of the transcription criteria for professions, the mechanism of construction of the first documented corpus promoted an obvious terminological simplification of the complex professional universe of the provincial settings in the places of origin during the second half of the 1800s. The implementation of a more direct method of recording information on the immigratory movement in 1888 (complemented by the so-called Consular Reports since 1901) has allowed the limited occupational realm indicated by the first statistical series to be enlarged, thus achieving a more inclusive representation of the female professional world that was "mobilized."[20]

From the middle of the nineteenth century and during the years prior to the massive boom in Italian immigration (1850–1876), the Italians who set a course for Argentina were incorporated within a diversified sociopolitical framework, balanced between professions of greater specificity within the female occupational setting and those that referred to provincial settings in a more general way. On a strictly local level, the list of the professional people from Chiavari is illuminating of the professional modalities from the Ligurian area, emphasizing the balance between jobs identified with traditional household industries—*ricamatrice* (embroiderer) and *lavoratrice in seta* (silk worker)—and those that responded to urban demand within the domestic service sector, such as laundress, cook, or domestic servant, and the "rural professions," such as farmhand, farmer, and countrywoman (see Table 2).

In contrast, the occupational table for Italians who left for Argentina during the final decades of the nineteenth century revolves around the dominant group of rural farmers. By the 1890s this group already included laborers and agricultural day laborers who were tied to the seasonal demand in River Plate agriculture and the growth of a demand for unskilled workers in the expanding urban centers. Table 3 illustrates the occupational distribution of Italian women to Argentina at the end of the nineteenth century.

This phenomenon had already been observed on a worldwide scale in the Italian emigration statistics. The transformations produced in the quality of the flow from the 1880s until the first decade of the 1900s (manifested in the drop in number of farmers compared to the rise in the proportion of day laborers and the manual sectors) also modified and diversified the profile of the Italian immigrants. By 1899 the number of Italians not included in the subgroup of farmers and agricultural workers had already risen significantly (from 8.5 percent in 1883 to 23 percent in 1899).

Table 3. Italian Female Migratory Flow to Argentina: Occupational Distribution (1885, 1898)

Women's Occupations	1885 %	1898 %
Farmers	40	51
Day laborers, laborers, and unskilled laborers	46	25
No profession	11	7
Landladies, housewives, and wealthy women	—	13
"Female" professions (seamstresses, dressmakers, spinners, tailors, and weavers)	2.5	3
Maids, servants, and domestic servants	0.5	1
Total	**100** (N=10,300)	**100** (N=4,210)

Source: Produced by the author. República Argentina, Dirección General de Migraciones, Passenger Lists (1885, 1898), CEMLA database.

The second statistical series (1888–1923) gives a more nuanced account of women's occupations, contributing a more accurate perspective on the complex female professional world. This group included a range of jobs that can be classified as "minor" in numerical terms, among which are included both the professions that identify female work (domestic services, confectionery, spinning, etc.) and those that are included in the shared professional world of the sexes (bakers, artists, merchants, carpenters, shoemakers, etc.). [21]

Although of modest scope at the start of the Italian migration to Argentina, the proportion of Italian women who declared themselves active within the majority professions experienced an obvious increase toward the end of the 1890s. This phenomenon was also recorded in the case of Spanish female immigrants.[22] Within this group, the professions representative of rural household industry reached a wide level of diffusion in the northern and central regions of the peninsula. These women also took their place in the emigratory movement. The crisis in home services framed a good part of the circumstances that accompanied the migratory exodus. The continuity of their effect on women's migration, even in the first decade of the 1890s, underlines the solidity of this professional model within the female flow, even if their presence appears excessively moderate in relation to the real weight of domestic work in the places of origin. [23]

The demographic-structural attributes (age and marital status) in which such professions as weaving and spinning are inscribed are indicative of the magnitude of the transformations that occurred in the traditional world of work from the places of origin. The case of the spinners (see Graph 3) is the most illustrative. In the sample corresponding to 1889 single women spinners were in evidence throughout the life cycle, while married women were more likely to respond to the exigencies of family life. Therefore, female work "adjusted" to the individual life cycle and the cadences of fecundity. However, spinning manifests greater persistency throughout the years of the stages of the cycle as well as a certain independence in relation to marital status; the seamstresses and weavers, in contrast, were concentrated in the younger age groups (20–35). This phenomenon effectively demonstrates the extent of the general crisis of the traditional professional frameworks and its repercussions within the Italian women's current to Argentina.[24]

The second statistical series suggests a less schematic reading of the general profile of the Italian women's migration pattern to Argentina. It provides us with information not only about those who practiced a profession or trade but also about the larger group who declared themselves inactive. Within this latter group are included both those registered as of "no profession" and those who for reasons of status (landladies, housewives, and wealthy women) or due to a temporary interruption in their work cycle were not regarded as contributing to the family's occupational entrance into Argentina. Table 3 demonstrates the relative weight of this subgroup.

Graph 3. Italian Female Spinners According to Age and Marital Status (1889)

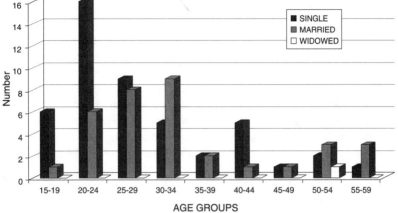

Source: Produced by the author. Argentina, Dirección General de Migraciones, Passenger Lists, CEMLA database, Cases = 82.

The presence of elements that linked migratory mobility models (migration in families), demographic structure (importance of younger cohorts, high proportion of married women), and occupational profiles played an important role in the incorporation of Italian women into the urban professional world of the River Plate. The migration of whole families, on one hand, and the existence of consistent village networks of relatives at the destination, on the other, maintained a significant role for extra-domestic activity. The migration patterns that the Italian women immigrants shared with other groups of Europeans contributed to attenuating the effects of the critical events (for example, loss of husband or illegitimate relations) that conditioned the female social environment in the second half of the 1800s.

Those Who Arrived at the Port: Italian Women in the River Plate World of Work

If we were to provide a brief list of the elements that identified the experience of Italian women in nineteenth-century Argentina, it would include references to the early and enduring contact that they had already established with the migratory movement by the middle of the century. However, not even when transatlantic immigration exploded in the River Plate area in the 1880s was the demographic predominance of Italian women over other European women discussed. Furthermore, by this time, the Italian women who had been settled the longest in Argentina and the fin-de-siécle latecomers could barely recognize one another. This difference was due not only to the different regional origins that separated them (northern versus southern Italians) but also to the diversity of options that Argentina was able to offer, whether in rural areas or in the emergent urban centers in the second half of the 1880s.

For those who chose to remain in the large cities, the urban experience suggested different forms of social integration. This experience was formulated in most cases by access to a labor market that was promoted in Buenos Aires, Rosario, and other urban centers by the intensive expansion of productive activities and the sustained growth of demand for nonspecialized women workers.[25] Nonetheless, viewed from a gendered perspective, the process showed significant contrasts in relation to models of incorporation within the various alternatives offered by the River Plate labor market. As such, while the male workforce was incorporated into a highly flexible and mobile model, the women's program was restricted to the urban work space. The male model was activated by the existent balance between agricultural seasonal demand and the growing demand brought about by the expansion of secondary and tertiary centers within the urban environments.

The arrival of the European immigrants was framed by a setting that had been significantly altered. The traditional structure of female labor demand changed over time. During the first half of the nineteenth century there were high levels of female employment in both rural and urban areas.[26] The retransformation of the economic participation of the active population as a result of international migrations, and the consequent growth of the male workforce, added to the fall in household production. The impact also manifested itself in changes in organization and levels of productivity in the traditional sectors where women's activities were concentrated (particularly in the confectionery and handmade cigar industries), and this led to the decline of female participation in the labor market.[27]

Although there is a fairly general consensus with .egard to the importance of modernization in the evolving female labor market in the second half of the 1800s and in the early 1900s, there is less agreement on the place occupied by the Europeans in such a development. The earliest works on the subject were written within the framework of modernization theory and attributed a central role to European immigration within the processes of the transformation of the traditional structures of Argentinean society into a modern society. Reviewing the criteria elaborated by the migratory statistics, which tend to emphasize the hegemonic role of the male immigrant population in this process, the greater part of these studies persisted with the traditional view that barely emphasized the active character of the migrants. [28]

Carried out from within this tradition but simultaneously demonstrating a partial rupture with it, the study by Donna Guy on women and industrialization in Argentina proposed a new interpretation of the role played by European immigrants in the constitution of the female labor market.[29] Focusing more on women's roles in the process of modernization and industrialization in Latin America, Guy attributes to European women the same transforming character as the followers of the school of modernization had given to male immigrants. Similarly, she explained the high level of European activity as a product of the greater employment possibilities created by their qualifications as well as the greater number of work opportunities opened up by ethnic rifts in the recruitment of the workforce.

At present, a number of studies have approached to any degree some of these subjects from the experience of Italian women, such as the study of R. Gandolfo on the Molisanas from Agnone and the cases of southern Italian women in the neighborhood of La Boca, in the city of Buenos Aires, and in Luján.[30] These studies indicate a lesser participation of such groups in extra-domestic labor activity, even if in the latter case the arguments suggest cultural reasons (the lesser proclivity of the southerners for taking on tasks outside the family structure). In contrast, the absence of effective responses to the Buenos Aires labor market would have derived not only from cultural *imperatives* but also from an intense process of social mobility experienced by the group that emigrated from Agnone.

The city of Rosario is no exception to the general structure of the female labor market in the urban centers of Argentina during the final decades of the 1800s and the early 1900s (Buenos Aires, Córdoba, La Plata, and Bahía Blanca). At the time, this urban setting offered a few female activities of low qualification and demand, linked to the domestic services sector, to clothing manufacture (shirtmakers, tailors, makers of footwear), and to those subsidiary productive activities linked to the commercialization of agricultural products (bag makers).[31] With the predominance of the small workshop as well as retail trade and industrial activity still intimately linked to craft production (and family), the "industrial" universe of Rosario contrasted with the "modern" centers that were concentrated in the massive industry of fin-de-siécle Buenos Aires. Within the latter, textile mills and food-processing plants (liquor, biscuits, and food in general) constituted important centers of demand for women's labor.[32] Rosario also had a few factories that employed women, such as the Argentine Refinery (1888), which processed sugar, and the cereal bag and cigar factories that were established in the city in the late nineteenth century.[33] In this "industrial world," high turnover coexisted with seasonal and low-skilled activities (such as the manufacture of bags), contrasting with those in which specialization inferred a more selective recruitment according to the type of labor activity involved. In all cases, the same nationality of origin between company owners and workers was linked to strategies for recruiting and controlling the workforce through interaction negotiated within an ethnic framework.

The heterogeneous nature of the female labor market was also identified by the existence of a diversified demographic structure, in which the protagonists (provincial and interprovincial migrants as well as immigrants from Europe and neighboring counties, both provincial and city born) coexisted within alternative family and migratory models, offering notably different responses to labor demand. In order to examine such differences, the patterns of Italian and Argentine women's participation in productive activities were reconstructed from a group of indicators (national origin, marital status, and age) and from variables related to more general processes of social integration (socio-professional diversification of the migrant group and the socio-occupational status of married couples).

The reconstruction of the *female* professional sphere in the late 1800s centers on an analysis of the information contained in the manuscript schedules of two reviews of industry in Rosario, carried out during the 1887 and 1895 censuses.[34] The period under study between the two censuses coincides with an economic crisis and, at the same time, a high level of potential supply of female labor. The crisis of 1890 had selective effects on global economic activity (stagnation of the industries with the greatest aggregated value of the era [metallurgical, construction], growth of the activities associated with consumption [food, clothing]). Moreover, the extensive and rapid demographic growth of Rosario caused, in turn, an excess in labor supply, compensated for with difficulty by a parallel growth of global demand in the sectors of traditional and nontraditional female employment (domestic services and sewing in the former case, and industry and commerce in the latter).

The female labor market in Rosario was made up of migrants from various Argentine provinces and neighboring countries (Uruguay, Paraguay, and Chile) as well as from Europe. The internal migrants and those from South America represented an important component of the population of the city in 1887 (25.5 percent of the total female population of Rosario [21,942] and 56 percent of the active workforce). Foreign women also constituted a substantial proportion of the local population (28 percent of the total women in the city).

An analysis of the age structure of the subgroups examined here (Italian women and internal migrants) also confirms this diversity in the female labor group (see Graph 4). The age structure of the internal migrant group (the majority from Córdoba and Buenos Aires province) demonstrate a pattern of settlement of longer duration (expressed in the narrowness of their base and the extent of their presence in more advanced age groups), while the Italian women's group suggests a more recent settlement pattern.

Graph 4. Italian and Argentinean Migrant Women by Age Groups, Rosario, 1887

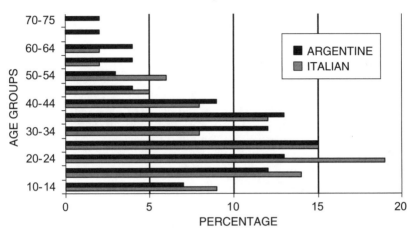

Source: Produced by the author. Manuscript schedules, Census of the Province of Santa Fe, 1887, Rosario, Urban District.

The response of Italian women to participation in extra-domestic activity translated into different behavior with respect to the native and local migrant population (see Table 4).[35] In order to identify the dynamic behind such behavior, I have revised the models of labor activity of Italian women, using both demographic-structural analyses and elements more closely linked to the processes of incorporation of the Italian migratory group that settled in Rosario (social mobility and socio-occupational integration).

Table 4. Percent of Women Employed by Place of Origin, Rosario, 1887

Place of Origin	% Employed	Number
Italian women	39.6	696
Interprovincial migrants	70.2	732
Santa Fe women	43.2	556
Immigrants from neighboring countries	47.6	204
Total		**2,188**

Source: Produced by the author. Manuscript schedules, Census of the Province of Santa Fe, 1887, Rosario, Urban District.

The familial typologies in which the Italians were inscribed (mainly nuclear family units and legal unions) constitute an important variable in the configuration of the indicators of Italian activity vis-à-vis those observed for Argentine women, in particular those from other provinces. In the latter case, the presence of examples of illegitimacy and common-law marriages among Argentine women (single women with children accounted for 17 percent and common-law marriages for 8 percent of the total for internal migrants) suggests a contrast with the family models of the Italian women. Exactly as is suggested by the structure of the migratory flow and the census records, the absence of single Italian women with families is significant, and only widows and a minimum proportion of married women were recorded as heads of households. These observations are therefore revealing of the presence of differential patterns of female labor participation according to the place of origin of the protagonists.

The internal migrants' activity proved to be significantly high; the level of activity of the group reaches 70.2 percent (see Table 4). This phenomenon reproduced models similar to those manifested by the Buenos Aires province migrants settled in the city of Buenos Aires in 1855, as well as to those of female immigrants from neighboring countries among whom there is a strong incidence of illegitimacy (9.8 percent of all single women). The behavior of the women from Santa Fe conforms to a more balanced pattern (with a level of activity of 43.2 percent), with less incidence of illegitimate pregnancy (only 6.3 percent of the total), a uniform distribution in its cohorts, and a more diversified socio-occupational profile than is manifested by their internal migrant co-nationals registering instead the presence of married couples declaring themselves as specialized workers. In far lesser proportions, this also records the lack of dependent (employees of the public sector) and independent manual sectors (merchants, stockholders, proprietors).

The Italian women, however, conform to a less participatory model, manifested in the lowest values for activity in the census sample for the entire female group studied (39.6 percent in 1887) (see Graph 5). In evident contrast with the Argentine migrants for whom entry into the professional world was the axis around which the migratory project turned, the Italian women who created their family cores in the new spaces of their destinations or who emigrated within a network of relatives observed a less direct response to labor supply.[36]

The differences between these models and those followed by their Argentine counterparts also can be seen in the distribution of activity according to the variables of age and marital status. In the case of Italian women, a pronounced participation of minors and of young single adults is clear, declining with married women between 35 and 45 years old (see Graph 6). The results make it necessary to revise the schemes that rigidly link reproductive cycle, labor cycle and inactivity of the immigrants.

**Graph 5. Rates of Female Economic Activity According to Origin and
Marital Status, Rosario, 1887**

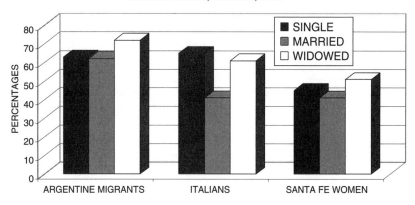

Source: Produced by the author. Manuscript schedules, Census of the Province of
Santa Fe, 1887, Rosario, Urban District, Cases = 2,188.

**Graph 6. Italian Women: Rates of Economic Activity According to Age and
Marital Status, Rosario, 1887**

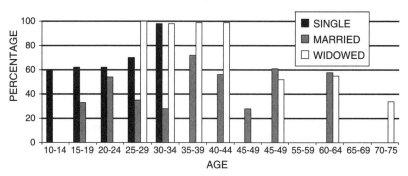

Source: Produced by the author. Manuscript schedules, Census of the Province of
Santa Fe, 1887, Rosario, Urban District, Cases = 696.

Other factors intervene or modify the traditional patterns throughout
the process of incorporation of the migratory family groups. Both the
family migratory model and the relative length of settlement (a variable
which is not possible to measure with the available information) constitute factors of considerable impact in the formulation of models of female labor activities. Precisely in the manner indicated, the immigration
of family groups (whether in groups or by long-awaited reunions) suggests the adoption at first of a greater number of strategies designed to
facilitate the family's settlement and to balance the costs of installation

required in the earliest stages of the migratory experience. This phenomenon could explain the activity of married women in early stages of the
reproductive cycle. The existence of high levels of minors working in
family groups (with or without active mothers) reaffirms, in turn, this
process and must be borne in mind in relation to their impact on the world
of the active female population. The anticipation of entry into labor activity is revealing of the implementation of family strategies designed to
reestablish the consumption/reproduction equilibrium in the critical stages
of the family and migratory cycles.[37] A more prolonged stay (or, failing
this, a successful occupational incorporation) of the family group at the
destination could suggest, however, more contingent models in relation
to the access of immigrants to the female labor market.

These responses must also be examined within the more general framework of social integration of the original migratory group. The Italians
who settled in Rosario maintained a pronounced socio-professional diversification, starting with their early incorporation into the new opportunities opened up in the city by commerce and crafts from the middle of
the 1800s. A consistent number of women merchants and proprietors
(11.6 percent of the total of all occupations in 1887) indicates the extent
to which the professional profile of women accompanied the presence of
movements of occupational and social mobility within the Italian national
group as a whole (see Table 5). [38]

**Table 5. Most Represented Professions of Employed Italian Women,
Rosario (1869, 1887, 1895)**

Profession	1869 %	Profession	1887 %	Profession	1895 %
Seamstress	30.5	Seamstress	31.0	Maid	34.0
Merchant	16.5	Laundress	23.0	Seamstress	21.0
Maid	12.0	Maid	11.6	Cook	9.0
Cook	10.0	Merchant	11.6	Dressmaker	8.0
Laundress	6.0	Ironer	6.5	Laundress	9.0
Fruitier	6.0	Dressmaker	4.3	Teacher	5.0
Restaurateur	6.0	Farmer	3.9	Ironer	5.0
Farmer	4.0	Cook	2.6	Merchant	6.0
Ironer	4.0	Window dresser	2.6	Cigarmaker	2.0
Greengrocer	4.0	Weaver	2.6	Clerk	1.0
Total	**99***		**99.7***		**100**
	(N=49)		(N=232)		(N=290)

Source: Produced by the author. República Argentina, Primer Censo Nacional,
1869. *Censo de la Provincia de Santa Fe, 1887*. República Argentina, *Segundo
Censo Nacional, 1895*, Rosario, Urban District.
*Totals may not add to 100 percent due to rounding.

For the vast majority of women linked to the manual sectors (both specialized and of low or no skills), extra-domestic work was related to the group of strategies that the family nucleus used to define its modalities of incorporation—that is, saving, structure of the family's integration, or critical moments in the family cycle.

Family industry concealed a more intricate and broader presence of women in the world of work and certainly involved a far from negligible proportion of "industrial" employees. This fact assumes even greater dimensions if we bear in mind the high proportion of small business people and proprietors of workshops and industries of Italian origin who, in turn, were the largest employers of foreign labor in the city of Rosario.

If we examine the same occupational structure, paying attention now to the broader framework of the family professional world (and restricting our analysis to the occupations practiced by spouses), it is possible to put forward a more integrated image of the spaces and the social itineraries of the female professional world at the end of the 1800s. Unsurprisingly, Table 6 confirms a correspondence between a married couple's occupational statuses, both in the less-skilled professions (cooks, ironers, and servants) and in the more qualified ones. In contrast, seamstresses appear to have been connected to a diversified range of social and professional spaces.

The exodus of Italian women to Argentina displays precise borders with regard to the models of the female protagonists, privileging those able to pay the series of "investments" involved in the migratory process, while for those with unavoidable family leadership it increased the uncertainty of the project.

The challenge of approaching the complex professional universe of the immigrants on both sides of the Atlantic is far from answered. On this side at least, the identification of models of the activities of Italian women in the River Plate area confirms the need to increase the precision regarding the traditional images of immigrants and work. There is also a need to critically revise the models that, from the global perspective, have projected their conceptual schemes onto specific migratory social settings. Access to extra-domestic work remained firmly linked to the expected responses of the same migratory family nuclei now faced with the possibilities offered in the local socio-economic contexts. Rather than explaining the labor activity of women from rigid causal models (socio-professional status and national origin), it is necessary to offer a more complex view of the urban migratory experience of the second half of the 1800s. In this process the norms of consumption, the savings plans, and the migratory family structures that accompanied various models of female labor activity had a significant influence.

Italian women went through their migratory experiences on both sides of the Atlantic in a plurality of settings that have yet to be recovered and

Table 6. Occupation of Married Italian Women's Spouses by the Wife's Profession, Rosario (1895)

Seamstresses		Dressmakers		Ironers		Laundresses	
Tailor	5	Tailor	2	Worker		Day laborer	7
Mailman		Merchant				Unskilled	
						laborer	2
Spaghetti maker		Cabinetmaker		Bricklayer	4		
Bricklayer	3	Blacksmith		Knife			
				grinder			
Shoemaker	3			Launderer			
Clerk				Carpenter			
Fisherman				Clerk	2		
Mechanic				Market			
				gardener			
Waiter				Shoemaker			
Saddler				Sailor			
Painter				Cleaner	2		
Carpenter							
Plasterer							
Bookseller							
Broker							
Sailor							

Servants		Cooks		Merchants		Midwives	
Servant		Unskilled					
		laborer		Merchant	4	Pharmacist	
Unskilled laborer	2	Spaghetti					
		maker		Restaurateur		Blacksmith	
Cook	2	Maid		Storekeeper	2	Printer	
		Bricklayer					
		Painter					

Cigar Makers		Window Dresser	Mattress Maker	
Cook		Shoemaker	Mattress maker	
Landlord				

Source: Produced by the author. Samples from manuscript schedules, *Segundo Censo Nacional, 1895*, Rosario, Urban District.

NOTE: Numbers have been inserted only in the cases where there was more than one marriage with the listed combination of professions. N=77.

understood through studies of gender and migration. The contribution of future approaches on a micro-analytical scale (based on regional and micro-regional groups from places of origin) and comparative work with other River Plate (and South Atlantic) urban spaces will surely enable the reformulation of the results presented here in a provisional fashion.

Notes

1. F. Devoto, *Movimientos migratorios: Historiografía y problemas* (Buenos Aires: CEAL, 1992).

2. N. C. Hollander, "Women: The Forgotten Half of Argentine History," in A. Pescatello, *Female and Male in Latin America: Essays* (Pittsburgh: University of Pittsburgh Press, 1973), 142–58; C. Frid de Silberstein, "Inmigración europea y mundo del trabajo en Argentina: Desarrollos historiográficos y cuestiones en debate desde una perspectiva del género," *Anais* (Universidade do Vale do Rio del Sinos, RS), 1997.

3. P. Corti, "Donne che vanno, donne che restano: Emigrazione e comportamenti femminili," *Annali Istituto "Alcide Cervi"* 12 (1990): 213–36; C. Brettell, *Men Who Migrate, Women Who Wait: Population and History in a Portuguese Parish* (Princeton: Princeton University Press, 1986).

4. On the interpretative difficulties presented by the statistics on professions in countries of origin and destination during the period of massive immigration, especially in relation to the Spanish case, see B. Sánchez Alonso, *La inmigración española en Argentina: Siglos XIX y XX*, Colección Cruzar el Charco (Barcelona: Júcar, 1992), 94–108.

5. On the historiographic significance of these conceptualizations, see Z. Recchini de Lattes, "Las mujeres en las migraciones internas e internacionales, con especial referencia a América Latina," *Cuaderno 41* (Buenos Aires: CENEP, 1989).

6. G. Beyhaut, "Los inmigrantes en el sistema ocupacional argentino," in T. Di Tella, G. Germani, and J. Graciarena, *Argentina, sociedad de masas* (Buenos Aires: Eudeba, 1965), 85–123; G. Germani, *Política y sociedad en una época de transición* (Buenos Aires: Paidós, 1965), 197–210.

7. R. Gandolfo, "Del Alto Molise al centro de Buenos Aires: Las mujeres agnonsesas y la primera emigración transatlántica (1870–1900)," *Estudios Migratorios Latinoamericanos* 20 (1992): 71–98; M. C. Cacopardo and J. L. Moreno. *La familia italiana y meridional en la emigración a la Argentina* (Naples: Edizione Scientifiche Italiane, 1994), 42–45.

8. G. Massé, "Migrantes interprovinciales en la ciudad de Buenos Aires al promediar el siglo XIX," *Cuadernos de Historia: Serie Población* (Universidad de Córdoba, 1994): 85–110; idem, "Mercado de trabajo e inserción socio-ocupacional de los migrantes en el partido de Luján a fines del siglo XIX," *Cuadernos de Historia Regional* 5 (1992): 97–124.

9. L. Favero, " Fonti per lo studio dell'emigrazione in Argentina," in G. Rosoli, *Identità degli italiani in Argentina: Reti sociali, famiglia, lavors* (Rome: Edizioni Studium, 1993), 1–22; A. Bernasconi, "Aproximación al estudio de las redes migratorias a través de las listas de desembarco: Posibilidades y problemas," in M. Bjerg and H. Otero, *Inmigración y redes sociales en la Argentina moderna* (Buenos Aires: CEMLA-IEHS, 1995), 191–201.

10. On migratory typologies and the concept of the migratory cycle, see F. Devoto, "Las migraciones de las Marcas a la Argentina, la cuestión de la escala y las posibilidades de una tipología regional," in E. Sori, ed., *Le Marche fuori dalle Marche: Migrazioni interne ed emigrazione all estero tra XVIII e XX secolo*, book 1:68–111, *Quaderni di "Proposte e ricerche"* 24 (1998).

11. We can only rely upon systematic information on the marital status of the women departees for the period 1882–1887. This information is crucial for the structural analysis of the female trend. As of that date the record is much less complete.

12. The criteria followed for obtaining the samples were based on the examination of the female population per steamer (understood as the unit of analysis), varying the dates of entrance in order to control possible seasonal distortions. For 1883 the lists of the following boats that arrived at the port of Buenos Aires were reviewed: the *Braunschweig* (7/1/1883), the *Lassel* (29/2/1883), the *Río Grande* (5/7/1883), and the *Montevideo* (12/11/1883). For the year 1889 the sample consisted of the *Nord America* (22/2/1889), the *Napoli* (12/4/1889), and the *Amérique* (7/9/1889). Only the lists from the port of Genoa were included, as they constitute a superior qualitative record to those from Naples or even Marseilles.

13. Both the *nulla osta* and passport records are petitions for permission to leave initiated by potential emigrants to Italian communal authorities. Even if they represent a way of approaching the emigratory universe, they should not be understood as representative of its totality, as not all the requests were confirmed by the authorities or the applicants themselves. On the importance and limits of these sources, see Gandolfo, "Del Alto Molise," 328. The utilization of passport records for the analysis of migratory models has already provided abundant evidence of their utility. See Cacopardo and Moreno, *La familia italiana y meridional*, 78–91; Gandolfo, "Del Alto Molise," 82–85.

14. Archivio Comunale di Chiavari, Stato Civile, Nulla Osta (1870–71), Cartella 1.110.

15. The information was obtained from the Immigrant Data Base (CEMLA), (1882–1900).

16. During the lengthy period of "open door" migratory policies there were no clauses that restricted the arrival of family groups headed by widows or of other elements lacking in provable means of livelihood. The Argentine government did not limit the entrance of single women with children under fifteen years old until much later.

17. This is the term that is used in the columns of the Passenger Lists and the Consular Reports (1901–1936) for those who embarked in Italy. The interchangeability of "profession" or "trade" is indicative of the ambiguities that surround the records, the utilization of one or the other label in the same list being a matter of chance.

18. Using similar criteria, the census takers were advised to register small family businesses and agricultural families as productive units from 1880 onward, assigning the same profession to the wife and children as that of the head of the family (farmer, merchant). G. Carrasco, "Modo de empadronar," *Censo de la Provincia de Santa Fe, 1887*, Book I (1988), 167.

19. The first statistical series recorded the age, marital status, profession, nationality, education, and religion of the arrivals, by name and in alphabetical order for every steamer. The nominative and sequential order permits the reconstruction of effective and presumed collateral nuclear family groups (uncles and aunts, cousins, brothers- and sisters-in-law). Bernasconi, "Aproximación al estudio," 191–202.

20. The Consular Reports constitute a valuable parallel source, available from 1901 until 1938 only. They add to the nominative data known from the Passenger Lists relative to place of birth, last place of residence, and date and place of passport application by the emigrants. These involve documents granted by the Argentine consular authorities at the port of embarkation that were added to the passenger lists of the ships that transported the immigrants. Favero, "Fonti per lo studio dell'emigrazione in Argentina," in G. Rosoli, *Identità degli italiani in Argentina*, 1–22.

21. A large part of these occupations refer either to the activities of the family group or to the profession of the head of the family, an extremely widespread phenomenon in the Italian case, such as *carrozziere, cavallerizza, carrettiere, massaia* (coachman, horsewoman, carter, housewife). Others, however, are more closely identified with a single activity such as artist, *cameriere* (waiter), merchant, *fruttivendola* (fruit vendor).

22. Sánchez Alonso, *La inmigración española*, 102–4.

23. The continuity of this professional current (spinners and weavers) can be attested to during the early years of the century, according to information gleaned from an analysis of the Immigrants Lists from the first decade of the 1900s. Directory General of Immigration, *Listas Pasajeros: Llegadas de Ultramar (1882–1926)*.

24. A. Angeli, "Mestieri, ruoli femminili, aggregati domestici in un'area mezzadrile," in P. Corti, *Annali Istituto "Alcide Cervi"* 12 (1990): 92–93.

25. G. Bourdé, *Buenos Aires: Urbanización e inmigración* (Buenos Aires: Ed. Huemul, 1977); H. Sábato, *Los trabajadores de Buenos Aires: La experiencia del mercado, 1850–1880* (Buenos Aires: Sudamericana, 1992); M. Johns, "The Urbanization of a Secondary City: The Case of Rosario, Argentina, 1877–1920," *Journal of Latin American Studies* 23 (1989): 489–513.

26. In 1855 the Census of the City of Buenos Aires recorded rates of female activity at close to 55 percent, observing a fall of nearly 10 percent (to 45.55 percent) by 1869. In contrast, and notwithstanding the drop in the secular movement, the provinces of the interior maintained high levels of female activity participation. Z. Recchini de Lattes, *La población de Buenos Aires: Componentes demográficos del crecimiento entre 1855 y 1960* (Buenos Aires: Ediciones del Instituto, 1971); E. Kritz, "La formación de la fuerza de trabajo en la Argentina, 1869–1914," *Cuadernos del CENEP* 30 (Buenos Aires, 1985).

27. H. Sábato, "La formación del mercado de trabajo en Buenos Aires, 1850–1880," *Desarrollo Económico* 24 (1985); D. Guy, *El sexo peligroso* (Buenos Aires: Sudamericana, 1994), 86–88; R. Korznekiewicz, "Labor Unrest in Argentina, 1887–1907," *Latin American Research Review* 3 (1989): 71–98; Z. Recchini de Lattes and C. Wainerman, "Empleo femenino y desarrollo económico: Algunas evidencias," *Desarrollo Económico* 66 (1977): 301–17.

28. Beyhaut, "Los inmigrantes en el sistema ocupacional," 95–96; M. Bejarano, "Inmigración y estructuras tradicionales en Buenos Aires (1854–1930)," in T. Di Tella and T. Halperín Donghi, *Los fragmentos del poder* (Buenos Aires: Editorial Jorge Alvarez, 1969).

29. D. Guy, "Women, Peonage, and Industrialization: Argentina, 1810–1914," *Latin American Research Review* 16 (1981): 65–89.

30. Gandolfo, "Del Alto Molise al centro de Buenos Aires"; Cacopardo and Moreno, *La famiglia italiana y meridional*, 30–72.

31. G. Carrasco, *Anales de la ciudad de Rosario* (Rosario: Imp. J. Olivé, 1897); E. Gómez Rivara, *Gran guía del Rosario de Santa Fe* (Rosario, 1896); Johns, "The Urbanization of a Secondary City," 489–513.

32. M. C. Feijoó, "Las trabajadoras porteñas a comienzos del siglo," in D. Armus, *Mundo urbano y cultura popular* (Buenos Aires: Sudamericana, 1990), 281–312; F. Rocchi, "Concentración de capital, concentración de mujeres: Industria y trabajo femenino en Buenos Aires, 1890–1930," in *Historia de las mujeres en la Argentina*, vol. 2, *Siglo XX* (Buenos Aires: Cedal, 2000), 223–44; M. Lobato, "Mujeres obreras, protesta y acción gremial en la Argentina: Los casos de la industria frigorífica y textil en Berisso," in D. Barrancos, *Historia y género* (Buenos Aires: Cedal, 1993), 65–97.

33. D. Guy, "Refinería Argentina, 1888–1930: Límites de la tecnología azucarera en una economía periférica," *Desarrollo Económico* 28 (1988).

34. *Censo de la Provincia de Santa Fe, 1887*, Industries Census, manuscripts, Rosario, vol. 232, Bulletins 15, 19, 32; República Argentina, *Segundo Censo Nacional de 1895*, Industrial Census, manuscript schedules, Rosario.

35. The samples collected correspond to the five districts or sections of the city. The difficulties in discriminating between interprovincial migrants and the Argentines born in Rosario has made it necessary to join both domains in a single category (women of Santa Fe).

36. In the 1890s work participation of Italian-born women in Rosario decreased (the Second National Census of 1895 registered 34.9 percent). The demand for work decreased in the early 1890s as a result of the Argentine financial crisis of 1890. The effects of the crisis on female work are also evident in Buenos Aires. In the capital city of Argentina, female foreign workers participation in 1887 totaled 40.4 percent, while in 1895 it decreased to 32 percent. Hilda Sábato and Luis Alberto Romero, *Los trabajadores de Buenos Aires: La experienceia del Mercado, 1850–1880* (Buenos Aires: Sudamericana, 1992) Apendice, Cuardro 12; Roberto Cortes Conde, *Dinero, deuda y crisis: Evolucion fiscal y monetaria en la Argentina* (Buenos Aires: Sudamericana, 1989).

37. The censuses of the second half of the nineteenth century only recognized people older than fifteen years of age as active. The analysis presented here includes ages greater than ten, not only because of the importance this group holds within the active female population but also in order to make compatible the criteria used in the analysis of the migratory flow.

38. For a reconstruction of the occupational framework of the Italian women, see A. Bernasconi and C. F. de Silberstein, "Le altre protagoniste: Italiane a Santa Fe," *AltreItalia* 9 (1993): 116–38.

III

Brazil

STORY THREE

Santo Codo (1861–1942), an Italian Immigrant on a Brazilian Coffee Plantation

Maria Silvia C. Beozzo Bassanezi

This section on Brazil opens with the story of a farmer from Rovigo, Italy, who, in 1895—with the help of free passage offered by the government of the state of São Paulo—migrated with his family to a coffee plantation in the interior of the state. Although Santo Codo left no written records, as did the protagonists in our two previous stories, Brazilian scholar Maria Silvia Bassanezi has skillfully reconstructed his migration experiences from official documents (birth, marriage, death, and parish records, plantation records). Thus, we are able to learn much about the daily life of an immigrant family on a coffee plantation: the deaths of two of their young children; caring for the coffee trees; the influence of religion and the customs of Rovigo on marriage, work, and the cohesion of the community; the importance of personal social networks; and the family's remarkable ability to save and eventually to purchase their own farm.

In the European autumn of 1895, Santo Codo (aged 34), his wife Ludovica Piccelli (aged 28), and their two small children, Giacomo and Giuseppina, left their small village in Rovigo in Italy's Veneto, crossed the ocean, and arrived in the state of São Paulo, Brazil. They followed hundreds of other Italians at the end of the nineteenth century who were fleeing from bad socioeconomic conditions in their homeland and who were looking for a new and better life overseas in Brazil. Like many Italians, Santo Codo and his family were lured by the advertising campaign and the travel subsidies offered by the Brazilian government to those who wanted to work on the coffee plantations. Moreover, they were attracted by the opportunity of finding work and by the possibility of having a dream come true: owning a small farm. The Codos originally belonged to agricultural families in the Veneto, although at the moment of his departure Santo was a coachman.

After enduring a long and uncomfortable trip in third class on a crowded steamship, they traveled by train from the port of Santos to the city of São Paulo, where they spent a few days at the immigrant hostel in collective accommodations. Then they were transferred by train to Santa Gertrudes plantation, their final destination, where they joined some of their Italian relatives and acquaintances.

The plantation where Codo's family lived and worked for almost thirty years was extremely large. It was one of the most important in the west coffee region of the state of São Paulo and was located about 200 kilometers from the city of São Paulo. Its owner, Count Eduardo Prates, had received his title from the Pope. The plantation chapel had special privileges from the Catholic Church; most priests who served the Prates family and the workers were also Italian.

Santo and Ludovica did not leave any written memoirs, diaries, or letters that could help us know more about their lives. Like other Italian immigrants in their same situation, it is likely that Santo Codo had a basic knowledge of reading and writing. His wife might have been able to sign her name and read a few words, or she could have been illiterate, as were the majority of the Italian immigrant women on the coffee plantation.

The history told here is the result of research in official documents such as birth, marriage, and death certificates, in parish registers (baptism and marriage), and also in books that registered the accounts and daily life of Santa Gertrudes and its workers between 1895 and 1930. An incomplete genealogy of the Codo family based on information given by their descendants has contributed as well.*

At first, life at Santa Gertrudes was not what Santo Codo and his family had expected. According to the bookkeeping records, as soon as they arrived they went into debt to buy food and tools at the plantation store. Soon their 3-year-old son Giacomo died of bronchitis in January 1896. In December of that same year their 2-year-old daughter Giuseppina succumbed to intestinal problems. Both children died without medical attention. Moreover, Italian mothers had difficulties in dealing with the tropical weather and unfamiliar foods as far as their children were concerned. Santo and Ludovica had already lost two other children in Italy before migrating. As a devout Catholic, Santo Codo made a promise that if God sent more children to the couple, he would grow a beard and keep it all his life. After his son Guerino was born in 1898, Santo Codo ceased to shave. His long, dense beard became his most distinctive feature.

Santo and Ludovica had three more boys and one girl: Domingos (1899), José (1902), Albino (1907), and Tereza (1910). The children were

*L. C. Pignataro, *Imigrantes italianos em Rio Claro e seus descendentes* (Rio Claro: Arquivo Publico e Histórico do Município/Imprensa Oficial do Estado de São Paulo, 1982), 65–89.

baptized as soon as possible, usually between one to three months after birth. The boys' godfathers and godmothers were chosen from among the family relatives. Tereza's godparents did not belong to the family, although they were also from Rovigo. They had lived for many years at Santa Gertrudes at Colónia São Joaquim (one of the eight "colonies" that housed the immigrants), where Codo's family lived too. Santo and Ludovica also were godparents to children of relatives and acquaintances from Rovigo who worked on the same farm. The choice of godparents among relatives and acquaintances helped to reinforce the relationship between families as the immigrants faced the new land. This Italian custom would continue in Brazil in the next Codo generation.

The work at Santa Gertrudes plantation was hard and involved the entire family. They usually woke up at 5 A.M. By the time the *colónia* bell rang an hour later, they were ready to go to the fields, where they stayed until 6 P.M. There were only short breaks for meals, and the schedule was strictly followed under threat of punishment from the *colónia* manager. Children from the age of six helped their parents by doing small jobs: feeding the livestock, helping the mother with the family's bean and corn crops, taking care of younger siblings, helping with the coffee harvest, and so on. When they reached the age of sixteen, they were considered full-time members of the farm labor force.

Santo Codo, by his work contract, was in charge of about 3,000 coffee trees when he had only his wife to help him. Later, when their children grew up, they all took care of 8,000 trees. With his family, he weeded each tree five or six times per year. For this work he was paid an annual fixed wage that was divided in installments. From May to August or September he and his family brought in the harvest, with their pay determined by the volume of coffee beans. Their harvest usually amounted to between 400 and 900 *alqueires* per year (one *alqueire* equals fifty liters). Sometimes, Santo Codo and his sons received extra payment (called *diária*) for other jobs such as fixing fences, castrating livestock, transporting goods, eliminating ant nests, and drying coffee beans. Nevertheless, there was no bonus for opening or maintaining roads, getting rid of locust hordes that damaged coffee trees, or putting out fires; these jobs were included in the work contract.

Codo's family and other workers learned that the start of the harvest was the best time to make the farm owner improve conditions or raise their pay. Coffee beans would rot if the harvests were delayed, so sometimes the laborers refused to work and even threatened the owner with a strike to get what they wanted.

Santo Codo and his family could plant their own beans and corn, and sometimes rice and cotton, between the coffee trees or on other plots of land. This practice was established in a contract that was renewed each year. The family also raised one or two cows, several pigs, and chickens. Any excess from this subsistence production was sold in the town market on Sundays.

Santo Codo and his wife were used to keeping the family on a tight budget. They did not buy much food or other items in the plantation store and did not spend much money in the town shops. Sometimes they gave some money to the church, the poor, and the victims of some calamity in Italy. They paid a small amount to a medical cooperative and rarely spent money to see a private doctor, which was expensive. Only once, in 1909, did Santo Codo pay a fine because he was in a fight, an activity that was prohibited by the plantation rules. By hard work and by avoiding the health or alcoholism problems somewhat common in immigrant families, Santo Codo already had a savings account in a São Paulo bank by 1904. His savings had doubled by 1921 and kept on increasing in the 1930s. Many of his relatives and friends were not so lucky.

Codo's sons learned how to read and write, but their only daughter, Tereza, remained illiterate. When his sons married, they brought their wives to live in the family house, as was the usual practice in their Italian homeland. According to the same practice, Tereza, after marrying in 1930, went to live with her husband's family, who also worked at Santa Gertrudes plantation.

Guerino, the oldest son, and Domingos, the second one, married women from the Gasparini family, who lived at Colónia Santo Antônio on the same plantation, in 1917 and 1920, respectively. Santo Codo and Ludovica's first grandchild, Albino, was born in 1919, beginning an extensive Brazilian second generation of the Codos. (Their five children gave them thirty-three grandchildren, and the third generation accounts for ninety-five great-grandchildren!) The Gasparini family originally had come from Treviso, a town near Rovigo, and so had Tereza's husband's family, the Marinos. The other two sons, who married in the 1920s, also chose spouses of Italian descent, probably from the Veneto. They also lived not far from Santa Gertrudes plantation.

Choosing a spouse from their own group—a fellow countryman/woman or a descendant thereof—was common among Italian immigrants. Like the choice of godparents, marriage was important in maintaining and reinforcing the cohesion and solidarity of the group that helped immigrants face a difficult life in their new land. Marriage also joined together two labor forces, so the choice of a spouse included the search for a partner who was strong, healthy, and a good worker—someone who could take advantage of the opportunities offered in the new land.

During the long years that the Codo family stayed at Santa Gertrudes, they saw many relatives and friends go away to other farms or cities or even return to Italy, without hope of seeing them again. The majority of workers did not spend many years at the same farm. Several of them, in poor health or with no strength to face hard conditions, died. Others stayed in the neighborhood and continued the friendship with the Codos.

Fortunately, the Codo family escaped the many epidemics that devastated the coffee region: yellow fever at the end of the nineteenth century, measles in 1905, smallpox in 1910, and Spanish influenza in 1918. Perhaps the family's good health was due to the farm owner's precautions: he provided vaccines and kept persons from leaving or entering the plantation during times of epidemics. However, the severe frost of 1918 brought serious trouble to the São Paulo coffee economy and to Codos and other workers' families, who depended on a bountiful harvest to increase their income and savings or allow them to pay their debts.

At Santa Gertrudes plantation, Santo Codo and his family had a religious, social, and cultural life. Like other immigrants there, they attended every religious rite or ceremony held at the farm: Easter, Christmas, New Year, Holy Communion, confession, Sunday and holiday Masses, triduums, and novenas. At June parties the feast days of Saint Anthony (the 13th), Saint John (the 24th), and Saints Peter and Paul (the 29th) were celebrated. They took part in processions to ask God for rain, a common practice among peasants when there were long periods of drought that threatened their livelihood.

By the mid-1920s, when the youngest boys were married, the Codos had already left Santa Gertrudes. They went to work on a neighboring plantation called Itaúna, which probably offered better working conditions, or perhaps the Codos had some problems on the old plantation. But Santo Codo had an old dream: to be a landowner. Finally, in the 1930s, when the crisis in the coffee economy lowered land prices and when he was about seventy years old, he became the proprietor of Sítio Mombuca, a small farm near Santa Gertrudes plantation. Santo Codo and his family repeated at Sítio Mombuca some of the old habits from rural northern Italy; he brought his four sons and their families to live with him and his wife at Mombuca. He left his daughter with her husband's family at Santa Gertrudes. According to tradition, as an elderly man he went to live in his youngest son's house.

The work at Sítio Mombuca was done only by the family labor force. Under Santo Codo's orders his entire family—wife, sons, daughters-in-law, and grandchildren—raised their own subsistence and farm products to sell in the local market. The women, as they had done before on the coffee plantations, were not only in charge of the household chores but also worked on the land, mainly getting rid of weeds. Apart from helping with the coffee trees, women also planted small crops and raised livestock.

Time passed. Santo Codo divided Sítio Mombuca among his five children, but he and his wife had the use of the land during their lifetime. Santo Codo died in 1942, and Ludovica lived another eleven years, until 1953, in her youngest son's house. At that time, Brazil went through great economic transformations; coffee culture and rural areas started to lose space to industrialization and urbanization. After Santo Codo's death, his sons started to diversify. Little by little they moved to the urban nucleus, working in commerce and factories in Santa Gertrudes village, where they took part in local politics, or in nearby Rio Claro city. A few descendants of Santo Codo continued to till the land; the rest went to town. Almost all of them continued to live and work in the region of Santa Gertrudes and Rio Claro.

Santo Codo and his wife had left Italy for Brazil in search of a job, a good life for their children, and their own piece of land. They lost their first babies, they faced poverty, but they fought against misery and hardship. They had more children, they left a large number of descendants, and they made an old dream come true. They were ordinary people but, in their own way, they were winners.

10

German Immigration and Brazil's Colonization Policy*

Giralda Seyferth

The Germans, like the Jews in Brazil and the Danes in Argentina, were small in number compared to the Italians, Spaniards, and Portuguese, but they had a significant impact on immigration policy. In this essay Giralda Seyferth shows how German colonists in the nineteenth century became the model of the efficient settler who would help transform the Brazilian south into a productive area. Indeed, they did contribute much to the development of agriculture and industry, but they also presented problems for twentieth-century Brazilians who saw them as inassimilable. German-Brazilians developed strong ethnic community institutions that, along with the widespread use of the German language, defined much of their identity. This persistence led the Brazilian government in the late 1930s to nationalize the German schools and to compel the use of Portuguese. Thus, what seemed so promising initially in terms of economic goals came to clash in the long run with cultural issues of the meaning of Brazilian identity.

German immigrants started to settle in Brazil in 1824 with the founding of Colónia São Leopoldo in Río Grande do Sul in the vicinity of Pôrto Alegre. That same year, about 340 persons of German origin arrived in Brazil. This number was far less than the 1,750 Swiss who in 1819 had participated in the first colonial undertaking of immigrants in Brazil subsidized by the state. This initial colony was named Nova Friburgo.

The "founding act" of German immigration[1]—the settlement of the first colonists or São Leopoldo—is linked to Brazilian colonization policy for the south. Even before independence in 1822 there had been interest in promoting the occupation of the territory in the south of Brazil and in

---

*This article is a translated and revised version of "La inmigración alemana y la política brasileña de colonización," *Estudios Migratorios Latinoamericanos* 10 (1995): 53–75. Please see this text for complete references.

developing an agricultural industry through immigration and colonization. To this end, in the second half of the eighteenth century, families from the Azores islands were settled both in the south and in the extreme north of Brazil. This approach was rapidly exhausted, for the number of islanders was insufficient to populate the empty spaces in Brazil, including those of Río Grande do Sul.

While the colonizing experience in Nova Friburgo was successful, there were no new settlements after 1820; only in the second half of the nineteenth century did Swiss immigration start again but in very low numbers. Moreover, the settlement of Germans in Bahía and Pernambuco (between 1818 and 1822) failed; subsequently, these immigrants returned to their countries of origin. After independence, the increased concern with the occupation of the national territory, combined with the failure of the northern colonies, determined the imperial government's policy of colonization. This policy gave preference to immigrant projects in the south of the country. Until 1850 the majority of colonists were of German origin. With the increase in settlements and the growing restrictions on emigration to Brazil imposed by the Prussian government (eventually formalized in a decree of 1859), other immigrant groups—especially Italians—numerically surpassed Germans beginning in the 1870s.[2] The Prussian restrictions were abolished for the southern region, and German immigration then continued until the 1940s.

German colonization was the favored model in Brazil's colonization system because it fulfilled some of the goals of the country's immigration policy. Nevertheless, it also produced results contrary to this policy, especially results related to the ideals of immigrant assimilation and nation-building. In this essay, the two-sided nature of German immigration to Brazil during the period from 1824 to the 1940s will be analyzed, with the focus on the Germans' participation in the system of small property colonization and the organization of the German ethnic community. This colonization effort resulted in the establishment of 200 colonies in the south and in Espíritu Santo, and German immigrant community organization helped shape the German-Brazilian population as a paradigm of ethnic clustering.

The Representativeness of German Immigration

There are differing opinions about the number of German immigrants who actually entered Brazil between 1818 and 1940.[3] Scholars disagree on who should be counted. Some argue that German-speaking Austrians and the Germanic minorities in Eastern Europe who emigrated to Brazil should be included in the totals. Others count only those emigrating directly from Germany. Scholars can agree that Germans were a small portion (between 5 and 7 percent) of the more than 4 million immigrants whom Brazil received between 1886 and the 1940s.

In spite of the numerical insignificance of these numbers vis-à-vis the three main immigrant groups—Italians, Spaniards, and Portuguese—that represented more than 70 percent of the total immigration to Brazil, German immigration was fundamental in the articulation of the colonization system. Until the middle of the 1870s, the majority of the colonies established in the south were German. Colonization policy during the empire held Germans to be the ideal colonists. This preference was later criticized for a number of reasons: religious and cultural differences as well as the difficulty of assimilating the Germans. In spite of the evident official desire to link immigration and colonization, we should emphasize that not all Germans who arrived as immigrants were colonists. The documents produced by the directors of the colonies mention that many immigrants left their plots in search of better living conditions in provincial capitals, returned to their country of origin, or re-emigrated to other nations in the Americas. These same documents also indicate high death rates as well as overall discontent, escapes, and conflicts in many colonies. These indications reflect the extremely poor conditions and the lack of resources for the organization of public services.[4]

Such information helps us refine the statistics about German immigration: we know that many Germans arrived as immigrants to Brazil, but some left. On the other hand, at different times the empire recruited German mercenaries in the Brazilian army, and, although these soldiers were not included in the immigration totals, many of them remained in Brazil. A few of them played a significant role as journalists and politicians in the German-Brazilian communities of the south (for example, Karl von Koseritz, founder of an important German periodical in Pôrto Alegre and the first German-Brazilian to be elected provincial representative). In addition, even during the empire, and outside the context of colonization, German immigrants settled in São Paulo and Río de Janeiro. In the urban context this small but significant group has had an important role in the development of commerce in Río de Janeiro since 1808.

What is not in dispute is that language played an important role in the definition of German ethnicity in Brazil: Germans from the Volga, from Poland, from the different sections of the Austro-Hungarian Empire, and from the Danube, for example, assumed an ethnic identity in which the defining element was origin and the use of the German language. They ended up under the common denomination of German-Brazilians. J. F. Carneiro emphasizes the fact that official data are problematic because the constant change in European borderlines made classification according to nationality difficult.[5] This fact explains the relatively high numbers included in Carneiro's data in categories such as "miscellaneous," "Russians" (including Polish immigrants and Germans from the Volga), "Austrians" (including northern Italians and Germanic minorities), and the absence of Polish immigrants until 1920.

The relative difficulty of settling on an absolute number of German immigrants does not preclude the possibility of having a more or less precise vision of the migratory flow. In the first period, between 1824 and 1829, about 2,000 Germans participated in the founding of the first agricultural colonies in Río Grande do Sul, Santa Catarina, and Paraná. Recruiting was interrupted in 1830 because of a dearth of public resources and in 1835 by the civil war, and only started again in 1845. From 1845 onward, the flow became constant, with annual entry registrations that oscillated between 10,000 and 15,000 per decade until the outbreak of World War II. Two intense periods account for one-third of all immigrants: the five years before World War I (1909–1913), and the decade of the 1920s (during the economic crisis of the Weimar Republic). An exceptional number of Germans (22,170) registered in 1924, the record for an immigration flow that had never exceeded 2,000 per year.

Statistically, German immigrants to Brazil were a minuscule portion of the 5 million people who left Germany from the beginning of the nineteenth century. The major reason that German immigration was both visible and important in the Brazilian context was because of the immigrants' concentration in some regions—notably in the south of the country. As we shall see, the cultural, socioeconomic, and ethnic characteristics of this community that developed from the process of colonization in the south diverged from the national Brazilian ideals during this period of almost 120 years of immigration.

Immigration and Colonization

German immigration to Brazil cannot be considered a spontaneous movement. Propaganda and the action of representatives of the imperial Brazilian government and of private colonization companies (formed either in Germany or Brazil) directed at the less favored social classes (peasants and urban workers) attracted to Brazil individuals and families in search of better living conditions. Both the propaganda and the agents emphasized the virtues of the colonization system and promised subsidies and fertile lands in temperate regions—a kind of paradise for German peasants living in many agricultural districts in crisis (especially in Pomerania) and for proletarians subject to the worst working conditions.

However, not every German immigrant was of peasant or proletarian origin. Those favored by the immigration policy associated with colonization were agriculturalists, and different studies of specific colonies tell us that there was a certain predominance of farmers. But the system also incorporated artisans, laborers, and even a small proportion of political emigrants besides individuals who had some resources (usually modest) to be invested in agricultural ventures or in artisanal or commercial activities.

It must be emphasized that the social origin of the immigrants had little importance in the context of colonization. The official rhetoric of Brazilian immigration policy mentioned "undesirables" and held as privileged the peasant model of ideal colonization, but it did not exclude the entry of those who socially did not meet this norm.[6] In fact, those who entered the system, with some exceptions, became colonists even though not all of them remained so.

The relative success of this process of colonization with small family properties provided evidence for the discussion of immigration policy that preceded the promulgation of the Law of the Lands of 1850.[7] Colonization consisted of the occupation of the hilly terrain scorned by the ranchers and was implemented within a pioneer model. It was therefore a policy of peopling and agrarian development, initially focused on the regions around the provincial capitals. This development resulted in a nearly continuous system of territorial occupation of the main river valleys and, with the occupation of public lands, left the colonies at the margins of the great extensive ranching properties.

A quick overview of the process of occupation shows continuity and breadth from 1824 onward, in spite of a fifteen-year interruption between 1830 and 1845. The first colony, São Leopoldo, was founded in 1824 in an area located twenty-five kilometers north of Pôrto Alegre on the banks of the Dos Sinos River. However, starting in 1849 and until the end of the empire in 1889, colonization intensified and the main colonies such as Santa Cruz (1847), Santo Angelo (1857), Nova Petrópolis (1858), and Monte Alverne (1859) were established. Dozens of other nuclei were started by the initiatives of government or private companies; Blumenau (1850), D. Francisca/Joinville (1851), and São Bento do Sul (1873), among others, resulted from private initiative in Santa Catarina, where the provincial government also participated in the founding of colonies. German colonies outside of the southern region were restricted to the formation of a few nuclei in Minas Gerais, Santo Spirito, and Río de Janeiro.

Except for the colonies of Espíritu Santo, Río de Janeiro, and Minas Gerais, which only received immigrants in the imperial period (1822–1889), the occupation of the other areas continued through the republic (1889–1930). In the three states of Rio Grande do Sul, Santa Catarina, and Paraná, immigrants and their descendants established themselves in the plateau, in a system of colonization where private initiative predominated. This process formed some ethnically homogeneous nuclei. The most recent cases are located in Paraná: the colony of Mennonites in Witmarsum was founded in 1951 in the municipality of Palmeira; and the colonies of Swabians from the Danube, in Guarapuava and Entre Ríos, were founded after World War II with refugees of Germanic origin from Yugoslavia. However, the majority of the colonies developed after 1889, receiving people of different European nationalities.

In addition, German immigrants participated in the establishment of colonial nuclei along the railroads built in Paraná, Santa Catarina, and Río Grande do Sul at the beginning of the twentieth century. This colonization was implemented both by the state and by private agencies and resulted in the expropriation of those lands from traditional occupants, or *caboclos*, people who remained at the fringes of the process of colonization. Thus we see that German immigrants along with other Europeans participated in the occupation of a substantial part of the southern region. In spite of the substantial presence of private enterprises formed with the goal of promoting settlements in areas set aside for colonization, the Brazilian state created and controlled this system.

The first German colonies were the product of the initiative of the imperial government. The relative success of these German colonies was an element in the debate that preceded the promulgation of the Land Law in 1850. With the legal regulation of the sale of land to foreigners guaranteed by this law and by the normalization of the colonization system through a number of additional laws, decrees, and edicts, settlement increased with a predominance of German immigrants up to the middle of the 1870s. Starting in 1850, the provinces assumed the responsibility for colonizing their territories,[8] responding to legislation and rules set by the Ministry of Agriculture.

The first private initiatives were taken in the decade of the 1850s, with enterprises formed by farmers with European capital. The private companies were merely intermediaries between the state and the colonists: they bought public lands by means of a concession from the state to sell them later in parcels to the colonists. Although there were very few cases of colonization on private lands, these too ended up following the official model governed by the rules of the Ministry of Agriculture.

The characteristics of the system established in the legislation, therefore, were the same in both state and private forms. What was different was that the law changed the way land was granted from that during the first phase of German immigration (1824–1829), particularly in the form of land concession and the size of plots. Before the 1830s, the plots were bigger (about 75 hectares [one hectare equals 2.471 acres]), and they were handed over for free. In the decade of the 1840s, no longer were the grants free but were revised in favor of a system of installment payments that was considered more efficient in establishing the immigrant/colonists.

The formation of a peasantry on the frontier was the first distinctive characteristic of the colonization system, and it reminds us of the relative isolation of the colonists. The location of the first colonies in areas around the provincial capitals did not mean an immediate closeness to Brazilian society. Isolation was not just geographic. The term *colónia alemão* was more than a simple reference to the pioneer colonists. Some regions received immigrants continuously for more than fifty years—the majority of whom were of German origin. If there were other nationalities (such as Polish or Italians) in the German colonies, these newcomers were numerically less significant because there were similar "Italian," "Polish," and other colonies nearby.

Brazilians, in their turn, were relegated by the state and by the private companies to insignificant participation as colonists. Even if there were references to indigenous occupants and to the colonization with national workers in the legislation of the 1850s, racial considerations restricted the entrance of Brazilians into the system of small landholdings. Prejudice was not visible in the laws and decrees, but edicts and reports had restrictions that discriminated against the Brazilians. Works published under the Ministry of Agriculture manifested a racist ideology that influenced the Brazilian elite toward the end of the empire and during the republic. This ideology classified the vast majority of the Brazilian population within the so-called "inferior" or "primitive" races. From this starting point of supposed inferiority those consigned to the outcast category of "national workers"—including blacks, mestizos, and native peoples—were considered incapable of succeeding in enterprises based on free initiative, which ownership of land represented.

Colonization, thus, was always identified as an immigrant project and with a specific population model for the country. Germans had a central role in this process, which was based on the recruitment of colonists carried out by agents at the service of the imperial or provincial governments or by private enterprises. The second phase of colonization, at the end of the nineteenth century, was a period in which private colonization dominated the stage. The "old colonies" (formed during the imperial period from 1824 to 1888) later supplied a portion of the new colonists who settled in the western region of Río Grande do Sul and Santa Catarina, in the highlands of Paraná.

This point illustrates another characteristic of the system: the geographic mobility of the immigrants and especially of their descendants. The changes in legislation principally affected the form of payment and the subsidies of land. During the republic, the Land and Colonization Bureau under the Settlement Service of the Ministry of Agriculture gave legal guidelines to the provinces and private enterprises. Neither the change in political regime nor the continual revisions of the immigration laws and decrees altered the system substantially. Starting in 1850, the occupation of land of the so-called German colonies (as in the rest of the colonies) was carried out by means of grants of about 25 hectares, bordered by lines that paralleled the shores of rivers and streams. The standard size of the plot, the way in which it was delimited, and the price of the land were constant items in the legislation after the Land Law was promulgated. The lengthened shape of the plots was related to the uneven topography in almost all regions, a model that presumably gave colonists access to water and communication lines. The occupation of communities took place starting from those areas designated as "urban centers," which were much smaller and designed to contain the administration merchants, artisans, schools, and churches. This pattern was reflected in the layout of different cities.

In the official colonies, each immigrant family received its plot by means of an installment purchase, contracting a "colonial debt" that could include the price of the land and any subsidies that may have been eventually granted. In the act of concession, therefore, the head of the family assumed a debt with the state, receiving a provisional title where the obligations and the number of payments were registered (almost always in five yearly installments). Colonists were obliged within six months to cultivate a plot of cleared land and to build a dwelling (designated by the term "permanent dwelling"), actions that implied the intention of permanent occupation.

The basic parameter of the colonial model was the small plot of 25 hectares worked exclusively by the members of the family of the grantee who had to reside on the plot (and not in those lands classified as "urban"). This model made access to the land more difficult for single immigrants and for the children of colonists who already had a land grant. However, the idealized image found in the land maps and reproduced in the laudatory historiography of German colonization really hid a large variety of adverse circumstances, which affected a great proportion of public and private colonization projects. In plots destined for colonization, the demarcation of plots in straight lines on the maps of surveyors did not precisely match the uneven terrain, covered with vegetation, that the colonists found. These discrepancies produced conflicts, especially at the time of issuing final property titles, when a new mediation would have to be undertaken.

The standard size of 25 hectares stipulated beginning in 1850, according to the principle of exclusive use of family labor, ignored what would become the main reason for the later geographic mobility of the colonists: the poor quality of the government land set aside for colonization projects. In his studies of agricultural systems practiced in different periods during the European colonization, geographer Leo Waibel affirmed that plots should have had at least 55 hectares of fertile land, and between 85 and 105 hectares for lands less adequate for farming.[9] The standard of 25 hectares was also used in colonies administered by private companies, even though there were no other restrictions to land access as in government projects.

Obscured by an almost idealized image of the self-sufficiency of family-owned small landholdings, the colonization plan did not take into account the difficulties of cultivation in jungle areas and of the great distances from consumer markets. In addition, with few exceptions the farming techniques used by the settlers did not contribute much to the modernization of Brazilian agriculture in the way those who created the system had hoped. Instead of introducing their own European farming procedures in keeping with the designs of those who created the colonization policy, they adopted the native methods of *coivara* (clearing of the trees followed by razing). They also initially found problems in plowing. Waibel talks about the slow progression of rotating the land and crops to avoid the rapid depletion of the soil. However, as other authors on this subject point out, there are innumerable references to the use of a farming technique considered "primitive" and to the geographic mobility of the colonists that resulted from their failure to farm the land.[10]

There were no advanced preparations of the areas designated to be settled. Work to demarcate the lines and the opening of the means of communication happened simultaneously with the arrival of the immigrants. Therefore, those who bought or were given the colonial lots were hired to put up fences, construct bridges, clear the land, and set up public lands. These services should have existed as a precondition for the settlements. Consequently, in the pioneer cycle (even during the most recent stages of colonization), immigrants expected concessions of six to twelve months with regard to payments based on their farm's productivity. In addition, settlers could only count on their family's labor, while labor traditionally had been collective in their country of origin. In this precarious situation, many settlers depended dramatically on subsidies from the state or from private companies as the best way to escape from dependence on the local merchants' system of credit (and consequent indebtedness) and to survive until their farms showed a profit.

This brief description of the colonial system does not include the everyday hardships, partly related to the lack of essential public services, that appear in autobiographical writings, administrators' correspondence, and local historical accounts.[11] The information on the colonial system shows that implementation of the model for colonial farms in the south of Brazil was thought up in an official environment but was far from the harsh reality. Nevertheless, official numbers registered in provincial presidents' reports pointed out the success and prosperity of the colonists' endeavors.

In spite of these difficulties, up until the first decades of the twentieth century, the main objective set by immigration policy regarding colonization was the development of an agriculture that was oriented to providing for the cities in the south. This agriculture was an almost exclusive activity of immigrants and their descendants. The demand for land associated with immigration flow plus a high birth rate in the older colonies led to the occupation of part of three states in the south and resulted in the formation of a peasantry whose economic base was the small, family-owned, mixed-farming property. Germans were not the only historical actors; they shared this role with other European immigrants.

The term *colónia* is significant in this historical tradition: it refers to a colonized area as a whole (including the urban groups or *Stadtplatz*) and its minimum unit, the small property. The plot also was given the name of colony, and its holders the official designation of *colono*. This colonial complex of farmers represents a unique combination of domestic and corporate economy, an essential characteristic in the theoretical definition of the peasantry. In it there are no permanent wage workers; productive tasks were done by family members where, in the division of labor, criteria of sex and age prevailed. The colony existed as a unit of mixed farming production, combining crops destined for the family and for the market as well as the breeding of domestic animals (poultry, pigs, and dairy cattle). When we idealize the pioneer past, the traditional colony appears as a self-sufficient unit. However, in reality it depended on ties with the market run by merchants represented in the *Stadtplatz*, who almost always were of the same ethnic origin. The production surplus was sold in commercial houses of the villages and towns in the colonized areas. This fact signaled another characteristic of the peasantry—their dependence on those who were not farmers.

In a general sense, farming techniques and the kind of crops that were chosen by the settlers had nothing to do with the traditions of the German peasantry. Plots were developed characteristically by the use of the *coivara*, planting solely by a plow and hoe; after five or six years, the rotation of crops was used as a way of keeping the land productive. Finally, the colonists planted the basic Brazilian crops such as corn, manioc, sugarcane, tobacco, and beans. As pointed out in the immigration literature, in the colony as well as in the villages and cities, it was intense artisanal activity that made a difference and in some sectors led to industrialization.[12] In the historical period we are considering, there was an industrial transformation of colonial products—goods produced by the settlers themselves—by specialized artisans and by merchants with capital.

Among the activities of the small family-owned property were the manufacture of lard, cigars, wine, and dairy products; settlers who owned sugar and wheat mills lent their services to the others. Thus, the artisan remained attached to agriculture; goods were not produced by specialized artisans but by farmers within the economic system based on family production. Artisan work was an activity complementary to this system and necessary to produce enough to sell outside the borders of the colonial regions. Many flour and sugar mills belonged to the local merchants rather than to the farmers.

Small artisan-based industry proliferated in the rural environment and in urban areas. It was considerably diversified: breweries, delicatessens, soap and oil factories, distilleries, smithies, leather works, shoe manufacturers, and canning factories among others were fairly usual up to the 1940s. In addition, a process of industrialization began in various centers of German colonization at the end of the nineteenth century, independently from these small artisan enterprises. The textile and metallurgical industries in the valley of Itajaí and Joinville and the leather industry in the region of São Leopoldo are examples. In addition, German immigrants were responsible for the first industries in Pôrto Alegre (shipyards, breweries, and ironworks). Certainly the beginning of industry cannot be attributed to the artisans: the accumulation of capital by German-Brazilian merchants fostered this development, although there were some exceptions.[13]

These brief observations show the social differentiation in the colonies, even among farmers, with the consolidation of a rural and urban middle class, and an upper class made up of merchants and industrialists. In some towns (Blumenau, Joinville, Novo Hamburgo, São Leopoldo), industrialization helped to absorb part of the excess rural population, even though migration from one colony to another may have been numerically much more important before the 1940s. In fact, this process of industrialization began at the end of the nineteenth century, but the main industries developed more systematically only after World War I. After the 1930s, the process of industrial development played a leading role in the rural-urban migration, with the formation of a significant working class of rural origin. In some regions, as in the Itajaí Valley, there was a specific segment of farmers partially proletarianized who combined wage labor in industry with work on a small rural property that was by itself too small to sustain the peasant family.

If we go back to the idealized image in Brazilian policy that the immigrants would assimilate into the broader nation, one can say that the historical process of colonization showed significant differences in the efficiency of colonizers/immigrants compared to the patterns of Brazilian nationals. Differences with regard to Brazilian society go much further than the socio-economic aspects already mentioned. These differences between the German colonists and the Brazilian majority are found in the fields of urban planning, in architecture, in food habits, in working organization, in the type of rural family (which kept a Germanic family structure), and in class structure, just to mention the most important. Brazilian immigration policy, nevertheless, was marked by the assimilationist ideal. These economic and social differences resulting from the colonization process were in general not as visible as the cultural characteristics and ethnic institutions that served as the basis for German immigrant community organization and for the constitution of a German-Brazilian identity.

German-Brazilian Community Organization and the Construction of an Ethnic Identity

In an article titled "O Brasil e a imigração," included as an appendix to his *Historia do Brasil* published in 1859, Heirich Handelmann said: "the German race . . . is not one of those that lets itself be absorbed and assimilated."[14] The reforms that emerged to attract a spontaneous immigration flow to Brazil in large part coincided with the proposals of Brazilians favoring immigration. Both, for example, supported efforts to foster naturalization, religious freedom, civil marriage, changes in the structure of land ownership, and the abolition of slavery. However, Handelmann notes that the reforms diverged from Brazilian ideas on a fundamental point: the intended assimilation of the immigrants would be an impediment to German immigrants because they would transfer to their adopted country the "love for the fatherland," but they would never renounce their "nationality, language, and customs."[15] This German author, therefore, anticipates the discussion about ethnic pluralism and German-Brazilian identity that would become the main point of contention between Brazilians and the German colonists

The situation of the colonies on the frontier favored the emergence of a strong, organized ethnic community; its principal cause, however, was certainly not isolation. *Deutschtum* (Germanity), a word frequently used in newspaper editorials and German-Brazilian magazines, was summarized in Handelmann's recommendation: Brazilians were expected to give up their "native whims" if they wished to "receive German immigration." *Deutschtum* expresses a very simple idea: ethnic nationality is based in the *Volksgeist* (spirit of the people), the *Kultur* (culture), and the *Muttersprache* (mother tongue), and assimilation meant destruction of all three. German immigrants therefore considered Brazil their *Vaterland* (fatherland), took citizenship in the terms of the *jus soli* (based on residence instead of blood), acquired a *Bodenstandigkeisgefuhl* (they became attached to the land as expressed in the literature produced by intellectuals linked to the colonies), but they did not renounce their *Deutschtum*. The *Heimat* (homeland) built in the colonies in Brazil ought to have "a German character." In this case, formalized ethnic boundaries included the daily use of the language and the creation of institutions to preserve the culture—in elementary schools that taught the German language, in the German-Brazilian press, and in German recreational, sporting, and cultural associations.

The first community schools flourished simultaneously with the foundation of the colonies, partly because there was either a partial or complete lack of public schools. Settlers frequently asserted their rights to a quality education, and the large number of German elementary schools was attributed to the fact that the state did not provide schools for the immigrants. Emilio Willems points out the difficulties that arose from the implantation of a Germanic-Brazilian school system and its heterogeneity, stating that "German immigrants were more concerned with themselves than with solving the problem of education."[16] However, in the context of *Deutschtum*, school represented a sure way to maintain the mother tongue: it helped to stimulate the daily use of the German language. The fact that the language survived in the presence of the public school (free) system was due to its character as an ethnic boundary rather than to its much-vaunted excellence. For this reason, the German-Brazilian press during the 1930s defended German teaching from a Brazilian offensive against the so-called ethnic schools, all of which finally became nationalized in 1937. When the nationalization of schools started, there were approximately 1,500 German-language schools, many of which were concentrated in Río Grande do Sul and in Santa Catarina, with the Catholic, Lutheran, and Evangelical churches maintaining most of them. These churches had a leading role in preserving ethnic values, since community schools were fewer and existed in the rural environment. Each of these systems of teaching drew their orientation from Germany through different associations and pedagogical publications.

The German-Brazilian press and other periodicals in German also had a leading role in the construction of an ethnic identity. Since the first publication—*Der Kolonist*—in Pôrto Alegre in 1852, more than fifty newspapers flourished in different cities (including Pôrto Alegre, Curitiba, São Paulo, and Río de Janeiro). Two significant newspapers began in the 1860s: the *Deutsche Zeitung* (1861) in Pôrto Alegre, and the *Kolonie Zeitung* (1862) in Joinville. In 1931, H. Gehse listed a total of twenty-six newspapers in Río Grande do Sul, fifteen in Santa Catarina, ten in Paraná, ten in Río de Janeiro (five of which were in Petrópolis), and seven in São Paulo that had been established since 1852.[17] Some lasted a short time; others, such as the *Kolonie Zeitung*, circulated more than half a century. In the 1930s there were thirteen newspapers, three of which were in Pôrto Alegre and five in the region colonized in the valley of Itajaí and five more in Joinville. The newspapers *Der Kompass* (Curitiba), *Deutsche Zeitung* and its predecessor *Germánia* (which circulated between 1878 and 1921), of which the latter two were in São Paulo, also were distributed in the colonial regions by local wholesale merchants.

Besides the newspapers, in the 1930s there were various publications in the German language: several monthly religious magazines (two Catholic, ten Evangelical, and two Lutheran from the Missouri Synod), pedagogical magazines (a total of five, edited in Pôrto Alegre, São Leopoldo, and Blumenau), monthly newspapers directed specifically at colonists with technical information for agriculture and cooperatives, newspapers directed toward families, and yearly almanacs, among which was the *Kalender für die Deutschen in Brasilien*. In one way or another, they were all committed to Germanic ideals.

Depending on the kind of publication, there was local, national, and international news alongside articles dealing with ethnic issues, useful information aimed at the small rural producer, transcriptions of poetry, stories, and short novels written by either German or German-Brazilian writers, and even Brazilian novels translated into German. Eventually, there was active participation related to specific community institutions, such as the defense of German schools during the 1920s and 1930s or the July 25th "Day of the Colony," which celebrated the founding of São Leopoldo.

In a text about the school issue, Marcos Konder (belonging to a German-Brazilian political family in Itajaí) attributed "the greatest accomplishments of colonization to the excellent education at home as well as in schools" as a clear reference to the two principal poles of the formation of ethnicity. Konder includes his ethnocentric stand in his volume commemorating the 100 years of German immigration in Santa Catarina, which is a synthesis of *Deutschtum*, a term that also expresses the Germanic contribution to Brazilian progress (colonization and economical success).[18] However, as noted earlier, *Deutschtum* also meant the preservation of German culture. Various clubs and associations had the goal of preserving German traditions not only in sports but also in music, singing, poetry, literature, and theater. The intense activity of these associations was remarkable in all colonial regions, precisely because of their organization into federations, which established a true network of social relations among different segments of the rural and urban German-Brazilian population, ensured also by the press as well as by the schools. This structure of the ethnic group could be observed not only in the rural areas of the colonies but also in Río de Janeiro, Pôrto Alegre, Curitiba, and São Paulo. These cities received German immigrants, but, more important, they became poles of attraction for those who abandoned the colonial system under which they had originally immigrated to Brazil.

All of this suggests that German-Brazilian ethnicity arose within an urban context, marked by a number of symbols linked to the process of establishing colonies and to the preservation of German culture in those colonies. An intellectual and political elite connected with the press and other associations established the category of identity *Deutschbrasilianer*, which reflected a double preference for German ethnicity and the Brazilian state. The core elements of this ethnic condition were related to everyday life—the use of the German language and a strong German element in clubs and organizations, the home, the customs, and the *habitus* (the Weberian notion of "a subjective belief in a common background"). In its condition as an ethnic symbol, colonization was presented as a result of German diligence that transformed the "Brazilian jungle" into a civilized place.

Taken as a type of ethnic ideology, the idea of *Deutschtum* linked the population of German origin with an ancestral fatherland (*Urheimat*): the German nation conceived as a racial and cultural entity. However, *Deutschtum* also embodied the idea that the colonists were "Germans in Brazil": therefore Brazilians, but different from the rest. The pluralist claim contained in this ideology clashed with the idea of assimilation set forth by the official state immigration policies. The pluralist discourse of the German-Brazilian elite with political aspirations, begun by Karl von Koseritz even during the empire, had a negative consequence in the midst of Brazil. It did so because any plural identity would be inconceivable given that the ideal of nationality in Brazil was unequivocally Brazilian. Those who were not assimilated could only be classified as "foreign" or *alienígenas*.

In the period under consideration, the German colonies appeared to the Brazilians as unassimilated ethnic communities, dangerous to national integrity. A strong feeling of group and an ethnic ideology created from *Deutschtum*, in addition to political aspirations and other rights of citizenship systematically claimed through the press, gave an argument to those critical of the German presence in the south of the country. Critics were worried about the "German Danger" (that is, the possibility of the secession of the colonies) and produced a series of crises that were progressively aggravated by pan-Germanist ideology before World War I and Nazi ideology in the 1930s. The moments of greatest tension happened during the First Republic (1889–1930) and the Estado Novo (1937–1945).[19] For example, during the First Republic, there was pan-Germanist propaganda, the *Panther* case in 1905 (a controversy over the treatment of a German sailor in a Brazilian port), the Delbruck Law in Germany that facilitated the access of the sons and daughters of German immigrants to German citizenship, the racist tone of some newspapers (such as *Der Urwaldsbote* in Blumenau), accusations about German imperialist interests in South America, and a declaration of a state of war against Germany during World War I. During the Getúlio Vargas regime and the Estado Novo, there was the presence of leaders of the Nazi Party and other typical Nazi manifestations of the 1930s and, finally, the nationalization campaign that began in 1939 and that was aggravated during World War II.[20]

The nationalization campaign, a major crisis, counted on the participation of the army. It attacked the ethnic bases of community organization, prohibited the public use of German, closed German schools and associations, and required the publication of German newspapers in Portuguese and insisted on Brazilian publishers (a measure that resulted in the almost total extinction of the regular publications of the German community). The compulsory use of Portuguese also destroyed the so-called *Deutschbrasilianische Literatur* (German-Brazilian literature), which had as its main subject the daily life in the colonies. Despite this nationalizing action (which affected all the other immigrant groups), ethnicity persisted in the cognitive construction of collective belonging, re-elaborating continually the historical experience of colonization and common origin as symbols of identity. Finally, what becomes clear from the German experience in Brazil is that the belief in a community of origin is important in the formation of ethnic communities, and immigration is one of its processes.

Final Considerations

The distinct qualities in the construction of a common German-Brazilian identity are defined by ethnic boundaries, according to the concept of F. Barth.[21] The existence of this identity, shaped by a concrete social reality (the so-called German colonies) served as an argument for the imposition of another identity, attributed by the Brazilians, that of "non-assimilated foreigner." The concept of nationality, based on the *jus soli*, was no longer enough to transform ethnic individuals into Brazilians, and the campaign of nationalization (which ended in 1945) was a practical act of condemnation of such plural identities.

There are similarities between the conception of ethnic identity and national identity; in both of them, elements such as a presumed common historical origin or a common linguistic and cultural community appear as symbols of unity. However, in the ideas that sustained the nationalization campaign in Brazil, only those people could be considered Brazilian who were not in conflict with the "national goals" based on miscegenation, the assimilation of all aliens, and the use of only one language in all the territory covered by the Brazilian nation.

The two themes briefly analyzed in this work are indicative of the paradigmatic character of German immigrants in the discussion and execution of the politics of colonization. In spite of their relative lack of significance in the overall immigrant statistics, Germans in Brazil have been the object of fierce nationalist debates since the middle of the nineteenth century. On the one hand, they were regarded as efficient settlers, although sometimes as too demanding in their claims; but, on the other hand, they were seen as inassimilable ethnic individuals who occupied the south of Brazil.[22]

Notes

1. Celebrations of German colonization ignore the failed experiences in the northeast (both at the beginning of the process in 1818 and 1822 as well as in the 1870s in Bahía's cacao-producing region); the commemorated date is the founding of São Leopoldo, July 25, 1824.

2. Several German groups spread a series of accusations: about the working conditions in the system in São Paulo's *colonato*, about the adversities faced by German immigrants in the colonial projects of the south, about the existence of a slave regime, and the restrictions imposed on non-Catholics. These issues, among others, were the determining causes in the promulgation of the decree of Heydt, which prohibited emigration to Brazil. It is also significant that one of those who formed the idea of one of the most important private colonization projects in Santa Catarina—Dr. Hermann Blumenau—came to Brazil for the first time in the 1840s to observe the living conditions of Germans in the *colonias* in Santa Catarina and Río Grande do Sul as a representative of the Society for the Protection of German Immigrants in the South of Brazil.

3. Data in this section come from these sources: J. F. Carneiro, *Imigração e colonização no Brasil* (Río de Janeiro: Faculdade Nacional de Filosofía, Cadeira de Geografia do Brasil, Publicações Avulsas, 1950); Emilio Willems, *Assimilação e populações marginais no Brasil* (São Paulo: Cia Editora Nacional, 1940); Emilio Williams, *Aculturação dos alemães no Brasil* (São Paulo: Cia Editora Nacional, 1946); M. Diegues Junior, *Imigração, urbanização e industrialização* (Río de Janeiro: CBPE/INEP, 1964).

4. G. Seyferth, "Colonização e conflicto," in *PPGAS/Comunicação* 10 (1988).

5. Carneiro, *Imigração e colonização*.

6. The ideal immigrant invariably seems to have been white, a farmer or artisan, healthy and industrious. These "qualities" placed Germans at the top of the immigrant hierarchy. At the same time, ministerial authorities and colonial directors condemned the introduction of such "subversives" as Socialists, Communists, and the revolutionaries of 1848, who were labeled the "dross of Europe" and accused of being the guiding forces behind all the conflicts and protests that took place in colonial areas. See Jean Roche, *A colonização alemã e o Río Grande do Sul*, 2 vols. (Pôrto Alegre: Ed. Globo, 1969); G. Seyferth, "Os paradoxos da miscigenação," in *Estudios Afro-asiáticos* 20 (1991); Seyferth, "Colonização e conflicto," 1988.

7. Law 601 of September 18, 1850, linked to immigration policy, regulated fiscal land and colonization. Its regulation can be found in Decree No. 1318 of January 30, 1854. This law abolished the existing regime of land tenure. The fiscal land was transformed into property sold by the state, and the concession of colonial plots was obtained by means of an installment purchase.

8. Initially, the provinces were only concessionaires because the lands belonged to the Brazilian state. The control of fiscal lands was only turned over to the provinces at the beginning of the Republic (in 1891).

9. Leo Waibel, *Capítulos de geografia tropical e do Brasil* (Rio de Janeiro: IBGE, 1958).

10. Ibid.; Willems, *Assimilação e populações marginais*; Willems, *Aculturação dos alemães no Brasil*.

11. The settlers' main claims (individual or collective) were related to medical and religious assistance, primary education, adequate means of transportation for their produced goods, delayed wages, and a clearer view of their colonial debt. Frequently they mentioned losses due to periodic floods, information about

epidemics such as smallpox, yellow fever, and typhus as well as malaria and other illnesses that considerably increased the mortality index.

12. Willems, *Aculturação dos alemães no Brasil*; Diegues Junior, *Imigração, urbanização e industrialização*; Roche, *A colonização alemã*.

13. Immigrants who brought family resources from Germany to initiate industrial enterprises were the exception; the best-known case is that of the Hering brothers, who established a textile mill in Blumenau in the 1880s.

14. Heirich Handelmann, *Historia do Brasil* (Río de Janeiro: Imprensa Nacional/ IHGB, 1931).

15. Ibid., 994.

16. Willems, *Aculturação dos alemães no Brasil*, 390.

17. H. Gehse, *Die deutsche Presse in Brasilien von 1852 bis zur Gegenwart* (Münster: Aschendorf, 1931).

18. G. Entres, *Gedenkbuch zur Jahrhundertfeier deutscher Einwanderung in Santa Catharina* (Florianópolis: Livraria Central, 1929).

19. One of the first anti-German outbursts occurred during the empire in the episode known as the "Christie matter," in 1863. On that occasion, *Deutsche Zeitung* published some articles defending the position of William Christie, the English ambassador, who demanded reparations from the Brazilian government for the looting of a vessel that was shipwrecked off the coast of Río Grande do Sul. In Pôrto Alegre, there were nationalist manifestations against German-Brazilian institutions, including one against the newspaper's editorial office.

20. The forced nationalization of the German-Brazilians was being proposed by some Brazilians, such as Silvio Romero, from the beginning of the Republic. The *Panther* case—a sailor from the crew of a German warship, which was visiting the port of Itajaí, deserted and was taken back to the ship by another sailor without Brazilian authorization—opened the polemic over the question of assimilation. See G. Seyferth, "O incidente do *Panther* (Itajaí, SC 1905); "Estudio sobre idologias étnicas," *Antropologia Social/Communicações do PPGAS* 4 (1994). But the proposal to "eradicate external influences," by means of compulsory assimilation, was only carried out during the Estado Novo and targeted mainly Germans and Japanese.

21. F. Barth, "Introduction," in F. Barth, ed., *Ethnic Groups and Boundaries* (Bergen: Oslo Universitetsforlaget; London: G. Allen and Unwin, 1969).

22. In his 1906 anti-German pamphlet, "Allemanismo no sul do Brasil," Silvio Romero compares the German settling movement to the barbaric invasion of the Roman Empire.

11

Jewish Immigration to Brazil*

Jeffrey Lesser

Jewish immigration to Brazil differed from that of the Italians and Portuguese in at least two important respects: it was much smaller, and it involved a religion that was different from that of the host society. Jeffrey Lesser takes us through the evolution of the Brazilian Jewish community in the colonial period and the nineteenth century, but he concentrates on the work of the Jewish Colonization Association in the twentieth century. Due in part to the match between the skills of the newcomers and the needs of the Brazilian economy, the Jewish immigrants as a group did better than most immigrants in Brazil and better than their counterparts in the United States and Argentina. Yet despite this success, Brazilian Jews are ambivalent about their place within the nation.

Jews have been a presence in Brazil since the colonial era. Variously called *judaizantes, marranos, conversos,* and *cristãos novos* (New Christians), Jews came in limited numbers to escape the Inquisition as well as the economic, social, and religious persecution of the Church and Crown in Portugal. While New Christians may have made up as much as 20 percent of the white population of the colonial capital of Salvador, Bahía, large-scale Jewish immigration to colonial Brazil never took place.

Brazilian independence, achieved in 1822, brought about the end of official persecution of Jews, even though non-Catholics were not permitted public exercise of their faith. With the creation of the republic in 1889, the state was secularized and all legal distinction of religious affiliation ended. Throughout the early nineteenth century, Jews entered in small numbers as part of a general European migration to Brazil and made significant social and economic progress in the capital of Rio de Janeiro.

*This essay is based on Jeffrey Lesser, *Welcoming the Undesirables: Brazil and the Jewish Question* (Berkeley: University of California Press, 1994); and idem, *Negotiating National Identity: Immigrants, Minorities, and the Struggle for Ethnicity in Brazil* (Durham, NC: Duke University Press, 1999). The author thanks René Decol and Samuel Baily for their helpful comments.

The small numbers of Jews entering Brazil did not compare with the masses arriving in other American nations. In the United States, Canada, and Argentina, countries with the largest Jewish communities in the hemisphere, dislocations in midnineteenth-century Central Europe led to the settlement of German speakers who were followed at the end of the century by East European, primarily Yiddish-speaking, Jews. The former group emigrated with urban and acculturated life-styles, and it was these Central Europeans who formed the corporate base of Jewish life in the communities in the United States, Canada, and Argentina. By the latter decades of the nineteenth century, the dominant forces in Jewish communal/organizational life in all three countries were German-Jewish based, even though the population was increasingly East European in origin.

Brazil has a variant in Jewish immigration unlike that in the aforementioned nations. Those who arrived before the establishment of the republic in 1889 consisted of about 2,000 North Africans in Amazonia as well as some Alsatians, English, and Germans who lived in Rio de Janeiro. In 1903 the Jewish Colonization Association founded a group of colonies that eventually attracted another 1, 500 Jews to Brazil. In 1910 the American Jewish Yearbook estimated the Jewish population there at 3,000, and by 1920 the figure had only risen to 6,000.

Within fifteen years, however, the situation would change. Immigration restrictions throughout the hemisphere and an alteration in European images of Brazil made the country an attractive destination. Between 1924 and 1933, East European immigration to Brazil jumped almost 1,000 percent to over 90,000 people, and almost 50 percent of these new arrivals were Jews. By 1930, Brazil's Jewish population was reported at about 30,000, and it was only after 1935 that Central European Jews, already populous and powerful in the United States, Canada, and Argentina, began arriving in significant numbers as war refugees, eventually comprising about one-quarter of the Ashkenazic population.[1] While Jewish entry to Brazil was reduced notably during World War II, it rose again as Arab nationalism impelled large numbers of Sephardic Jews to emigrate, and between 1950 and 1960 another 15,000 Jews settled in Brazil, creating a community that in 2000 had between 100,000 and 120,000 members.

The Roots of Brazil's Jewish Community

The establishment of a modern Brazilian Jewish community can be traced to the early nineteenth century, when North African (Maghribi) Jews began settling at the mouth of the Amazon. Jews were driven from Morocco by a profound sense of minority status that was emphasized as economic opportunity diminished and Muslim merchants became increasingly xenophobic and resentful of the economic ties that many Jewish merchants had to the French. At the same time, Maghribi Jews were prime candidates for emigration because of their transnational perspective and multi-lingualism: Arabic and Spanish were used for business, French and Hebrew were studied at Alliance Israélite Universelle schools that had been set up in many Moroccan towns, and Haquitia was spoken at home.

By 1890 more than 1,000 Maghribi Jews had migrated to the state of Pará. The Brazilian rubber economy was booming, and Belém do Pará, a city located at the mouth of the Amazon, was filled with peddlers and small merchants. Many Jews settled in small towns along the banks of the river where they traded city goods such as clothes, medicine, tobacco, and *cachaça* (a sugarcane-based liquor) for fish, Brazil nuts, rubber, and copaiba oil. Prosperity, however, was only one of the attractions for Morocco's Jews: they soon discovered that they could easily obtain Brazilian naturalization certificates. For Jews, becoming Brazilian meant both economic advancement and a sense of security.

The number of Moroccan Jews who remained permanently in Brazil was modest, perhaps no more than 1,000 people, yet the existence of this community was well known and elite impressions of it were not always positive. Indeed, the Brazilian government worked hard to discourage the entry of Maghribi Jews, eventually breaking diplomatic ties with Morocco over the issue. Just at this time, however, European Jewish refugee organizations began to look toward South America for mass resettlement when Tsar Nicholas II expelled all Jews from Moscow as part of his "Russification" plan.

In Germany, Jewish communal leaders, fearful that the Russians might resettle among them and interfere with the process of acculturation begun so auspiciously under Napoleon's emancipation decree, set out to find alternate places of residence for the refugees. They quickly set up an agency, the Deutsches Zentral Komitee für die Russischen Juden (German Central Committee for Russian Jews), and sent Oswald Boxer, a Viennese journalist and friend of Zionist leader Theodor Herzl, to Brazil to investigate possibilities for the resettlement of Russian Jews as farmers.[2] Notions of a return to the land, then popular among European Jewish intellectuals, led many in the Deutsches Zentral Komitee to ignore the fact that most Muscovite Jews were urban tradespeople and not farmers. Regardless of this difficulty, Boxer reported enthusiastically to the Komitee after visiting São Paulo and Rio de Janeiro in May 1891.

The high hopes were dashed when a series of late nineteenth-century political changes in Brazil discouraged the Deutsches Zentral Komitee from sending any immigrants. Indeed, the secular nature of the new Brazilian republic, which, as noted, included the end of all legal distinction of religious affiliation, did not soothe other fears about the safety of Brazil that were confirmed in 1892, when Boxer died of yellow fever in Rio de Janeiro.

In the early twentieth century, few European Jews went to Brazil since the more desirable locations—the United States, Canada, and Argentina—erected no barriers to Jewish entry. As the numbers of Jews leaving Europe increased after 1900, however, Baron Maurice de Hirsch, a Bavarian-born Jewish philanthropist living in Brussels, decided "to stake my wealth and intellectual powers . . . to give a portion of my companions in faith the possibility of finding a new existence, primarily as farmers and also as artisans, in those lands where the laws and religious tolerance permit them to carry on the struggle for existence."[3] Finding that money was available from a number of European sources, the baron founded the Jewish Colonization Association (Yidishe kolonizatsye gezelshaft, or JCA), in 1891 with the specific purpose of aiding poverty-stricken East European and Balkan Jews by establishing farming colonies in the Americas.

In 1893 the JCA set up its first colony in Moisesville, Argentina, to provide for Russian Jews already in the area. Thereafter, boatloads of JCA-sponsored Jews arrived in the country. In 1896, Hirsch died, bequeathing the funds needed to broaden the organization's scope. In early 1901 the JCA began to investigate expansion into Brazil's southernmost state, Rio Grande do Sul. Because of its proximity to the Argentine settlements and the state government's desire for new colonists, the state was thought to be a good home for Russian Jews. It was also attractive because the Positivist-influenced Rio Grande do Sul Republican Party (PRR) was tolerant in matters of religion, an important factor for immigrants being persecuted for their religious beliefs in the Russian empire.

Between 1904 and 1924 the JCA formed two Jewish agricultural colonies on the frontier of Rio Grande do Sul.[4] The new colonists fled daily persecution and accepted farming, with which they had little or no experience, as a condition of their escape from Europe. They never shared the dream of returning wealthy to their homeland—the dream of *fazer a América*—with other immigrants. The East European Jews who settled in Brazil never amounted to more than a few thousand people, yet they played two critical roles. First, the mere existence of the agricultural colonies contested elite notions of urban Jews as exclusively oriented toward finance and capital. Second, the residents of the colonies committed themselves to life in Brazil. This dedication challenged elite images of Jews as a closed group uninterested in becoming citizens of the countries where they resided. The two farming colonies were thus the first step in the regular and organized migration to Brazil.

The JCA brought Jewish immigration to the official attention of Brazilian political leaders for the first time since the Inquisition. This interest arose for a number of reasons. First, the Association enjoyed the diplomatic support of a British government committed to ensuring that emigrating Russian Jews would resettle outside of the United Kingdom.

As a consequence, in times of crisis, the Rio Grande do Sul government would often find the Jewish colonies represented by powerful English diplomats. Furthermore, some of the JCA's directors were also heavy investors in the Brazilian economy. Thus, the JCA provided legitimate refugee relief even while representing foreign interests in Brazil. As a result, a particularly strong relationship developed between the JCA, committed to Jewish resettlement, and the Rio Grande do Sul government, interested in subsidizing and sponsoring agricultural colonization and encouraging foreign investment.

There is no doubt that the Jewish colonies held special meaning for Rio Grande do Sul's politicians. When the state government decided to promote colonization at the St. Louis International Exhibition (World's Fair) of 1904, the official English-language *Descriptive Memorial of the State of Rio Grande do Sul* singled out the Jewish colonies, and no others, as examples of the positive results of colonization in the area.[5] This interest in Jewish immigration was important since many members of the Rio Grande do Sul government in the first few decades of the twentieth century would become federal leaders when Getúlio Vargas, a one-time governor of the state, led a coup and appointed himself president following his defeat in the 1930 presidential elections. Indeed, the positive images of Jewish immigration were in many ways unrelated to ethnic or religious factors. Simply by chance, the JCA began setting up its colonies during a period when immigration to Brazil fell significantly, a situation resulting in large part because of a crisis in the coffee industry generated by overproduction. Colonists, including Jewish ones, were welcomed with open arms.

Few people knew much about Jews in early twentieth-century Brazil, and politicians and large landowners (often the same people) were happy to support any group that would work the land in frontier regions. The positive attitude, however, was modified as more Jews entered the country in the next three decades. Those opposed to Brazil's changing economic order pointed to the regular out-migration of Jews from the Rio Grande do Sul colonies to urban areas as evidence that Jews could not fit into Brazil's agricultural orientation. Those on the left cited the European-based Jewish Colonization Association as an example of an alleged international Jewish capitalist conspiracy. For those on the right, the JCA's international and domestic connections gave the impression of an insular, powerful, and not easily identifiable group.

The Impact of World War I

The pattern of immigration to Brazil, both general and Jewish, changed when the violence and dislocation of World War I were unleashed. Although not militarily involved, Brazil suffered inflation, shortages, and capital market dislocations that scarred its already troubled social and economic face. Yet a quieter, more subtle change also occurred with the coming of global war. Throughout the Americas the streams of immigrants that had poured from Europe to new promised lands were shut off. In Europe, World War I temporarily strengthened local economies, demanded men to fill its armies, and commandeered shipping and passenger space for military purposes. With the end of the war, immigration restriction became the rule; and as nativist movements rose throughout the Western Hemisphere, immigration decreased.

Such was almost the case in Brazil. The number of migrants entering its ports fell by over 50 percent between 1913 and 1914 and by another 60 percent in the following year. In 1918 fewer than 20,000 immigrants entered Brazil, a low that would not again be approached until 1936. But, with the end of World War I, large numbers of people renewed their migration in part because Brazil did not respond to its local nationalist movements with immigration quotas. Between 1918 and 1919 the number of arrivals to Brazil's ports almost doubled, and in 1920 it almost doubled again, reaching 69,000.

Postwar immigrants differed in many ways from the prewar group, both in national origin and in their view of success and opportunity. Although Portuguese, Italians, Spanish, and German immigrants continued to predominate, two new groups now entered in growing numbers: Japanese and East Europeans. Population pressures on Japan's islands and the growing unrest among its rural people, led the Meiji regime and its Taisho successors to encourage emigration. These "push" factors combined with growing legislative and popular anti-Asian movements throughout the rest of the Americas. When Japanese entry into the United States was banned in 1907, Brazil became the center of an ever-growing Japanese diaspora. In the two decades following World War I, more than 150,000 Japanese immigrants entered Brazil.

With the end of the war, Jews began arriving in Brazil in ever-growing numbers (see Table 1). The upheavals caused by the establishment of the new state of Poland encouraged this emigration, as did legislation in the United States, Canada, and South Africa, where restrictive immigration quotas reduced Jewish entry. In Argentina the decision to issue visas to applicants only in their country of birth reduced the numbers of Jews in a position to make legal requests to emigrate. Brazil was left as one of the few large American republics without many impediments to immigration, and the Jewish Colonization Association targeted the country for migrant relocation. At the same time, Brazil's image among East European Jews was improving markedly. Its relatively strong economy was attractive, and newly formed communal and religious institutions provided funding and social help for newcomers. As Jews prospered in small and large cities throughout the states of Rio Grande do Sul, São Paulo, Rio de Janeiro, and Paraná, they sent a clear message back to Europe: Brazil was a land of prosperity and little religious conflict.

Between 1924 and 1934, East European immigration to Brazil increased almost ten times as more than 93,000 entered. Jews made up 45 to 50 percent of the group. Like all East Europeans, Jews reevaluated Brazil's potential as a country of resettlement as the economy seemed increasingly prosperous in the face of a shift toward industrial development after World War I. Jews, however, were not simply "pulled" toward Brazil; their increasingly precarious position in Eastern Europe certainly encouraged them to leave. By the mid-1920s more than 10 percent of the Jews emigrating from Europe chose Brazil as their destination; by the early 1930s the Jewish population of Brazil approached 60,000.

Table 1. Overall Jewish Immigration to Brazil, 1881–1942

	Overall Immigration to Brazil	Jewish Immigration to Brazil	%	As % of World Jewish Migration
1881–1900	1,654,101	1,000	.06	0.1
1901–1914	1,252,678	8,750	.07	0.5
1915–1920	189,417	2,000	1.0	2.2
1921–1925	386,631	7,139	1.8	1.7
1926–1930	453,584	22,296	4.9	12.9
1931–1935	180,652	13,075	7.2	5.5
1936–1942	120,318	14,576	12.1	3.6

Sources: Maria Stella Ferreira Levy, "O papel da migração internacional na evolução da população brasileira (1872–1972)," *Revista de Saúde Pública*, Supplement 8 (1974): 72; Jacob Lestschinsky, "Jewish Migrations, 1840–1956," in Louis Finkelstein, ed., *The Jews: Their History, Culture, and Religion*, 3d ed. (New York: Harper and Brothers, 1960), 2:1554.

Jewish Success and Community Building, 1920–1945

The East European Jews who arrived in Brazil after World War I and the Russian Revolution settled primarily in the states of São Paulo, Rio Grande do Sul, and Rio de Janeiro. They achieved a level of economic success matched by only a few other immigrant groups in Brazil, notably those from Japan and the Middle East. This success occurred for a number of reasons. Many Jewish immigrants settled in or near urban centers because refugee relief was most available there. This "step up," which included everything from help with housing to small loans, gave many Jews access to economic opportunities not available to other immigrants. The possibility of a real income combined with the communal and ethnic-based nature of the immigration process led Jewish immigrants to establish burial societies, youth groups, schools, and synagogues. The existence of these institutions made Jewish families more likely to invest their time and capital in a Brazilian future and less likely to leave. While never holding the allure of the United States or Argentina, by the mid-1920s Brazil was seen by Jews as an attractive nation of relocation. Indeed, the Jewish community, in the aggregate, was able to succeed economically in Brazil more than in any other American republic.

Jews rarely saw their migration to Brazil as an attempt to get rich overseas and return home. Economic opportunity, however, was an important component of the migratory process. In their homeland, many Jews had lived in towns and thus had some experience in small business and trade. An ever-increasing match between East European economic skills and the demands of the Brazilian economy for commercial and industrial activity helped many Jews rise to positions of financial security. Peddling and textiles, not farming, were the keys to success. By the end of the 1920s, European Jews saw that Brazil provided positive options for both secular and religious life. As other American republics restricted immigration through nationality quotas, Brazil, with its huge expanses of underpopulated land, growing urban centers, relatively open immigration laws, and apparent lack of anti-Semitism, seemed to be *o país do futuro* (the country of the future).

By the mid-1920s, Brazil was indeed a land of the future for Jewish emigrants. Between 1920 and 1930 about 30,000 Jews settled, making it the third most important receiving country in the Americas after the United States and Argentina. In one five-year period almost 13 percent of all emigrating Jews went to Brazil. As one relief worker commented in 1929, "The European Jew has adopted a new slogan: 'Go South, young man, go South!' "[6]

Most Jews arriving in Brazil in the 1920s came from Poland. Comprising a little over 10 percent of Poland's population, Jews were relatively urbanized and concentrated in manufacturing and trade.[7] Those with experience and skills, such as tailors, mechanics, and shoemakers, were needed, especially in the industrializing cities of the south, but Jewish immigrants rarely had the capital to buy a shop or factory upon arrival in one of Brazil's urban centers. These immigrants were often aided by *laispar kasses*, loan societies that provided them with the funds to purchase goods or to open a small shop or factory.

About 35 percent of the Jews arriving in Brazil had no professions or saleable skills and thus entered the life of the *clientelchik* (Brazilian Yiddish for peddler; the Brazilian Portuguese equivalent was *mascate*), an occupation that did not demand a large initial capital investment. Peddling was a prototype of Jewish economic integration in Brazil. Jewish store or factory owners would sell piece goods or housewares on credit to the newcomers, often choosing agents who were relatives or townspeople in their countries of origin. In cities with small Jewish populations, as many as 80 percent of the newly arriving males worked as peddlers, although the percentages were considerably lower in Rio de Janeiro and São Paulo. Peddling was so lucrative that it often led to small shop or factory ownership and more rapid accumulation of capital.

Brazil was fertile ground for peddling. Some European immigrants peddled clandestinely in the midnineteenth century, but legal peddling began on a large scale in the very late 1800s with Syrian and Lebanese immigrants, who found wider markets created by the abolition of slavery. When still more Syrians and Lebanese immigrated during the coffee boom, they also set the stage for the acceptance of Jewish peddlers a generation later.[8] As Brazil experienced significant population growth in the 1920s, the nascent middle class desired previously unavailable goods. Product distribution did not progress as efficiently as industrial growth and capital redistribution, so peddlers picked up the slack, efficiently and cheaply.

Jewish *clientelchiks* often purchased goods wholesale from former Syrian and Lebanese peddlers who had become wholesalers. Like these earlier immigrants, Jews often traveled in pairs: an experienced peddler helped the newcomer earn some income while teaching him Portuguese phrases and a sales pitch. Since many Jews had had experience in textiles prior to migration, they gravitated to the peddling of cloth, clothing, and sewing materials. By the late 1930s, 54 percent of the industries in Luz, a São Paulo district with a high Jewish population, produced clothing and cloth articles.

In cities across Brazil, from Curitiba in the south to Natal in the northeast, Jewish immigrants worked as peddlers and began to integrate into the Brazilian economy, much as did Jews in the United States and elsewhere. Indeed, one of the striking features of Jewish, Middle Eastern, and Japanese immigrant life in Brazil before World War II, and Korean and Chinese immigrant life afterward, is how ethnic banking and rotating credit were used to rapidly move even poor members of the community into self-sufficiency.

Saúl Givelder's story is typical. Born in 1906 in Moguilev, Russia, near the Dniester River, Givelder moved with his parents to Bessarabia when his father became manager of a small nail factory. Saúl attempted to emigrate to Palestine in his late teens but was unable to procure the necessary visa from the Soviet government. He first considered moving to Brazil because he "had many friends [there], and I had heard they became rich because [it] was a country where you could earn a lot of money." In 1930 he made his way to Marseilles, where he purchased his passage with an advance from the Jewish Colonization Association. Upon arrival in Rio de Janeiro, he became a peddler after a friend arranged for him to buy umbrellas on credit from a Jewish immigrant loan society. "In truth [Givelder] was not very good" at peddling, but soon he formed a partnership with a friend who owned a shop. This expanded the line of goods he peddled and increased his income. When Givelder's wife came to Rio ten months after his arrival, he already "had a house . . . and the basic necessities were satisfied."[9]

While it would not be accurate to suggest that Jewish economic success in Brazil was unique (it was certainly matched by Middle Easterners and Japanese), it would be correct to say that Jews, as a group, did better than most immigrants, and that Jewish immigrants in Brazil rose up the economic ladder higher and more rapidly than did Jews in the United States or Argentina. There are a number of reasons. Most notable was timing: Jews arriving in Brazil after World War I and settling in urban areas were able to take advantage of a new national focus on industry and provide goods and services that a growing middle class desired. At the same time, Jews stepped off the boat with a racial advantage—that of being "white" or at least "non-black"—in a nation where discrimination against people of color was commonplace.

Despite economic success and the support that community institutions, friends, and compatriots gave to the *clientelchiks*, peddling elicited dubious approval from Jewish leaders in Brazil. As was the case throughout the Americas, the Jewish establishment worried that the popular association of Jews with peddling would lead to a rise in anti-Semitism, fears that were not unfounded.

In 1929 the highly regarded poet Guilherme de Almeida, a member of Brazil's prestigious Academy of Letters, termed Bom Retiro, a São Paulo neighborhood with a significant concentration of East European Jews, "the Ghetto" in an article for the mass circulation newspaper, *O Estado de S. Paulo*. He conjured up a dual image that combined the notion of a Central European urban neighborhood where Jews were clearly segregated from the surrounding society with the poverty and otherness that non-Jews often associated with the East European *shtetl*. Bom Retiro, however, was neither a legislated Jewish residential area nor was it particularly poverty stricken. In fact, it had been an immigrant neighborhood since 1881, when São Paulo's provincial assembly placed an immigrant receiving station there. Almeida's description of the residents of Bom Retiro, however, suggests that he believed Jews were somehow less than completely human: "I found myself face to face with the first face (I saw) in the São Paulo ghetto. Face? Beard: beard and nose. The first Jew."[10]

Swelled by the numbers and relative success of immigrants arriving after World War I, Brazilian Jews created an extensive network of communal, social, economic, and political institutions. This rapid expansion of Jewish institutions did not only take place in São Paulo, Rio de Janeiro, and Pôrto Alegre, where the majority of Jews were settling. In the early 1920s Jewish schools also could be found throughout Brazil, even in such small communities as Campinas, Niterói, and Curitiba. By 1930 the Jewish Colonization Association had twenty-five schools with more than 1,600 students.

Newspapers also served the community. Brazil's first Yiddish-language newspaper, *Di Menscheit* (Humanity), began publication in 1915 in Pôrto Alegre. In 1916 the first Portuguese-language Jewish newspaper was founded by a Rio de Janeiro intellectual, David Pérez, whose Moroccan parents had arrived in the Amazon in the middle of the nineteenth century. Pérez, a lawyer who identified himself as a Brazilian Zionist, founded *A Columna* to combine a Zionist line with a desire to defend the interests of the country's Jews. The decade after World War I witnessed an expansion of the Jewish press. Most newspapers were printed in Yiddish and served as political and informational tools that helped the growing Jewish community integrate into Brazilian social and economic life. The Jewish press also helped facilitate immigration since much published information was related to the bringing of family members to Brazil from Eastern Europe.

The establishment of Jewish institutions made Brazil an increasingly desirable place for East European Jews, most of whom arrived after 1925 with their passage prepaid by relatives already in the country. These capital expenditures, and the establishment of a relief system to help newcomers find jobs, indicate how quickly many Jews found economic success. Thus, even as community leaders continued to worry about a negative backlash against Jewish entry, Brazil remained a focus of relocation efforts. These efforts included a new promotion of Sephardic immigration, and by the 1930s Brazil received between 10 and 20 percent of all the Jews leaving Constantinople. The Sephardic community quickly grew in size and importance. With this nucleus in place, a later migration, mainly from Egypt following the Suez crisis of the mid-1950s, was to find a recognizable communal life already in place.

By the early 1930s the Jewish community had changed significantly. Whereas a decade earlier, Jews viewed Brazil merely as a station on their way to fortunes elsewhere, now remigration was rare. Yet as integration progressed and Brazil's economy stagnated as part of the Great Depression, politicians began to see the Jewish presence as a key issue in gaining the support of a middle class whose economic expectations were not met. Policymakers and intellectuals harped on the fact that while immigrants were expected to save Brazil's agricultural economy and Europeanize the culture at the same time, Jews seemed to do neither. The middle classes resented both Jewish financial success and cultural difference. By 1934 immigration quotas had been established via a new constitution, and criticism of Jewish immigration was becoming a regular component of political discourse. As popular and political nationalism grew, Jews found themselves targeted for negative treatment by the Brazilian government.

The growing Jewish immigrant population, a worsening economy, and rising nativism made the so-called Jewish Question an important topic among intellectuals, state politicians from urban areas, and federal leaders. This sentiment was reinforced when the rise of National Socialism in Germany and Fascism in Italy simultaneously provided a model for Brazilian anti-Semitism and became widespread among intellectuals and federal policymakers in the 1930s. The existence of Nazi ideology made anti-Semitism respectable and surely played a role in how Brazilian policymakers reacted when confronted with growing pressure to accept Jewish immigrants and refugees. Modern European racial theories encouraged the view of Jews as an undesirable race.

Beginning in 1935, Brazil began sporadically to deny visas to Jews. Yet it was not until 1937, as the country moved swiftly toward authoritarian rule, that the discussion of Jews moved fully into the policy sphere. In late September the "Cohen Plan," a forgery by a rightwing political group that allegedly had plans for a violent Communist overthrow of the government that specifically included the burning of churches, was "discovered" by the offices of President Vargas.[11] The title, "Cohen Plan," was meant to suggest a linkage of Judaism and communism, and in September it was made public together with an executive decree suspending numerous civil rights. In November, Vargas led an *auto-golpe* (internal coup) as the cavalry surrounded the presidential palace and copies of the Estado Novo (New State) constitution were distributed.

Nativism was a critical part of political discourse during the Estado Novo. Yet the growing opposition to Jewish entry and the prohibition on Jewish entrances in late 1937 neither stopped them nor particularly changed their pattern. Indeed, only 11 percent more Jews, representing about 3,000 people, entered Brazil between 1920 and 1930 than did between 1930 and 1940. There are a number of reasons. Jewish tourists and businesspeople from the United States, Canada, Britain, and South Africa who were denied visas complained to their political representatives, who in turn pushed the British and U.S. governments to pressure Brazil to modify its restrictions. Furthermore, the appointment of former Ambassador to the United States Oswaldo Aranha as foreign minister helped a pro-Semitic vision of "the Jew" to gain credence within the government. From this perspective, German, Italian, and Austrian (but not East European) Jewish refugees were increasingly seen as bringing skills and capital to Brazil. International pressure to accept these refugees was matched by a change in perception among some of the country's most important immigration policymakers. By 1938 new rules regarding Jewish immigration reopened Brazil's gates to such an extent that more Jews were to enter than in any of the ten years previously.

With the immigration of Central European, primarily German, Jews to Brazil in the 1930s, a series of new institutions were created. German

Jews generally followed the Liberal tradition of worship, a form that grew out of the midnineteenth century emancipation when Jews were made citizens with full rights and that was based on the idea that Jews should be religious at home and citizens in public. The Liberal tradition, which included religious services conducted in the national language rather than in Hebrew or Yiddish, was seen as inappropriate by many Jews whose economic and political situation in Eastern Europe had left them with a highly traditionalized form of worship. As early as 1934, splits between Central and East European Jews in Brazil were apparent.

It was in the larger cities that the first large-scale German Jewish communal religious organizations were created. All emphasized the teaching of Portuguese, since most of the German Jewish leaders were of bourgeois background and fervently believed that people should be both good Jews and good citizens. A knowledge of Portuguese helped the German Jewish community to integrate socially and economically. Integration was also political, and the strong relationship between German Jewish leaders and Brazilian politicians often positively influenced the government's attitude toward Jewish refugees. The desire for integration should not indicate a declining attachment to German high culture, even among refugees from Nazism. Indeed, it was the "whiteness" of Central European Jews, often expressed via the relationship to European cultural norms, that created a scenario in which anti-Semitism, and the extraction of many refugees from the "Jewish" category, went hand in hand.

Brazil's Post-World War II Jewish Community

Brazil's postwar Jewish community, while in many ways similar to that in the other American republics, is far from a replication of those in the United States and Argentina. Jews in Brazil, for example, are more concentrated in the upper economic classes than in other places, but exogamy rates are as high as elsewhere. Zionism, although important in postwar Brazilian Jewish life, has never played the same role that it did in other communities in Latin America, notably Argentina, Uruguay, and Chile. For example, a preparatory *kibbutz* (agricultural community) of Brazilian Jews thinking of making *aliyah* ("returning" to Israel) was only founded in 1948, much later than in many other countries. The lack of participation in the agricultural Zionist movement led one Jewish leader to complain that because "the economic situation of Brazilian Jewry is fantastic . . . one finds [the group] in the process of complete assimilation."[12] Between 1948 and 1977, only 6,268 Brazilian Jews made *aliyah*, a number that compares (in percentages) more to the United States than to Argentina.[13] This statistic can be explained by a number of factors, but most notable are the integration of Jews into the upper and upper-middle classes and the lack of widespread violence (in either language or action) against Jews in Brazil.

Following the Suez crisis and the rise of Arab nationalism in the 1950s, about 5,000 Jews from Egypt and other Arab countries emigrated to Brazil (see Table 2). The established non-Jewish Syrian and Lebanese community became important facilitators for these new Jewish arrivals into Brazil's economic and political worlds. While the Sephardic newcomers initially had little contact with the established Ashkenazic community, this distance narrowed among the generation born in Brazil. Intermarriage between Sephardic and Ashkenazic Jews became common, and it is significant that the former German congregations in Rio de Janeiro and São Paulo elected Sephardic presidents in the 1980s. Today, most Jews in Brazil identify themselves as East European Ashkenazim, with about 20 percent falling into the German Ashkenazic category and another 15 percent into the Sephardic one.

The establishment of a military regime in Brazil in 1964 brought new challenges to the Jewish community. Although many Jews were prominent members of the opposition, most saw the twenty-one-year military regime as defenders of their class interests. Moreover, many Jews believed that state suppression of political movements would ensure that the level of anti-Semitism would remain low, an additional motive for Jewish support. Brazil's new military government never provided the expected protection for minority groups, and political violence against dissenters led many Jews to relocate to Israel where the Brazilian-born population doubled between 1977 and 1982. The regime's foreign policy also made many Jews uncomfortable, especially after 1975, when Brazil voted in favor of the United Nations resolution equating Zionism with racism.

Table 2. Jewish Population of Brazil, 1940–1991

Year	Number
1940	55,666
1950	69,957
1960	96,199
1980	91,795
1991	86,417

Sources: Instituto Brasileiro Geográfico e Estatístico (various censuses); U. O. Schmelz and Sergio Della Pergola, "The Demography of Latin American Jewry," *American Jewish Year Book 85* (New York: American Jewish Committee, 1985), 74.

While it is unclear exactly how many Jews live in Brazil today, in part because the definition of "who is a Jew" is highly debated, the figure is between 100,000 and 150,000. The Congregação Israelita Paulista is the largest synagogue in South America, boasting a membership of over 2,000 families, and affiliated Jews have a wide variety of options in their religious practice in all of Brazil's major cities. Jews are widely integrated into the political system at its highest levels. The 1988 presidential elections saw Brazil's most famous television personality, Silvio Santos (Senhor Abravanel), the son of Sephardic Jews from Greece, briefly enter the race. His public acknowledgment, but non-practice, of Judaism appears not to have hurt his base of support among the poor and urban working classes. More recently, Jews have held political posts, including that of foreign minister. They have also been promoted to the higher ranks of the Armed Forces, including as military commander of one of the largest states. Even so, a 1977 confidential report by the Army's Division of Security and Information, written at the height of the controversy over Brazil's proposed nuclear agreement with West Germany, claimed that Jews opposed to the agreement were Zionists.[14] While the Jewish Question may no longer be asked, questions about "Jewish issues" still exist.

Brazil has little popular or open anti-Semitism (in spite of a tiny skinhead movement and a few active Holocaust deniers), in part as the result of the limited contact between a relatively small community of Jews and the mass of the country's impoverished urban and rural people. Jewish issues (as opposed to ones related to Israel) are kept out of the spotlight, and Brazil's rhetoric of ethnic, cultural, and racial tolerance is backed up by law, making public anti-Semitism a crime. The current president, Fernando Henrique Cardoso (PDSB, Social Democratic Party of Brazil), a sociologist, was strongly supported by the Jewish community. As a senator he openly opposed Brazil's support for the United Nations' "Zionism equals racism" policy, which has since been overturned. Moreover, he made stops at Jewish communal institutions a regular part of his political routine. If any contemporary challenges exist, they come from the fundamental contradictions between antiracist electoral democracies and the rights of anti-Semitic and anti-Zionist groups under freedom-of-speech and -press guarantees. Yet recent moves toward peace in the Middle East have created a positive image of the Jewish State and by extension, Jews. In addition, the active involvement of some Jewish community leaders in popular movements to combat hunger, poverty, and discrimination have been widely publicized and have presented Brazil's Jews in a socially conscious light.

Conclusion

From the perspective of an outsider, Jewish life in Brazil is very good. One could make a small list of annual anti-Semitic incidents, but they are minor and the reactions to them are strong. Jews as a group are in the small privileged class and seem to suffer no political or economic discrimination, yet their place within the nation is marked by ambivalence. The result is that Jews in Brazil are extremely concerned about security even though the 1988 constitution makes the public expression of religious or racial prejudice a crime; there is even a law banning the display of the swastika.[15] However, the widespread elite position that the country is uniquely free of racism and bigotry, and the realization by ethnic and racial minorities that prohibiting an attitude does not make it disappear, weaves discrimination or, in this case, negative stereotypes of Jews deeply into Brazilian culture. One indicator is that Jewish institutions in Brazil are almost always hidden behind high walls and gates, which is not the case with, say, Japanese-Brazilian ones in which "Japaneseness" is proudly exhibited.

The history of Jewish immigration to Brazil stands well apart from that to the rest of the Americas because of its lack of mass nineteenth-century migration. Because of the numerical dominance of Polish Jews who emigrated after World War I and the Russian Revolution, as well as the significant number of Central Europeans fleeing the Shoah (Holocaust), and Middle Eastern Jews who departed following the 1954 Suez crisis, the contemporary Jewish community has significant numbers of people who remember the pre-migratory experiences of anti-Semitism. This collective memory helps to explain why so many Jews appear ambivalent about their place in Brazilian society in spite of access to education, generally high levels of social mobility, and apparently wide integration in both the social and economic spheres. Over the last decade, some Jewish community leaders have played an active role in popular movements to combat hunger, poverty, and discrimination. This involvement has been widely publicized and thus presents Brazil's Jews in a socially conscious light. For many Jews, however, the answer to the Jewish Question continues to be less than satisfactory.

Notes

1. Ashkenazim are generally understood to be the descendants of Jews from Western and Eastern Europe. Sephardim are descendants of the large community living in Spain and Portugal in the Middle Ages who were expelled in 1492.

2. For more on early schemes to settle Jews in Brazil, see Egon and Frieda Wolff, *Dicionário Biográfico II: Judeus non Brasil—Século XIX* (Rio de Janeiro: Egon and Frieda Wolff, 1987); and Nachman Falbel, *Estudos sobre a comunidade judaica no Brasil* (São Paulo: Federação Israelita de São Paulo, 1984).

3. Maurice de Hirsch, "My Views on Philanthropy," *North American Review* 153 (1889): 2.

4. Jeffrey Lesser, *Jewish Colonization in Rio Grande do Sul, 1904–1925* (São Paulo: Centro de Estudos de Demografia Histórica de América Latina, Universidade de São Paulo, 1991).

5. Eugenio Dahne, ed., *Descriptive Memorial of the State of Rio Grande do Sul, Brazil* (Pórto Alegre: Commercial Library, 1904), 29.

6. Cecilia Razovsky, "The Jew Re-Discovers America (Jewish Immigration to Latin American Countries)," *Jewish Social Service Quarterly* 5 (1928–29): 127.

7. Jacob Lestschinsky, "The Industrial and Social Structure of the Jewish Population of Interbellum Poland," *YIVO Annual of Jewish Social Science* 11 (1957): Table 1, 246.

8. Jeffrey Lesser, "From Pedlars to Proprietors: Lebanese, Syrian, and Jewish Immigrants in Brazil," in *The Lebanese in the World: A Century of Emigration*, Albert Hourani and Nadim Shehadi, eds. (London and New York: I. B. Tauris and St. Martin's Press, 1992), 393–410.

9. Interview with Saúl Givelder by Avram Milgram and Janette Engelbaum, November 31, 1985, Rio de Janeiro. Interview 13, American Jewish Archives (Cincinnati).

10. Guilherme de Almeida, "Cosmópolis: O 'Ghetto.' " Republished in *Cosmópolis: São Paulo/29* (São Paulo: Companhia Editora Nacional, 1962).

11. Hélio Silva with Maria Cecília Carneiro and José Augusto Drummond, *A Ameaça Vermelha: O Plano Cohen* (Pórto Alegre: L and PM Editores, 1980); Robert M. Levine, *The Vargas Regime: The Critical Years, 1934–1938* (New York: Columbia University Press, 1970), 145; Carlos Lacerda, *A Missão da Imprensa* (Rio de Janeiro: Livraria AGIR Editora, 1950), 61.

12. Sigue Friesel, *Bror Chail: História do Movimento e do Kibbutz Brasileiros* (Jerusalem: Departamento da Juventude e do Chalutz da Organização Sionista Mundial, 1956), 13.

13. Donald L. Herman, *The Latin-American Community of Israel* (New York: Praeger, 1984), Table 2.1, 32.

14. *Latin American Weekly Report*, June 20, 1980.

15. *Constituição da República Federativa do Brasil, 1988*, Article 5, XLII.

12

Family and Immigration in the Brazilian Past

Maria Silvia C. Beozzo Bassanezi

Maria Silvia Bassanezi focuses on the impact of migration on the Italian families who went to Brazil. Government subsidies, the ratio of men to women in the migration flow, the timing of emigration, the nature of the labor markets, the attitudes of the receiving society, and the places where the newcomers settled all had an impact on the family. A distinctly non-European marriage pattern developed in the coffee-growing regions of Brazil in which more people married and the partners married at a younger age than in the areas of Italy from which the migrants came. There was also a difference between the immigrant families on the coffee-growing plantations of São Paulo and those in the colonies in the south. The latter tended to be larger. In both cases, size was a response to the necessary adjustments immigrants made to the new society in which they settled.

In the period of international mass migration—the latter decades of the nineteenth century and the early decades of the twentieth century—Brazil was among the major receiving nations of immigrants. One of the characteristics that distinguished Brazil from other receiving nations was that the government exerted considerable influence in shaping the immigrant flow as a predominantly family-dominated one. In fact, its policies gave preference and incentives to family migration for different reasons. These policies were designed to support agricultural colonization that was aimed at promoting national defense, peopling the territory, and supplying the internal market. Moreover, the policies were meant to meet the great demand for labor on the coffee plantations, where immigrant wage labor was replacing slave labor.

The issue of the immigrant family in Brazil, however, has not yet received adequate attention from migration or family scholars. The "photo album" of the immigrant family in Brazil remains incomplete. Leafing through the imaginary pages of this album, we find some pictures in focus and some blurred: of families choosing to migrate, arriving in the new land, growing and multiplying, finding work, and, in the process, weaving social networks. Among the photographs we can also see images that reveal gender and intergenerational relations as well as relations of power and group solidarity.

Deciding to Emigrate

The migration flow to the Paulista (state of São Paulo) coffee region confirms the theory that the general reasons both for the migrants to leave their homelands and for societies to seek immigrants were similar. This movement was part of a common economic system and global demographic transformation that made millions of individuals and families choose to cross the ocean in search of better living and working conditions. In Brazil the rapid growth of the coffee business generated capital to subsidize foreign immigration and to finance not only the expansion of rail links but also the industrialization and urbanization of São Paulo state. These factors, when added to important political and institutional reforms such as the abolition of slavery and the establishment of a decentralized republican system, generated favorable conditions for massive immigration to São Paulo.

A major advertising campaign throughout Europe as well as travel subsidies for emigrant families were key incentives for Europeans—especially those most impoverished ones—to leave their countries of origin to work at least initially on the coffee *fazendas* under the *colonato* labor system,[1] as subsidies were restricted to that system. Work on the *fazenda* offered access to land that produced subsistence for the family and a surplus that could be sold in local markets. It fed migrants' expectations of better living conditions as well as stimulated dreams of future land or business ownership. Even the propaganda suggested that the *fazenda* was the place where immigrants initially adapted and learned about their new environment.

By accepting work on the *fazendas* in exchange for travel subsidies, the immigrants were assuring the migration of whole family units. Sometimes families were accompanied by others who were either related by kinship or were acquaintances who had accepted work in the same place. Once they settled on the *fazenda*, they could send home a *carta de chamada*[2] that made possible the immigration of relatives who had stayed in the native land. Documents found in our research show that *fazenda* owners were interested in hiring relatives and acquaintances of good *colonos* (workers under the *colonato* system) and reveal the practice of lodging relatives and friends within the same *colônia*[3] wherever possible.

In the European agricultural societies from which the immigrants came, the family was the fundamental unit around which work was organized. In Italy, which supplied the majority of the workforce for the Paulista *fazendas*, both among the peasants and the *braccianti* (proletarianized farm labor), family work was a value to be preserved. The *colonato* system further reinforced this expectation that the family would remain the main unit of production. The likelihood that these values would be respected on the coffee *fazendas* without doubt weighed in the decision to emigrate and in the choice of destination.

The letters and narratives that the immigrants left us show that, regardless of the force of historical circumstances and social-economic determinants, there was room in the migration process for the decisions of the historical actors involved (individuals and/or families). These documents show that the decision to migrate was generally made by the family as a whole. Even when individuals departed alone, the decision to leave was rarely an isolated one. Furthermore, in the context of family life in those places, particularly Portugal and Italy, that sent migrants to Brazil for a long time migration had been a strategy to improve the family's living conditions as well as its occupational and economic situation. Migration could be considered a way of surviving.

In the decision to migrate, gender, generation, and power relations played an important role. The initiative was often in the hands of the family head or father. He was listed in the family's collective passports as the person responsible for the wife and children when they migrated together. However, women influenced the migratory process when they refused to accompany their husbands at the time of departure or when they failed to respond to the *cartas de chamada*—thus remaining in their countries of origin. At times when the decision to migrate was made by family consensus, the women coordinated the process.[4] Travel subsidies were granted on the condition that at least one member of the family was a male between 12 and 45 years old. In addition, travel subsidies restricted which members of the family could migrate together.

Arriving in the New Land

We know from passport records, boarding lists, and immigration registers that the vast majority of the newly arrived family units who went to the coffee plantations were originally from agricultural communities. Most families had a nuclear structure formed by a couple only or by a couple with unmarried children, and even by a husband or a wife with some or all of his or her children. Of a group of sixty-three Italian families who went directly from the government-sponsored immigrant hostel in São Paulo to the Santa Gertrudes *fazenda* between 1897 and 1902,[5] fifty-one were nuclear families; in forty-two of these cases the couple and their children migrated; in three cases it was the couple only; and in two cases, only one of the spouses with children migrated. The average size of these families was five persons. Those families that did not fit this description most often brought with them the father and/or mother of the head of the family and, less often, a married son, the daughter-in-law, the grandchildren, or nephews of the family head. Married daughters or the father- or mother-in-law of the family head were not included. The women who made up these family units were under 50 years old, and the men were under 56. Married women averaged 33.8 years of age, married men 37.4, and the children 7.2. Nonnuclear families were comparatively older. They had more members over 50 years of age; of these nonnuclear families 59 percent of men and 55 percent of women were married, and 23 percent of men and 18 percent of women were widowed.[6]

The composition of these family units was shaped by the requirements set for obtaining travel subsidies. Besides the family head with his spouse and children, the parents, grandparents, unmarried brothers, brothers-in-law, or orphaned nephews of the head of the family could be included on the ticket. Married women who were to join their husbands in Brazil could be included, but not cousins or more distant relatives.

Many families who migrated spontaneously—without subsidies—and who went to areas with small properties were of similar structure and composition.[7] Most of these were young people in the reproductive phase of their life cycle and therefore were likely to expand their families in the new land.

A closer look finds some differences between the size and structure of immigrant families of the different ethnic groups that arrived in Brazil. From a total of twenty-five families who went directly from the immigrant hostel to the Santa Gertrudes *fazenda* between 1903 to 1914, seven Italian families had an average size of 6.3 persons, three Austrian families 4.4, five Portuguese families 5.3, and five Spanish families 5.4. Japanese families arriving at the *fazenda* between 1917 and 1919 were of smaller size, about three persons. However, many of these Japanese families were artificially formed as they incorporated other people into the unit in order to satisfy contractual requirements.

In the years from 1908 to 1936, in the state of São Paulo as a whole, the Italian family had an average size of 4.1 persons. The Portuguese and Spanish families averaged 3.7 and 5.1 respectively, and the Japanese 5.4.[8] By 1902, Italy had already prohibited subsided migration to Brazil, and those Italians who arrived subsequently came primarily from the south. Portuguese and Spanish migrations then predominated, and other groups, such as East Europeans or Japanese, increased their share of the migrant flow to Brazil.

Another question regarding the Italian immigrant family was whether differences among patterns found in Italy were reproduced in the New World. The historiography regarding the family in Italy indicates that household complexity differed among the various regions of the country and, within the same region, between different social groups. The same differences occurred regarding residential arrangements after marriage.

In the rural areas of the center-north of Italy, for example, the majority of the agricultural population followed patrilocal postmarital residence norms (that is, the woman going to her husband's family house after marriage) and spent most of their lives in homes consisting of three generations. Two, three, and even four nuclear family units resided together. The level of complexity of the household depended upon the nature of the property, the means of production, and the agricultural contracts. Salaried workers, the *braccianti*, generally lived in single nuclear family homes, while the *mezzadros* (sharecroppers), small landowners, and tenant farmers frequently were in multiple family units. In the rural areas of the south the situation was entirely different. In Puglia, the region about which there is more information, a high proportion of people used to live in nuclear households after marriage (neolocal postmarital residence). Most households revealed simple structures.

It is difficult to say what happened to these family patterns in Brazil. These differences cannot be seen in our portrait of the immigrant family at the time of their arrival. Since the *braccianti* made up the majority of those Italians who came to work on the coffee plantations, nuclear families predominated. The pattern of patrilocal residency could also explain the absence of married daughters or of parents-in-law of the family head among the immigrants.

However, it is possible to imagine that the existing migration norms, which are revealed in the granting of passports and in other documents, may have divided the family groups that made up complex households. Kinship- and/or neighbor-based groups, including the *braccianti*, could emigrate together, indicating a migration broader than just nuclear families. The *carta de chamada* for relatives permitted the development of traditional patterns of life for the immigrants in the New World. It is also possible to imagine that in the coffee-growing regions, with time and depending on the circumstances, complex households would form again. This formation happened in the areas of small properties in the south of Brazil, starting in the second generation.[9]

Finally, we should mention that at the time of arrival, the immigrants generally had little money saved; some families crossed the ocean with nothing in their pockets. The majority dreamed about landownership (immigrants from the Veneto, for instance), but the goal of a significant number of the families (southern Italians) was to live and work in the city. Many saw immigration as permanent, particularly Veneto and German families; others, such as the first Japanese arrivals, emigrated with the not always fulfilled goal of returning some day to their country of origin.

Growing and Multiplying: Marriages and Offspring

Once in Brazil, those immigrants and their descendants who wished to marry chose a spouse in their own group, a fellow countryman or woman. This practice (endogamy) was important in maintaining and reinforcing the cohesion and solidarity of the immigrant group. A marriage within one's own culture also could facilitate a possible return to the native country, but this practice sometimes was used as a way to resist inclusion in the new society. However, the opportunity to marry within one's ethnic group was not the same for all immigrants and their descendants. Several factors encouraged or discouraged endogamy.

Immigration in family units in coffee-growing areas reduced the gap between total male and female migrant flows. In the coffee-growing municipality of Rio Claro,[10] the civil registry of marriages between 1890 and 1930 shows that opportunities for male and female immigrants to choose spouses in their new community were high during the first few years of residence in Brazil (see Table 1).

Table 1. Endogamy Indexes According to Nationality: Municipality of Rio Claro, São Paulo, 1890–1930

Period	Italians	Portuguese	Spaniards
1890–1899	0.843	0.506	0.635
1900–1909	0.702	0.425	0.545
1910–1919	0.406	0.364	0.450
1920–1930	0.211	0.251	0.304

Source: Municipality of Rio Claro, Civil Registry Office: Marriages, 1890–1930.
NOTE: An endogamy index indicates intragroup marriage; the higher the index, the greater the intragroup marriages.

From 1890 to 1930 the Italians, followed by the Spanish and then the Portuguese, had the highest endogamy rate. In the latter periods, the ebbing of the migratory movement brought about a decrease in the endogamy indexes. Then, immigrant endogamy gave way to ethnic endogamy, especially among the Italians. In other words, with time, marriages united foreigners with Brazilian children of foreigners of the same nationality or Brazilian children of foreigners of the same nationality between themselves.

The greater proportion of men vis-à-vis women (high masculinity index) benefited women more than men, as the women had greater opportunities for finding a spouse from within their group. Because of the scarcity of eligible women, many immigrant men had to compete with Brazilians and other foreigners or else had to look for a mate in other places, even in their country of origin. In other cases, they remained celibate. Among the Portuguese, for instance, individual male migration was dominant, a fact that made it impossible for a significant proportion of these immigrants (75 percent) to find Portuguese wives in the Brazilian marriage market.

Besides the country of origin and the high masculinity index, other factors shaped matrimonial choices. Even if there were numerous immigrant men in the marriage market, just one-half of the Portuguese women married men of the same nationality; among Spaniards, only 40 percent of the men and 59 percent of the women married within their ethnic group. Where immigrants settled may have played a role in their marriage choices. The concentration of the same nationality in the same spaces—the dominant style on the *fazendas* and in small property areas—facilitated marriage between nationals.

The organization of space and work in the great coffee-producing *fazendas* served to isolate families in the *colônias*, since people of the same origin were generally grouped together to live and work in the coffee fields. This organization, in addition to a rigid system of vigilance maintained by the *fazenda* manager, served to limit the opportunities for immigrants to meet and choose partners, to circumscribe the marriage market to the property boundaries, and, within them, to the small colonies within the larger *fazenda*. In the marriages performed between Italian *colonos* of Santa Gertrudes, 83 percent of Italian women married Italian men, while 70 percent of Italian men married their compatriots.[11]

In the small rural properties of the municipality of Rio Claro, endogamy predominated, but it was less rigid than on the coffee *fazendas* and less strong than in colonization areas in the south of the country. Marriage, in addition to preserving and increasing family resources, also sought to increase work resources. In this situation, preference was given to co-nationals, those who were in the position to satisfy the interests of the group.

In the urban core, even if the possibilities of encounters with a diversity of people were greater, the trend of endogamy continued with more or less intensity according to the group. There were neighborhoods that concentrated people of the same origin, thus making the selection of a spouse from the same group easy. The immigrant community made efforts to facilitate the marriage of people of the same nationality. Women were taken to certain clubs and parties to find husbands; other clubs kept out people not born within a given region or country.

From genealogies of wealthy Italian families in Rio Claro it is possible to infer the important role of socioeconomic conditions along with ethnicity in the practice of endogamy. This factor is evident in the case of families linked to local commerce, where Italians and their descendants occupied a significant position. The unions in which ethnic, social, and religious factors coincided were frequent. Furthermore, religious endogamy was significant not only in the Catholic majority but also in the

Presbyterian and Lutheran minorities. Catholic parish registries in the sixty-year period show only twenty-seven marriages between Catholics and people of other denominations.

Table 2. Median Age at Marriage of Immigrants and Brazilians in Rio Claro, Brazil, versus Median Age for Selected Nations/Regions in Europe, 1890–1930

| Rio Claro Immigrants and Brazilians | | | European Residents | | |
Nationality	Men	Women	Nationality	Men	Women
Italians	24.4	19.8	Veneto, 1881	28.3	24.6
Portuguese	26.3	20.7	Veneto, 1901	27.5	24.7
Spaniards	24.3	19.7	Italy, 1901 (other regions)	25.3–30.1	21.7–25.4
Germans	26.4	21.1	Minho (Portugal)*	29.1	27.0
Other Foreigners	27.1	20.4	Andalucia (Spain)*	27.4	23.4
Brazilians (children of Brazilian parents)	23.9	20.1	Galicia (Spain)*	29.6	26.1
Brazilians (children of Italian parents)	23.2	20.1	Germany 1850–1874	29.5	26.9
Brazilians (children of foreign other than Italian)	23.7	20.2	Germany 1875–1899	28.3	25.5

Sources: Municipality of Rio Claro, Civil Registry Office: Marriages, 1890–1930; European data from R. Rettaroli, "Age at Marriage in Nineteenth-Century Italy," *Journal of Family History* 15 (1990): 417; R. Rowland, "Sistemas matrimoniales en la peninsula iberica (siglos XVI-XIX): Una perspectiva regional," in V. Y. Pérez-Morera and D. S. Reher, eds., *Demografía Historica en España* (Madrid: El Arquero, 1989), 100; J. Kondel, "Demographic Transitions in German Villages," in A. J. Coale and S. C. Watkins, eds., *The Decline of Fertility in Europe* (Princeton: Princeton University Press, 1986), 352.
*Second half of nineteenth century.

Our research shows that Italians had with some frequency multiple marriages between two families (two siblings from one family marrying two siblings from another) or, less often, intermarriage between their children, forming veritable networks. Many times these unions solidified old links of friendship or *compadrio*,[12] which joined people from one region, or *paese*, in Italy. It is probable that arrangements of this kind also occurred in other immigrant groups. Marriage within the same family rarely happened in the immigrant families of Rio Claro.

What we find in Rio Claro is a non-European pattern. On average, spouses in the New World married younger and were more likely to wed than those in their homelands. As Table 2 illustrates, the immigrants of each nationality in Rio Claro married at a younger age than did their counterparts in their society of origin and a little later than the Brazilians. This finding was not only true for the men but also for the women. Besides marrying younger, immigrants were more likely to marry than were those in their countries of origin. We still do not know the exact level of celibacy in the areas we looked into. Here we define permanent celibacy in demographic terms—that is, as the person who remains unmarried until the age of 50.

Between 1890 and 1900, at the moment the immigrants arrived in Rio Claro, Italians who had chosen permanent celibacy represented 7.4 percent of the total male population and 3.4 percent of the female population. We also know that the unmarried between ages 40 and 49 were 9.4 and 3.4 percent of men and women, respectively. In 1891 in the Veneto, the proportions of those age 40 to 49 were 10.9 percent for men and 10.2 percent for women; in 1901 these proportions were 10.8 and 10.4, respectively.[13] These data indicate that the pattern of celibacy of immigrants was lower for those arriving in Brazil and did not conform to the pattern observed in their native land. The women who were considered celibate, more than the men in the same situation, either had difficulties in migrating to the coffee-producing regions or chose not to do so.

Both age at marriage and patterns of permanent celibacy in the New World thus were at variance with the patterns in the old country. This marriage pattern of the Brazilian immigrants of all nationalities may have been a mechanism utilized by the group in their new land to face conditions that generally did not pose obstacles to unions. Job offers, access to the possibility of free or inexpensive land in rural areas, and the existence of an ample and diversified labor market in the cities facilitated the adoption of this pattern of marriage at younger ages. The pattern of marrying at ages younger than in Italy is maintained whether the setting was rural or urban, although the marriage age of the first wedding varied according to whether the place of residence was urban or rural. In the majority of cases the variation in marriage age was related to the occupation of the groom and/or his parents insofar as different occupations were related to different places of residence.

According to the data in Table 3, Italian men who resided in the urban areas and worked in the secondary or tertiary sector married later (at 26 years) than the inhabitants of the rural areas (23.2). Women followed a similar pattern, but with a smaller difference between urban and rural dwellers. The Brazilian children of Italians, at the time of marriage, were also younger in the country than in the city. However, Brazilian sons married at younger ages than immigrant men born in Italy. Conversely, the Brazilian daughters of Italian immigrants married a little later than women who were born in the peninsula and then married in Brazil.

Table 3. Median Age of Italian Immigrants and Their Descendants at the Time of Marriage According to Their Place of Residency, Rio Claro, 1890–1930

	Age at Marriage			
			Italian Children	
Place of	*Italians*		*Born in Brazil*	
Residence	*Men*	*Women*	*Men*	*Women*
Urban core	26.1	20.5	24.1	20.7
Fazendas	23.2	19.4	22.4	19.9
Small rural	24.5	19.8	23.0	19.9

Source: Municipality of Rio Claro, Civil Registry Office: Marriages, 1890–1930.

The absence of deliberate birth control—which seems to have happened with the immigrant population at first—and the frequency with which nuptials occurred placed a larger number of women at risk of becoming pregnant. At the same time, a precocious marriage age placed immigrant women at an even higher risk of pregnancy than nonimmigrant women, thus allowing immigrant women to give birth to more children.

The impact of international immigration on the natural increase in the coffee-producing areas was considerable. In Rio Claro, for instance, 13,664 children were born alive from 1900 to 1910. Half of these were born to foreign mothers; Italian mothers alone represented 40 percent of all these births. Between 1911 and 1920, we have no data by specific nationality—only data referring to foreign mothers, which represent 45 percent of the total of births in those years. Also there are no data that permit us to know the percentage of foreign and Italian mothers in the Rio Claro population in the same period. Nevertheless, the 1920 census shows that foreign females represented 25 percent of the total female population between 15 and 69 years of age. This is the group who could have given birth to live babies between 1900 and 1920 in Rio Claro. The same census also shows that Italian women represented about 60 percent of the total foreign women in Rio Claro municipality.

On the other hand, for the coffee-growing region of São Paulo, we also lack empirical studies to confirm that immigrant women gave birth to large families at levels higher than the women who remained in the countries of origin. We do, however, have evidence to show that this was so in the regions of colonization in the south of Brazil. The Italian families in Rio Grande do Sul, for instance, in the period 1875–1910, had as many as an average of 10.8 children. The families in Santa Felicidade

(Curitiba in Paraná,1888–1909) had an average of 9.9 children, and the German Lutheran families who began their marriage cycles between 1866 and 1894 produced an average of from six to seven children.[14] The authors who analyzed these communities have unanimously affirmed that Italians and Germans in the New World maintained a reproductive pattern similar to those of their parents and grandparents in their lands of origin. What was different in the New World was that the young marriage age of women led to a greater number of offspring in Brazil.[15]

If we take into account that the immigrant families who went to the coffee-growing areas came from the same European regions as those in the colonization areas in southern Brazil, then we can assume that the reproductive pattern of immigrants should have been repeated in São Paulo. However, other reasons advanced to justify the existence of numerous progeny among the immigrants in the south seem not to be applicable in the same way to immigrants in the coffee regions.

Studies about the Italian family in the south of Brazil highlight the strong influence of religion and the presence of the Church, through its priests, in the reproductive behavior of the immigrants. In addition, these studies either rule out or minimize the economic advantages of having a large number of children. As R. Costa explains, "According to the religious outlook of the immigrants, a child was God's gift who should always be welcomed as something sacred. No one spoke then of limitations [of birth], . . . that one should accept all the children sent by God. Large families were explained by natural evolution, thus contradicting the commonplace idea that the immigrant in our environment [the south of Brazil] sought a larger number of children because they [the children] represented more labor for agriculture."[16]

In the south the church was the only meeting place for immigrants and, in consequence, religion became a fundamental factor in the Italians' process of cultural identification. The priest had a special status: he was the most cultivated person in the community. Moreover, he was the delegate of those natural powers that emanated from his "ministry of God." Therefore, he was in a position to pressure the immigrants not to practice birth control.

In the coffee-producing areas, the situation was very different. On the majority of the coffee *fazendas*, the presence of a priest was not continuous. Religious control was in the hands of the proprietor (or his manager): he owned the land, the chapel, the work, and the houses of the *colonos*. It was he who sanctioned the presence of a priest on the *fazenda*, took charge of the priest's salary and related religious expenses, and determined the rhythm of religious activity. For these reasons the immigrants sometimes had less confidence in the priests.

Even among the small property owners in the coffee region, the presence of a priest was sporadic. In this context, it seems improbable that religion and the priests had the same impact that they had in the south in influencing the reproductive behavior of the immigrants. The studies of German Lutherans in Curitiba (state of Paraná) affirm that "the size of the progeny was fundamental for the survival of the *colono*; they [children] constituted a necessary and lucrative investment . . . in the mental universe of the peasant, taking advantage of the fecundity of a union meant social and economic advantages, and, in a reciprocal relationship, shelter in old age."[17] For the immigrant on the coffee *fazendas* the *colonato* was associated with large Italian families because the economic advantages of family work meant as much for the immigrant as for the plantation owner.

Nevertheless, the idea that lack of control over fertility is linked to the organization of production is questionable for several reasons. First, it does not take into account the phases of family development vis-à-vis its effects on a large family. As M. C. F. A. de Oliveira and F. Madeira explain, "the expansion of the size of the family means that for an extended period the family unit was made up of a minority of producers. . . . It is only when the family unit can take advantage of a high proportion of producers that its enlarged size acts as a benefit. . . . Then, the concentration of the benefits in one limited time period raises doubts about the efficiency of a large family." Second, "because given the characteristics of coffee production, the adjustment of the family to the productive system may be achieved, either with a simple reorganization of work, or by means of mechanisms of land redistribution allotted to grow foodstuffs.[18] Therefore, the complexity resulting from the action of these factors indicates that the *colonato* was a much more flexible system, more capable of absorbing the workforce of even large families than of determining their size.

The evidence from Santa Gertrudes offers clues that reinforce this hypothesis and that indicate that the families were not as large as may have been initially assumed. This evidence shows that on the *fazenda* an average family size of seven predominated. This average, however, corresponds to those families, whether nuclear or nonnuclear, who found themselves in different phases of the life cycle. On the other hand, it was possible to verify that the families who were considered large were not so because of their numerous children, but because of the addition of daughters-in-law, grandchildren, and/or the parents of the head of household. One analysis of this evidence has demonstrated that the *colonato* would successfully accommodate, for a limited period of time, families who were in a favorable phase of the life cycle in which the ratio of producer to consumer was fairly close to one. Moreover, small and medium-sized families in those conditions managed to obtain balances relatively higher than larger families.

In considering such evidence we are inclined to think that in the coffee areas, especially on the *fazendas*, immigrant women were generating an average number of children higher than that observed in their native lands and lower than that encountered among the women who emigrated to the south of Brazil. This question, nevertheless, remains an open one.

Conclusion

Many ingredients were present in the decision to emigrate: difficult living conditions in the country of origin, family resources (both human and material), personal expectations, and available opportunities (travel subsidies, access to land and work, preservation of the family unit and family work, the presence of family and friends). These factors affected the type of family that made the decision to go (the majority were rural, nuclear, not very numerous, and young) and also affected the choice of destination (coffee-growing areas). When added to the volume, structure, and composition of the migratory flow, to the timing of the family's arrival, to its intersection with the labor market, and to other possibilities offered by the receiving society (access to religious practices, for instance), these factors had a significant role in the formation of the immigrant family of the first and second generations.

The immigrant's choice of a spouse shows that the internal cohesion of the group was much stronger during the initial years of settlement. In these years, the ties that linked the migrant to his native land still existed, the hope of a future return was still strong, and the migration flow was most intense. The concentration of immigrants of the same origin in a given space facilitated endogamous marriages. These marriages varied in frequency as a product of demographic and/or socioeconomic factors. The high proportion of male immigrants benefited women because the women had a greater chance of finding a spouse within the ethnic group; Spanish women were more prone to endogamy than Portuguese, but less so than Italians.

In the coffee-producing areas, immigrants demonstrated a non-European marriage pattern—they married younger and more frequently than those remaining in the countries of origin. Without deliberately using birth control, immigrant women had more children than their counterparts in the homeland. The evidence gathered indicates that there were some behavioral differentials in family size between immigrants who went to the coffee-growing areas and those who went to the south: families of the former do not seem to have been as large as those of the latter.

Among the factors that played an important role in the migratory process and in the adaptation of immigrants and families to their chosen land were the attitude of the family toward work, the interaction of family networks, friendship and solidarity in the mutual support of family members, the immigrant associations, and the Church and religion. Simultaneously, the items that made up the cultural baggage brought by the immigrants were crucial in the acceleration as well as the slowing down of immigration processes. These factors, however, remain outside the scope of the present paper.

Nevertheless, we have been able to show the importance of taking into account in the analysis of immigrant families the complexity of factors that affect the migratory process and the life of the immigrants and their descendants in Brazil. This complexity exists precisely because in addition to historical circumstances and socioeconomic and demographic determinants, there was a space for the decisions and actions of the historical subjects.

Notes

1. The *colonato* has been defined as a system based on family labor that combined different forms of production. The *colono* and his family performed all the work related to coffee production: planting and harvesting. They were responsible for directly producing for their own subsistence as well as for carrying out a number of other duties, either with or without payment, on the *fazenda*.
2. The *Carta de chamada* was a letter that immigrants in São Paulo state sent to their relatives or acquaintances in their native country inviting them to emigrate to Brazil. The remittance of the letter was often encouraged by farm owners and was organized by state officials to ease the immigration process. The statistics about these letters, published by the Brazilian secretary of agriculture, show the interest of the state in using the letter to promote immigration.
3. The *colônia* was a group of houses where the immigrants lived. Several of these compounds were located on the coffee plantation.
4. J. Scarano, "Migração italiana para a área urbana: Estudo de caso," in L. A. De Boni, ed., *A presença italiana no Brasil*, vol. 3 (Pôrto Alegre/ Turin: Edições EST/Fondazione Giovanni Agnelli, 1996), 255–61; J. F. Alves, *Os brasileiros: Emigração e retorno no Pórto Oitocentista* (Pôrto: N.p., 1994); E. Sonino et al., "Italian report," in A. Eiras Roel, "Long-distance migration, 1500–1900," *XVII International Congress of Historical Sciences* (Madrid: International Commission on Historical Demography, 1992); R. Rowland, "La migración a grandes distancias y sus contextos: Portugal y Brasil," *Estudios Migratorios Latinoamericanos* 7 (1992); C. de M. S. Cunha, "Emigração familiar para o Brasil: Concelho de Guimarães, 1890–1914 (uma perspectiva microanalítica)" (Master's thesis: Instituto de Cíncias Sociais/Universidade do Minho, 1997); R. Costa, "A família italiana da área agrícola do Rio Grande do Sul," in De Boni, ed., *A presença italiana no Brasil*, 3:252–66.
5. This property, which at the time belonged to the town of Rio Claro, was one of the most important coffee *fazendas* in the state of São Paulo. Santa Gertrudes is a well-documented case.
6. M. S. C. B. Bassanezi, "Família e força de trabalho no colonato: Subsídios para a compreensão da dinámica demográfica no período cafeeiro," *Texto Nepo 8* (Campinas: UNICAMP, 1986), 25–28.

7. The families from the Veneto who went to the areas of colonization in the state of Espírito Santo had an average of 4.8 persons in 1894 and 4.6 in 1895. A. Castiglioni, "A imigração italiana no Espírito Santo: Análise das características dos imigrantes," in A. Castiglioni, ed., *Imigração italiana no Espírito Santo: Uma aventura colonizadora* (Vitória: UFES, 1998), 107–8; T. Holloway, *Imigrantes para o café* (Rio de Janeiro: Paz e Terra, 1984); Herbert Klein, "A integração social e econÙmica dos imigrantes portugueses no Brasil do fim do século XIX e no século XX," *Revista Brasileira de Estudos de Populacão* 6 (1989); idem, "A integração dos imigrantes italianos no Brasil, na Argentina e Estados Unidos," *Novos Estudos* CEBRAP 25 (1989); idem, "A integração social e económica dos imigrantes espanhóis no Brasil," *Estudos Económicos* (São Paulo) 19 (1989); M. R. G. C. G. Silva, "A vocação religiosa como estratégia familiar de reprodução da vida camponesa entre italianos do vale do Itajaí/SC" (Doctoral thesis, UNICAMP, Campinas, 1998); Costa, "A família italiana"; A. Balhana, *Famílias coloniais: Fecundidade e descendíncia* (Curitiba: A. M. Cavalcanti & Cia., 1977).

8. These averages were calculated from Klein, "A integração social e económica dos imigrantes portugueses"; idem, "A integração dos imigrantes italianos"; and idem, "A integração social e económica."

9. Silva, "A vocação religiosa," 120–21.

10. This municipality received a large contingent of foreign immigrants. Rio Claro was characterized not only by its large coffee-growing *fazendas* but also by the predominance of small properties dedicated mainly to subsistence and to some commercial coffee production, by a well-developed urban core, and by linkage to the Paulista railroad network. Therefore, it was a region that offered a variety of opportunities to immigrants and immigrant families.

11. M. S. C. B. Bassanezi, "O casamento na colónia no tempo do café," *Anais do VI Encontro Nacional de Estudos Populacionais* 1 (Olinda-PE), 1988.

12. *Compadrio* was the relationship established (and /or reinforced) between parents and godparents by a child's christening.

13. R. Rettaroli, "Age at Marriage in Nineteenth-Century Italy," *Journal of Family History* 15 (1990): 417.

14. Respectively, Costa, "A família italiana"; Balhana, *Famílias coloniais*; M. L. Andreazza and S. O. Nadalin, "O cenário da colonização no Brasil Meridional e a família imigrante," *Revista Brasileira de Estudos de População* 11 (1994): 61–87.

15. Ibid.

16. Costa, "A família italiana," 254.

17. Andreazzaa and Nadalin, "O cenário da colonização no Brasil Meridional," 76–78.

18. M. C. F. A de Oliveira and F. Madeira, "População e força de trabalho: O caso da cafeicultura paulista," *Revista Brasileira de Estudos de População* 3 (1986): 54–55.

Conclusion: Common Themes and Future Directions

Samuel L. Baily

The collection of essays presented here provides us with fresh insights into many of the important issues of migration as well as with confirmation of findings that others have made in different spatial and temporal contexts. Among the common themes are the concept of migration as a long-term, open-ended process, the ongoing interaction between cultural persistence and integration and the crucial role of social networks in both processes, and the importance of comparison. Let us begin by discussing these three points and then turn to some issues raised by the essays that suggest the need for additional exploration.

The authors in this book testify to the fact that overseas migration indeed is a long-term, open-ended process that results in no single given outcome such as assimilation. It starts in the villages or regions of origin where the decision to emigrate is made, and continues with the actual move to a larger city within the same country or directly to destinations abroad. Once in the new society the immigrants need to find jobs and places to live, to recreate social lives, to protect their interests, and to maximize their material well-being. Some individuals remain permanently in the adopted society while others return home; others move back and forth a number of times, and still others go from one destination abroad to another. The movement from one phase in the migration process to another is not, however, inevitable or irreversible.

Although the authors focus on different aspects and phases of the migration process, the process as a whole is what we are ultimately trying to understand. José Moya and Maria Baganha examine the global context in which it takes place, then through the move, and on to adjustment and integration into the new societies. Fernando Devoto and Maria Bassanezi analyze issues relating to the societies of origin: Who left and why? How did they choose a destination and how did they get there? All of the authors focus to some extent on aspects of what happened to the immigrants once they arrived in their new destinations abroad. María Bjerg, Jeffrey Lesser, and Giralda Seyferth evaluate the experiences of numerically smaller groups as they sought to find a niche for themselves. Samuel Baily, Carina Frid de Silberstein, Maria Baganha, and Daniel Masterson with Sayaka Funada focus on some of the larger groups—the Italians, the Portuguese, and the Japanese. Hernán Otero with Adela Pellgrino and Míguez probe the specific issues of settlement and marriage among a number of groups. All, however, elucidate aspects of the larger process of migration.

No part of the migration process receives more attention than the relationship of the immigrants to the host societies. In this two-way relationship, immigrants and host societies changed and were changed by the presence of the other. Most current migration scholars both in the United States and Latin America have rejected the classic assimilationist paradigm represented by the concept of the "melting pot" and instead have adopted some form of the model of "cultural pluralism." Nevertheless, what is obvious from reading these essays is that both of these perspectives contain at least some part of the truth. Migration definitely was not totally uprooting, as the assimilationists have argued, and the immigrants were active participants in the process who contributed much to their new societies. At the same time we must not overlook the very real and often traumatic dislocation involved. Even under the best of circumstances, immigrants left friends and a familiar situation behind them and moved to what was for the most part unknown.

What is also clear is that almost all of the immigrants used personal networks to help them mediate the process and overcome the worst difficulties of dislocation. One figure from the U.S. Immigration Commission Report of 1910 strikingly indicates how important these networks were— in 1908 and 1909, 98.7 percent of southern Italians and 92.6 percent of northern Italians arriving in the United States went to relatives or friends.[1] We do not have such precise figures on every immigrant group or on the Latin American countries, but existing evidence indicates that the large majority of immigrants did join relatives and friends. For example, Juan Alsina, the Argentine director of migration during the 1890s, noted that the majority of immigrants to that country had been greatly assisted by such networks.[2] To survive, prosper, and contribute, the immigrants needed to build on their traditional culture as well as to make the necessary adjustments to and accommodations with the host societies.

A third common theme in this book is the use of comparison as an analytical framework. Comparison has enabled the authors to identify more clearly significant similarities and differences, to ask new questions, and to formulate generalizations and causal explanations with greater confidence. Moya, Devoto, Baily, Baganha, Otero and Pellegrino, Masterson and Funada, and Bassanezi have compared immigrant groups in two or more countries. In addition, Lesser compares Jews and Japanese within Brazil; Frid de Silberstein, Italian women in Rosario and other cities of Argentina; Bjerg, initial and later community formation patterns of Danes in the province of Buenos Aires; Seyferth, the development of German colonies in various parts of southern Brazil; and Míguez, both the marriage patterns in Tandil (the "Tandil model") with those of other Argentine urban centers such as Buenos Aires, Córdoba, and Rosario, and the marriage patterns of different immigrant communities.

One of the most suggestive overall comparisons this book enables us to make, at least on a preliminary basis, is that between the experiences of the major Latin America immigration countries (Argentina, Brazil, and Uruguay), on the one hand, and the United States, on the other. There are a number of important similarities. In both areas, migration was characterized by the predominance of young, single, unskilled males, especially in the early phases. In addition, personal networks of kin and fellow townspeople were a critical factor at every phase of the migration process. And in both areas, economic opportunity played a major role in determining the fate of the immigrants; it established the parameters in which they would attempt to improve their financial positions.

The differences, however, seem to be most illuminating regarding our understanding of the process of migration. One of the major differences, as Míguez notes in his introductory overview, is in the timing of mass migration to the two areas. In the United States the first great wave occurred from the 1830s to the beginning of the Civil War, and a second one took place from the 1870s to the restriction laws of the 1920s, interrupted only briefly by World War I. In the three Latin American countries, however, the first great wave of immigration occurred from the 1870s to 1930 while the second great wave was developing in the United States. This difference in the timing of mass immigration meant that conditions in the societies of origin and of reception also were different; this difference, in turn, influenced such important factors as who left and why and the nature of integration into the receiving countries.

Another major difference between the two areas is that the Latin American economies were less developed at the time of mass migration (1870–1914) than was the economy of the United States. As a result, the respective opportunity structures in the two areas differed significantly. The United States in 1900 was becoming a major world industrial power and needed unskilled labor for its factories and for construction projects. The Latin American countries, on the other hand, were primarily commercial agricultural economies and needed artisans, skilled workers, commercial employees, and agriculturists (who could become independent farmers on their own or rented land) as well as unskilled factory and construction workers. The Latin American labor markets therefore offered greater opportunity at the middle and upper end of the job hierarchy than did that of the United States.

The nature of competition with other immigrant groups differed as well between the two areas. When the Portuguese, Spaniards, and Italians

arrived in mass numbers in Latin America after 1870, there was no substantial number of previously settled immigrants with whom they had to
compete for jobs and places to live. In the United States during the same
period, new immigrants faced competition with well-established earlier
groups such as the English, the Germans, and the Irish. Furthermore, in
Latin America there were only two or three major groups of migrants,
compared to more than a half-dozen in the United States; and in countries
such as Argentina, Uruguay, and Brazil, immigrants were also important
employers of other newcomers. This fact meant that the Latin American
immigrant groups could be played off less easily against each other and
therefore were less vulnerable to the dictates of employers and others
within the host society.

The differing levels of economic development and the different patterns of migration had a major impact on the insertion of the migrants
into the respective host societies. Most notably, immigrants become the
central component of the developing middle classes in Argentina, Brazil,
and Uruguay, whereas in the United States the middle class was well developed by the post-Civil War period of mass immigration. The greater
economic and social mobility in Latin America clearly defined the immigrants' process of integration into their new societies in different ways
than took place in the United States at the same time.

Another major difference was the level of cultural distinction between
the immigrants and the respective host societies. In Latin America the
three major immigrant groups—the Spanirds, the Italians, and the Portuguese—all shared a similar Latin culture with the Argentines, Uruguayans, Brazilians, and other nationalities. The Catholic religion was the same.
This similarity, of course, did not apply to the smaller immigrant groups
such as the Danes, Germans, and Jews or to the more numerous Japanese.
In the United States, Protestant English immigrants had been in a similar
cultural relation to the host society as the Italians, Spaniards, and Portuguese in Latin America, but increasingly immigrants to the United States
were Catholic and non-English speaking. The cultural divide between those
immigrants and their host society was much wider, and thus it made adjustment in the United States difficult.

The role that the respective governments played in the migration process differed between the United States and Latin America. The United
States, Argentina, Brazil, and Uruguay all passed legislation at various
time to regulate the process, and in the 1920s and 1930s they all restricted
immigration in some form. The Latin American governments, however,
took a more active role in recruiting immigrants and attempting to determine the nature of the migrant flow. The Argentine and Brazilian governments—both national and state—used agents as recruiters. Brazil provided
subsidized passage and help in settlement for immigrants who were members of families. The agents were not very successful in attracting signifi-

cant numbers of the Northern European immigrants whom both countries preferred, but the family subsidy policy was effective. As a result, Brazil was able to attract a greater percentage of families who, as opposed to single men, were more likely to remain permanently in their adopted society than those going either to the United States or to Argentina.

The ratios of the immigrant population to the base population of the receiving societies also differed between the two areas. In Argentina, southern Brazil, and Uruguay, the base society to which the immigrants were expected to assimilate was much smaller than it was in the United States. Thus, in 1914, for example, 30 percent of the Argentine population and 80 percent of the active population of Buenos Aires were foreign born. In the United States at the same time only 14 percent of the population and approximately 50 percent of the active population of New York City were foreign born. Solidarity among ethnic groups was not always a given, although the elites frequently were successful in constructing this identity and solidarity. Thus, because the immigrant population in Latin America was relatively large and, as mentioned previously, was divided into only two or three major groups, it was in a stronger position to negotiate with the members of the host society than was the case in the United States.

Settlement patterns also differed between the United States and the Latin American countries. Although, as we noted, there was a higher percentage of immigrants in the cities of Argentina, southern Brazil, and Uruguay than was the case in the large eastern cities of the United States, the Latin American immigrants were more evenly dispersed within these cities. This greater dispersion in addition to the lesser social and cultural distances between the immigrants and the members of the host society facilitated greater interaction among the various groups.

Finally, there was a difference in the host society's perceptions of immigrants in the two areas. In the United States, immigrants were seen primarily as a source of labor to help the country develop. Immigrants, who for the most part were looked down upon, were expected to assimilate to the "superior" institutions and culture of the host society. In Brazil and especially in Argentina, on the other hand, immigration was viewed as a way to change the composition of the existing host society. In Brazil with its large number of black former slaves, the Portuguese, Spaniards, and Italians would help "whiten" and civilize the country. In Argentina the coastal European-oriented elites believed that the Italians and Spaniards would help them replace the "barbarism" of the gauchos of the interior. Thus, in both Brazil and Argentina, immigrants were seen in more positive terms than in the United States. This attitude, in turn, helped ease their way in the new societies.

This comparison of the United States and the major Latin American countries of immigration brings us back to the question of cultural persistence and social integration. The difference in stages of economic development, the economic opportunity structures, and competition with earlier groups enabled the Latin American immigrants during the decades before World War I to become an essential element of the developing middle classes of these countries. These factors plus the role of the governments, the settlement patterns, the greater percentage of immigrants, and the positive perceptions all helped facilitate the entrance of the immigrants into their new societies. There was some dislocation in the move, to be sure, but there were advantages in the South American countries that helped the migrants deal more effectively with these dislocations.

Although these and many other themes are discussed in this volume, the authors also raise issues that are, as yet, only partially resolved. These issues therefore need further attention from scholars as we move into the twenty-first century. In the remaining pages of this essay, let us turn to these questions and to some possible future directions for migration research.

One such issue raised by Otero and Pellegrino is how migration scholarship should relate to the broader national and global histories of which it is a part. In other words, how can we avoid being trapped in what the Argentine Hilda Sábato has called "the ethnic capsule"?[3] In the past many migration scholars have focused on fairly narrow case studies in order to develop the necessary knowledge about the experiences of various ethnic groups in multiple temporal and spatial contexts. This research indeed has been an important step in developing our knowledge of the process of migration. One of our future tasks, however, is to integrate this information both practically and conceptually into the relevant national and global histories. Any specific migration experience is part of one or more national histories and at the same time fits into a larger global historical context. Those of us interested in Latin American migration will therefore need to demonstrate several points more clearly: 1) how migration is an integral part of the histories of Argentina, Brazil, Uruguay, Cuba, the United States, Spain, Portugal, and Italy, among other countries; 2) how the histories of migration and of these countries are part of larger transnational forces such as the Atlantic economy; and 3) how knowledge of the migration process helps us to understand these broader national and global histories.

One way to do this, for example, is to focus on the relationship between the migration process and some of the broad social issues of these national and regional or global histories. Frid de Silberstein, using the Italians in Rosario as a case study, documents the important but neglected role of women in the migration experience as well as in Argentine history. Yet much more needs to be done regarding both women and gender in migration and Argentine history. Have the patterns that Frid de Silberstein found for Italians in Rosario been the same with other immigrant groups and in other temporal and spatial settings? How do the patterns for immigrant women compare to those of Argentine women in general? We need to examine more closely not only how women participated in the migration process but also how this participation changes our understanding of the process. The United States, which has a longer tradition of women's and gender history, has produced considerably more literature on these topics than have the Latin American countries. How useful are North American and/or European models to those who are studying Latin America? How do the Latin American models apply to the United States, to Europe, and to other regions?

Another area that needs more attention is that of race and discrimination. Masterson and Funada, writing on the Japanese, and Lesser, writing on the Jews, point out the historical discrimination and racism in Brazil against these groups. In both cases the immigrant group was at once economically successful yet remained somewhat isolated from the host society. The reaction against these groups came to a head in the late 1930s during Getúlio Vargas's Estado Novo. The government launched a campaign that nationalized the foreign schools and prohibited the use of languages other than Portuguese. The German and Italian communities of Brazil were also subjected to this nationalization campaign.

We need to know more about the causes of such nativism and its particular expressions. Where and under what circumstances has nativism manifested itself in the various Latin American countries? In what ways was Vargas's nationalization program similar to the anti-Italian demonstrations in São Paulo in August 1896 or the antiforeign marauding of Tata Dios and his followers in Tandil on January 1, 1872? How did the Brazilian anti-Japanese campaign differ from the one in Peru at the same time? In what ways is nativism in Latin America similar to that in the United States? Was it aimed only at certain groups? Or was it a racist or nativist phenomenon, or both? To what degree was the involvement of the Roosevelt administration in sending Peruvian Japanese to relocation camps in the United States during World War II important in shaping Latin American attitudes toward the Japanese?

There are other issues of racism and discrimination to which the study of migration might contribute. Brazil and Cuba both had large black populations. How did immigrants (Spaniards, Portuguese, and Italians) react to and interact with blacks? How did the Japanese and Jews in Brazil, themselves the victims of racial discrimination, respond to the situation of Afro-Brazilians? To what degree do such immigration concepts as persistence and integration apply to Afro-Brazilians? In what ways, as mentioned above, did the different perception of immigrants influence ideas of race, and vice versa? The joint analysis of race and ethnicity would benefit both fields.

We also need to know more about the participation of immigrants in host society politics. As Bjerg documents, the immigrant pioneer Hans

Fugl became active in local Tandil politics and skillfully used his role as ethnic leader to further his political career and thence to strengthen his position. Bjerg notes that this was possible because the early Danes in Tandil thought of themselves as neighbors of the Argentines rather than as ethnics in a foreign land who were seeking to preserve their culture. This relationship changed with time and with the coming of the Lutheran pastors to the Danish community of Tandil and other towns in the south of the province of Buenos Aires. The larger questions this example suggests are: Under what circumstances do immigrants participate in host society politics? What impact does this participation have on the ethnic community and on the host society? Is the Danish example in Tandil typical, or are the nonelectoral forms of participation such as demonstrations, protests, and petition signing most common? Obviously the integrity and influence of elections have a lot to do with electoral participation; a much higher percentage of immigrants took part in electoral politics in the United States, where there were relatively free and meaningful elections, than, for example, in pre-1912 Argentina, where most elections were fraudulent. A greater understanding of immigrant participation in politics of all kinds will give us new insight into the complex process of the integration of ethnic communities into the host society.

The relation among European immigrants, Latin American immigrants, and internal migrants is another issue of importance. Otero and Pellegrino as well as Frid de Silberstein compare with great effect the experiences of European immigrants with those from other nearby South American countries together with internal migrants. They are able to show significant differences along with some similarities among the three groups. The similarities are especially important because they suggest a more general pattern of migration that cuts across these various groups, but we need to pursue this kind of comparison to determine the limits, if any, of such models. Do the similarities extend to all immigrant groups, including Asians and those Europeans not dealt with by the authors?

Míguez and others raise another issue of importance that needs more attention, and that is the second generation, the children of the immigrants. We need to study them to know more about how long and in what ways immigrants maintain their cultures of origin and how much they integrate into the culture of the host society. The problem is that the Latin American censuses record second-generation immigrants born in Argentina or Brazil as Argentines or Brazilians and not as Italo-Argentines or Portuguese-Brazilians. Thus it is difficult to trace this second generation and to determine such factors as their marriage patterns, their participation in politics, or their patterns of geographic and economic mobility. We need to devise ways to identify the second generation and even the third and fourth ones. As we do so, we will greatly increase our knowledge of cultural persistence and integration.

Finally, let us touch on the issue of the transnational and subnational nature of migration that Devoto, Baily, and others raise. The nation-state was a significant influence on the process of migration (laws, economy, opportunity structure), but from the point of view of the migrant, it probably was not the most important one. This was especially true during the period of mass migration between 1870 and the 1920s, when there were few restrictions of any kind on the movement of people. Rather, as Devoto and others in this book demonstrate, the migrant has seen the world in local terms. The family, kinship, and *paesani*-based personal networks that operate in specific local villages and regions of origin and in specific destinations abroad are of most importance to the migrant. The concepts of Italy, Spain, or Portugal as nation-states to which one owed ultimate loyalty had little meaning. The local villages or towns or regions within these entities were the basis of identity and the crucible in which decisions were tested.

We need more research on if and how these original local loyalties broadened during the process of migration. Did individuals whose primary identities were to towns and villages become Italians or Spaniards or Portuguese, and, if so, how? How, then, did they become Argentines or Brazilians? In addition, how did such transnational forces as personal networks and global economic systems influence the migrants and their identities? The whole question of the construction of national identity and the emergence of nationalism among the descendants of the immigrants is still a largely unresolved one in countries of massive immigration such as Argentina and Brazil.

These essays demonstrate that the field of Latin American migration history has come a long way in the last fifteen years and that it has a bright future. The growth of the field enables us to make comparisons between Latin America and the other immigration receiving societies of the world. And this growth, in turn, will contribute significantly to our knowledge of the complex process of migration.

Notes

1. U.S. Senate, Reports of the Immigration Commission (Dillingham Commission) (Washington, DC, 1911), 4, 59.

2. Juan Alsina, *La immigración en el primer siglo de la independencia* (Buenos Aires, 1910), 245.

3. H. Sábato, "El pluralismo cultural en la Argentina: Un balance crítico," *Historiografía argentina, 1958–1988* (Buenos Aires: Comité Internacional de Ciencias Históricas, Comité Argentino, 1989).

Suggested Readings

There is very little literature in English specifically on the subject of migration in Latin America, which, of course, is why we published this volume. Below are some of the few books in English that do directly address the topic. Others, such as James Scobie's *Buenos Aires: Plaza to Suburb* and Warren Dean's *The Industrialization of São Paulo*, are not primarily immigration history, but immigrants play a significant part. For additional information as well as the Spanish- and Portuguese-language sources, please refer to the notes that conclude the various chapters in our book and the works listed below. Another important source is the leading journal on migration in Latin America, *Estudios Migratorios Latinoamericanos*, published in Buenos Aires since 1985.

Baganha, Maria Ioannis B. *Portuguese Emigration to the United States.* New York: Garland, 1990.

Baily, Samuel L. *Immigrants in the Lands of Promise: Italians in Buenos Aires and New York City, 1870 to 1914.* Ithaca: Cornell University Press, 1999.

Gardiner, C. Harvey. *The Japanese and Peru, 1873–1973.* Albuquerque: University of New Mexico Press, 1973.

Higashide, Seiichi. *Adios to Tears: The Memoirs of a Japanese-Peruvian Internee in a U.S. Concentration Camp.* Seattle: University of Washington Press, 2000.

Holloway, Thomas H. *Immigrants on the Land: Coffee and Society in São Paulo, 1886–1934.* Chapel Hill: Duke University Press, 1980.

Lesser, Jeffrey. *Welcoming the Undesirables: Brazil and the Jewish Question.* Berkeley: University of California Press, 1994.

———. *Negotiating National Identity: Immigrants, Minorities, and the Struggle for Ethnicity in Brazil.* Durham: Duke University Press, 1999.

Luebke, Frederick C. *Germans in Brazil: A Comparative History of Cultural Conflict during World War I.* Baton Rouge: Louisiana State University Press, 1987.

Masterson, Daniel M., with Sayaka Funada. *The Japanese in Latin America: Immigration, Settlement, and the Sojourner Tradition.* Urbana: University of Illinois Press, 2003.

Morner, Magnus, with the collaboration of Harold Sims. *Adventurers and Proletarians: The Story of Migrants in Latin America.* Pittsburgh: University of Pittsburgh Press, 1985.

Moya, José. *Cousins and Strangers: Spanish Immigrants in Buenos Aires, 1850–1930*. Berkeley: University of California Press, 1998.

Newton, Ronald C. *German Buenos Aires, 1900–1933: Social Change and Cultural Crisis*. Austin: University of Texas Press, 1977.

Sofer, Eugene. *From Pale to Pampa: A Social History of the Jews in Buenos Aires*. New York: Holmes and Meier, 1982.

Szuchman, Mark D. *Mobility and Integration in Urban Argentina: Córdoba in the Liberal Era*. Austin: University of Texas Press, 1980.

Young, George F. W. *Germans in Chile: Immigration and Colonization, 1849–1914*. New York: Center for Migration Studies, 1974.

About the Contributors

Maria Ioannis B. Baganha is an associate professor of demography, history, and sociology of migration in the Department of Sociology, Faculty of Economics, University of Coimbra. She has written extensively on Portuguese emigration to Europe and the Americas. Among her more recent publications is *Immigration in Southern Europe* (1996).

Maria Silvia C. Beozzo Bassanezi is with the Núcleo de Estudos de População (NEPO, Center of Population Studies), Universidade Estadual de Campinas (UNICAMP), São Paulo, Brazil. Her fields of interest are historical demography and international migration. She has published a number of articles in journals in Brazil and Italy.

María Bjerg, of the Universidad Nacional de Quilmes, is a researcher at the Consejo Nacional de Investigaciones Científicas y Técnicas (CONICET, the National Research Council of Argentina). She is co-editor with Hernán Otero of *Inmigración y redes sociales en la Argentina moderna* (1995). Her articles have appeared, among other places, in *Hispanic American Historical Review*, *Studi Emigrazione*, *Revista de las Indias*, *Estudios Migratorios Latinoamericanos*, and *Uppsala Multi-ethnic Papers*.

Fernando J. Devoto is professor of history at the University of Buenos Aires as well as at the University of Mar del Plata. He has published five books and edited eight more in addition to being the associate editor and the driving force behind *Estudios Migratorios Latinoamericanos* since 1985. He has been a visiting professor at universities in Paris and throughout Italy, Spain, and Uruguay. Eighty of his articles have appeared in journals in the United States, Canada, Italy, Spain, the Chechan Republic, Argentina, and Uruguay.

Sayaka Funada is completing her Ph.D. in international relations at Tsuda University in Tokyo. She is the author of a number of articles on international relations in Africa and has conducted extensive research on the Japanese of Brazil.

Jeffrey Lesser is professor of history and director of the Latin American and Caribbean Studies Program at Emory University. His research focuses on issues of ethnicity, immigration, and national identity. A specialist in Brazilian history, he is the author of *Negotiating National Identity: Immigrants, Minorities, and the Struggle for Ethnicity in Brazil* (1999), winner of the Best Book Prize, Brazil Section, Latin American Studies Association. His *Welcoming the Undesirables: Brazil and the Jewish Question* (1994) won the Best Book Prize, New England Council on Latin American Studies. He is also co-editor of *Arab and Jewish Immigrants in Latin America: Images and Realities* (1998).

Daniel M. Masterson is professor of history at the United States Naval Academy. He has authored or edited four books including *Militarism in Latin America, Peru from Sánchez Cerro to Sendero Luminoso*, and his recently published *Fuerza armada y sociedad en el Perú moderno*. His completed book-length manuscript on the Japanese experience in Latin America will be published by the University of Illinois Press in 2003.

José C. Moya is an associate professor of Latin American history at the University of California, Los Angeles. His book, *Cousins and Strangers: Spanish Immigrants in Buenos Aires, 1850–1930* (1998), received the Bolton Prize from the American Historical Association's CLAH, *Choice's* Outstanding Academic Book Award, an honorable mention for the Bryce Wood prize from LASA, the Herring Prize from the Pacific Council on Latin American Studies, and the Sharlin Memorial Award from the Social Science History Association. His next project is an intellectual, social, and cultural history of anarchism in *belle époque* Buenos Aires.

Hernán Otero, a historian and demographer, is a researcher at CONICET and director of the "Population and Society" Program at the Institute of Historical and Social Studies, Universidad Nacional del Centro de la Provincia de Buenos Aires, Tandil, Argentina. His areas of investigation concern the history of population, especially international migration and the formation of the Argentine statistical system. He has published, among others, *Poblaciones argentinas: Estudios de demografía diferencial*, edited with Guillermo Velázquez (1997), and *Inmigración y redes sociales en la Argentina moderna*, edited with María Bjerg (1995).

Adela Pellegrino is director of the Population Program at the Faculty of Social Sciences, University of the Republic, Uruguay. Her research interests include the history of population and international migration. Between 1994 and 1998 she was a member of the South-North Migration Committee of the International Union for the Scientific Study of Population (IUSSP). She has published *Latin American and Caribbean Migration: Recent Trends and Historical Perspectives* (2001).

Giralda Seyferth, a professor of anthropology and a researcher at the National Historical Museum, Federal University of Rio de Janeiro, has written numerous articles and books on immigration, German colonization, and ethnic identity in Brazil. Among her more recent publications is *Imigração e cultura no Brasil* (1990).

Carina L. Frid de Silberstein is professor of history of economic thought at the Universidad Nacional de Rosario, a researcher at CONICET, and an associate at the Centro de Studios Migratorios Latinoamericanos (CEMLA). She has published many articles on immigration and women. She is now working on the impact of European immigration on Argentine culture, with special reference to the emergence of art markets and the participation of Spanish and Italian intellectuals.